PRAISE FO

RIMBAUD CO

POETR

"It's quite likely that [the season's] most exciting new book of verse was stamped Made in France more than a century ago. . . . *Rimbaud Complete,* Wyatt Mason's bouncy new translation of the avant-garde poet's hallucinatory corpus, finds new music in the writing, revealing a classical artist."

—*Entertainment Weekly,* Editor's Choice, A-

"An important new rendering of a major poet." —*Library Journal*

"Mason's translations are confident and contemporary—muscular but without muscling in on the originals. There is no crabby diction, but neither is there that self-conscious pseudo-hipness with which it's all too tempting to render Rimbaud's lolling truculence of pose. Mason's approach has been to aim for common (as distinct from middle) ground between the literalist and the free, and the decision to translate successive versions and drafts pays off too, letting English-speaking readers see the genesis of poems and trace their often substantial alterations. Mason gets Rimbaud's range across impressively." —*The Times Literary Supplement*

"Mason does a splendid job in arrangement and translation."

—*The Tampa Tribune*

"Wyatt Mason's translations of Rimbaud's literary works manage, more than any others, to convey to contemporary ears the real sense of the work. Previous attempts had strained to maintain a sense of the French style or an equivalence in rhyme and form. For all their good intentions, these ideals forced the renderings into awkward locutions or pretentiously formal tropes, making Rimbaud sound as much like a biblical elder as a modern poet. Mason has finally given us an English Rimbaud we can read as we should, as if he were kin to Jack Kerouac, to Charles Bukowski, to Jim Morrison. . . . His *Rimbaud Complete* will surely live on as the standard edition. —*Toronto Star*

"Wyatt Mason's [translations] capture the rigours of the original." —*London Review of Books*

"Exceptional new translator Wyatt Mason limns the afterlife of Arthur Rimbaud's 37 chaotic years on Earth. . . . There is no small literary excitement in this, one of the best Rimbaud translations in English and certainly the most complete."
—*The Buffalo News,* Editor's Choice

"A monumental achievement . . . a book to treasure."
—*Scotland on Sunday*

"The best opportunity thus far to experience Rimbaud as fully as possible in English. Here is Rimbaud uncensored: the savage maker, the scathing satirist, the rigorous Alchemist of the Word, the master of metrics and innovator of the prose poem, the figure who made himself absolutely modern, the poetic visionary whose work systematically disorders the senses and resonates with a strange beauty, an exultant splendor."
—Edward Hirsch

PRAISE FOR WYATT MASON'S

RIMBAUD COMPLETE, VOLUME II: I PROMISE TO BE GOOD, THE LETTERS

"Perhaps you know him only by myth: Bad boy rebel poet, possibly gay but probably bisexual, lover of the lesser poet Paul Verlaine, survivor of literary and romantic scenes worthy of Norman Mailer.... Wyatt Mason, in a word, detests all that; he shows us, in his straightforward translations of these letters from the second half of Rimbaud's life (ages 19 to 37), a man dedicated to factual information, a simple but elegant describer of the foreign lands . . . a man who gives up poetry to look at the world with a disciplined eye, who sleeps outdoors for the last 20 years of his life—now there's a writer you can sink your teeth into." —*Los Angeles Times*

"The book is fascinating for the voice it reveals . . . the post-poetic Rimbaud, the man glimpsed in bracingly cold letters sent to his family. . . . Mason's translation is crisp and lively, and his clear-eyed introduction is essential reading for anyone besotted with the image of the poet as tragic figure."

—*Time Out New York*

"Mason, the American translator who last year published Rimbaud's collected poems in English [unveils] an Apollonian craftsman, one who took infinite pains to achieve perfection of expression.... Mason's an agile, skillful translator."

—*Publishers Weekly*

"Thanks to Wyatt Mason's masterly translations, Rimbaud has, after a century and a half, recovered his gift."

—Askold Melnyczuk

"Modern Library's *Rimbaud Complete*, translated and edited by Wyatt Mason . . . includes all of Rimbaud's poetry as well as uncollected writings ranging from Latin school compositions to fragments of poems reconstructed by his acquaintances. This is now joined by *I Promise to Be Good: The Letters of Arthur Rimbaud*, the largest sampling of the poet's correspondence yet to appear in English."

—*The New Yorker*

"Mason's elegant translations flow smoothly off the page."

—*Library Journal*

"Wyatt Mason's translation of Rimbaud's letters is a swashbuckler of a book, nothing less than a resurrection of a remarkable life. As such, it is a worthy companion to Mason's fine translation of the poems. No admirer of Rimbaud will want to be without it."

—Arthur Goldhammer

"The letters themselves are bizarre, twisted, and oddly welcoming. . . . Mason's introduction is invaluable. It grounds the details from Rimbaud's letters in a concrete narrative, filling in gaps without the benefit of other people's return letters, the other half of Rimbaud's conversations. Mason acts as conductor, whispering into our ears through footnotes that treat their subject playfully and respectfully at the same time."

—*The San Francisco Bay Guardian*

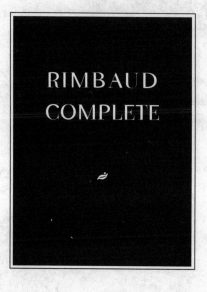

RIMBAUD
COMPLETE

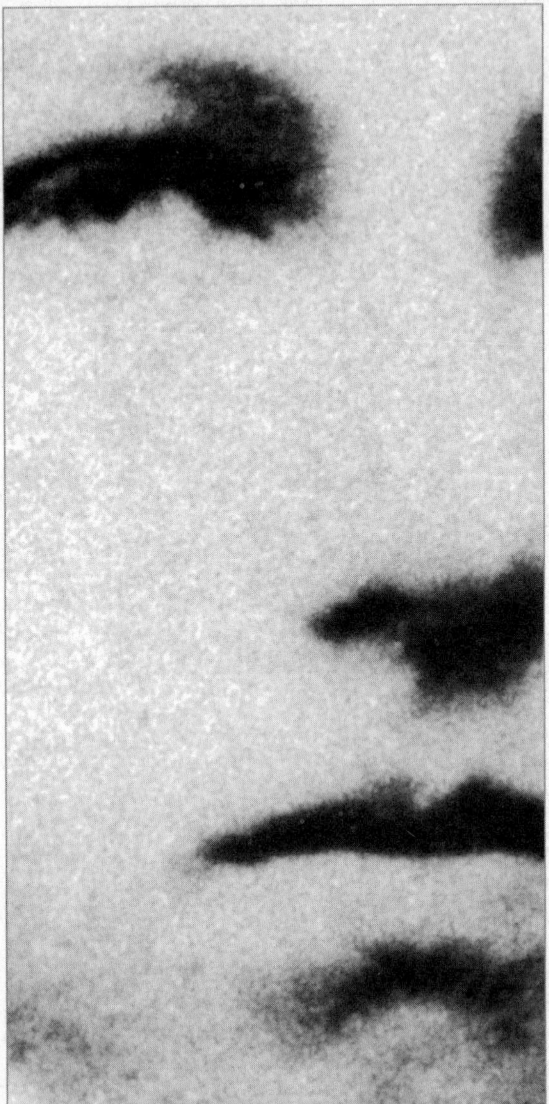

ARTHUR RIMBAUD

RIMBAUD COMPLETE

VOLUME I: POETRY AND PROSE

TRANSLATED, EDITED, AND
WITH AN INTRODUCTION BY
WYATT MASON

THE MODERN LIBRARY
NEW YORK

2003 Modern Library Paperback Edition

All images courtesy of the Musée-Bibliothèque Rimbaud de Charleville-Mézières (France).

Published in the United States by Modern Library, an imprint of The Random House Publishing Group, a division of Random House, Inc., New York, and simultaneously in Canada by Random House of Canada Limited, Toronto.

This work was originally published in hardcover by Modern Library, a division of Random House, Inc., in 2002.

LIBRARY OF CONGRESS CATALOGING-IN-PUBLICATION DATA

Rimbaud, Arthur, 1854–1891.
[Works. English. 2002]
Rimbaud complete/translated, edited, and with an introduction by Wyatt Mason.
p. cm.
Includes bibliographical references.
ISBN 0-375-75770-8 (pbk.)
1. Rimbaud, Arthur, 1854–1891—Translations into English. I. Mason, Wyatt Alexander, 1969- II. Title.

PQ2387.R5 A264 2002
841'.8—dc21 2001051389

Modern Library website address: www.modernlibrary.com

Printed in the United States of America

6 8 9 7 5

To Suzanne and William Mason

What will become of the world when you leave?
No matter what happens, no trace of now will remain.

—"Youth, IV"

ILLUMINATIONS

CONTENTS

Introduction • xxvii

A Note to the Reader • xlv

Rimbaud Complete

POETRY

I. 1869

THE ORPHANS' NEW YEAR'S GIFTS • 5

II. 1870

SENSATION • 11

SUN AND FLESH • 12

OPHELIA • 17

VENUS ANADYOMENE • 19

FIRST NIGHT • 20

NINA REPLIES • 22

"DEAD OF NINETY-TWO AND NINETY-THREE" • 27

FROZEN IN FEAR • 28

NOVEL • 30

WINTER DREAM • 32

THE SIDEBOARD • 33

THE STUNNING VICTORY AT SAARBRÜCKEN • 34

CLEVER GIRL • 35

AT THE CABARET-VERT, FIVE P.M. • 36

A Sleeper in the Valley • 37
To Music • 38
Hanged Men, Dancing • 40
Tartufe Undone • 42
The Blacksmith • 43
My Bohemia • 49
Evil • 50
Caesar's Rage • 51

III. 1871
Stolen Heart • 55
The Battle Song of Paris • 56
My Little Loves • 58
Squatting • 60
Parisian Orgy or The Repopulation of Paris • 62
Poets, Age Seven • 65
The Poor at Church • 68
Sisters of Charity • 70
First Communion • 72
On the Subject of Flowers: Remarks, Addressed to the Poet • 78
The Drunken Boat • 85
"The Righteous Man..." • 89
Jeanne-Marie's Hands • 92

IV. UNDATED POEMS, c. 1870–1872
Sitting Men • 97
Lice Hunters • 99

Customs Men • 100
"The Star Wept . . ." • 101
Evening Prayer • 102
Faun's Head • 103
Vowels • 104

V. 1872
Comedy of Thirst • 107
Good Morning Thoughts • 110
River Cassis • 111
Tear • 112
Patience Celebrated • 113
1. may banners • 113
2. song from the tallest tower • 114
3. eternity • 115
4. golden age • 116
Young Coupledom • 119
"Is She a Dancer . . . ?" • 120
Hunger Celebrated • 121
Crows • 122
"Blankets of Blood . . ." • 123
"Flowerbeds of Amaranths . . ." • 124
"In April, Listen . . ." • 126
Michel and Christine • 127
Shame • 129
Memory • 130
"O Seasons, O Châteaux" • 132

VI. 1871–1872: FROM THE *ALBUM ZUTIQUE*

SONNET TO AN ASSHOLE • 135

LILY • 136

SEEN IN ROME • 137

FEAST OF LOVE • 138

"I WAS IN A THIRD-CLASS COMPARTMENT . . ." • 139

"DOUBTLESS I PREFER . . ." • 140

"HUMANITY TIED . . ." • 141

NONSENSE/NONSENSE, PART 2 • 142

THE OLD WOMAN'S OLD MAN! • 143

UNDER SIEGE? • 144

THE BRUSH • 145

EXILE • 146

FALLEN CHERUB • 147

"ON SUMMER NIGHTS . . ." • 148

"TO BEDSIDE BOOKS . . ." • 149

SATURNINE HYPOTYPOSES, VIA BELMONTET • 150

REMEMBRANCES OF AN OLD IDIOT • 151

RECOLLECTION • 153

PROSE

I. 1866: "THE SUN WAS STILL HOT . . ." • 157

II. 1870: A HEART UNDER A CASSOCK • 163

III. 1871: DESERTS OF LOVE • 181

IV. 1872: GOSPELS • 187

V. 1873: A SEASON IN HELL • 193

"LONG AGO, IF MY MEMORY SERVES [...]" • 195

BAD BLOOD • 196

NIGHT IN HELL • 202

DELIRIA • 204

I. FOOLISH VIRGIN • 204

II. ALCHEMY OF THE WORD • 208

THE IMPOSSIBLE • 215

LIGHTNING • 217

MORNING • 218

FAREWELL • 219

VI. 1872–1874: ILLUMINATIONS • 221

AFTER THE FLOOD • 223

CHILDHOOD • 224

TALE • 227

SIDESHOW • 228

ANTIQUE • 229

BEING BEAUTEOUS • 230

LIVES • 231

DEPARTURE • 233

ROYALTY • 234

FOR A REASON • 235

DRUNKEN MORNING • 236

LINES • 237

Untitled Fragments • 238
Workers • 239
Bridges • 240
City • 241
Ruts •242
Cities [I] • 243
Vagabonds • 244
Cities [II] • 245
Vigils • 247
Mystic • 248
Dawn • 249
Flowers • 250
Common Nocturne • 251
Seascape • 252
Winter Celebrated • 253
Anguish • 254
Metropolitan • 255
Barbarian • 256
Fairy • 257
War • 258
Advt. • 259
Youth • 260
Promontory • 262
Devotion • 263
Democracy • 264
Stages • 265
Historic Evening • 266

Bottom • 267

H • 268

Movement • 269

Genius • 270

UNCOLLECTED WRITINGS

I. SCHOOLWORK • 275

"It was spring . . ." • 277

"And the new year had already begun . . ." • 280

"A very big baby was born . . ." • 283

"Long ago . . ." • 287

"In those days . . ." • 289

Apollonius the Greek Speaks of Marcus Cicero • 291

Invocation to Venus • 295

"Sire, time has abandoned his raincoat . . ." • 297

II. FROM A SCHOOL NOTEBOOK • 301

III. FRAGMENTS AND RECONSTRUCTIONS • 323

A. Via Rimbaud • 325

from CREDO IN UNAM • 325

"THE CHILD WHO GATHERED BULLETS . . ." • 327

from A LETTER TO ERNEST DELAHAYE, OCTOBER 14, 1875 • 328

B. Via Paul Verlaine • 329

VERSES FOR BATHROOM WALLS • 329

"IT RAINED SOFTLY . . ." • 330

C. Via Ernest Delahaye • 331

two sonnets • 331

"ancient animals sullied themselves . . ." • 331

"our asses aren't like theirs." • 332

"oh if the bells are bronze!" • 333

"at the feet of dark walls . . ." • 333

"in back, the porter leapt . . ." • 333

"a brunette, just sixteen . . ." • 334

"you lied . . ." • 334

[grocers' gripes] • 335

D. Via Labarrière • 336

E. Via P. Arnoult and Jean Richepin • 337

"when the iranian caravan stopped . . ." • 337

F. Errant Manuscript Phrases • 338

"take heed, o absent life of mine!" • 338

G. Fragments from the *Album Zutique* • 339

bouts-rimés (poem in set rhymes) • 339

"but . . ." • 340

IV. A DRAFT OF *A SEASON IN HELL* • 341

[*from* bad blood] • 343

false conversion • 345

[*from* deliria ii: alchemy of the word] • 347

hunger • 348

eternity • 349

golden age • 350

MEMORY • 351

ENDS OF THE EARTH • 352

BL[IS]S • 353

V. FOUR SEASONS • 355

VI. LETTERS: "THE ARTIST AS CRITIC" • 361

LETTER TO THÉODORE DE BANVILLE, MAY 24, 1870 • 363

LETTER TO GEORGE IZAMBARD, MAY 13, 1871 • 364

LETTER TO PAUL DEMENY, MAY 15, 1871 • 366

LETTER TO PAUL DEMENY, JUNE 10, 1871 • 371

LETTER TO THÉODORE DE BANVILLE, AUGUST 15, 1871 • 372

Œuvres Complètes

POÉSIES

I. 1869

LES ÉTRENNES DES ORPHELINS • 376

II. 1870

SENSATION • 379

SOLEIL ET CHAIR • 379

OPHÉLIE • 383

VÉNUS ANADYOMÈNE • 384

PREMIÈRE SOIRÉE • 384

LES REPARTIES DE NINA • 385

"MORTS DE QUATRE-VINGT-DOUZE [. . .]" • 389

Les Effarés • 390

Roman • 391

Rêvé pour l'hiver • 392

Le buffet • 393

L'éclatante victoire de Saarebrück • 393

La Maline • 394

Au Cabaret-Vert, cinq heures du soir • 394

Le Dormeur du Val • 395

À la Musique • 396

Bal des pendus • 397

Le châtiment de Tartufe • 398

Le Forgeron • 399

Ma Bohême (Fantaisie) • 403

Le Mal • 404

Rages de Césars • 404

III. 1871

Le Cœur volé • 406

Chant de guerre Parisien • 407

Mes Petites amoureuses • 408

Accroupissements • 409

L'Orgie parisienne ou Paris se repeuple • 410

Les Poètes de sept ans • 413

Les Pauvres à l'église • 414

Les Sœurs de charité • 416

Les Premières Communions • 417

Ce qu'on dit au Poète à propos de fleurs • 421

Le Bateau ivre • 426

L'Homme juste • 429

Les Mains de Jeanne-Marie • 431

IV. POEMES NON DATÉS, C. 1870–1872

Les Assis • 434

Les Chercheuses de poux • 435

Les Douaniers • 436

"L'étoile a pleuré rose [. . .]" • 436

Oraison du soir • 437

Tête de faune • 437

Voyelles • 438

V. 1872

Comédie de la Soif • 439

Bonne Pensée du matin • 441

La Rivière de Cassis • 442

Larme • 443

Fêtes de la patience • 443

1. bannières de mai • 444

2. chanson de la plus haute tour • 444

3. l'éternité • 445

4. âge d'or • 446

Jeune ménage • 448

"Est-elle almée? [. . .]" • 448

Fêtes de la faim • 449

Les Corbeaux • 450

"Qu'est-ce pour nous, mon cœur [. . .]" • 450

"Plates-bandes d'amarantes [. . .]" • 451
"Entends comme brame [. . .]" • 452
Michel et Christine • 453
Honte • 454
Mémoire • 454
"O saisons, ô châteaux [. . .]" • 456

VI. 1871–1872: POEMES DE L'*ALBUM ZUTIQUE* • 457
L'idole. Sonnet de Trou du Cul • 457
Lys • 457
Vu à Rome • 458
Fête galante • 458
"J'occupais un wagon de troisième [. . .]" • 459
"Je préfère sans doute [. . .]" • 459
"L'Humanité chaussait [. . .]" • 459
Conneries/Conneries, deuxième série • 460
Vieux de la vieille! • 460
Etat de siège? • 460
Le balai • 461
Exil • 461
L'angelot maudit • 462
"Les soirs d'été [. . .]" • 462
"Aux livres de chevet [. . .]" • 463
Hypotyposes saturniennes, ex Belmontet • 463
Les Remembrances du vieillard idiot • 463
Ressouvenir • 465

PROSES

I. 1866: "LE SOLEIL ÉTAIT ENCORE CHAUD [. . .]" • 468

II. 1870: UN CŒUR SOUS UNE SOUTANE • 470

III. 1871: LES DÉSERTS DE L'AMOUR • 481

IV. 1872: PROSES ÉVANGELIQUES • 483

V. 1873: UNE SAISON EN ENFER • 485

"Jadis, si je me souviens bien [. . .]" • 485

Mauvais sang • 485

Nuit de l'enfer • 490

Délires • 491

I. vierge folle • 491

II. alchimie du verbe • 494

L'Impossible • 499

L'Éclair • 501

Matin • 501

Adieu • 502

VI. 1872–1874: ILLUMINATIONS • 503

Après le Déluge • 503

Enfance • 504

Conte • 505

Parade • 506

Antique • 507

Being Beauteous • 507
Vies • 507
Départ • 508
Royauté • 508
À une Raison • 509
Matinée d'ivresse • 509
Phrases • 509
Fragments sans titre • 510
Ouvriers • 511
Les Ponts • 511
Ville • 511
Ornières • 512
Villes [I] • 512
Vagabonds • 513
Villes [II] • 513
Veillées • 514
Mystique • 515
Aube • 515
Fleurs • 516
Nocturne vulgaire • 516
Marine • 517
Fête d'hiver • 517
Angoisse • 517
Métropolitain • 518
Barbare • 518
Fairy • 519
Guerre • 519
Solde • 519

Jeunesse • 520
Promontoire • 521
Dévotion • 522
Démocratie • 522
Scènes • 523
Soir historique • 523
Bottom • 524
H • 524
Mouvement • 524
Génie • 525

ŒUVRES DIVERSES

I. COMPOSITIONS D'ÉCOLE • 528
"Ver erat [...]" • 528
"Jamque novus [...]" • 529
"Nascitur Arabiis [...]" • 531
"Olim inflatus [...]" • 534
"Tempus erat [...]" • 535
Verba Apollonii de Marco Cicerone • 536
Invocation à Venus • 538
"Sire, le temps a laissé [...]" • 539

II. D'UN CAHIER D'ÉCOLIER • 542

III. FRAGMENTS ET RECONSTITUTIONS • 557
A. Fragments de Rimbaud • 557
credo in unam • 557
"l'enfant qui ramassa les balles[...]" • 558
"on a faim dans la chambrée[...]" • 558

B. Reconstitutions par Verlaine • 559
vers pour les lieux • 559
"il pleut doucement sur la ville [...]" • 559
C. Reconstitutions par Ernest Delahaye • 560
deux sonnets • 560
"les anciens animaux saillissaient [...]" • 560
"nos fesses ne sont pas les leurs [...]" • 560
"oh! si les cloches sont de bronze [...]" • 561
"au pied des sombres murs [...]" • 561
"derrière tressautait en des hoquets grotesques [...]" • 561
"brune, elle avait seize ans [...]" • 561
"vous avez menti [...]" • 561
la plainte des épiciers • 561
D. Reconstitutions par Labarrière • 562
E. Reconstitutions par P. Arnoult et Jean Richepin • 563
"quand s'arrêta la caravane [...]" • 563
F. Phrase • 563
"prends-y garde, ô ma vie absente!" • 563
G. Fragments de *L'Album Zutique* • 563
bouts-rimés • 563
"mais enfin [...]" • 564

IV. BROUILLON D'*UNE SAISON EN ENFER* • 565
Mauvais sang • 565
Fausse conversion • 566
Délires II: Alchimie du verbe • 566
Faim • 567
Éternité • 567

ÂGE D'OR • 568

MÉMOIRE • 568

CONFINS DU MONDE • 568

BONR • 569

V. LETTRES CHOISIES • 570

À THÉODORE DE BANVILLE, 24 MAI 1870 • 570

À GEORGE IZAMBARD, 13 MAI 1871 • 571

À PAUL DEMENY, 15 MAI 1871 • 572

À PAUL DEMENY, 10 JUIN 1871 • 575

À THÉODORE DE BANVILLE, 15 AOÛT 1871 • 576

Acknowledgments • 577

Selected Bibliography • 579

Index of Titles and First Lines (English) • 583

Index of Titles and First Lines (French) • 593

INTRODUCTION

Fame is, after all, only the sum
of all the misunderstandings
that gather around a new name.
—RAINER MARIA RILKE[1]

I

WE KNOW THE FACE: the delicate features, the pale eyes, the uninflected expression. We know the slight turn of the head, the shadow clouding one cheek. We know the stare, forever directed past us, above us, focusing on some unknown something out of frame. It is an attractive face, but the more we examine it, the more it eludes us. And although it seems somehow benevolent, or at the very least unimposing, it tells us very little. It could belong to a matinee idol, a prince, or the boy next door. It could even belong to Arthur Rimbaud.

---

1. Mitchell, 308.

The face—which comes down to us in a photograph snapped by Etienne Carjat in December 1871—was not the Paris photographer's only stab at Rimbaud. Two months earlier, the poet had visited Carjat's studio a first time. A very different face emerged from that session, one we rarely see.

In this photo, Rimbaud is dressed just as he would be in the second: the neat, dark coat; the pale vest, buttoned all the way up; the haphazardly knotted tie. But delicate features are not in evidence. The poet's cheeks are chubby. His nose looks twice as wide. His mouth, an inarticulate line later on, is full, its corners downturned. It looks like a bruise. Then there are his eyes. While still notably pale, this time they stare directly at us. Open, but like a wound. The expression seems to say: look at me, come on, *I dare you.* Were we not assured that this is Arthur Rimbaud, we would be hard-pressed to recognize him. As it happens, this is the photo Rimbaud's contemporaries said resembled him most.[2]

Yet in the century since his death, the December photo has *become* Rimbaud, reproduced in nearly every book devoted to him or his work.

2. Robb, 140. Rimbaud's childhood friend Ernest Delahaye and his professor George Izambard believed the earlier photo the better likeness.

The October photo has fallen away. Our preference for the later image is not, therefore, a reflection of how Rimbaud looked in his time, rather how we have come to prefer him to look in ours. Jean Cocteau, describing the appeal of the December portrait, wrote: "He looks like an angel... His eyes are stars."[3] Enid Starkie, an early biographer, found a "look of extraordinary purity... an astonishing and spiritual beauty."[4] Thus a beautiful face, like how many others before it, helped launch a thousand myths.

For in the short span of the century since his death, Rimbaud has been memorialized in song and story as few in history: a half-dozen biographies in English; fictional accounts in celluloid and print; documentaries; popular songs in many languages; numerous settings of his poems to music; even an opera. The thumbnail of his legend has proved irresistible: the boy genius who abandoned writing at twenty; the rapscallion who seduced a married Paul Verlaine; the thug who bullied everyone, even stabbed Carjat; the visionary who took drugs to expand his creative consciousness; the scoundrel who sold slaves in Africa; the martyr who died young.

Some of these tantalizing elements may even be true. But while the critical and biographical debate continues, readers are faced with an ancillary difficulty. So accustomed have we become to these variations on the Myth of Rimbaud, that when we turn to the poems themselves it is difficult to keep our preconceptions at bay. We find ourselves looking for the Adolescent Poet here, the Hallucinogenic Poet there, the Gay Poet everywhere. The problem with all of these adjectives is that they put too plain a face on the poems. And the poems—vessels of indeterminacy, ambiguity and frequently strange beauty—are easily disfigured by a blunt critical blade.

But: if we can manage to ignore what we know about Rimbaud or believe we know, if we can focus briefly on what he made rather than what he may have done, the opportunity to explore one of the most varied troves of individual expression in literature awaits us.

---

3. Ibid., 140.
4. Starkie, 166.

II

This much is sure: Jean-Nicolas-Arthur Rimbaud was born in 1854, in the French town of Charleville, some 200 miles northeast of Paris, near the Belgian border. He had a brother, and three sisters, two of whom died young. The father was a military officer rarely home during Rimbaud's earliest years, leaving for good when the boy was six. Thereafter, Arthur and his siblings were raised by their mother, by all accounts a person of considerable sternness. At thirteen, Rimbaud wrote a sixty-line poem in Latin, which he sent to Emperor Napoleon III's son (the poem is said to have reached the prince, but no copy of it remains). By age fourteen, Rimbaud was winning nearly every academic competition he entered, and by fifteen, had his first poem published in a literary review. He wrote to famous poets of the day, sending them his work in hope of publication. They declined to publish him but they did write back. Invitations followed, and Rimbaud fled, repeatedly, to Paris. For the remainder of his teens, he traveled, often on foot, and not infrequently with police escort or interest. He also wrote. That the police took an interest in his movements is confirmed by official municipal records; that he wrote is confirmed by fellow poets and friends who retained the manuscripts he gave them, despite, in one instance, his request to *"burn all the poems I was dumb enough to give you."*[5] Such friendly defiance turned out to be very important: without it, you and I would not be sitting here together.

For during Rimbaud's life, he actively achieved posterity for only two poems, "The Orphans' New Year's Gifts" and "First Night," published in reviews, and one prose poem, *A Season in Hell,* self-published. Everything else that fattens the book in your hands passed through a great many others, of which Rimbaud scrupulously washed his: shortly after his twentieth birthday, he began a five-year period of peregrinations through England, Scotland, Germany, Switzerland, Italy, Holland, Sweden, Denmark, and Egypt, ostensibly in pursuit of work, whether as tutor, soldier, or foreman, before departing Europe for Africa, living all but his final

5. See "Letter to Paul Demeny," p. 366.

days in Abyssinia as a trader of goods (coffee, cloth, guns), and dying at thirty-seven in Marseilles after the amputation of an ailing leg failed to restore his health. Thus it is true that after his twenty-first birthday, the only writing we have from Rimbaud's hand takes the form of letters that offer some literary, and much biographical, interest.

In constructing this skeleton of Rimbaud's life, I have made every attempt to sidestep the many colorful secondary characters, strenuously avoiding the brand of sentimentality that has made Rimbaud a patron saint of precocity. That said, it is only human of us to want to probe these bones further, with an anthropological eye. "Published at fourteen" puts us in mind of other prodigies: Mozart on his fiddle at four, before all of Europe's royalty; Picasso at his easel, painting impossibly well at nine; insert your favorite here. The fact of his genius, undeniable and remarkable, is as interesting to remember as it is essential to forget: if Rimbaud's poems are worth reading—and they are—it is not because they were a circus trick performed by an immensely clever bear, but because their artistry warrants our attention.

What might have been responsible for Rimbaud's "abandonment of poetry," deemed in one hyperbolic assessment as having "caused more lasting, widespread consternation than the break-up of the Beatles," is a question without an answer, though another poet has made some useful admissions:

> Trying to learn to use words, and every attempt
> Is a wholly new start, and a different kind of failure
> Because one has only learnt to get the better of words
> For the thing one no longer has to say, or the way in which
> One is no longer disposed to say it. And so each venture
> Is a new beginning, a raid on the inarticulate
> With shabby equipment always deteriorating
> In the general mess of imprecision of feeling,
> Undisciplined squads of emotion. And what there is to conquer
> By strength and submission, has already been discovered
> Once or twice, or several times, by men whom one cannot hope

To emulate—but there is no competition—
There is only the fight to recover what has been lost
And found and lost again and again: and now, under conditions
That seem unpropitious. But perhaps neither gain nor loss.
For us, there is only the trying. The rest is not our business.
—*from* FOUR QUARTETS, T. S. Eliot

Nor, in the end, is the question of why Rimbaud's literary trail ends well before that of his life any of our business.

Let our business be Rimbaud's poetry.

III

"Some poems which I wrote and, unfortunately, published, I have thrown out because they were dishonest, or bad-mannered, or boring." So wrote W. H. Auden in the Introduction to his *Collected Shorter Poems.* If it seems oxymoronic to the reader that a volume could be termed *Collected* and still elect to omit, the practice has become a sort of poetic quid pro quo. T. S. Eliot and W. B. Yeats, among others, supervised very elastic definitions of such a seemingly inflexible word as *complete.* When preparing their posterities, they dropped poems altogether or revised others written half a century earlier, bringing them into congruence with the whole body of a life's work. Auden, on the subject of revision, wrote: "I can only say that I have never, consciously at any rate, attempted to revise my former thoughts or feelings, only the language in which they were first expressed when, on further consideration, it seemed to me inaccurate, lifeless, prolix or painful to the ear."[6]

As we have grown accustomed to this luster upon our poets' coffins, if we expect the same from Rimbaud we will be disappointed, or, at the very least, perplexed. For when reading Rimbaud, we encounter the occasional poem that may well be dishonest, bad-mannered, or boring,

6. Auden, 16.

written in language that is lifeless, prolix, or painful to the ear. Rather than seeing this as a condition that can be solved editorially—by omitting bad poems, or by offering translations that seek to "improve" uneven passages—it is wiser, I believe, to view Rimbaud's occasional lack of good grooming as a unique opportunity to experience the uneven, vivid, and rapid progression of his verse. His brief stint as a neophyte making smart copies and parodies (if not outright thefts) of earlier poets' work is followed by almost ceaseless innovation. Rimbaud repeatedly shreds metrical and musical corsets on his way to the restraint and reserve of the late poems called *Illuminations*. Rimbaud does not have a single style that unites the works within this volume; rather, styles often appear very briefly as he toys with a particular verse form to which he never again returns.

The earliest of Rimbaud's poems, published on January 2, 1870, begins:

> The room is full of shadow; you vaguely hear
> Two children whispering, sadly, softly.
> Heavy with sleep, their heads are bowed
> Beneath the long white curtain that trembles and rises...
> —Outside, birds huddle against the cold;
> Wings benumbed beneath the sky's gray shade;
> And the New Year, trailing mist,
> Drags the folds of her snowy train behind her,
> Smiling through tears, shivering as she sings...
>
> —*from* THE ORPHANS' NEW YEAR'S GIFTS

A few months later, in March of 1870, he wrote the second of his poems to reach us:

> Through blue summer nights I will pass along paths,
> Pricked by wheat, trampling short grass:
> Dreaming, I will feel coolness underfoot,
> Will let breezes bathe my bare head.

Not a word, not a thought:
Boundless love will surge through my soul,
And I will wander far away, a vagabond
In Nature—as happily as with a woman.
—SENSATION

And a little over a year later, during the summer of 1871, he produced a poem that begins:

While swept downstream on indifferent Rivers,
I felt the boatmen's tow-ropes slacken:
Yawping Redskins took them as targets
Nailing them naked to totem poles.

I never gave much thought to my crews,
To holds of Flemish wheat or English cotton.
So when the cries of boatmen and Redskins receded
The Rivers left me to chart my course.
—*from* THE DRUNKEN BOAT

The first, "The Orphans' New Year's Gifts," is a highly polished pastiche of a style of sentimental poetry prevalent in the day (angels, orphans, poverty), the wistful poet casting a misty eye on the misanthropic, at which Hugo was master. The second, "Sensation," roots the reader in an entirely different and far more individual voice. Abandoned is the guise of impersonal, all-knowing Poet descanting from the empyrean; adopted is a sensual, personal directness of sensory experience. It is a love poem, written to Nature, but without Nature being mediated through the mythic: no Venus intercedes to garland the young bard with rings of flowers.[7] In the third, "The Drunken Boat," Rimbaud removes the poet from the poem al-

7. For an example of Rimbaud writing in this older, less individual mode, see "It was spring . . . ," p. 277.

together: instead, a boat, having lost its crew, drifts through the wreck of the world's waters recounting its own journey, a leap from simile to anthropomorphization that was, in its time, a radically new means of poetic expression. In just eighteen months, Rimbaud moved from the method of poetic apprenticeship favored by Dr. Johnson—that of scrupulous imitation—to utter originality. And he was by no means done.

In the summer of 1873, Rimbaud's production of rhyming poetry begins to wane. He turns his attention to prose. Rimbaud had experimented with prose forms since he was a very small boy, and by the autumn of that same year he published the only work he deemed finished, *A Season in Hell:* a complex, polyphonic, highly compressed collection of dramatic monologues. *A Season in Hell* tends to polarize those who wish to read Rimbaud's work chiefly as a road map to his life: some view it as an account of Rimbaud's experiences with French poet Paul Verlaine, the poet's most infamous intimate; others prefer to interpret the work as proof of Rimbaud as Seer, predicting his African future. It is clear that travel, adventure, and departure on various levels are thematic concerns that run through much of Rimbaud, including *A Season in Hell,* but what advantage can be gained by viewing the work through any single prism is for the reader to decide. No matter how one elects to read *A Season in Hell,* it presents a struggle both in its content and its form. The poem is as articulate a document of existential ambivalence as we have, and its method, for better and worse, is expressive of that very ambivalence.

The last of Rimbaud's major works are the *Illuminations,* most of which are prose poems, with a scattering of verse. While the prose poem had been exploited as a form by Baudelaire, Mallarmé, and others before Rimbaud, his efforts are nonetheless distinctive within such distinguished company. The advent of the prose poem represented a liberation from the strictures of established verse forms. Rimbaud, who quickly mastered and moved past many such forms while pioneering his own, must have found the formally informal liberty of prose ideally suited to a thematic quest for liberty, perennially present at all stages in his artistic development.

In the winter of 1875, Verlaine visited Rimbaud in Stuttgart and was handed a pile of manuscripts. Verlaine gathered them together, named them *Illuminations,* and saw to it they were published, a decade later. "Illuminations" is meant in the double sense of epiphany and of "pictures in books." The order of its forty-two parts is definitely not of Rimbaud's choosing, but they are unquestionably all of a piece. Some have suggested that there were more than forty-two, that some were lost. This cannot be confirmed. Since Verlaine's time, editors have arranged the poems in numerous ways, most of which are as good as any other. Paul Schmidt's decision to present them not as prose but as blank verse, with line breaks determined according to Schmidt's excellent ear for the musical qualities of a poem, seems, while enjoyable, wrongheaded. All major French editions of the *Illuminations,* based on the original manuscripts, present them as a mix of prose and poetry. I have, too.

The *Illuminations* contain some of Rimbaud's most vivid and direct imagery, Graham Robb noting their "almost total absence of comparisons and analogies. Every image exists in its own right." Scholars have often described them as perplexing and abstruse. It is true that they defy tidy explication; perhaps for this reason, it seems to me that of all Rimbaud's work they are the most immune to the Myth, the least prone to being read only as vessels into which the poet pours the ashes of self.

Scattered throughout these monuments are a not-unreasonable share of ruins. Some are structures no one would recommend on an itinerary as compulsory viewing; others are suggestions of what might well have been beauty beyond imagining.

IV

The excavation of Rimbaud's writing has been a century-long detective story full of dead ends, red herrings, and shocking reversals. *Rimbaud Complete* is thus a deceptively tidy title. It would be more appropriately named *Everything We Could Find That He Wrote.* In this regard, scholarly work on

Rimbaud's legacy is most similar to rescue missions run by classical scholars in which fragments of Sappho, written on shards of pottery or tatters of papyrus, are salvaged from oblivion.

While far less fragmentary than Sappho's output, Rimbaud's is similarly scattered. Most of it (in the form of manuscripts written in his neat, occasionally showy hand) comes to us from three sources: George Izambard, Rimbaud's teacher and early mentor at school; Paul Demeny, a Belgian poet and friend; and Verlaine. A variety of other individuals in Rimbaud's circle possessed manuscripts, few of which had been dated, adding exponentially to editorial difficulties when organizing any edition, as the dozens of competing French collections in the last century amply attest. Amid all that disagreement, one thing is certain: had Rimbaud elected to have anything to do with his posterity, many poems would have met the fate to which Auden consigned certain of his.

I have rejected nothing, arranging the poems and the prose in separate sections, chronologically, or as close to chronologically as current scholarly consensus allows. Another organizational option some have tried is a thematic grouping of poems based on the editor's critical judgment. Although such arrangements can prove engaging, they risk imposing too singular a reading of the works upon readers. The method I've chosen—an evolutionary presentation of the poet's work—seemed to be the most objective way of exhibiting Rimbaud's accomplishments, and the least likely to prevent the reader from coming away with his or her own Rimbaud. I make this statement while recognizing the outright impossibility of any real objectivity, given that Arthur Rimbaud wrote in French, and readers of this edition will, necessarily, be reading my English, which brings us to the matter of translation.

V

The number of ways in which any single line can be translated is exceeded only by the number of theories of translation that have been advanced over the years. Debates over opposing views have sometimes grown heated, occasionally boiling over into violence. William Tyndale, the greatest translator of the Bible since Jerome, whose work would later serve as the basis for the so-called King James version, was strangled by the hangman and, as if that were not enough, burned at the stake for his solitary act of faith. More recently, translators of Salman Rushdie's *The Satanic Verses,* that supposedly sacrilegious text which launched the fatwa heard 'round the world, have been attacked: Ettore Capriolo, Rushdie's Italian translator, was assaulted in his apartment but survived; Hitoshi Igarashi, who translated the book into Japanese, was slashed to death.

But religious reactionaries are not the only ones to throw stones. The fervor has carried over into the secular world, where polyglot writers hurl metaphors instead. Nabokov's is perhaps best known:

> What is translation? On a platter
> A poet's pale and glaring head,
> A parrot's screech, a monkey's chatter,
> And profanation of the dead.[8]

Milan Kundera, in his *Testaments Betrayed,* goes as far as to equate mistranslation of an author's work with sodomy performed upon the unwilling writer. There are countless such comparisons. All of them, whether witty or just plain weird, refer to the yin and yang of translation, its irreconcilable poles: literalism or liberty.

Kundera, Nabokov, et al are advocates of literalism, a theory founded on the notion that there exist, across languages, very nearly exact equivalents for words. The task of the translator is to find them, hewing as close a course as possible to the original author's expression while avoiding the howlers that ignorant allegiance engenders. There is Nabokov's classic example:

---

8. Nabokov, *Onegin,* 9.

> Insufficient acquaintance with the foreign language involved may transform a commonplace expression into some remarkable statement that the real author never intended to make. "*Bien être general*" ["general well-being"] becomes the manly assertion that "it is good to be a general."[9]

Translators, the literalists argue, are altogether too willing to depart from the texts they have in favor of blasphemous inventions of their own, made chiefly in order to bypass the appearance of awkwardness that rigorous fidelity can create, and which inevitably leads critics to conclude that the translation, because of its awkwardness, must therefore be poor, as Edmund Wilson famously concluded when reviewing Nabokov's translation of Pushkin's *Eugene Onegin,* prompting one of the most interesting and fiery exchanges in the history of literary translation.[10]

Translation, in the literalist model, turns a deaf ear to euphony in favor of sense, preparing not a work of art in its own right but a means of serving a work of art by rendering what has been written, not what the translator feels has been suggested, implied, or felt.

Borges, another heavyweight in the debate, takes the opposite view, believing that a translation should aspire to being viewed as an independent work of art. Literalism was born, Borges believed, with translations of the Bible:

> . . . because the Bible was supposed to have been written by the Holy Ghost. If we think of the Holy Ghost, if we think of the infinite intelligence of God undertaking a literary task, then we are not allowed to think of any chance elements—of any haphazard elements—in his work. No—if God writes a book, if God condescends to literature, then every word, every letter, as the Kabalists

9. Nabokov, *Lectures,* 315.

10. For further reading on this clash of titans, see Nabokov's essay "A Reply to My Critics" in *Strong Opinions*, pp. 241–67.

said, must have been thought out. It might be blasphemy to tamper with the text written by an endless, eternal intelligence....

—*from* THIS CRAFT OF VERSE[11]

That sacrosanct idea of the Word has carried over into the pagan world of letters, much to Borges's dismay. He looks forward to a time when "translation will be considered something in itself... when men will care for beauty, not for the circumstances of beauty."[12]

Many are in Borges's corner, believing that a translation is nothing if it does not become something in and of itself. Dr. Johnson claimed, "We must try its effect as an English poem, that is the way to judge the merit of a translation." William Gass, distinguished translator of Rilke, has written that the translator must aspire to rendering the poem the poet would have written had he or she written in our language.[13] And Paul Auster has declared that when translating a poem, given the choice between literalism and poetry, he unhesitatingly chooses poetry.[14]

Both camps, of course, are correct: philosophical broadsides not excluded, all translation is a compromise between the rival philosophies, requiring, as Nabokov wrote, "a poet's patience and scholastic passion blent."[15]

Three prior translators have mustered the patience and passion required to render Rimbaud's complete works into English. Two of the translations may safely be termed Nabokovian (for brevity's sake, only one of them will be addressed here), while another may safely be labeled Borgesian. To see these different philosophies in action, let us consider Rimbaud's poem "Jeune goinfre," from the *Album Zutique.* On the left is Rimbaud's original. On the right are three different renderings into English.

11. Borges, 72.
12. Borges, 76.
13. Gass, 113.
14. Auster, xlviii.
15. Nabokov, *Onegin,* 10.

Jeune goinfre	**Young Glutton**	**Young Glutton**	**Piglet**
Casquette	Cap	Two sick	Silky
De moire,	Of silk,	Young fruits.	Beanie
Quéquette	Prick	Drastic	Ivory
D'ivoire,	Of ivory.	Pursuits.	Weenie.
Toilette	Clothes	Big thick	Black
Très noire,	Very black,	Black boots,	Frocks,
Paul guette	Paul watches	Paul's trick	Paul stalks
L'armoire,	The cupboard,	Just suits.	The hutch,
Projette	Sticks out	"Don't kick,	Towards pear,
Languette	Small tongue	Just lick."	Turns
Sur poire,	At pear,	Disputes.	Tongue,
S'apprête	Prepares,	"Some prick."	Rod, at ready
Baguette,	Wand,	"Come quick!"	With
Et foire.	And diarrhea.	He shoots.	The runs.
	(Wallace Fowlie)[16]	(Paul Schmidt)[17]	(Wyatt Mason)

"Jeune goinfre" is Rimbaud at his most verbally playful, and sexual (or obscene, depending on your moral barometer). The first translation, by Wallace Fowlie, is a literal, line-by-line gloze, the method favored by Fowlie throughout his edition. Fowlie's is the ideal translation for a student of French who wishes to read the original but requires a crutch. As such, Rimbaud's poems are presented on facing pages, making it impossible to forget the translations' dependence upon them: they are joined at the hip. By design, Fowlie's method ignores rhyme, rhythm, and all of the arrows in the poet's quiver apart from bare-bones definitions (over which one is nonetheless bound to argue, for lexicography, however

16. Fowlie, 157.
17. Schmidt, 141.

scrupulous, is a matter of relatives, not absolutes). Fowlie's work also ignores the consequential fact that French grammar and English grammar are very different. If, as Fowlie does, one translates each word literally and maintains French word order, the translation, though no longer in French, cannot be truly said to be in English, either. Rather, it is in a third language that lies between the two, the language of translatorese that fuses (in this case) English words onto French grammar. "Cap of silk," while certainly correct as far as the word-by-word meaning of the French phrase, has, to modern ears, an antique quality that the phrase in French does not possess: *casquette de moire* is merely the way one would say "silk cap" in French.

The second translation, by Paul Schmidt, could not be more different. Schmidt has not translated the poem's words, but rather its style and apparent subject (erotic horseplay), while at the same time eschewing the presentation of French originals *en face.* Whereas Fowlie ignores rhyme and rhythm, Schmidt bravely holds to them. Read in English, Schmidt's translation gives the reader what Fowlie's doesn't: a feeling of what it is like to read Rimbaud's music. In so doing, however, Schmidt writes a totally new poem that may or may not be beautiful (each of us will decide that for ourselves), but which has little to do with the literal sense of what Rimbaud wrote. Schmidt's rendition is more explicitly sexual (as opposed to Rimbaud's tacit filth), offering us "Two sick young fruits," where "fruits" is a slangy substitute for homosexuals. Rimbaud makes no such indication of sexual preference, nor, for that matter, of two people at all: one—"Paul"—is mentioned; the other is implied.

The last translation, my own, strives to find common, rather than middle, ground between the two poles presented by Fowlie and Schmidt. My desire is to present, as closely as possible, a poem that Rimbaud *might* have written, rather than one he surely couldn't have, or one that someone else undoubtedly did. The first stanza finds me using words very similar to Fowlie's, substituting "beanie" for "cap" (as "beanie" is closer in meaning and disyllabic rhythm to *casquette*) and "weenie" for "prick" (for the same reasons). I have also, where possible, tried to have the lines scan in English, dropping the prepositions (*de*/of) that clutter the phrase and create odd inversions. Although I do invert common word order in stanza three, it is to serve the rhyme in the final line of stanza four. I justify this violation of my earlier dictum on the grounds that it *gains* something for the poem: a semblance of euphony, whereas Fowlie's inversions do not bring us closer to the original French, beyond its grammar. Where rhyme is available, I take it (in the first stanza, a matter of luck), but I do not allow the desire for rhyme to risk erasing all traces of the words Rimbaud chose. That, for me, would be going too far. Instead, I strive to use alternate means at my disposal (rhythm, sibilance, word order, internal consistency, etc.) to attempt to duplicate the effects Rimbaud was achieving.

The difficulty with any of these philosophies of translation—Fowlie's, Schmidt's, my own—is that none provides an indelible solution. Every translator struggles to convey Rimbaud in all his richness: he was a master of metrical and musical rigor unique to French poetry. The approximative nature of translation makes conveying such mastery an endless retreat: some degree of richness *must* be lost. The essential question becomes: how much loss is tolerable? When Borges hoped that translation "will be considered something in itself," he was addressing the endless tug of war between the tolerable and the ideal.

My translation, in so much as it strives to convey its source, is offered as an honest account of Rimbaud's work, not a replacement for it. What is certain beyond all philosophical considerations is the real wonder of so much of what Rimbaud wrote. I have therefore included all his French and Latin originals in this volume, in their own section, unfettered by my grapplings, so they may be enjoyed for what they are, not what I or anyone else reports them to be.

VI

Working forward from the principal of readerly enjoyment, I've included many hitherto untranslated parts of Rimbaud's legacy in this edition. As it turns out, none of these is a lost manuscript recently unearthed by a literary sleuth. Rather, a bafflingly rich range of writings that have been available in France throughout the twentieth century and that no one had bothered to put into English before. The reasons behind such omissions become thoroughly incomprehensible as soon as you've read these jewels.

The most important of these are Rimbaud's school compositions. Whereas only "It was spring..." ("Ver erat") had seen English, all the exercises are given here. They are, I believe, remarkable, not because of Rimbaud's age at their composition, but for their literary merit. Given a dusty old French poem or a few lines of Horace's Latin, Rimbaud reinvents the source in one fascinating performance after another. Of these, "Apollonius the Greek Speaks of Marcus Cicero" is a remarkably moving piece of thought and expression.

I also include the first translation of writings in a school notebook Rimbaud kept from age nine to eleven (approximately). It contains parts of lessons (arithmetic, Latin, Greek) and idle verbal wanderings. It is interesting as a showcase of the various texts to which the budding poet was exposed, and it provides some context for an excerpt long presented as Rimbaud's earliest work, "The sun was still hot..." (erroneously known as "Prologue"), a brief account of the sort of daydream one might imagine a young boy having (though not normally committing to paper). The piece appears in the middle of the notebook, stuck between some clumsy paraphrases of the Vulgate Bible. Readers now have the opportunity to read it in its original context.

I have translated a fragmentary early draft of *A Season in Hell,* which highlights the rigorous editing to which Rimbaud subjected the poem. While only a portion of the lost manuscript, it is suggestive of Rimbaud's method.

Four Seasons presents four different drafts of one of Rimbaud's best-loved poems, offering us a glimpse at overall editorial complexities. I have also included all of Rimbaud's fragments, including all the highly undependable bits of poems remembered by several of his friends, which are presented for the first time.

Finally, in *Letters: The Artist as Critic*, we read a few of Rimbaud's letters, in which he offers pronouncements on the proper path of modern verse, giving him, for once, the last word.

—Wyatt Mason
December 2001

A NOTE TO THE READER

The notes that accompany some of the poems are neither intended nor designed to explain Rimbaud's work: I only define specific references to French culture or history that an American dictionary is unlikely to illuminate.

When I refer to the work of prior Rimbaud scholars by last name only (e.g., "Murphy says..."), this is shorthand for full citations found in the bibliography.

The dates and signatures that follow some of the poems are transcriptions from the manuscripts. Rimbaud did not follow any consistent notational method: sometimes he abbreviates, sometimes he does not.

Occasionally, a horizontal series of dots will separate one of Rimbaud's stanzas from the next. These dots reproduce those Rimbaud wrote on his manuscripts and probably indicate cuts the author had made in earlier versions. Rather than replace them with an arbitrary typographical element, I have retained them, in keeping with all French editions of the poems.

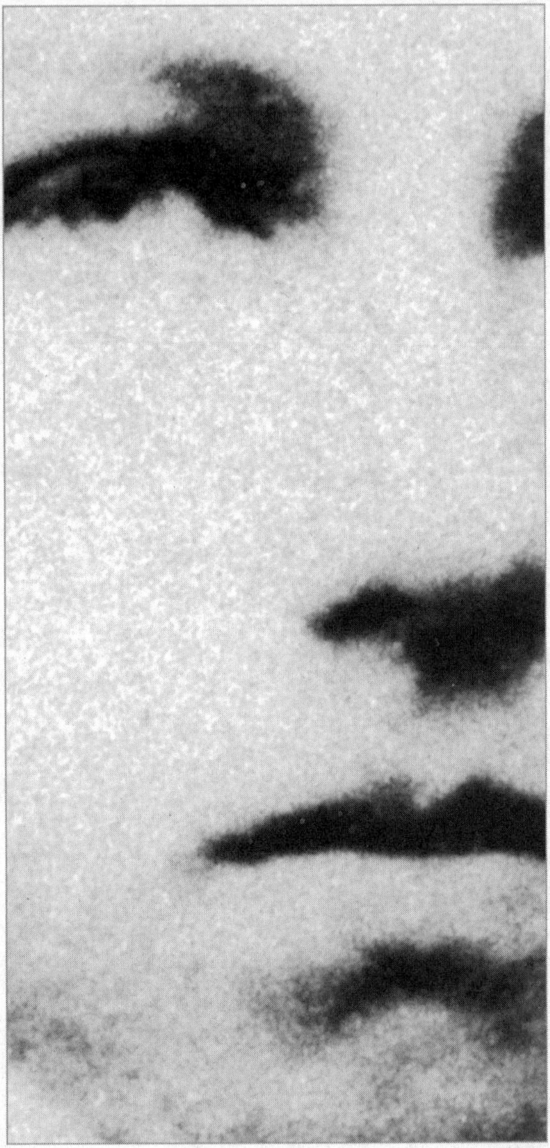

POETRY

I. 1869

THE ORPHANS' NEW YEAR'S GIFTS

I

The room is full of shadow; you vaguely hear
Two children whispering, sadly, softly.
Heavy with sleep, their heads are bowed
Beneath the long white curtain that trembles and rises…
—Outside, birds huddle against the cold;
Wings benumbed beneath the sky's gray shade;
And the New Year, trailing mist,
Drags the folds of her snowy train behind her,
Smiling through tears, shivering as she sings…

II

But beneath the fluttering curtain, the little ones
Speak as one does in the dark of night, softly.
Lost in thought, they listen as if to a distant murmur…
How they tremble at the clear golden voice
Of the morning bell, its metallic refrain striking
The glass globe again and again…
—Then…on the floor…strewn around their beds
In this frozen room, you notice mourning clothes:
The bitter winter wind wailing at the threshold
Blows its grim breath into the house.
You sense something missing in all of this…
—Where is their mother? Where is her triumphant
Maternal stare, her warm absolving smile?
One night, alone, bent over them
She must have forgotten to kindle a fire
From a dying ember, must have forgotten
To tuck blanket and quilt around them

Before leaving, while crying out: *forgive me.*
She couldn't have known how cold the next morning would be,
Nor how to keep the winter wind behind the door...
—This maternal dream is a warm blanket,
A cottony nest where children hide,
Like beautiful birds on swaying branches,
Sleeping a soft sleep brimming with white dreams...
—And here, the nest is featherless and cold,
And the little ones are cold, restless, afraid;
A nest frozen solid by bitter winds.

III

Your heart has understood: these are motherless children.
No mother near! —And father far away...
—So an old servant cares for them.
The little ones are all alone in this frozen house;
Four-year-old orphans who slowly
Awaken to a happy memory...
Like a rosary, a prayer made bead by bead:
—Oh what a beautiful morning! New Year's Morning!
During the night, each dreamt of his heart's loves,
Strange dreams of dancing toys
Gowned in gold, glittering jewels
Dancing a musical dance, disappearing
Under curtains and appearing again!
The next morning, they rose happily,
Mouths watering, rubbing their eyes...
With tousled hair and sparkling eyes
They made their way, brimming with holiday joy,
Little bare feet skimming across the floor,
Until softly tapping at their parents' door...
And in they went with nightshirted welcomes...
Endless kisses and every joy.

IV

Such a charming story, repeated how many times?
—How the old house has changed since then.
A great fire crackled brightly in the hearth,
Illuminating the old bedroom;
Vermilion reflections from the fireplace,
Dance over the furniture…
—The armoire was unlocked! Unlocked!
They had to stare at its dark black door…
Unlocked…! How strange… they so often dreamt
Of mysteries that slept within its ribs,
Thinking they could hear distant sounds
Through the keyhole's gaping depths,
A joyous, barely audible, murmur…
—Now the parents' bedroom is empty:
No vermilion reflections beneath the door;
No parents, no hearth, no keys to steal:
And no kisses when they leave, no sweet surprises!
How sad their New Year's Day will be!
—Lost in thought, while bitter tears fall…
Silently from big blue eyes, they murmur:
"When will mother return?"

V

Now the little ones are sleeping, sadly:
If you could see their puffy eyes and labored breaths
You'd say they were crying in their sleep…
Little children have such fragile hearts!
—But a guardian angel dries their eyes,
And slips a wonderful dream into heavy sleep,
A dream so wonderful that, smiling, their parted lips
Seem to murmur out loud…

—Resting on their little round arms, they dream
Of lifting their heads with morning's sweet motions
Until sleepy glances finally alight
On what must be a paradise of roses…
Fire sings merrily from a glowing hearth…
And a boundless blue sky peeks through the window;
Nature awakens, drunk with daylight…
The earth, half-naked, happily reborn,
Shivers with joy under sunbeam kisses…
And in the old house, everything is vermilion, and warm:
Dark clothes no longer carpet floors,
And the wind at their doorstep has finally fallen silent
As if a fairy had come…! —Perfectly happy,
The children cheer twice for joy… And there,
Near the maternal bed, beneath a beautiful rosy sunbeam,
There, on the great rug, something wonderful shines…
Silvery medals, one black, one white,
Both glittering, one jet, one mother-of-pearl;
Little black borders, little glass wreaths,
Each with three words, graven in gold:
"TO OUR MOTHER!"

—Published 2 January 1870

II. 1870

SENSATION

Through blue summer nights I will pass along paths,
Pricked by wheat, trampling short grass:
Dreaming, I will feel coolness underfoot,
Will let breezes bathe my bare head.

Not a word, not a thought:
Boundless love will surge through my soul,
And I will wander far away, a vagabond
In Nature—as happily as with a woman.

March 1870.

SUN AND FLESH

I

The sun, hearth of tenderness and life,
Spills molten love onto a grateful earth,
And, when you're asleep in a valley, you can feel
The earth beneath you, nubile and ripe with blood;
Her huge breast, rising with the soul within,
Is, like god, made of love; like woman, made of flesh;
Heavy with sap and sunlight,
And embryonic swarms.

How it all grows, how it all rises!

—O Venus, O Goddess!
I long for the lost days of youth,
For wanton satyrs and beastly fauns,
Gods who, for love, bit the bark of branches
And kissed blonde Nymphs in water-lily pools!
I long for lost days: when the rosy blood
Of green trees, the water in rivers,
When the world's sap flowed,
Pouring a universe into Pan's veins!
When the green ground breathed beneath his goat's feet;
When his lips, softly kissing his syrinx,
Sent a song of love into the sky;
When, standing on the plain, he heard
Nature respond to his call;
When the silent trees cradled the songbird,
When the earth cradled man, the blue seas
And the beloved beasts—beloved in God!
I long for lost days when great Cybele

In all her boundless beauty was said
To cut across magnificent cities
In a great bronze chariot, both of her breasts
Spilling the pure stream of eternal life
Unto the breach. Mankind suckled
Her blessed breast like a delighted little child.
—Because he was strong, Man was gentle and chaste.

Misery! For now he says: I know everything,
And therefore wanders, eyes closed, ears shut. —And yet,
No more gods! No more gods! Man is King!
Man is God! But Love remains our Faith!
O Cybele! O grandmother of gods and men,
If only man could linger at your breast,
If only he hadn't forsaken immortal Astarte
Who, flower of flesh, odor of oceans,
Once rose from the vast brightness of the blue waves,
Baring a rosy belly snowing foam, goddess
With great black conquering eyes
Who made the nightingale sing in forests
And love in human hearts.

II

I believe in you! I believe in you! Divine mother,
Aphrodite of the sea! Oh the way is bitter
Now that another God has yoked us to his cross;
Flesh, Marble, Flower, Venus: I believe in you!
—Man is sad and ugly, sad beneath an enormous sky,
He is clothed for he is no longer chaste,
He has sullied his godly head,
And his Olympian body is stooped
In dirty servitude, an idol in the fire!
Yes, even in death, even as a pale skeleton

He would live on, an insult to his original beauty!
—And the Idol upon whom you lavished your virginity,
In whom you made mere clay divine, Woman,
So that Man might illuminate his poor soul
And slowly climb, in limitless love,
From the earthy prison to the beauty of light—
Woman has forgotten her virtue.
—Such a farce! And now the world snickers
At the sacred name of mother Venus!

III

If only lost time would return!
—Man is done for, has played his part.
In the light, weary of smashing his idols
He revives, free from his Gods,
And, as if he were from heaven, searches the skies!
The idea of an invincible, eternal Ideal,
The god who endures within clayey flesh,
Will rise and rise until he burns his brow.
And when you see him sound the horizon,
Shrugging off old yokes, free from fear,
You will offer him divine Redemption!
—Splendid, radiant in the bosom of endless oceans
You will rise, releasing infinite love across
An expanding universe with an infinite smile!
The World will quiver like an enormous lyre
In the tremblings of an enormous kiss!

—The World thirsts for love: you slake it.

. . . .

IV

The splendor of flesh! The splendor of the *Ideal*!
The renewal of love, a triumphant dawn
When, Gods and Heroes kneeling at their feet,
White Callipyge and little Eros
Blanketed in a snow of roses,
Will lightly touch women and flowers
Blossoming beneath their beautiful feet!
O great Ariadne whose tears water
The shoreline at the sight of Theseus' sail,
White in sun and wind. O sweet virgin
By a single night undone, be silent!
Lysios in his golden chariot embroidered
With black grapes, strolling in the Phrygian fields
Among wanton tigers and russet panthers,
Reddens the moss along blue rivers.
Zeus, the Bull, cradles the naked, childlike body of Europa
Around his neck as she throws a white arm
Around the God's sinewy shoulders, trembling in a wave,
He slowly turns his bottomless stare upon her;
Her pale cheek brushes his brow like a blossom;
Her eyes close; she dies
In a divine kiss; and the murmuring wave's
Golden spume blossoms through her hair.
—Through oleander and lotus
Lovingly glides the great dreaming Swan
Enfolding Leda in the whiteness of his wing;
—And while Cypris, so strangely lovely, passes,
And, arching her richly rounded hips,
Proudly bares her large golden breasts
And her snow white belly embroidered with dark moss,
Hercules—Tamer of Beasts, who as if with a nimbus
Girds his powerful form with a lion skin, his face
Both terrible and kind—heads for the horizon!

In the muted light of the summer moon,
Standing naked and dreaming in the gilded pallor
Staining the heavy wave of her long blue hair,
In the dark clearing where the moss is stung with stars,
The Dryad stares at the silent sky...
—White Selene floats her veil
Timidly across the feet of fair Endymion,
And sends him a kiss in a pale beam of light...
—The distant Spring weeps in endless ecstasy...
Our Nymph, elbow on her urn, dreams
Of the fair white lad her wave had touched.
—A breeze of love passed in the night,
And in the sacred woods, surrounded
By terrible trees, majestic marble forms,
Gods whose brows the Bullfinch makes his nest,
—Gods watch over Man and the unending Earth.

May [18]70

OPHELIA

I

On calm black waters filled with sleeping stars
White Ophelia floats like a lily,
Floating so slowly, bedded in long veils...
—Hunting horns rise from the distant forest.

A thousand years without sad Ophelia,
A white ghost on the long black river;
A thousand years of her sweet madness
Murmuring its ballad in the evening breeze.

The wind kisses her breasts, arranges her veils
In a wreath softly cradled by waters;
Shivering willows weep at her shoulder,
Reeds bend over her broad dreaming brow.

Rumpled water lilies sigh around her;
And up in a sleeping alder she sometimes stirs,
A nest from which a tiny shiver of wings escapes:
—A mysterious song falls from golden stars.

II

O pale Ophelia! Beautiful as snow!
You died, child, borne away upon waters!
Winds from high Norwegian mountains
Whispered warnings of liberty's sting;

Because a breath carried strange sounds
To your restless soul, twisting your long hair,

Your heart listened to Nature's song
In grumbling trees and nocturnal sighs,

Because deafening voices of wild seas
Broke your infant breast, too human and too soft;
Because one April morning, a pale, handsome knight,
A poor fool, sat silent at your feet!

Sky! Love! Liberty! What dreams, poor Ophelia!
You melted upon him like snow in flame:
Visions strangled your words
—Fear of the Infinite flared in your eyes.

III

—And the poet says you visit after dark
In starlight, seeking the flowers you gathered,
And that on the water, sleeping in long veils
He saw white Ophelia floating like a lily.

15 May 1870

VENUS ANADYOMENE

As if from a green tin coffin, a woman's head
Rises from an old bathtub, slow and dumb,
Hair greased back to hide bald patches
And not succeeding very well;

First: a fat gray neck, jutting shoulder blades,
A squat back with all kinds of curves;
Then: her heavy hips begin and never seem to end;
Folds of fat shift beneath her skin;

Her spine's a little raw, and the whole mass
Reeks; above all, you notice irregularities
Better appreciated under a microscope . . .

Two words are engraved across her ass: *Clara Venus;*
—And then her body shifts and offers up her ample rump
For view: a repellent frame for the ulcer on her anus.

27 July 1870

FIRST NIGHT

She was almost undressed
And tall trees peeked indiscreetly
Throwing their leaves cleverly
Against the panes, so near, so near.

She sat half-naked
In my big chair, hands clasped.
Her little feet trembled on the floor,
Pleasurably, so delicate, so delicate.

—I watched as a wayward sunbeam
The color of wax fluttered
Across her smile, over her breasts.
A fly on a rose.

I kissed her delicate ankles.
She released a soft, sharp laugh
That rippled with trills,
Lovely laughter crystal clear.

The little feet fled beneath
Her nightshirt. "Enough of that!"
—Having gone this far,
Laughter only feigned reproach.

—Poor quivering things, her lids
Under my lips, gently kissed:
She tossed back her head
"Now you've done it ... *Monsieur!*

"I've got just two words for you..."
—But I put an end to that with kisses
Across her breasts, which brought a laugh
That augured well the rest...

She was almost undressed
And tall trees peeked indiscreetly
Throwing their leaves cleverly
Against the panes, so near, so near.

—Published 13 August 1870

REPLIES

HE: —Your breast on my breast,
Yes? We would walk
Through cool sunbeams,
Our nostrils full

Of fine blue morning air, bathing us
In the wine of day.
Lovestruck and dumb,
The trembling forest bleeds

Green drops from every branch,
Pale burgeoning buds
All agape; you feel their
Quivering flesh:

You plunge into alfalfa, your white dress
Blushing in the air,
Blue rimming
Your big black eyes

In love with the land,
Sowing it
With laughter, bubbling
Like champagne:

Laughing at me, drunk and wild,
I'd take you
Just like that—by your beautiful hair
How deeply I'd drink

Your berried breath,
Your flowery flesh.

Laughing as the chill breeze kissed you
        Like a thief,

Wild roses tease you
        Sweetly, laughing
Madly, mostly, at your lover—
        Me!

. . . .

Seventeen! How happy you'll be!
        Endless meadows
And endless amorous hills.
        So don't be shy . . .

—Your breast on my breast,
        Our voices mingling
We'd finally reach the ravine,
        And then the forest . . .

And like a little death,
        Your heart overcome,
You'd say: carry me.
        Eyes barely open . . .

And I would, tremblingly,
        Into the woods:
A bird whistling an air:
        By the hazelnut tree . . .

I would speak into your lips;
        Stepping tirelessly, cradling
Your body like a baby by its cradle,
        Drunk with blood

That flows beneath your white skin
As it blossoms rose:
I speak my mind
That your mind knows…

Our forest smells of sap
And the sun
Sprinkles gold-dust over
This green vermilion dream.

. . . .

And at night?… We head back
Along the white road that wanders
Like a grazing flock,
Wander through

The blue grass of obliging orchards
And gnarled trees
Their scents fill the air
Endlessly

We return to the village
Beneath a black sky;
Scents of milk and milking
Fill the night air;

We smell stables
Full of warm manure,
Full of rhythmic breathing breaths
And broad-shouldered backs

Whitening in the lamplight;
And, way over there,
A cow dunging dung
With each proud step…

—Grandmother's glasses
And her long nose
In her missal; a jug of beer
Rung with pewter,

Foaming between pipes
Billowing smoke
Horrible lips
Enfold fat forkfuls

Of ham while smoking,
And drinking, and . . . :
The fire illuminates bunks
And cupboards.

Glossy fat cheeks
Of the baby's fat butt
Who, on all fours, sticks
His white snout into cups

Brushed by a muzzle, growling
gently and
Licking the round face
Of the adorable child . . .

Black, pompously perched on the edge
of her chair, her profile
A nightmare, an old woman spins
Thread before the fire;

What things we shall see, my sweet,
In dives like these
When fires ignite
Gray windowpanes . . .

—Then, tiny and tucked
Within a lilac clutch
Cool and black: a little window
Laughing in back . . .

Come to me, come to me.
To my love, beautifully.
Come to me, so that we—

SHE: *And miss work?*

15 August 1870

"DEAD OF NINETY-TWO AND NINETY-THREE"

"... Frenchmen of 1870, Bonapartists, Republicans, remember your forefathers of 1792 ..." etc.

—PAUL DE CASSAGNAC, *LE PAYS*

Dead of ninety-two and ninety-three,
Weak from liberty's rough kiss,
Calmly broke the yoke beneath your clogs
That weighs on humanity's soul and brow;

Exalted soldiers stood tall despite storm,
Whose hearts leapt with love beneath rags,
And whom Death—noble Lover—has sown
In every ditch so they can rise again;

You, whose blood washed over every ruined hill,
Dead of Valmy, of Fleurus, of Italy,
A million Christs with soft, dark eyes;

We left you to sleep alongside the Republic,
We who bend beneath a King as if a club;
—As Cassagnac and sons invoke you once again!

Set down in Mazas, 3 September, 1870

Valmy: site of a battle between the French and the Prussians, on September 20, 1792. *Fleurus:* site of a French victory by General Jourdan, June 26, 1794. *Italy:* reference to the Napoleonic campaign of 1796, which ended well for Bonaparte and the French. *Cassagnac:* The irony here is that the Cassagnacs were Bonapartists who ran the newspaper from which Rimbaud got his epigraph. *Mazas:* Murphy points out that Hugo, whom Rimbaud would have been reading, wrote, "The more often one is in Mazas, the more deeply one is a part of the Republic." Mazas was a Paris prison to which Rimbaud was sent for vagrancy.

FROZEN IN FEAR

In snow and fog
Against a basement grate aglow
    Five black butts, in a row

Little kids on their knees—poor things!—
Watch the baker, making
    Heavy golden bread, baking...

They watch the strong white arm knead
And thrust gray dough deep
    Within the luminous hole.

They listen to the sound of baking bread.
The baker sings an old air
    With a jowly grin.

None moves as they huddle together
In the warm breath of the glowing grate,
    Warm as a breast.

And when midnight comes,
The bread emerges
    Sculpted, gleaming, gold

And fragrant crusts sing
Beneath the smoky beams,
    And crickets too,

When this hot pit breathes life
Their souls breathe too
    Beneath their rags,

They feel reborn,
Poor frozen fellows!
        But they're there, all of them,

Their pink little snouts stuck
To the grate, singing
        Through the holes,

As softly as prayer...
Bowed down to a light
        Like heaven rent open,

—Bowed so low their pants finally split,
And their underwear flutters
        In the winter wind.

20 September 1870
revised June 1871

NOVEL

I

No one's serious at seventeen.
—On beautiful nights when beer and lemonade
And loud, blinding cafés are the last thing you need
—You stroll beneath green lindens on the promenade.

Lindens smell fine on fine June nights!
Sometimes the air is so sweet that you close your eyes;
The wind brings sounds—the town is near—
And carries scents of vineyards and beer...

II

—Over there, framed by a branch
You can see a little patch of dark blue
Stung by a sinister star that fades
With faint quiverings, so small and white...

June nights! Seventeen! —Drink it in.
Sap is champagne; it goes to your head...
The mind wanders; you feel a kiss
On your lips, quivering like a living thing...

III

The wild heart Crusoes through a thousand novels
—And when a young girl walks alluringly
Through a streetlamp's pale light, beneath the ominous shadow
Of her father's starched collar...

Because as she passes by, boot-heels tapping,
She turns on a dime, eyes wide,
Finding you too sweet to resist…
—And cavatinas die on your lips.

IV

You're in love. Off the market till August.
You're in love. —Your sonnets make Her laugh.
Your friends are gone, you're *bad news.*
—Then, one night, your beloved, writes…!

That night… you return to the blinding cafés;
You order beer or lemonade…
—No one's serious at seventeen
When lindens line the promenade.

29 September 1870

WINTER DREAM

to... Her

One winter, we'll take a train, a little rose-colored car
        Upholstered blue.
We'll be so comfortable. A nest
        Of wild kisses awaits in every cushioned corner.

You'll close your eyes to shadows
        Grimacing through windows
This belligerent nocturnal realm, inhabited
        By black demons and black wolves.

Then you'll feel a tickle on your cheek...
A little kiss like a crazed spider
        Fleeing down your neck...

Bending your head backwards, you'll say: "Get it!"
—And we'll take our time finding the beast
        —While it roams...

Written on a train, 7 *October 1870*

THE SIDEBOARD

A broad carved sideboard; its dark, aged oak
Has taken on the wonderful weathered air of old people;
The sideboard stands open, and sweet scents
Swim in its shadows like a tide of old wine;

It's filled with a jumble of old knickknacks,
Fragrant yellowing linens, women's
And children's clothes, faded lace,
Grandmotherly scarves embroidered with griffins;

—You'll find medallions inside, blonde and white
Locks of hair, portraits, dried flowers
Whose scents mix with the scent of fruit.

Old sideboard, you've seen more than a little
And have tales to tell, and speak each time
Your big black doors slowly swing open.

October 1870

THE STUNNING VICTORY AT SAARBRÜCKEN

Accompanied by shouts of "Long Live the Emperor!"
Pretty color postcard, sells for 35 centimes in Charleroi

In the middle, the Emperor, in an apotheosis
Of blue and yellow, rides stiffly away,
Sitting pretty on his extravagant nag—
Fierce as Zeus and sweet as daddy;

Beneath him, good grunts napping
Near golden drums and red cannons
Gently rise. Pitou dons his jacket tipsily
And, turning towards the Chief, dreams of greater things.

On the right, Dumanet leans on the stock of his
Chassepot, feels the hairs on his nape perk up,
And then: "Long Live the Emperor!"—While
The fellow next to him says nothing...

A shako rises like a black sun...—At the center,
Shallow as the day is long, red and blue Bouquillon
Gets to his feet, flashes his can, and says: "Long live *this*."

October 1870

Saarbrücken: a much ballyhooed battle of the Franco-German War (1871) won by the French, who nonetheless went on to lose the war. *Pitou* is slang for a grunt. *Dumanet* is a clumsy, Gomer Pyle–like soldier who was ridiculed in cartoons of the era. *Chassepot* was a brand of rifle used by the French army from 1866–1874. *Boquillon* comes from *La Lanterne de Boquillon,* a satirical newspaper in which Dumanets would have figured.

CLEVER GIRL

In the brown dining room, brimming
With sweet scents of varnish and fruit,
I casually filled my plate with Belgian
Morsels and sank into an easy chair.

I listened to the clock as I ate, happy and still.
Then the kitchen door opened with a warm gust
—And a servant girl emerged, who knows why,
Her scarf loose, her hair temptingly arranged.

And while brushing a trembling finger across
The velvety pink peach of her cheek,
Her little-girl lips affected a pout

And she leaned towards me, adjusting my plates
Just so; then, casually, angling for a kiss—
Said softly, "My cheek is *so* cold. Here, feel..."

Charleroi, October 1870

AT THE CABARET-VERT, FIVE P.M.

Eight days of shredding my boots
On bad roads. Then, Charleroi.
—And into the Cabaret-Vert. I ordered:
Bread and butter with lukewarm ham.

I felt good, and stretched my legs
Under the green table: I was staring
At a tapestry's simple scenes
When a girl with huge tits and bright eyes

—No kiss could scare her off!—
Cheerily brought my bread and butter
And lukewarm ham on a colorful plate,

Pink and white ham rubbed with garlic—
And then filled my giant mug with foamy beer
That glowed gold with late-day light.

October 1870

A SLEEPER IN THE VALLEY

A green hole where a river sings;
Silver tatters tangling in the grass;
Sun shining down from a proud mountain:
A little valley bubbling with light.

A young soldier sleeps, lips apart, head bare,
Neck bathing in cool blue watercress,
Reclined in the grass beneath the clouds,
Pale in his green bed showered with light.

He sleeps with his feet in the gladiolas.
Smiling like a sick child, he naps:
Nature, cradle him in warmth: he's cold.

Sweet scents don't tickle his nose;
He sleeps in the sun, a hand on his motionless chest,
Two red holes on his right side.

October 1870

TO MUSIC

Railway square, Charleville

Pruned into stingy plots of grass, the public square,
Where trees and flowers and everything is just so,
Finds wheezy bourgeois strangling in the heat,
Trotting out petty jealousies on Thursday nights.

—The military band, in the middle of the garden,
Balance their shakos while playing the "Waltz of Fifes."
—Around them, in the first rows, dandies strut;
The notary hangs from his own monogrammed fob:

Women wearing ruffles like advertisements
For themselves flounce like elephant wranglers
Around bloated bureaucrats and bloated wives:
Petty bourgeois with lorgnettes hang on every clinker;

On green benches, clubs of retired grocers rest
Poking the sand with knobbed canes,
Discussing treaties with great sobriety,
Taking snuff from silver boxes, saying: "And so . . . !"

Spreading the roundness of his rump across the bench,
A bourgeois with bright buttons and a Flemish gut
Savors his pricey Onnaing pipe overflowing with tobacco:
"This stuff's still illegal, don't-you-know?"

All along the green lawn, little hoodlums sneer;
Naïve young soldiers smoking roses,

Onnaing: A French town known for making pipes of the finest quality.

Made lovesick by the sad trombones,
Pat the heads of babies to charm their nannies...

Me? Looking like a scattered student
I follow exuberant girls through the green chestnuts:
They know I'm there, and turn towards me
Laughing, eyes brimming with indiscretion.

I don't say a word: I just stare at the flesh
Of their white necks framed by tresses:
I follow the curve of their shoulders down
Their divine backs, hidden by bodices and flimsy finery.

Soon I'm ogling their boots and socks...
Burning with fever, yearning for flesh.
They think I'm silly. They whisper to each other...
—And I feel kisses blossom on my lips...

There is debate regarding the last line of this poem. Prior translations depend on an earlier manuscript source that has never surfaced, described by Rimbaud's teacher and friend George Izambard in his memoir *Rimbaud tel que je l'ai connu (Rimbaud As I Knew Him).* Izambard claims that Rimbaud's original last line was *"—Et mes désirs brutaux s'accrochent à leurs lèvres,"* rendered by Fowlie as "—And my fierce desires fasten onto their lips." Shortly after the poem was written, Izambard went over the poem with its young author and explained that he felt the tone of the line was off, was the sort of thing uttered by a cad, not by a timid schoolboy. Rimbaud agreed. Izambard happened to have a line in his head with the same beat and rhyme, *"—Et je sens les basiers qui me viennent aux lèvres,"* which, writes Izambard, he "gave" to Rimbaud "the way you give someone a cigarette" (Murphy, 307–09). Editors and translators, arguing that Rimbaud's supposed original is more in keeping with our idea of the poet, have preferred the alleged line to "Izambard's." But if we accept Rimbaud as the author of the poem, I think it better, as Alain Borer argues, to accept the version the author approved and sent to others subsequently, rather than what readers feel the author should have chosen initially.

HANGED MEN, DANCING

Cheerful, one-armed, and black,
The gallows dangles paladins,
Satan's skinny skeletons
Dancing bones of Saladins.

Christmas carols fill the air,
Small black puppets face the sky;
Messer Beelzebub makes them dance
Smacking heads and yanking ties.

Quaking puppets join spindly arms:
Black organ pipes swaying high above,
Their chests once pressed to maidens' breasts
Now coitally collide, disgustingly in love.

Three cheers for dancers disemboweled!
There's room to writhe on the killing floor.
Is it a battle... or is it a dance? Who cares:
Mad Beelzebub fiddles, evermore.

Heels this hard don't need replacing.
Chests have shrugged off shirts of skin:
There's nothing shocking left to see.
Skulls bear snowcaps, white and thin.

Crows crown heads, feather cracks;
Fleshy chunks quiver on chins:

Saladin (also Salāh Ad-dīn, 1138–93) was a Muslim sultan of Egypt who opposed Richard the Lion-Hearted, among other crusaders.

They look like knights in paper armor
Colliding in darkness and nocturnal winds.

Breezes blow these hanged men, dancing.
Like an iron organ, the black gallows groans.
Along the horizon, the sky turns hellish red.
From violet forests rise lupine moans...

Someone unstring these grim commanders
Who, underhanded, read rosaries of love.
Broken fingers count pale vertebrae.
No monastery this, for the dead above!

And in this *danse macabre*'s midst
One mad skeleton can't stay in check,
Like a spooked horse he leaps into the red sky:
Stiff noose still coiled around his neck,

His little fingers grip a bony thigh
Squeezing out laughter more like moans,
And like an actor lost in drama,
Retakes the stage to the applause of bones.

Cheerful, one-armed, and black,
The gallows dangles paladins,
Satan's skinny skeletons
Dancing bones of Saladins.

TARTUFE UNDONE

One day as he walked happily along, raking
A gloved hand across his heart like a claw
Hidden beneath chaste black robes, yellow piety
Dribbled, sickly sweet, from his toothless maw,

One day as he walked piously to pray—a Lout
Grabbed him roughly by his saintly ear
And yelled obscenities therein, rending
Chaste black robe from pale moist skin!

Undone!... Habiliment assailed!
And as a rosary of pardoned sins
Ungirded in his heart, Saint Tartufe went pale...!

Then, he confessed and prayed with woe
The Lout content to take his clothes...
Leaving Tartufe naked—ugh!—head to toe!

THE BLACKSMITH

Palais des Tuileries, around August 10th, 1792

One arm wields a giant hammer, enormous,
Terrifying, and drunk, while the broad brow brims
With laughter like a bronze trumpet, mouth agape,
Staring hard at that fat man over there: So it was
That the Blacksmith spoke to Louis XVI, on a day
When the People milled all around them, dragging
Their dirty jackets across gilded wainscoting.
And the good king looked pale, standing there with his paunch,
As pale as a condemned man on the way to the gallows,
And like a beaten dog, he didn't whimper,
Because this broad-shouldered rogue at the forge
Was full of piss and vinegar, telling bawdy old tales
That had the king no less transfixed
Than if the smith's meaty fist held his ear.

"Now, *Monsieur*, who better than you to know
How we used to sing: *Tra la la! Tra la la!*
And graze our cattle in any field we wished:
The Canon would spin out paternosters in the sun
The clear beads of his rosary glinting gold.
The Lord would pass on horseback, blowing his horn,
When suddenly one fellow with a noose, and another
A whip, would lash us. —Like dazed cattle,
We were rendered mute; and roamed, and roamed,
And once we had plowed the limits of the land,
When our very flesh had been sewn into the black earth,
We were given our reward: our homes, our hovels
Burned in the night; our children cooked like cakes.

“Lord knows I’m not complaining! Between us,
I’m just getting things off my chest, not that you need agree.
But we must agree about June: how inspiring it is,
The sight of enormous wagons freighted
With wheat on their way to the barns.
To smell the scent of growing things,
Orchards after a touch of rain, and hayfields, too.
Wheatfields and cornstalks, their shafts and ears full,
And think of the bread it will all bake! Oh!
Fortified we enter the glowing forge,
Singing while hammering at the anvil,
And, being men, were there only some guarantee
Of keeping some of what God gives in the end!
—But so much for that; always the same old story!

“But now I know! And yet can hardly believe—
Given my two strong hands, my hammer and head—
That a man can waltz in here with a dagger under his coat
And say: Boy, speed that plow, seed that land;
Or that another can enter my home during a war
And take my son, just like that! —So just imagine:
I’m a man; you’re a king; and you say:
Hand It Over . . . ! —You see how stupid that is, right?
You think I want any part of your extravagant dump,
Your gilded officers and thousand rogues,
Your but-for-the-grace-of-god bastards
Primping like peacocks: They’ve feathered
Your nest with the scent of our daughters
And with your little writs, your *lettres de cachet*,
That lock us away in your bastilles. Nevertheless,
We say Fair Enough: we poor on our knees!
Let us gild your Louvre with our extra pennies!
While you get drunk and have a high time.
—And while your Gentlemen will laugh,
Their asses resting on our heads.

"No. Our fathers had to put up with that crap.
The People are done being whores. It took
Just three steps to topple your Bastille into dust.
The thing sweated blood from its stones
And was intolerable to see erect, in one piece,
With leprous walls that spoke volumes
And whose shadow hung over us all!
—Citizens! Citizens! That dark past crumbled,
A death rattle that roared when we took the tower!
Something like love rose in our hearts.
We hugged our sons to our chests.
And like snuffling horses we marched proud and strong
We marched in the sun with his feeling beating in our blood,
Our heads held high—like this—into Paris!
And they came out to greet us in our dusty clothes.
At last we felt like Men! We were pale, Sire,
And drunk with terrible hope: and when
We finally arrived before the black towers,
Waving our bugles and oak leaves with
Pikes in our hands, we forgot our hate.
—We felt so strong that we wanted only to be gentle.

. . . .

. . . .

"And since that day we've been nuts!
Heaps of workers pile up in the streets,
A purgatorial horde forever embarking, swelling
With dark ghosts at the doors of the rich.
I beat up your snitches with them: I go
To Paris, my face all black, a hammer over my shoulder,
Savagely swinging at scamps in the streets,
And I'd kill you if you laughed in my face!
—For you can count on one thing: you'll pay a price
For all your men in black who take our petitions
And bat them around, your clever lads who
Lower their voices as they look our way and say: 'Idiots!'

While cooking up laws and serving up
Pretty pink decrees to be plastered on walls,
Sugar-coated pills they ram down our throats,
Taking pleasure in knocking us down to size,
And holding their noses as we pass:
Our honorable representatives find us foul!
And they fear nothing, nothing but bayonets...
It's all well and good. To hell with their cant!
We've had enough of their empty heads
And full bellies. Enough of the cake
You bourgeois bake and expect us to eat,
While we run with rage, shattering
Scepters and crosiers, in our wake."

. . . .

The blacksmith takes him by the arm, yanks the velvet
Curtains back, and has him look at the courtyard below,
A mob rising and falling and seething, and seething,
An unthinkable mob with the voice of a storm,
Howling like a dog, howling like the sea,
With heavy clubs, and iron pikes, and drums,
Shouts of the marketplace, shouts of the slums,
A dark mass of bloody rags and red bonnets:
Through the window, the Man shows the scene
To the pale and sweaty king who wobbles,
Sick at the sight!

"There's the Scum,
Sire. Slobbering at the walls, spreading like disease:
—Since they don't eat, Sire, they beg!
I am a blacksmith: but my wife is with them,
She's mad: she believes she'll find bread at the Tuileries!
—No one wants our kind in the boulangeries.
I have three little ones: I'm scum. —I know
Old women who walk through the streets, weeping
Under their hats, weeping for lost daughters or sons:

Scum. —One man was in the Bastille,
Another a galley slave: and both were citizens
Honest to a fault. Free, they run like dogs:
They're driven and derided! Something
Must be chasing them! It's wrong, and since
They feel hunted, they feel damned,
There they are, right now, screaming in your face!
Scum. —There are even some notorious girls down below,
Notorious because—you know women are weak—
Certain Gentlemen of the Court (who are always game)
Have spit on their souls as if it were nothing!
Today your girls are down there. Scum, every one.

. . . .

"Oh such suffering! Those whose backs burn
Beneath the hot sun, and who wander, who wander,
Who toil until their heads border on bursting...
Doff your caps, O bourgeois! These are Men!
We are Workers, Sire! Workers! We are
Made for new times when men will wonder:
Where will Man forge from dawn until dusk?
Where will Man hunt for great ends and means?
Where—as victories stack up—will Man tame time
And mount Life as he would a horse!
Such light gleams from the forges! The end of evil:
Done! —The Unknown is horrible: but,
We will know! —Hammers in hand, we'll sort
It all out: then, Brothers, we will move forward!
Now and again we must have this heartbreaking dream
Of living simply, ardently, without
Grumbling, traveling under the august smile
Of a woman you love, with nobility:
And we would work proudly through such a day,
Answering the call of duty like the ring of a trumpet:
And we would feel so happy, and no one—

Above all—no one could make us kneel!
For we would have guns hanging over our hearths...

. . . .

"But the air is heavy with the breath of battle!
What did I tell you? I'm part of the rabble!
Snitches and thieves about! Yet,
We are free! There are moments of terror
When nonetheless we feel well, so well! Just now
I spoke of peaceful work, of a home...
Just look at the sky! —It's too low,
We'd die of heat, we'd have to kneel!
Just look at the sky! —I'm going back to the mob,
Into the terrible crowd, Sire
Rolling your old cannons over dirty streets:
—Oh the streets will be clean when we die!
—And if in the wake of our cries and our vengeance,
The claws of old bronze kings drive
Regiments ready for battle across France,
Then, all of you, what then? Then, you dogs,
Get ready to eat shit!"

. . . .

—He swung his hammer onto his shoulder.
The soul
Of the mob felt drunk in his presence,
And, in the courtyard, in the apartments,
Wherever Paris panted and cried,
A shudder shook the teeming populace.
Then, his great hand gleaming with grime,
While the potbellied king sweated away,
The Blacksmith, terrifying to behold, tossed
His red bonnet onto the king's head!

MY BOHEMIA
A Fantasy

And so off I went, fists thrust in the torn pockets
Of a coat held together by no more than its name.
O Muse, how I served you beneath the blue;
And *oh* what dreams of dazzling love I dreamed!

My only pair of pants had a huge hole.
—Like some dreaming Tom Thumb, I sowed
Rhyme with each step. My inn was the Big Dipper.
—My stars rustled in the sky.

Roadside on warm September nights
I listened as drops of dew fell
On my forehead like fortifying wine;

And there, surrounded by streaming shadows, I rhymed
Aloud, and as if they were lyres, plucked the laces
Of my wounded shoes, one foot beneath my heart.

EVIL

When the cannon's red spittle
Whistles through limitless blue skies;
When scarlet and green forces crumble
In fiery heaps at the feet of a jeering King;

When an impossible madness grinds
A hundred thousand men into a smoldering mass;
—Such woeful dead in the summer grass!
O Nature who makes saints of men.

—A God laughs away the finery
Of the holy see, the incense and golden
Goblets, a God who dozes to hosannas,

And then stirs when mothers gather
In grief, crying in their black hats,
Offering him pennies from their pockets.

CAESAR'S RAGE

A pale man in black, cigar in moue,
Paces the flowering lawns:
The pale man recalls flowers in the Tuileries
And, at times, his dull eyes gleam . . .

The emperor is drunk from an orgy of years.
He once said, "Liberty? I shall snuff
As gently as a candle!" Liberty
Lives again! He has been broken!

And bound. —Oh what name trembles
On his mute lips? What implacable remorse
Has hold of him? We'll never know.
The Imperial eyes are dead.

Perhaps he recalls his bespectacled Accomplice . . .
—As he watches a fine blue cloud rise
From his cigar as it used to
On nights at St. Cloud.

A pale man in black: Emperor Napoleon III (1808–73) who, suffering defeat in the Franco-German War (1870), was confined to the Prussian Château de Wilhelmshohe. The *Accomplice* is Émile Ollivier, the justice minister under Napoleon who declared the war, soon after resigned, and went on to write history, rather than make it. *St. Cloud* was an imperial residence just outside of Paris, and remains a fine place to spend an afternoon.

III. 1871

STOLEN HEART

My sad heart drools on deck,
A heart splattered with chaw:
A target for bowls of soup,
My sad heart drools on deck:
Soldiers jeer and guffaw.
My sad heart drools on deck,
A heart splattered with chaw!

Ithyphallic and soldierly,
Their jeers have soiled me!
Painted on the tiller
Ithyphallic and soldierly.
Abracadabric seas,
Cleanse my heart of this disease.
Ithyphallic and soldierly,
Their jeers have soiled me!

When they've shot their wads,
How will my stolen heart react?
Bacchic fits and bacchic starts
When they've shot their wads:
I'll retch to see my heart
Trampled by these clods.
What will my stolen heart do
When they've shot their wads?

May 1871

THE BATTLE SONG OF PARIS

Spring is here, plain as day,
Thiers and Picard steal away
From what they stole: green Estates
With vernal splendors on display.

May: a jubilee of nudity, asses on parade.
Sèvres, Meudon, Bagneux, Asnières—
New arrivals make their way,
Sowing springtime everywhere.

They've got shakos, sabers, and tom-toms,
Not those useless old smoldering stakes,
And skiffs *"That nev-nev-never did cut..."*
Through the reddening waters of lakes.

Now more than ever we'll band together
When golden gems blow out our knees.
Watch as they burst on our crumbling heaps:
You've never seen dawns like these.

This poem, "Chante de guerre parisien," refers semiparodically to the "Chante de guerre circassian" of François Coppée (1842–1908), who was later a regular object of parody for Rimbaud in the *Album Zutique.* In a letter to his friend Paul Demeny (see p. 366), Rimbaud introduced the poem as "a psalm on current events." While Coppée's poem concerns the Turks, Rimbaud's antagonists are the leaders of France's Third Republic who took refuge in Versailles during the Franco-Prussian War. In the vacuum of the governmental flight, the French Communards (communists) rose up to claim the city as their own, an attempt at rekindling the egalitarian ideals of the French Revolution. *Thiers:* Louis-Adolphe Thiers (1797–1877), the first president of the Third Republic ordered his troops to retake the city. They bombed the suburbs (*Sèvres, Meudon, Bagneux, Asnières*), before leveling the rebellion in Paris. *Picard:* Ernest Picard (1821–77), Thiers's interior minister. *"Nev-nev-never did cut...":* an allusion to a French song of the era, "Il était un petit navire" ("A Little Boat"), that tells of a shipwrecked crew in dire straits.

Thiers and Picard think they're artists
Painting Corots with gasoline.
They pick flowers from public gardens,
Their tropes traipsing from seam to seam…

They're intimates of the Big Man, and Favre,
From the flowerbeds where he's sleeping,
Undams an aqeductal flow of tears: a pinch
Of pepper prompts adequate weeping…

The stones of the city are hot,
Despite all of your gasoline showers.
Doubtless an appropriate moment
To roust your kind from power…

And the Nouveau Riche lolling peacefully
Beneath the shade of ancient trees,
Will hear boughs break overhead:
Red rustlings that won't be leaves!

Corots: Jean-Baptiste-Camille Corot (1796–1875), French painter noted for his landscapes. *Favre:* Jules Favre (1809–80), foreign minister famous for negotiating the French surrender to Prussia while, supposedly, in tears.

MY LITTLE LOVES

A teary tincture slops
        Over cabbage-green skies:
Beneath saplings' dewy drops,
        Your white raincoats rise

With strange moons
        And ripe spheres,
Knock your knees together,
        My ugly little dears.

How we loved each other once:
        Eating chickweed
And soft-boiled eggs,
        My ugly, blue-eyed dear…

One night you hailed me *poet:*
        You hopped on my lap
For a spanking,
        My ugly, blonde dear…

Your brilliantine made me puke:
        Your heavy brow
Could break a guitar,
        My ugly, dark-haired dear…

My dry jets of sputum,
        Fester between
Your round breasts,
        My ugly, red-headed dear…

My little loves:
    I hate you.
I hope your ugly tits blossom
    With painful sores.

You trample my stores
    Of feeling;
And then, *voilà:* you dance
    For me once more.

Your shoulders dislocate,
    My loves.
Stars brand your hobbled hips
    While you do your worst.

And yet, for these sides of beef,
    I made the lines above:
Hips I should have broken,
    I filled with acts of love.

Guileless clumps of fallen stars
    Accumulate below;
Saddled with trifling concerns
    You'll die with God, alone.

Beneath strange moons
    And ripe spheres,
Knock your knees together
    My ugly little dears!

A.R.
15 May 1871

SQUATTING

Later, when he feels his stomach grumble,
Brother Milotus—an eye on the skylight
Where, bright as a scoured pot, the sun
Shoots him a migraine and briefly blinds him—
Shifts his priestly belly beneath the sheets.

He thrashes around under the covers
And sits up, knees against his trembling belly,
Upset like an old man who's swallowed his snuff,
Because he still must hike his nightshirt up
Over his hips, one hand on the handle of the chamberpot.

Now, squatted, shaking, toes curled, shivering
In the bright sunlight that plasters
Brioche-yellow patches on paper windowpanes;
And the fellow's shiny nose ignites
With light, like a fleshy polyp.

. . . .

He simmers by the fire, his arms in a knot, his lip hanging
Down to his belly: he feels his thighs slipping towards the fire,
Chausses glow, pipe goes cold;
Something like a bird softly stirs in his belly,
Serene as a heap of tripe!

Around him, a jumble of beaten furniture sleeps
With filthy rags and dirty bellies;
Stools like toads sit hunched
In corners: sideboards with mouths like cantors
Gape in carnivorous sleep.

Sickening heat floods the narrow room;
The fellow's head is stuffed with rags.
He listens to the hairs growing on his moist skin,
And, at times, ridiculous hiccups
Escape, shaking his wobbly perch . . .

. . . .

And at night, in moonlight drooling
Beams onto the curves of his ass,
A shadow squats, etched onto a backdrop
Of rosy snow, like hollyhock . . .
Surreal: a nose seeking Venus in the deep dark sky.

May 1871

PARISIAN ORGY OR THE REPOPULATION OF PARIS

Cowards, behold! Spill from the stations!
The sun's hot breath blew streets dry
That teemed with Barbarians only nights before.
Behold the Holy City, the Western throne!

Come! We'll snuff smoldering fires!
See the quays, the boulevards,
Houses in relief against radiating blue
That nights before was starred red with bombs!

Board up the dead palaces!
Bask in the terror of dying daylight.
Behold these droves of redheads shaking their asses:
Be as crazy as you like: go wild!

Bitches in heat eat poultices in packs,
Who can resist golden houses' calls: so rob!
Eat! Behold the joyous night descends in spasms,
Deep into the street. O desolate drinkers,

Drink! When blinding light shines
Streams of luxury across your sides,
Will you drool into your glasses,
Immobile and mute, eyes lost in the distance?

Knock one back for the Queen and her fat ass!
Listen to belches tear through flesh!

Barbarians: The barbarians of whom Rimbaud writes are not the Goths sacking Rome, but the Germans of the Franco-German War, who paraded through Paris on March 1, 1871. The Tuileries, as well as part of the Louvre, which Rimbaud alludes to in the third stanza, the "dead palaces," were destroyed a few months later.

Listen to idiots and old codgers, groaning
Puppets and lackeys leaping into the burning night.

O filthy hearts and wretched mouths,
Belting shouts from reeking mouths!
Wine for everyone! We drink to this empty sloth...
O conquerors, your bellies dissolve with shame!

Open your nostrils to this incomparable nausea!
Drown your gullets in potent poison!
Laying his crossed hands onto your necks
The Poet says: "Cowards, show me your fury!"

Because you grope around in Woman's guts,
You fear another shrieking contraction
That would smother the nest you've made
In her breast beneath an unbearable weight.

Syphilitics, madmen, kings, puppets, ventriloquists,
Why would Paris—that old whore—care
About your bodies and souls, your poisons and rags?
She's well rid of you, you rabble.

And when you're doubled over, gripping your guts,
Sides numb, demanding money, bewildered,
The red whore, breasts fat from battle,
Will shake raised fists far from your pain!

O Paris! When your feet danced with indignation!
When you were knifed how many times?
And when you fell, your clear eyes still retained
A vision of ruddy spring,

O sorrowful city! O half dead city,
Face and breasts thrust boldly towards the Future

Opening a million doors onto your pallor,
A city only the dark Past could bless:

Your body galvanized against suffering,
Again you drink from wretched life! Again you feel
The flux of worms writhing in your veins,
And icy fingers groping your grip on pure love!

But: that's not so bad. Worms, pale worms
Can no more halt the breath of Progress
Than the Styx could put out eyes of Caryatids
Whose astral tears fell golden from the blue above.

While unbearable to see you overrun again;
While no city has been so befouled in all history—
A fetid ulcer on Nature's greenery—
The poet nonetheless proclaims, "Your Beauty is magnificent!"

By storm, you have been consecrated Supreme Poetry.
The vast stirring of strength succors you;
O Chosen City! Your works boil, death moans!
Gather soundings in your deaf horn.

The poet will collect the tears of the Wrong,
The hate of Convicts, the clamor of the Damned;
And his rays of love will whip our Women.
His stanzas will shout: Thieves, behold!

—Society is restored: Orgies weep
Their ancient sob in ancient whoreries:
Gaslights blaze deliriously on reddened walls,
Sinister flares against a paling blue!

May 1871

POETS, AGE SEVEN

And the Mother, closing the workbook,
Departed satisfied and proud, without noticing,
In blue eyes beneath a pimply forehead,
The loathing freighting her child's soul.

All day he sweated obedience; clearly
Intelligent; and yet, black rumblings, hints
Of bitter hypocrisies, hidden, underneath.
In shadowy corridors hung with moldy drapes
He'd stick out his tongue, thrust his fists
In his pockets, shut his eyes till he saw spots.
A door opened onto the night: by lamplight
You could see him, up there, moaning from the banister,
Beneath a bay of light under the roof. Above all,
In summer, beaten and dumb, he was bent
On locking himself in cool latrines:
He could think there, peacefully, filling his lungs.
In winter, when the garden behind the house
Was bathed in the day's fragrances, illunating,
Lying down at the foot of a wall, interred in clay
He pushed on his eyes until they swam with visions,
Listening to the rustling of mangy espaliers.
What a shame! His only friends were bareheaded runts
Whose eyes leaked onto their cheeks, who hid
Skinny fingers mottled yellow-black with mud
Beneath ragged clothes that stunk of the shits,
And who spoke as blandly as idiots!
And when his Mother found him wallowing among them
She was shocked; but seeing such tenderness

---

illunating: sic.

In her child muted her surprise. For an instant:
Her blue eyes lied!

At seven years old, he wrote novels
About life in the desert, where Freedom reigns,
Forests, suns, riverbanks, plains! —Inspiration
Came in the form of illustrated papers where he
Blushingly saw laughing girls, from Italy and Spain.
When the daughter of the laborers next door
Came by, eight years old, wild brown eyes,
In a calico dress, he backed her into a corner
And the little brute pounced onto his back,
Pulling his hair, and so, while under her,
He bit her ass, since she never wore panties;
—And bruised by her fists and heels,
He carried the taste of her skin back to his room.

He hated dreary December Sundays,
His hair greased flat, sitting on a high mahogany table,
Reading from a Bible with cabbage-green edges;
Dreams overwhelmed him each night in his little room.
He didn't love God; instead, the men returning to the suburbs
After dark, in jackets, in the tawny dusk,
Where the town criers, after a trio of drumrolls,
Would stir up crowds with edicts and laughter.
He dreamt meadows of love, where luminous swells
Of nourishing scents and golden pubescence
All move about calmly and take wing!

And as he especially relished darkness,
When he was alone in his room, shutters shut,
High and blue, painfully pierced by damp,
He read his endlessly pondered novel,
Overflowing with heavy ochre skies and drowning forests,

Flowers of flesh scattered through the starry woods,
Vertigo, collapse, routs in battle and lasting pity.
—While the noise in the neighborhood continued
Below—alone, reclined on cream canvas,
He had a violent vision of setting sail.

A.R. 26 May 1871

THE POOR AT CHURCH

Parked on oak benches in church corners
Warmed by stale breath, eyes fixed
On the chancel's glittering gold, the choir's
Twenty mouths mumble pious hymns;

Inhaling the scent of melting wax like the aroma
Of baking bread, the Happy Poor
Humiliated like beaten dogs, make stubborn prayers
To the good Lord, their patron and master.

After six dark days of suffering in God's name,
The women don't mind wearing the benchwood smooth.
In dark cloaks they cradle ugly children
Who cry as if on the brink of death.

Dirty dogs dangle from these soup eaters,
Prayer in their eyes but without a prayer
They watch as a group of girls parades by
Wearing ugly hats.

Outside: cold; hunger; carousing men.
But for now all's well. One more hour; then,
Unmentionable evils! —For now, wattled old women
Surround them groaning, whining, whispering:

Idiots abound, and epileptics
You'd avoid in the street; blind men
Led by dogs through the squares
Nose through crumbling missals.

And all of them, drooling a dumb beggar's faith,
Recite an endless litany to a yellow Jesus
Who dreams on high amidst stained glass,
Far from gaunt troublemakers and miserable gluttons,

Far from scents of flesh and moldy fabric,
This dark defeated farce of foul gestures;
—And prayer blossoms with choice expressions,
And mysticisms take on hurried tones,

Then, from the darkened naves where sunlight dies,
Women from better neighborhoods emerge,
All dim silk, green smiles, and bad livers—O Jesus!—
Dipping their long yellow fingers in the stoups.

June 1871

SISTERS OF CHARITY

The young man with shining eyes and brown skin,
A beautiful, twenty-year-old body best seen bare
That some nameless Persian Genius in a copper crown
Would have worshipped beneath the moon,

Impetuous, but with sweetness, virginal
But dark, proud of his first contumacies
Like young seas, tears on summer nights
Which turn to diamonds in your bed;

In the face of the world's ugliness,
The young man's angry heart flutters,
And burdened with a wound that never heals,
Begins to desire his Sister of Charity.

O sweet merciful Woman—but a heap of entrails—
You are never a sister of charity, never, neither
Your dark stare, nor your belly where a red shadow sleeps,
Not your little fingers, nor your perfect breasts.

An unwaking sightless thing with giant pupils:
Our every embrace shapes a question:
You and your breasts lean over us;
We nurse you, your sweet and solemn Passion.

You give it all back: your ancient sins
And sufferings, your hates and easy apathy;
You give it all back at night, without malice,
Like a monthly shedding of blood.

—When woman, briefly inspired, frightens him
With love—call of life, song of action—
The Green Muse and ardent Justice come
To draw and quarter him with venerable obsession.

Ceaselessly thirsting for splendor and peace,
Forsaken by two unappeasable sisters, whimpering
Tenderly for the knowledge of someone's loving arms,
He arrives with a bloody brow before blossoming Nature.

But black alchemy and sacred studies
Repulse this wounded soul; pride's dark scholar,
He feels an unbearable solitude bearing down.
No less beautifully, and with no fear of the grave,

Let him believe in open endings, Dreams
Or endless Promenades through nights of Truth,
And may he call you to his soul and sickly limbs,
O Sister of charity, O mystery, O Death!

June 1871

FIRST COMMUNION

I

Be honest, these village churches are a joke:
You get fifteen little brats with filthy fingers
Listening to divine esophageal twaddle
Spouted by a black gargoyle with rotting shoes:
But between the leaves, the sun awakens
The old colors of the crude stained glass.

The stones still smell of maternal earth.
You see heaps of these earthy stones
Strewn through a landscape that trembles
Solemnly beneath the burden of wheat,
Bearing burned trees where blackthorns blossom blue,
Knots of black mulberry and rue.

Every hundred years, they slap another coat of
Watery blue or milky white distemper on their barns:
If any creepy relics lurk within
Near Our Lady or our stuffed Saint,
Flies smelling of inns and stables gorge
On wax from the sunny floors.

Children's duty is to house and home, simple
Family life, hard work; they depart, forgetting
How their skin crawled at the firm fingers
Of the Priestly touch, for which the Priest
Is reimbursed with a shady porch from which
To shoo them to labor in the noonday sun.

The first long pants, the best baked treats, beneath
A framed Napoleon or Little Drummer Boy, or

An engraving where Josephs and Marthas stick out
Their tongues with a love that seems excessive and which
Later will be joined by two maps from science class.
Only these sweet memories will remain of the big Day.

The girls always go to church, glad
To hear the boys call them sluts, standing
On ceremony after mass or sung vespers.
Boys destined for life in the garrisons
Who'll sit in cafés and jeer at the better born,
Wearing new shirts, shouting scandalous songs.

Meanwhile, the Priest picks pictures
For the young; in his garden, after vespers, when
The air fills with the distant drone of dances
And he feels, despite his celestial taboo,
A toe begin to stir, then tap time.

—Night falls, black pirate disembarking from a golden sky.

II

The Priest, from among the catechumen, chooses
An unknown little girl with sad eyes and sallow skin
From a congregation drawn from the best and worst
Of neighborhoods. Her parents are humble porters.
"On the great Day, God will blizzard blessings
On this brow before all other catechumen."

III

On the eve of the great Day, the child's anxiousness
Makes her ill. Better at home than in the lofty church
With its doleful murmurs: first, shivers set in—bed
Exciting after all—a superhuman shiver which prompts: "I'm dying..."

And as if stealing love from her idiotic sisters,
She counts, exhausted, hands over her heart,
Angels, Jesuses, glittering Virgins, and
Her soul calmly drinks her conqueror whole.

Adonai . . . ! —Latin phrases fallen from
Shimmering green skies bathe vermilion Brows,
While great snowy sheets tumble across suns
Stained with heavenly breast's pure blood.

—In pursuit of present and future virginity
She bites into your cool Absolution,
So unlike water lilies, so unlike sweets:
Your Pardons chill like ice, o queen of Zion!

IV

And now the Virgin is nothing more than the virgin
In the book; occasionally, mystic spirits shatter. . . .
So follows the impoverishment of images forged
By boredom, awful engravings and old woodcuts;

Vaguely indecent curiosity
Rocks her chaste blue dream
With thoughts of celestial raiment
In which Jesus hides his nakedness.

Soul in distress, mute cries burying
Her brow into the pillow, she wants:
To prolong these supreme bursts of tenderness,
But drools . . . —Shadow fills houses and squares.

And the child cannot go on. She stirs, cants
Her hips, and opens the blue curtain with a hand

To let cool air under the covers,
Over her belly and her burning breast…

V

When she awoke at midnight, the window was white.
Before the blue slumber of lunated curtains
The vision filled her with thoughts of Sunday chastity;
She had dreamt red. Her nose bled,

And, feeling fully chaste and awash in weakness,
Savoring the return of her love of God,
She thirsted for night, where hearts leap
And fall beneath the sky's benevolent eye;

For night is that impalpable Virgin Mother, which bathes
All early emotion in gray silence; she thirsted
For night's strength in which, unwitnessed,
The bleeding heart spills its voiceless revolt.

Playing the victim and the little wife, her star
Saw her coming through the courtyard where
Her jacket hung drying like a white ghost, while
The candle in her hands raised black ghosts from rooftops.

VI

She spent her holy night on the toilet. White air
Streamed around her candle through holes
In the outhouse roof along with a purple-black vine
Invading through a breach in a crumbling wall outside.

---

lunated: sic.

The little window was a heart of live light
In the courtyard where low skies plastered windowpanes
With vermilion and gold; flagstones stank of detergent,
And endured shadows from walls welling with black sleep.

VII

Who—O filthy madmen—will tell of such languors
And fouled mercies, and what will she know of hate
When leprosy finally devours her benevolent body,
Whose holy work still distorts the world?

VIII

And when she's eased her knots of hysteria
She sees, beneath the sorrow of joy, her lover
Dreaming sadly of a thousand white Marys,
This very morning after their first night of love;

"Do you know I killed you? I took your mouth,
Your heart, everything, everything you have;
And I, I'm sick: Oh lay me down
Among the Dead in the sodden waters of night!

"I was young when Christ fouled my lips
By filling me with disgust!
You kissed my hair, thick as fleece,
And I let you... You've got no complaints,

"You men! So unaware that the most smitten of us
Feels, beneath her inner certainty of doom,
Like a whore, horribly sad and certain
That all our lurches your way are missteps!

"For my first Communion is done with
And I'll never know your kisses:
And my heart and my flesh held by your flesh
Crawl with the touch of Jesus' putrid lips!"

IX

So such souls, rotten and wronged,
Will feel your rain of curses.
—Having slept upon your Hate inviolate,
They chose death than be denied true passion.

Christ! O Christ, eternal thief of wills,
You God who, for two thousand years devoted
To Your pallor, has nailed the faces of women
To the earth, in shame, in migraine, in agony.

July 1871

ON THE SUBJECT OF FLOWERS: REMARKS, ADDRESSED TO THE POET

To Monsieur Théodore de Banville

I

There, bordering blue black skies
Where wavecrests tremble gold,
Lilies stimulate evening ecstasies,
Enemas thrust between bardic folds.

After all, times have changed:
Plants now labor—aloe and rose.
Lilies arranged in bunches
Decorate your religious prose.

Kerdrel disappeared behind them
In the Sonnet of eighteen thirty.
Poets are buried beneath them,
In amaranth and carnation flurries.

Lilies, lilies. So often mentioned,
So seldom seen. In your verses, though
They blossom like good intentions
As sinners' resolutions come and go.

Why, even when you bathe, Dear Sir,
Your sallow-pitted gown must bloom
With morning breezes: sleeves confer
High above forget-me-nots in swoon.

Yes: our garden gates let lilacs pass.
But such candied clichés have a cost:
Pollinating spit on petals looks like glass
But is still spit. Our poor flowers? Lost.

II

And when you get your hands on roses,
Windwhipped roses red on laurel stems,
Their effect upon you one supposes
Irresistible: bad versus just never end.

BANVILLE's roses fall like snow,
Their whiteness flecked with blood.
A pricking feeling readers know:
Incomprehension chafes and rubs.

Through grassy banks and wooded ways
Feast your shutterbugging eyes.
What they seize on sure amazes:
A monotony of pretty lies.

Why this mania for floral wrangling?
Why does it prompt such turgid lines?
Low-slung hounds with bellies dangling
French poets are tickled by muddy vines.

As if the lines weren't bad enough,
Consider the pictures they adjoin . . .
A first communion? Either option's rough:
Sunflowers or Lotuses? Flip a coin.

Can French poets resist an Ashokan ode?
Can addicts resist a bag of blow?
As if butterflies take the high road,
To avoid shitting on daisies below.

All this greenery is becoming mulch.
Blossoms plucked to raise the stakes.
Salons bedecked like a flowery gulch
Better for beetles than rattlesnakes.

Grandville's sentimental sketchings
Fill margins with mawkish blooms,
Caricatures of flowery retchings
Evening stars the dark consumes.

Saliva drooling from your pipings
Is all we have for nectar: Pan now dozes.
His song has become mere guttersniping
About Lilies, Ashokas, Lilacs, Roses.

III

O White Hunters: your barefoot excursions
Trample the pastoral into derision;
Shouldn't your flowery poetic diversions
Exhibit a modicum of botanical precision?

You deploy Crickets and Flies indiscriminately
Conflating Phylum and Genus. Rio's gold
And Rhine's blue are switched inadvertently,
Poor Norway becomes "Florida, but cold."

In the past, Dear Master, Art may have settled
For the alexandrine's hexametrical constrictions;

But now, shouldn't the stink of fallen petals
Rotting, make a clean sweep of our ambitions?

Our botanically challenged bards forever bungle:
Mahogany is "a flower found in the country":
Who could imagine that in the Guyan jungle
The real trees support armies of monkeys?

If decadent decoration is the answer that looms
To prettify your pages, the larger question's clear:
Is this riotous, ceaseless, vomitation of blooms
Worth a seagull's turd or one candle's tear?

I think I've made my point: sitting there,
A poet in his far-flung bamboo hut,
Draped with Persian rugs in the Sahara,
You resolutely keep the shutters shut:

And then describe the sands as full
Of flowers, ignoring barren dunes:
This sort of thing—so disgraceful—is bull.
Keep it up, and drive poetry to its doom.

IV

Heard of the notion of "keeping it real"?
Your efforts until now have been rotten.
Enough of this milk-fed literary veal:
Try describing tobacco and cotton.

Why not render Pedro Velazquez' face
And the dollars his cash-crop brings;
Let sun brown skin, your pallor erase,
Describe the shit on swans' white wings:

Yes: the Sorrento sea is full of feathers,
But an ocean of crap floats there too;
Are your stanzas equipped for all weathers?
Are there hydras in the waters with you?

Thrust quatrains into the bloody woods
And report the news that we need.
Expostulate on sugar and durable goods
Whether pansements or rubbers that bleed.

Your job? Deliver truth on these matters,
Such as what covers our tropical peaks;
Is what crowns them like snow-scatters
Lichen, or eggs from insectoid beaks?

O White Hunters, we really must insist
You find us perfumed madders' hues;
Nature nurtures, we gather: fat fists
Dye trousers our infantrymen abuse.

Find flowers that look like muzzles,
At forest fringes dead with sleep;
Unpack oozing botanical puzzles,
Ochre ointments that they leak.

Find calyxes full of fiery eggs
Cooking in their juices
In meadows gone insane with legs:
Pubescent insects Spring seduces.

Find cottony thistledown in bunches
By which donkeys' vision is impaired.
Nature never pulls her punches,
Some flowers even look like chairs.

Yes: find in the heart of dark divides
Flowers that look like precious gems;
Pistils and stamens the darkness hides
But crystally encrusts with faceted hems.

For once—Sad Jester—just serve it up;
Lay our table with a purple platter.
Fill it with a lily stew's sweet syrup:
Fill our spoons with the heart of the matter.

V

And, of course, we now arrive at *love:*
Surely it should be the poet's thing.
Yet Renan below and Murr above
Avoid all Dionysian blossoming.

Put your perfumes to good use:
Scent our stink of torpid lust;
Redeem the wanting we produce,
Lift us heavenward on verbal gusts.

Let *practicality* be a poetic criterion,
As for any Soldier, Psychic, or Salesman.
Awake us from thiopentalic delirium
Like rubber trees, tear us open.

Let strange fruit fall from stanzas,
Prismatic light refract from verses;
Black wings, lepidoptric memorandas,
Flutterings full of electric purpose.

An Age of Hell is now upon us:
The earthly body pierced with spears.

Telegraphic poles limn each Gowanus
Helplessly broadcasting silent tears.

Spin, my poet, tales of earthly blight,
Exalt, somehow, in the potato's sorry life;
Rhyme all ruin to make wrong right
Feed your poems on terrestrial strife—

Whether in Babylon or Bayonne—
Let them ramble, let them range
Over paper like low moans:
Graze the poem: make it strange.

Alcide Bava

A.R.

July 14, 1871

THE DRUNKEN BOAT

While swept downstream on indifferent Rivers,
I felt the boatmen's tow-ropes slacken:
Yawping Redskins took them as targets
Nailing them naked to totem poles.

I never gave much thought to my crews,
To holds of Flemish wheat or English cotton.
So when cries of boatmen and Redskins receded
The Rivers left me to chart my course.

Deafer than a dreaming child, I ran
Into winter's furious rippling tides.
Peninsulas wrenched from shore
Have never known such hurly-burly.

The tempest christened my maritime musings.
For ten nights I danced like a cork on waves
Whose victims call dread eternal breakers.
And I didn't miss the banished bowlights blinking.

Sweeter than sour apples are to infants
Were the green waters my pine hull drank,
As rudder and anchor were washed away: I was cleansed,
Rinsed of stains, of vomit and blue wine.

Thereafter I bathed in the Poem of the Sea,
Milky with reflected stars, devouring blue and green;
A drowned sailor sometimes floated by
Like some pale apotheosis, or flotsam lost in thought.

Love's bitter mystery suddenly blossoms
Beneath the blue, a slow delirium of rhythms,

A redness infecting the burgeoning day,
Stronger than spirits, louder than lyres!

I know skies split by lightning, waterspouts
And undertows, and tides: I know the night,
And dawn exulting like a crowd of doves.
I have even seen what man dreams he has.

I have seen the low sun stained with mystic horror,
Lit with long violet weals like actors
In some ancient play, waves unrolling
Their shuddering paddles into the distance.

I have dreamt green nights ablaze with snow,
Kisses climbing the eyes of the sea,
Unimaginable humors circulating freely,
Blue and yellow heavings of phosphorescent song!

I followed the swell for months on end,
Watched it storm reefs like hysterical herds,
Unaware that Marys' luminous feet
Could muzzle panting Seas.

You know I've stormed unimaginable Floridas,
Her flowers scattered with panthers' eyes
And human skin! Rainbows hung beneath horizons
Like bridles on blue-green broods.

I've seen Leviathan rotting whole
In reedy clots of putrid swamp; seen
Dead calm shattered by watery collapse;
Distant views caving beneath misty cataracts.

Silver suns, pearly waves, Glaciers and embered skies!
Shipwrecks at the borders of brown gulfs

Where giant serpents smelling of the dark
Tumble from twisted trees, a feast for bugs.

I would have liked to show daurades of the deep
Blue sea to children; shared these golden, singing fish.
—A foam of flowers was the only harbor I required
And indescribable winds have lent me wings.

At times, the sea's sobs tossed me gently,
Her dark, yellow petals brushed against me;
I was like a woman on her knees,
A martyr weary of poles and zones.

Like an island, my rails drew pale eyes,
Quarrels and droppings of gossiping birds,
And I drifted on, until drowned men bobbing
Through my flimsy lines sank down into sleep...

And I, a boat lost in inlets' tangled hair,
Tossed by hurricanes into birdless air, I
Whose water-drunken carcass Coast-Guard
And Hanseatic ships could not have dredged;

Free, on fire, crowned by violet mist,
I dug a hole in a reddening sky like a wall
Smeared with solar lichen and gobs
Of azure snot, irresistible poetic treats.

Scarred with electric crescent moons,
A lunatic plank escorted by black seahorses—
I fled, as July's hammering heat
Beat ultramarine skies into smoldering pits;

I, who trembled at groans fifty leagues away
Of Behemoth rutting and Maelstroms raging,

I, eternal weaver of immovable blues,
Finally missed Europe's ancient parapets!

I saw archipelagoes of stars, and islands
Whose delirious skies parted for the voyager:
O mounting vigor, o million golden birds exiled
In these bottomless nights: do you sleep?

Enough tears! Dawns break hearts.
Every moon is wrong, every sun bitter:
Love's bitter bite has left me swollen, drunk with heat.
Let my hull burst! Let me sink into the sea!

If I still long for Europe's waters, it's only for
One cold black puddle where a child crouches
Sadly at its brink and releases a boat,
Fragile as a May butterfly, into the fragrant dusk.

Bathed in your weary waves, I can no longer ride
In the wake of cargo ships of cotton,
Nor cross the pride of flags and flames,
Nor swim beneath the killing stare of prison ships.

Summer, 1871

“THE RIGHTEOUS MAN . . .”

[. . . . .]
The Righteous Man sat up on his heavy hips:
A beam of light gilded his shoulder; sweat
Gripped me: “Would you watch glimmering meteors?
Would you stand listening to droning floods
Of milky stars and asteroid swarms?

“O Righteous Man your brow is thorned
With these heavenly tricks! Find shelter. Pray,
Gently expiating beneath your sheets;
And if some lost soul shakes your sanctuary
Tell him: Move along, Brother, I am lame!”

And the Righteous stood on grass
So unbearably blue with the sun’s death:
“So would you sell your kneecaps,
Old Codger? Holy pilgrim! Bard of Armor!
Weeper of the Olives! Hand by pity gloved!

“Beard at home, fist in town,
Gently believing: a heart fallen in his chalice,
Majesties and virtues, love and blindness,
But Righteous? Fouler and more foolish than lice!
I’m the one who suffers and rebels!

“Fool! The vaunted prospect of your pardon
Makes me blubber on my belly and break out laughing!
You know I’m damned! I’m drunk, crazy, livid,

“The Righteous Man . . .” is an incomplete poem. Manuscript evidence indicates the first twenty lines are missing, along with a few words in the final stanza.

Whatever! But please, go to bed: Righteous?!
I don't want anything to do with your torpid thoughts.

"After all, you're Mr. Righteous! Right? Enough!
Sure: your serene tenderness and reason
Snuffle through the night like whales!
May your behavior see you banished, elegizing
On horns as if through beaks of grotesquely shattered birds!

"And you, coward, are the eye of God? When divine feet
Tread their cold soles upon my neck, still
You cower! Your brow streams with lice!
Socrates and Jesus, Holy and Righteous—foul!
Revere me: king of the Damned in the bloody dark!"

I screamed all this at the earth, and night
Filled the skies above my fever with pale calm.
I raised my brow: the ghost had gone,
Carrying my lips' atrocious ironies away...
—Nocturnal winds, visit the Damned! Speak to him!

All the while, silent under pillars of blue,
Order—the eternal watchman—rowed
Through luminous skies, trawling his fiery net
For streaming stars, speeding comets,
Celestial knots, upheaval, but without calamity...

Oh that he would leave—him—shame
Tied around his neck forever, mulling over
My boredom, sweet as sugar on rotten teeth.
—Like some bitch bitten by her litter
And left licking an entrail-dangling flank.

Enough of his dirty charity and progress…
—I'm sick of all these strange looks with […]
[…] that sing: happy as a heap of children on the brink
Of death, sweet idiots with unexpected songs:
O Righteous men, we shit in your bellies of stone […]

JEANNE-MARIE'S HANDS

Jeanne-Marie has strong hands
Dark hands tanned by summer,
Pale hands like dead hands.
—Do they belong to Juana?

Did they turn creamy brown
On swollen seas?
Did they dip in placid ponds
On distant moons?

Did they drink from savage skies,
Folded charmingly on knees?
Did they roll cigars
Or traffic diamonds?

Did they toss golden flowers
At Madonnas' ardent feet?
The black blood of belladonnas
Rests and blazes in their palms.

Hands hunting flies
Buzzing dawn's bluings
Nearing nectaries?
Hands decanting poisons?

Oh what Dream
Has gripped them?
A dream of Asia,
Of Khenghavars or Zions?

—These hands never sold an orange,
Nor turned brown at the feet of gods:

Nor washed the swaddling clothes
Of chubby, eyeless children.

These aren't a cousin's hands
Nor of workers whose heavy foreheads
Burn in some toxic forest factory
Where the sun drowns in tar.

These are shapers of spines,
Hands that do no harm,
More deadly than machines,
Stronger than a horse.

Restless as furnaces,
And shedding their shudders,
Their flesh sings Marseillaises
But never Eleisons!

They would wring the necks
Of evil women; pulverize the hands
Of noble women, vile hands
Mottled carmine and white.

The radiance of these loving hands
Turns the heads of lambs!
The sun sets rubies
Onto such delectable fingers!

A popular stain blots them brown
Like an ancient breast;
Upon the back of these Hands
Every rebel plants a kiss!

They have faded beautifully,
Under a love-laden sun.

On the bronze of machine guns
Throughout revolutionary Paris.

Sometimes, around your wrists
Cries a chain of shimmering links,
Hands where our trembling lips
Linger drunkenly, tirelessly.

And then sometimes a strange upheaval
Finds its way within us, and we wish
Your Angelic Hands were made paler still
By making your fingers bleed.

February 1872

IV. UNDATED POEMS, c. 1870–1872

SITTING MEN

Black wens, pockmarks, green bags
Under eyes; pudgy fingers clutching thighs,
Skulls tormented with angry blotches
Like leprous blossoms on old walls;

With epileptic affection they graft
Ghostly skeletons to chairs'
Black bones. Night and day
Their feet entwine with rickety rungs.

These old codgers are inseparable from their seats:
They sit stewing in sunlight searing their skin,
Trembling the painful tremble of toads,
Peering through the windows at melting snow.

Their seats are good to them: old and brown,
The straw gives against their angular rears;
The soul of old suns brightens, woven
Through braided ears which once cradled corn.

The sitting men gnaw their knees, ten fingers
Drum beneath their seats, green pianists listening
To the rhythmic rapping of sad barcaroles,
Noggins bobbing on waves of love.

—Oh don't tempt disaster and make them rise...
They hiss like cats caught by their tails, heaving up
And slowly spreading angry shoulders
As their pants balloon around swollen rears!

And you'll hear them bumping their bald heads
Against dark walls, stamping and stomping

Their crooked feet, their buttons ogling you
Down hallways like eyes of hungry beasts.

They can kill you wordlessly:
When they return, black venom seeps
Through stares that would down a dog:
And so you sweat, stuck in this horrible pit.

Seated again, their fists swim in dirty cuffs,
They stew upon whoever made them stand,
And from dawn until dusk their tonsils tremble
Nearly bursting beneath weak chins.

When stoic sleep finally finds their visors,
On folded arms they dream of pregnant chairs
And chair children sired in sleep,
Gathering around their regal desks;

Cradled by inky flowers spitting pollen commas,
They walk down rows of drooped calyxes,
Dragonflies through gladiolas. —And their members
Are stirred by the sharp straw of their seats.

LICE HUNTERS

When the child's forehead full of red torments
Begs the white swarm of vague dreams
To take him, two charming sisters loom
Above his bed, with fragile fingers and silver nails.

They sit him before a window opened wide
Where a jumble of flowers bathes in blue air,
And then, bewitching and terrible, the delicate fingers
Walk through his heavy, dew-matted hair.

He listens to the song of their uneasy breath,
Long earthy blossoms of rose-rich honey
Interrupted now and then by a salivary sucking,
Tongues licking lips, hungry for a kiss.

He hears their black lids bat beneath
The scented silence; their gentle pulsing fingers
Kill little lice beneath royal nails crackling
Sounds resounding through his gray stupor.

But the wine of Sloth is rising in him,
A harmonica's sigh that sets you reeling;
Beneath the slowness of their caresses, the child
Feels an urge to cry, welling and dying, endlessly.

CUSTOMS MEN

Soldiers, sailors, imperial rabble, even pensioners
Can't hold a candle to our Peace Keepers who yammer
"Awww Jeezis" and "Don't go nowhere" as they swing
Heavy axes though azure frontiers.

Pipes between teeth, knives in hand, happy as can be,
They set out with dogs tugging on leashes,
In search of an evening's evil fun, darkness
Drooling through the woods as if from a cow's maw.

They hassle female fauns,
Round up Fausts and Devils, saying
"None of that, fellas! Drop them bags!"

And when his highness the Customs Man happens
Upon young boys, he exacts more than a dutiful grope.
Hell for Delinquents pressed by his palm!

"THE STAR WEPT . . ."

The star wept rose into the heart of your ears,
An infinity of white rolled between your nape and hips;
The sea spumed red onto your vermilion breasts,
And Man bled black onto your sovereign side.

EVENING PRAYER

I live my life sitting, like an angel in a barber's chair,
A big fluted beer mug in my hand, neck and hypogastrus
Arched, a cheap Gambier pipe between my teeth,
And the air above me swollen with sails of smoke.

Like steaming droppings in an old dovecote
A thousand Dreams within me gently burn:
And at times my sad heart is like sapwood
Bleeding dark yellow gold where a branch is torn.

Then, when I've methodically drowned my dreams
With thirty or forty beers, I pull myself together
And release my bitter need:

Sweet as the Lord of Hyssop and Cedar,
I piss into the brown sky, far and wide,
Heliotropes blessing me below.

FAUN'S HEAD

Within the leaves, this gilded bower,
Within the leaves, uncertain and full
Of blossoming blooms and drowsy kisses,
The exquisite tapestry is suddenly shaken

And a frightened faun flashes its eyes
While biting red flowers between white teeth
Browned and bloodied like old wine, lips
Bursting with laughter beneath branches.

And when he flees like a squirrel
His laugh remains, beading on each leaf,
And the Golden Kiss of the Woods, startled
By a bullfinch, resolves once again to rest.

VOWELS

Black A, White E, Red I, Green U, Blue O: vowels.
Someday I'll explain your burgeoning births:
A, a corset; black and hairy, buzzing with flies
Bumbling like bees around a merciless stench,

And shadowy gulfs; E, white vapors and tents, proud
Glacial peaks, white kings, shivering Queen Anne's lace;
I, purples, bloody spittle, lips' lovely laughter
In anger or drunken contrition;

U, cycles, divine vibrations of viridian seas;
Peace of pastures sown with beasts, wrinkles
Stamped on studious brows as if by alchemy;

O, that last Trumpet, overflowing with strange discord,
Silences bridged by Worlds and Angels:
—O the Omega, the violet beam from His Eyes!

V. 1872

COMEDY OF THIRST

1. FOREBEARS

We are your Grandparents,
        Your elders.
Covered in cold sweat
From moon and leaves.
Our dry wines had soul.
What can a man do
Beneath a guileless sun? Drink.

MYSELF: Die in wild rivers.

We are your Grandparents,
        Your fields.
There is water beneath the willows:
The moat's waters are moving
Around the sodden château.
Go inside, into the cellars;
Soon, there'll be cider and milk.

MYSELF: Go where cows drink.

We are your Grandparents,
        Here,
Take these liquors from our stores
Of rare Tea and Coffee,
Quivering in kettles.
Look at the pictures, the flowers.
We return from the cemetery.

MYSELF: Drink the urns dry.

2. SOUL

Eternal water-nymphs
    Part the pure waters.
Blue sister Venus,
    Stir the glittering wave.

Wandering Jews of Norway,
    Tell me about your snows
Ancient exiles,
    Tell me about your seas.

MYSELF: No: forget these pure waters,
    And the waterflowers we drink from;
Neither legends nor faces
    Slake my thirst;

Songsmith, my wild thirst
    Is your daughterly ward,
A hydra, mouthless and near,
    That consumes and despoils.

3. FRIENDS

Come: wines beat the beaches,
Waves by the millions.
Look: Bitters run
Down mountains.

The green pillars of Absinthe
Are there for pilgrims' taking.

MYSELF: Enough of this.
Dear friends, what is drunkenness?
I would rather

Rot in a pond,
Beneath unbearable scum,
Near drifting logs.

4. A PAUPER DREAMS

Perhaps a Night awaits me
When I'll drink peacefully
In an old City,
And die happy:
Patience rewarded.

If my sufferings abate,
If I ever get some cash,
Will I choose the North,
Or the Land of Vines?
—These are the wrong dreams

Are hope for the wrong thing.
And if once again I
Become the traveler of yore
The green inn will never
Open its doors to me again.

5. CONCLUSION

Pigeons tremble in the prairie,
Game runs, watches the night,
Creatures of water, creatures enslaved,
And even butterflies . . . All thirst.

But to disappear with the wandering clouds . . .
—And to be blessed by cool . . .
And to die with these damp violets
That dawn dumps into the woods?

May 1872

GOOD MORNING THOUGHTS

At four in the morning, in summer,
Love's sleep slumbers on.
Beneath the bowers, dawn stirs
    The scent of evening celebrations.

But there, under the great oak,
Near the Hesperidean sun,
Carpenters in shirtsleeves
    Are already in motion.

At peace in their mossy desert,
They fashion precious woodwork
For rooms where the wealthy
    Will laugh beneath painted skies.

Ah Venus! For these dear Workers' sakes,
Subjects of some Babylonian king,
Leave the Lovers be,
    Their souls entwined.

        O Queen of Shepherds!
    Bring these workmen eau-de-vie
    To restore their vigor
For swimming in the noontime sea.

May 1872

A slightly different version of this poem appears in *A Season in Hell,* p. 209.

RIVER CASSIS

Unnoticed, the River Cassis streams
    Through strange valleys:
Accompanied by a hundred crows,
    Angelic voices good and true:
Pine groves sway
    When winds plunge.

Everything streams through ancient landscapes
    Brimming with terrible mysteries;
Visits to dungeons and important parks:
    By the banks we hear
Knights-errant praise lost passions:
    But the wind pays all debts.

Let a wanderer look through the leaves:
    He'll depart with courage restored.
Dear delicious crows, forest soldiers
    Sent by the Lord,
Drive treacherous peasants from this place
    Who toast with vestigial arms.

May 1872

TEAR

Far from birds, herds, and village girls,
I drank, crouched on a heath, surrounded
By hazelnut trees and
Warm green afternoon mist.

What was in this infant Oise I drank?
Voiceless elms, flowerless grass, cloudy sky?
What was in this colocasian gourd?
Its dull golden liquor makes me sweat.

As it was, I would have made a miserable tavern sign.
Storms kept changing the sky until nightfall.
These were dark lands, lakes, and poles,
Colonnades beneath the blue night, harbors.

Water from woods disappeared in virgin sands.
Wind from the heavens tossed ice onto ponds . . .
As if that would stop me from wanting a drink,
Like a panner for gold or diver for shells!

May 1872

A slightly different version of this poem appears in *A Season in Hell,* p. 208.

PATIENCE CELEBRATED

1. MAY BANNERS
2. SONG FROM THE TALLEST TOWER
3. ETERNITY
4. GOLDEN AGE

MAY BANNERS

The call of the kill dies feebly
In a linden's bright branches,
While heavenly songs flutter
Through currant bushes.
Blood laughs in our veins,
Amidst this tangle of vines.
The sky is an angel.
Wave and wind commune.
I leave. If a sunbeam strikes me
I'll die on the moss.

Patience and boredom are easy.
To hell with my suffering.
Let glorious summer bind me
To the back of its fated chariot.
O Nature! Let me die—less alone,
Less meaningless—with you.
So unlike Shepherds who, strangely, die
Almost anywhere in the world.

Let the seasons take me.
Nature, I give myself to you;
My hunger and my thirst.
Please; nourish; quench.

I have no illusions, none;
I laugh at the sun, a child at its parents;
But I don't want to laugh at anything;
And all this misfortune is free.

May 1872

SONG FROM THE TALLEST TOWER

Idle youth,
Slave to all,
Sensitivity
Was my fall.
Let the moment come
When hearts will be one.

Just say: let go,
Disappear:
Without hope
Of greater joy.
Let nothing impede
August retreat.

I've been so patient
I nearly forgot;
Fear and suffering
Have taken wing.
Unwholesome thirst
Stains my veins.

So the meadow
Surrendered,

A very different version of "Song from the Tallest Tower" appears in *A Season in Hell*, p. 210.

Lush and blossoming
With incense and weeds,
And the fierce buzzing
Of a hundred flies.

A thousand widowings
Of the indigent heart
Left with nothing
But our lady's face—Nôtre Dame!
Can one really pray
To the Virgin Mary, today?

Idle youth,
Slave to all,
Sensitivity
Was my fall.
Let the moment come
When hearts will be one.

May 1872

ETERNITY

Rediscovered.
What? —Eternity.
Sea and sun
As one.

Sentinel soul,
We'll confess
To empty night
And fiery day.

A slightly different version of "Eternity" appears in *A Season in Hell,* p. 212.

You break
From earthly approval
And common urges:
Then soar, accordingly.

Duty draws breath
From your silken embers,
Without anyone saying:
Enough.

No hope here,
Nul orietur.
Knowledge through patience,
Suffering is certain.

Rediscovered.
What? —Eternity.
Sea and sun
As one.

May 1872

GOLDEN AGE

One of these voices
—Speaking about me—
However angelically
Makes things clear:

The thousand questions
Reach like roots
And ensure no more,
Than drunken madness;

Nul orietur: "Nor will any arise."

It seems so simple and gay;
Don't be fooled,
By flowers and waves:
They're your family.

The voice sings. O
So simple and gay,
And seemingly clear
—I sing along—

Apparently simple and gay;
Don't be fooled,
By flowers and waves:
They're your family! Etc....

And then a voice
—Speaking about me—
So angelically
Makes things clear:

And suddenly sings:
Breathlessly, a sister
Sounding German,
Hot and full:

The world is vicious;
As if that's a surprise!
Live, and leave dark misfortune
To the flames.

O beautiful château!
O bright life!
What Age could claim

The princely nature
Of our big brother! Etc....

I, too, sing:
So many sisters!
Private voices!
Envelop me
In modest glory. Etc....

June 1872

YOUNG COUPLEDOM

The bedroom stands open to the turquoise sky;
Barely any room inside: just boxes and bins.
Outside, walls are thick with birthwort
And brimming with mumbling elfin gums.

Just like a genie, all this.
Frivolous expense and purposeless disorder!
The African fairy provides mulberry,
And hairnets high in corners.

Grumbling godmothers in skirts of light
Clamber into sideboards.
The couple leaves on some errand,
And nothing is put away.

In his absence, the bridegroom is betrayed
By winds that will not leave. Even water sprites
Make mischievously inside
To swim orbits in the alcove.

By sweet night, the honeymoon
Will amass their joys and spill
A thousand bands of copper through the sky.
A time will come to face the crafty rat.

—Unless a pale will-o'-the-wisp should alight
Like a shotgun blast at vespers.
—O white holy ghosts of Bethlehem,
Bless their window's blue view instead!

27 June 1872

"IS SHE A DANCER . . . ?"

Is she a dancer . . . ? In the first blue hours
Will she perish like wilting flowers . . .
Before the breathtaking vista, you feel
The burgeoning city's blossoming breath!

It's too beautiful! It's too beautiful! But essential . . .
—For the Fisherwoman and the Pirate's song,
And because the last masked souls still believed
In evening celebrations on a pure dark sea!

July 1872

HUNGER CELEBRATED

My hunger, Anne, Anne,
Flee on your mule if you can.

If I have any *taste,* it's for
Earth and stone.
Ding-dong! Ding-dong! Let's eat air,
Iron, rock, and loam.

May my hungers turn away,
Graze a field of sound!
Sample bindweed's poison;
It merrily abounds.

Rocks that paupers break,
Old church stones,
Pebbles from the flood,
Loaves in valleys all alone.

My hunger is black and tattered air,
Bells ringing in the blue;
—My stomach is my guide
To misfortune, all too true

Leaves appear upon the ground:
I look for rotten fruit.
I gather violets and baby lettuce
Along the furrow's swollen route.

My hunger, Anne, Anne,
Flee on your mule if you can.

August 1872

A different version of this poem appears in *A Season in Hell,* p. 211.

CROWS

When your meadows lie cold, O Lord,
When the endless Angelus falls silent
In every crumbling hamlet…
Strike down your dear delicious crows
From boundless skies above
To nature's deflowered ground.

Strange armies with cries that crack,
Cold nests that winds attack.
Along yellow rivers,
Along old cross roads,
Around ditches, around holes,
Mobilize and go.

By the thousands, wheel through winter air,
Above sleeping dead of yesteryear,
Across the fields of France
No passerby forgets.
Be our voice of duty,
O black funereal beauty.

Heavenly saints roosting in looming oaks,
Your matte-black lost in the enchanted dark,
Leave May warblers to the vanquished,
Deep in a wood or beneath the grass,
As promise of a future
We can't escape, alas.

"BLANKETS OF BLOOD..."

Blankets of blood, coalfires, a thousand murders,
Endless howls of rage, and all harmony undone
By every hellish tear: would any of this matter,
O heart of mine, while the Aquilon still stirs debris...?

But vengeance? Never! And yet we crave it.
Industrialists, princes, senators: die!
Power, justice, history: kneel! We're *due.*
We want blood. Blood, and golden flames.

My soul wants war; vengeance; terror! To war!
We writhe in its Bite: Enough republics!
We've had enough: of emperors,
Regiments, colonists, peoples—enough!

Who will stir the fiery whirlwinds' fury
If not ourselves and those we call our brothers?
It's our turn! Romantic friends: our fun begins.
O waves of fire, we'll never work again!

Europe, Asia, America—vanish. Our march
Of vengeance spreads across cities and over hills!
—And yet, we will be crushed!
Volcanoes will explode, oceans boil...

Oh my friends! —My heart knows its own brothers!
Dark strangers, what if we were to leave? So leave! Leave!
O misfortune! How the earth melts upon us,
How I shake as it melts on me and you,

But no matter: I'm here; I'm still here.

"FLOWERBEDS OF AMARANTHS..."

Brussels, July, Boulevart du Régent

Flowerbeds of amaranths stretching
All the way to the Palais de Jupiter.
—I know you blend Saharan blues
Into places such as this.

Then, as rose and fir and creepers
Play through sunlit plots
And a little widow's cage...!
What
Flocks of birds—hoo hee, hee hoo!

—Quiet houses, yesterday's passions!
Love made a woman mad, left her a house.
Rosebushes' backsides and, behind them,
Juliet's shadowy balcony.

Juliet reminds me of Henriette,
A charming railway station in the heart
Of a mountain as at the bottom of an orchard,
Where a thousand devils dance in the air!

A green bench where a pale Irish girl sings
And plays guitar for this stormy paradise.
Then from the Guianan dining room
Comes the chatter of children and cages.

A ducal window makes me think
Of snails' poison and boxwood
Sleeping in the sun.

And then
It's just too beautiful. Don't say a word.

—A boulevard without traffic or trade,
Every drama muted, every comedy stilled,
An infinite collection of scenes.
I know you, and stare at you in silence.

"IN APRIL, LISTEN . . ."

In April, listen
to the peas,
trellised and green
groaning beneath trees.

Saints of yesteryear
Turn their heads and peer
Towards Phoebe's mists
So bright and clear . . .

Far from capes' bright haystacks,
far from lovely roofs,
dear Ancients desire
perfidious proofs . . .

Neither holidays
nor starlight
constitute this
golden evening mist.

Nevertheless they remain
—Sicily, Germany—
despite pallor, fog and rain:
naturally!

MICHEL AND CHRISTINE

It would stink if the sun left our shores!
Shoo, bright flood! Seek shadowy roads instead.
The storm flings its first fat drops
Into the willows of the old courtyard.

O hundred lambs, O idyllic blonde soldiers,
Flee aqueducts and wasted heaths,
Deserts, prairies, plains, horizons—
Are rinsed red by storm.

Black dog, brown shepherd bundled up,
Flee lightning's finest hour;
Better perches lie below, blonde brood,
When sulfur and shadow swim.

But Lord! I see my Soul soar
Through frozen red skies, beneath
Celestial clouds that race and soar
Across a hundred Solognes, long as rails.

See a thousand wolves, a thousand wild seeds
Scattered by this religious afternoon of storm
That even blesses bindweed:
A hundred hordes cross our aged Europe.

And such moonlight when it's through! Crossing the moors,
Red brows rise towards black skies, warriors
Slowly advancing on pale horses.
Pebbles singing beneath the proud gang.

—O Gaul, will I see yellow woods and valleys bright,
Blue-eyed wife and red-browed man,

And at their cherished feet, all white, a Paschal lamb,
—Michel and Christine—with Christ!

—So our Idyll ends.

SHAME

If the knife has yet
To cut his head, or gut
This pale fat greenish mass
Of endless gas,

(Him? Let him lop
Off his nose, his lips, ears
And belly. While he's at it
Lose the legs! Better still.)

But, no, seriously: I think
If blade to neck
And stones to sides
And fires to gut

Have not yet cut, struck, or burned
This pain-in-the-ass kid,
Why should the bastard cease
To betray and cheat

Like a Rocky Mountain cat
Can't stop stinking up the world.
But when he dies, O Lord,
May someone say a prayer.

MEMORY

I

Clear water; like salt from childhood's tears,
the whiteness of women's bodies, rivaling the sun;
silk banners, droves of pure lilies
beneath walls a virgin once defended;

angels' games; —No . . . the coursing golden current
moves its grassy arms, heavy, black, and cool.
In darkness, blue sky as bed canopy, she draws
the shadows of hills and arches closed, like curtains.

II

So the moist square yields limpid bubbles.
Water fills the neat beds with pale bottomless gold.
Girls' faded green dresses conjure willows
Bursting with unfettered birds.

At high noon, the dear rose sphere
hot with jealousy into this dim mirror
peers; the marsh marigold—your wifely trust—
a hot yellow eyelid purer than a louis d'or.

III

Madame stands too upright in the neighboring field
where threads of work snow down; parasol
between fingers; trampling flowers; peacock proud;
children read Moroccan-leather books

in the flowering field! Alas, He, like
a thousand white angels dividing on the road,
flees to the mountain! She, perfectly
cold, and black, gives chase.

IV

Longing for strong young grassy arms!
April's lunar gold, the holy bed's heart!
Reveling in abandoned boatyards, prey
to August nights that sow their rot!

Now, let her weep beneath ramparts! Breath
from poplars is the only breeze. Then,
this dull gray sheet: no reflections, no source;
an old man struggles, dredging from a motionless boat.

V

I cannot reach a toy resting upon this sad watery eye.
O motionless boat! O short arms! Neither
one flower nor the other: neither bothersome yellow
nor blue, water's sister, color of ash.

Wings stir Dust from willows!
Roses rise from long-dead reeds!
My boat, stuck; its chain, caught
at what muddy bottom of this edgeless watery eye?

"O SEASONS, O CHÂTEAUX"

O seasons, o châteaux
Who possesses a perfect soul?

O seasons, o châteaux!

I made a magical study
Of inescapable Bliss.

All hail Bliss, throughout Gaul
When you hear the rooster's call.

Bliss has finally set me free
From desire's tyranny.

Its spell took soul and shape,
Letting every goal escape.

What do my words mean?
Meaning flees, takes wing!

o seasons, o châteaux

See *Uncollected Writings V: Four Seasons* (p. 355) for four different versions of this poem.

VI. 1871–1872
From the ALBUM ZUTIQUE

The Album Zutique *was a communal journal for the poets and artists with whom Rimbaud associated while living in Paris—a scrapbook for the out-at-the-elbows set. They called themselves* Zutistes, *a word coined from the French exclamation* "zut," *which, depending on context, can mean anything from "golly" to "damn." The album contained over sixty entries, twenty-one of which have been identified as being by Rimbaud. Most of his poems here are parodies of the work of other poets, and many are ribald in nature. As such, some scholars have dismissed them, which I think is wrong-headed: many are terrific.*

Below each of the entries, the name of the poet parodied is given, followed by its author. Rimbaud signs his name variously, and I've maintained these variations.

The album appeared on the collector's market in 1937, and represents the last substantial trove of Rimbaud manuscript discoveries of the twentieth century.

SONNET TO AN ASSHOLE

Dark and wrinkled like a violet carnation,
It breathes, humbly lurking in moss
Still moist from love following the sweet flight
Of white Buttocks to its rim's heart.

Strands like milky tears were wept
Beneath a cruel wind driving them back,
Between little clots of reddish clay
Losing themselves in the beckoning slope.

My Dream often mouthed its vent;
My soul, jealous of real coitus,
Made it a musky vessel for sobs and tears.

Swooning olive, tender flute, the tube
From which heavenly praline flows:
A womanly Canaan surrounded in moisture.

—Albert Mérat
Quatrains, Paul Verlaine
Tercets, Arthur Rimbaud

LILY

O swaying lilies! O silver enemas!
Contemptuous of work, contemptuous of famine!
Dawn fills you with love's cleansing wash!
A heavenly sweetness butters your stamens!

—Armand Silvestre
A.R.

SEEN IN ROME

In Rome, in the Sistine,
Ancient noses are drying
In a scarlet reliquary
Covered in Christian emblems:

In ascetics' noses from Thebes,
And Canons' from the Grail
Pale night is stiffening
To sounds of sepulchral wails.

Each day,
Foul schismatic dust
Is ground away and thrust
Inside occult decay.

—Léon Dierx
A.R.

FEAST OF LOVE

In Dreams, Babbit
Scratched a rabbit
beneath his cloak.

Courtesan
—Got it on!—
—*Do, mi*—flicked

The rabbit's eye
Which, tricked,
reels.

—Paul Verlaine
AR

"I WAS IN A THIRD-CLASS COMPARTMENT . . ."

I was in a third-class compartment: an old priest
Withdrew an old clay pipe and turned
His calm face and gray hair to the breeze.
Then, this Christian, risking reproach,
Turned and asked, in a manner both
Resolute and sad, for a pinch of tobacco—
He used to be chief chaplain
To a royal twice condemned—
To ease the boredom of the tunnel, dark vein
Available to travelers near Soissons,
A town in Aisne.

—François Coppée
A.R.

"DOUBTLESS I PREFER . . ."

Doubtless I prefer outdoor cafés in spring
Where dwarf chestnuts' bare branches bloom with buds
In May, along narrow communal greenswards.
Young dogs forever scolded approach drinkers,
Trampling hyacinths in their beds.
And all through these hyacinth nights,
At the slate table where, in 1720,
Some deacon carved his Latin nickname,
A meager scrawl like words in stained glass,
Black bottles cough, but never get them drunk.

—François Coppée
A.R.

"HUMANITY TIED . . ."

Humanity tied the shoes of Progress, that enormous child.

—Louis-Xavier de Ricard
A. Rimbaud

NONSENSE

I. Piglet

Silky
Beanie
Ivory
Weenie.

Black
Frocks,
Paul stalks
The hutch,

Towards pear,
Turns
Tongue,

Rod, at ready,
With
The runs.

A.R.

II. Paris

Al. Godillot, Gambier,
Galopeau, Volf-Pleyel,
—O Faucets!—Menier,
—O Christs!—Leperdriel!

Kinck, Jacob, Bonbonnel!
Veuillot, Tropmann, Augier!
Gill, Mendès, Manuel,
Guido Gonin!—A pannier

Of Graces! Hérissé!
Greasy shines!
Old bread, wines.

Blindmen! Who else?
Policemen, Engheins
At home!—Be good Christians!

A.R.

NONSENSE, PART 2

I. Drunk Driver

Dirtbag
Drinks:
Mother-of pearl
Watches;

Bitter
Law,
Carriage
Topples!

Woman
Falls:
Thigh

Bleeds:
Moan
Groan.

A.R.

II. Paris: A catalogue of Parisian names of the era. *Al. Godillot:* Alexis Godillot, shoemaker; *Gambier:* maker of Rimbaud's favorite pipes; *Galopeau:* manicures and pedicures; *Volf-Pleyel* [*sic*]: Wolff-Pleyel: piano sellers; *Menier:* chocolate maker; *Leperdriel* [*sic*]: Le Perdriel: maker of stockings for sufferers of varicose veins; *Kinck* and *Tropmann* [*sic*]: an Alsacian, Jean Kinck, killed by Troppman (corrected spelling), a famous serial killer who was guillotined; *Jacob:* known also as "*le Zouave Jacob*," an African healer (or, perhaps, a reference to another Parisian pipemaker); *Bonbonnel* [*sic*]: Charles-Laurent Bombonnel, a big-game hunter; *Veuillot:* Louis Veuillot, Catholic journalist; *Augier:* Émile Augier, playwright; *Gill:* André Gill, caricaturist; *Mendès:* Catulle Mendès, poet; *Manuel:* Eugène Manuel, poet; *Guido Gonin:* unknown; *Hérissé:* Al. Hérissé, hatmaker; *Engheins:* a purveyor of medicinal water; *At home:* their slogan.

THE OLD WOMAN'S OLD MAN!

To the peasants of the emperor!
To the emperor of the peasants!
To the son of March—
Glorious March 18th!
When Eugénie's sky blessed her womb!

Eugénie: Empress Eugénie de Montijo, wife of Napoleon III. Their son was born on March 16, 1856, not March 18.

UNDER SIEGE?

The poor driver, beneath the tin canopy,
Nursing a large chilblain under his glove
Following his heavy omnibus through the *rive gauche,*
Shifts his sack of fares from his aching groin.
And while the honest interior—the sweet shadow
Containing gendarmes—looks onto the deep sky
Where the moon nestles in cottony green,
And despite the edict, the delicate hour,
The bus returning to the Odéon, a bedraggled
Debaucher yaps away in the dark intersection!

—François Coppée
A.R.

THE BRUSH

A humble scrub brush, too coarse
For a bedroom or a wall. Its function
Is disconcerting and shouldn't encourage laughter.
Its roots still sunk in some old field while
Its inert bristles desiccate; its handle turning white,
Like island trees burned red by scorching heat.
Its little endloop looks like a chilly curl.
I love its forlorn taste, and I would, O Moon,
So like to scrub your broad milky borders
Where souls of our dead Sisters delight.

F.C.

EXILE

. . . .

My dear Conneau—
They took tireless interest in Little Ramponneau!
Even more than in our Conquering Uncle!
How every honest impulse deserts the bumbling Masses!
Alas! Who invited such dark worry!
It's high time we bolt the door—I think, don't you?—
Against a Wind children call Bari-barou!

. . . .

Fragment of a fictive letter in verse from Napoléon III, 1871

FALLEN CHERUB

Bluish roofs and white doors
Just like every nocturnal Sunday,

At the town's noiseless edge
The Street is white; it's night.

Angelic shutters shut
Strange houses on the street.

But, near a milemarker, look:
On the run, bad and chilled to the bone,

A black Cherub staggering around
After eating too many jujubes.

He poops: then poof! Disappears:
But, his fallen poop seems,

Beneath the hazy holy moon,
Like a delicate bog of dirty blood.

—Louis Ratisbonne
A. Rimbaud

"ON SUMMER NIGHTS . . ."

On summer nights, beneath shop windows' ardent eyes,
When sap trembles beneath dark networks
Reaching from the feet of spindly chestnuts,
Beyond these black groups, whether voluble or taciturn,
Pipe suckers or cigar kissers,
In the narrow, part-stone kiosque where I wander,
—As an Ibled poster glows above me,
I wonder if winter will freeze the Dribble
Of clean water that murmurs, appeasing the human wave,
—And if the bitter Aquilon will spare a single vein.

—Francis [*sic*] Coppée
A. Rimbaud

Ibled: a type of chocolate. *Dribble:* previous translations depended on a manuscript transcription that reads "Tibet." I have adopted Steve Murphy's reading.

"TO BEDSIDE BOOKS . . ."

To bedside books, placidly artful books,
Obermann and Genils, *Ver-Vert* and *The Lectern,*
I hope—old age finally come and at last bored
By grim gray novelty for its own sake—to add
The Treatise by Doctor Venutti. After
Experiencing enough of the dim-witted world,
I will know the ancient charm
Of the essential. A writer and engraver
Who gilded sexual sufferings: which is agreeable,
Isn't it? Dr. Venutti's *Treatise on Conjugal Love.*

F. Coppée
A.R.

Obermann: a novel by Étienne Pivert de Sénancour (1770–1846); *Genils:* Madame de Genlis (1746–1830), novelist; *Ver-Vert:* a poem by Jean-Baptiste-Louis Gresset (1709–77) from 1734, about a parrot among nuns; *The Lectern:* "Le Lutrin," a poem by Nicolas Boileau-Despréaux (1636–1711), well known and loved in Rimbaud's day.

SATURNINE HYPOTYPOSES, VIA BELMONTET

So what is this dark and impenetrable mystery?
Why, without even throwing up their white sails,
Does every rigged royal skiff sink?

Upend the grief in our lachrymatories.

. . . .

Love would live at the expense of its sister;
Friendship lives at the expense of its brother.

. . . .

The scepter, that we barely revere,
Is the cross from a great calvary
Crowning the volcano of nations!

. . . .

Oh! What distinction streams through your manly mustache. Belmontet,
Parnassian archetype.

REMEMBRANCES OF AN OLD IDIOT

Forgive me, father!
In youth, at country fairs,
I didn't seek out boring shooting galleries where every shot hits,
Rather, those loud places where donkeys
With weary flanks unfurled long bloody tubes
I still can't comprehend!
And my mother too,
Whose slip smelled sharply,
Rumpled and yellowed at its hem like fruit,
My mother who would climb noisily into bed
—A daughter of toil—my mother, with her
Ripe womanly thighs, her heavy hips
Creasing the sheets, got me hot in ways you shouldn't talk about!

A rawer, calmer guilt came
When my little sister, just back from class,
Her clogs worn down on the ice,
Pissed, and I watched a mawkish thread of urine!
Escape from her tight pink nether lips.

O forgive me!
Sometimes I would think about my father:
At night, card games and bawdy talk,
Our neighbor stopping by, me shoved aside, seeing certain things...
—Fathers can be frightening! —The things you imagine!
His lap, sometimes cuddly; his pants
My finger wanted to pry open at the fly... —Oh no!—
To touch my father's dark, fat, hard head,
Whose hairy hand had rocked me!
I shouldn't speak

Of the pot, that handled dish, glimpsed in the attic,
Among red almanacs, and the basket
Of rags, and the Bible, and the lavatories, and the maid,
The Holy Virgin and the crucifix...
                                        Oh! No one
Was so much disturbed as shocked!
And now pardon has been granted:
I am the victim of infected senses;
I confess my youthful crimes!

. . . .

Now! —Let me speak with the Lord!
Why did puberty come so late and why such suffering
At the hands of overactive glands? Why were shadows
So slow to cover my belly's base? And these innumerable terrors
Burying joy, as if beneath a black flood of stones?
It froze me in fear. What do I know?

. . . .

Forgiven...?
        Put your blue slippers back on
Father.
    O childhood! . . . .
. . . .
. . . . —let's just yank on our dicks!

François Coppée
A.R.

RECOLLECTION

The year the imperial Prince was born
Left me with an agreeable memory
Of a limpid Paris alive with golden N's and snow
On palace gates and equestrian steps,
Bursting, beribboned with the tricolors.
In the public swirl of faded hats,
Warm flowered vests, old frock-coats,
Workmen's songs in taverns,
Over shawl-strewn ground the Emperor strides, black
And proper, with the Holy Spaniardesse, at night.

—François Coppée

The year: 1856, when Rimbaud would have been one and a half years old. Coppée, however, born in 1846, and whose style Rimbaud is aping, would then have been old enough for an authentic memory of the day. *N's:* N is the first initial of the French emperor.

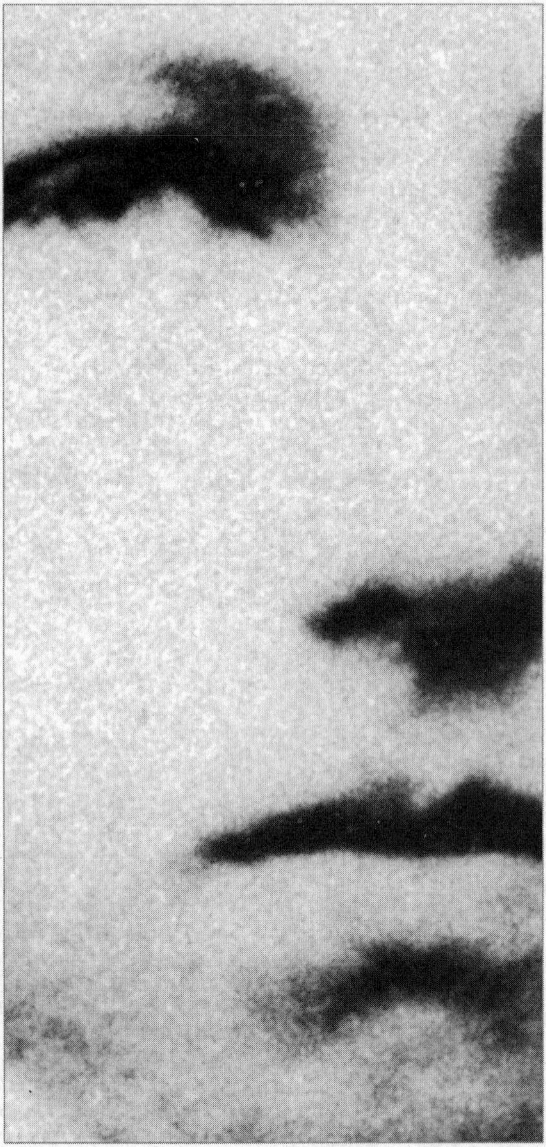

PROSE

I. 1866

"The Sun Was Still Hot…"

A very early prose fragment from Rimbaud's school notebook. In keeping with editorial tradition, spelling and punctuation have been regularized. For the original version, see also Uncollected Writings, *p. 316.*

I
PROLOGUE

The sun was still hot; nonetheless, now it barely illuminated the earth; like a torch placed before gigantic vaults casts no more than a weak glimmer. So the sun, earthly torch, is snuffed out while a final weak glimmer escapes its fiery body, nonetheless allowing us to see the trees' green leaves, little flowers that wilt, and gigantic summits of pines, poplars and age-old oaks. The refreshing wind, meaning a cool breeze, stirs the leaves of trees with a rustling nearly identical to the noise from silver streams which flow at my feet. The ferns bend their green foreheads to the wind. I slept, but not before drinking water from the stream.

II

I dreamt that... I was born in Reims in 1503. Reims was then a little town or better said a village nonetheless known for its beautiful cathedral, witness to the coronation of king Clovis.

My parents weren't very rich but very honest; they had just a little house that always belonged to them and which was in their possession twenty years before I was born and also a few thousand francs to which we should add a few louis d'or whose provenance was my mother's thrift. My father was an officer* in the king's army, he was a tall man, thin, black hair, beard, eyes, skin, all the same color... although when I was born he was only 48 or 50, one would have said he was easily 60 or... 58. He was brusque, hotheaded, often angry and never willing to suffer what displeased him. My mother was very different, a sweet woman, calm and easily startled who nonetheless kept the house in perfect order. She was so calm that my father entertained her like a little girl. They loved me

---

*Colonel of the *cent-gardes.* [Rimbaud's own footnote, appearing in the original text. The *Cent-Gardes,* or "hundred guards," were Napoleon III's personal military retinue, housed in residence.]

best. My brothers were less courageous than I though taller: I didn't like studying, meaning learning to read, write, and count... but fixing up a house, or gardening, or running errands; that's fine, I like doing all that.

I still remember a day my father promised me twenty sous if I did a division problem properly; I started; but I couldn't finish. Ah! How many times he promised me sous, toys, treats, even five francs one time if I could read something to him. Despite that, my father put me in school as soon as I turned ten. Why, I asked myself, learn Greek and Latin? I don't know. Really: who needs it? What do I care if I pass? What does it matter if I pass, right? Sure they say that you won't get a job if you don't pass. I don't want a job. I'll be independently wealthy anyway. Why learn Latin even if you want a job; no one even speaks it. Sometimes I see it in newspapers, but thank God I'll never be a journalist. Why learn history and geography? Sure you need to know that Paris is in France but no one ever asks what latitude. Learning about the lives of Chinaldon of Nabopolassar of Darius of Cyrus and of Alexander and their other historical pals with diabolical names,—it's torture? What do I care if Alexander was famous? Who cares. Who knows if the Latins even existed? Maybe it's some sort of made-up language and even if they had existed then why can't they just leave me to be independently wealthy and keep their language to themselves. What did I ever do to them that they torture me this way. And Greek? That dirty language isn't spoken by a single soul in the world! Ah *saperlipotte de saperlopopette sapristi.* I'll be independently wealthy. It's a waste to wear out the seat of your pants on the benches... *saperlipopettouille!* To be a shoeshine. To get a job as a shoeshine you have to take a test because the jobs you are offered are either shoeshine or swineherd or cattlehand. Thank god none of that's

---

saperlipotte de saperlopopette sapristi: Rimbaud is messing around here. *Sapristi* is along the lines of "odds bodkins," Graham Robb's excellent "gadzooks," or perhaps plain "fiddledeedee." Olivier reminds us that *sapristi* comes from *sacristie,* or sacristy, and thus there may be a whiff of the blasphemous. The rest is so much sound, but is also an impromptu, and fundamentally meaningless, portmanteau: *saper,* to crumble the bottom of a wall or, as metaphor, undermine; *popette,* a little girly pope; *pouille,* insults; etc.

for me: *saperlipouille!* You get paid with slaps in the face. They call you an animal which isn't true, a little fella etc.

More soon.

Ah *saperpopuillotte!*

—Arth . . . .

II. 1870

A Heart Under a Cassock

Another early prose piece. Little about its origin is known. On the manuscript, Rimbaud wrote the subtitle "Novel," which he crossed out, replacing it with "Short Story." The inconsistencies in the spelling of his protagonist's paramour's name are Rimbaud's, as are the endless variations in the writing of the date and the placement of punctuation (particularly ellipses and exclamation points).

A HEART UNDER A CASSOCK

A Seminarian's Innermost Thoughts

... O Thimothina Labinette! Now that I have donned the sacred robes, I can recall the passion—now cold and dead under my cassock—that, just last year, made my heart beat like a boy's under my seminarial cloak!...

... 1 May 18—...

... Spring. Abbot ____'s young vine is budding in its earthen pot: the branches of the tree in the courtyard are covered with little tender shoots like green drops; the other day, while leaving the study, I saw what looked like the Sup____'s big mushroom nose, poking out of a third-floor window. J____'s shoes smell; and I've noticed that the students often leave the room to ... in the courtyard; the same group that practically live in the study like moles, all packed inside, slumped over their bellies, their red faces turned towards the stove, breath as thick and hot as cows! Now, they stay outside forever, and when they snigger their way back in, very meticulously—sorry, I'm wrong: very slowly—closing the isthmus of their trousers with great ceremony, seemingly taking unconscious delight in a fundamentally futile endeavor...

2 May.

Yesterday, the Sup____ came down from his bedroom—timid, shivering, eyes closed, hands in pockets—and took a few shuffling steps through the courtyard in his canonical slippers!...

How my heart beats out time in my chest, as my chest beats against my grimy lectern! Oh! How I have grown to hate the days when, as students, we were fat sheep sweating into our dirty clothes, sleeping under the gaslights in the study's rank asthmosphere, enveloped in the stale heat of

---

Asthmosphere: sic.

the stove!...I stretch my arms! I sigh, I stretch my legs...I sense a world within me, oh! What a world!...

...4 May...

...Yesterday I reached my limit: I spread, like the angel Gabriel, the wings of my heart. The breath of the holy spirit filled me like a bellows! I picked up my lyre and sang:

Draw near
Mary dear!
Blessed mother!
Of sweet Jesus!
Sanctus Christus!
O pregnant Virgin,
O holy mother,
Hear our prayers!

O! If only you could experience the mysterious scents that shook my soul while I plucked this poetic rose! I grabbed my kithara and like a Psalmist raised my innocent voice into the celestial altitudes!!! *O altitudo altitudinum!...*

...7 May...

Alas! My poetry has folded its wings once again, but, like Galileo overcome with outrage and torture, I will say: It moves nonetheless! Or in this case, *they* move! I have been so imprudent as to let the preceding secrets fall to earth...Where J____ found them—J____, that most fervent Jansenist—the harshest of the Sup____'s henchmen, who then took it to his master, secretly: but the monster, to ensure I was plunged into universal ridicule, passed my poetry on to all his friends!

So yesterday, the Sup____ calls for me; I enter his rooms, I'm standing there in front of him, managing to keep a stiff upper lip. Like a flash of lightning across his bald brow, his very last red hair trembled; his calm eyes began to emerge peacefully from his fat face; his nose, like a washboard, wiggled perpetually; he was whispering an *oremus;* he licked the end of his thumb, flipped a few pages of a book, and removed a little dirty sheet of folded paper...

Maaaryyy deearrie!...
Bleeeeessed mummmy!

He was garbling my verse! He was spitting on my rose! Playing the Brid'oison, the Joseph, the fool, to sully and soil this virginal song! He stuttered and stretched each syllable, infusing them with hateful sniggers, and when he had gotten through the fifth line, *Pregnant Virgin!* he stopped, screwed up his nose, and...! He exploded:

—Pregnant Virgin! Pregnant Virgin!

Said with an unforgettable tone of voice, sucking in his bulging belly with a shudder, a tone of voice so terrible that my face flushed a modest rose. I fell to my knees, and with my arms raised to the ceiling, I cried:

—O My Father...!

. . . .

—Your lyyyre! Your kithara! Young man! Your kithara! Mysterious scents! That shook your soul! I would have adored seeing that! Young soul, I sense a certain worldliness in this blasphemous confession, a dangerous abandon, an impulsiveness, so to speak!—

He paused, belly jiggling from top to bottom, and solemnly continued:

—Young man, do you have faith?

—Father, why... why that word? Do your lips jest? Yes: I believe everything uttered by my Holy Mother Church.

—But... Pregnant Virgin...? That's conception, young man; conception!

—Father! I believe in the conception and...

Brid'oison: An idiotic character in Beaumarchais' *Le Mariage de Figaro.*

—And you should! Young man! It's something...

...He paused again... Then:

—Young J____ has alerted me that day by day he has seen you...spread your legs farther and farther while you sit and study; he says, he has seen you stretch out...completely, beneath your desk, like a discombobulated young lad... There's no point in denying any of this... So come, on your knees, before me; I wish to question you, gently; so answer me; do you often... spread your legs, while studying?

Then he settled a hand onto my shoulder, near my neck, his eyes brightening, as he made me tell him all about how I spread my legs... But I should just say it was disgusting, since I know what scenes like this are all about...!

So they'd spied on me and then slandered my heart and modesty both—and there wasn't a thing I could do about it: they had their reports, anonymous contradictory letters from students to the Sup____, all of it planned and condoned; and then I went into that chamber where I was f____ by the hand of that fat old man...! Oh the seminary...!

. . . .

10 May—

Oh my fellow students are unbelievably mean and unbelievably perverted. In study hall, these profanizers know the whole story about my verses, and as soon as I turn my head, I find D____'s wheezy little face whispering: And your kithara? And your kithara? And your journal? And then that idiot L____ starts with: And your Lyre, And your Kithara. And then three or four of them whisper a chorale: Mary dear... Mary dear... Blessed mother!

I'm such an idiot: and Jesus, it's not that I'm kicking myself over this, but I don't spy on the other students, I don't write anonymous indictments, and I keep my divine verses and my modesty to myself...!

12 May...

> Can't you guess why I'm dying of love?
> Flowers say hello; and birds above.

I greet the Spring! Angel of tenderness!
Can't you guess why I'm boiling with drunkenness!
From grandmothers to cradles
Runs a bright ring of angels.
But haven't you heard?
I'm becoming a bird!
My lyre quivers as my wings shiver
Like a swallow. . . . . . . ?

I wrote those lines yesterday, during break; I had gone into the chapel, locked myself in a confessional, and there, my young lines throbbed and took wing, in dream and silence, towards the amorous spheres. Then, since the least papers end up getting lifted from my pockets, night and day I keep these lines beneath my underwear, against my skin, and, while studying, I tug at these lines lodged under my clothes near my heart, and I dreamily hold my hand there as long as I can manage . . . . . .

15 May—

So much has happened since my last entry, so many solemn events, events that will impact upon my future inner life in the most unbearable ways!

Thimothina Labinette, I adore you!

Thimothina Labinette, I adore you! I adore you! Leave me to sing on my lute, like some sacred Psalmist at his Psaltery, of how I saw you and how my heart leapt onto yours as if onto everlasting love!

Thursday was our day off: we, we were allowed out for two hours; so I went out: my mother, in her last letter, had told me: ". . . you will go, my son, to spend your free time at the home of Monsieur Césarin Labinette, one of your departed father's intimates, to whom you should be introduced one day or another before your ordination . . ."

. . . I introduced myself to Monsieur Labinette, who kindly relegated me to his kitchen without so much as a word; his daughter, Thimothine, stayed with me, grabbing a dishrag and wiping a fat, bulbous pot that she held to her heart, and then, after a long silence, all of a sudden, said: So, Monsieur Léonard . . . ?

Up until that moment, and unsure what to think of being alone with that young thing in the solitude of that kitchen, I had lowered my eyes and invoked Mary's holy name over and again in my heart: I raised my reddening forehead, and, before my questioner's beauty, I could only manage to blubber a feeble: Mademoiselle . . . ?

Thimothine! You were lovely! Were I a painter, I would memorialize your holy features on a canvas titled: Virgin with Bowl! But I am only a poet, and my tongue can only incompletely honor you . . .

Embers burned in the black stove's openings like red eyes, and from its pots thin streams of steam escaped, diffusing a heavenly scent of cabbage and bean soup; and before it, inhaling the aroma of these vegetables with your sweet nose, staring at your fat cat with your beautiful green eyes, O Virgin with Bowl, you wiped your vessel! Your flat, bright braids were coiled around your head and plastered modestly to your yellow forehead like sunlight; bluish furrows ran from the corners of your eyes to the middle of your cheeks, just like Saint Teresa! Your delicate nostrils flared, filling with the scent of beans; a soft down circled your lips and contributed considerably to the effect of your face; and, on your chin, a beautiful brown mark shone whereupon a few frolicsome hairs quivered: your hair was wisely gathered at your nape; but a short tendril had broken free . . . I looked for your breasts in vain; you have none: such earthly ornaments are beneath you: your heart is all you need of breasts! When you turned to kick your golden cat with that big foot of yours, the sight of your shoulder blades jutting up under your dress and the graceful writhing of the two abundant arcs of your hips, pierced me with love!

From that moment on, I adored you: I adored, not your hair, not your shoulder blades, not the torquing of your . . . inferior posterior: what I love in a woman, in a virgin, is saintly modesty; modesty and piety make me leap with love; that—young shepherdess—is why I adore you!

I strove to show her my passion, for what's more, my heart, my heart betrayed me! My responses were repeatedly interrupted by her questions;

more than once my fluster made me mistakenly call her Madame instead of Mademoiselle! Little by little, under the influence of her magical inflections, I felt myself overcome; at last I resolved to give in, to give everything up: and I don't remember what question did it, but at some point I fell backwards off my chair, one hand over my heart, the other in my pocket grabbing at a rosary whose white crucifix I let hang out, and, with one eye fixed on Thimothine and another on the heavens, I responded dolorously and tenderly, like a buck to a doe:

—Oh! Yes! Mademoiselle . . . Thimothina!!!

Misery! Misery! —For as I was staring deliciously at the ceiling above from which hung a ham, a drop of brine from its bottom dripped into my wide-open eye, and red with shame and awakened to my passion, I lowered my forehead and noticed that my left hand no longer held the rosary, but a brown nipple instead; my mother had given it to me the year before to pass on to Mrs. What's-her-name's little one! From the eye that had been fixed on the ceiling dripped the bitter brine: but from the eye that stared at you, o Thimothina, flowed a tear, a tear of love, and a tear of pain!

. . . .

. . . .

A little later, perhaps an hour, when Thimothina offered me beans and a bacon omelet, I was so moved by her thoughtfulness that I responded, softly:

—My heart is so full that I have no appetite at all, as you can see! —But I sat at the table: Oh! I can remember how it felt as her heart replied to the call of my own: during our brief meal, she didn't eat a bite:

—Do you smell something too? She repeated over and over; her father didn't understand; but my heart did: it was the Rose of David, the Rose of Jesus, the mystical Rose of scripture; Love!

She rose with a start and went into the corner of the kitchen and, offering me a view of the double blossom of her hips, thrust her arms into a huge pile of bottles and mismatched shoes, sending her fat cat flying off what had been her perch; she threw the whole pile into an empty cupboard; then she returned to her seat, uneasily raising an inquisitive nostril to the air; suddenly, she wrinkled her brow and cried:

—It still smells!...

—Yes, it does, her father rather feebly responded: (he couldn't understand, the profaner!)

I did: it was coming from within me, my virgin flesh that boiled with passion for her! With supreme adoration, I lovingly savored that golden omelet as my hand beat time with the fork, and beneath the table my feet quivered with pleasure in my shoes!...

But the real flash of illumination came later, like proof of eternal love, a diamond of sweetness Thimothina bestowed upon me, when, just as I was leaving, she presented me with a pair of white socks with a smile, saying:

—Do you want these for your feet, Monsieur Léonard?

. . . .

16 May—Thimothina! I love you, you and your father, you and your cat...

Vas devotionis,
Rosa Mystica,
Thimothina, { Turris davidica, Ora pro nobis!
Cœli porta,
Stella maris,

17 May—

What do I care about the world's noises and those of the study? What do I care if my fellows are doubled over with laziness and sloth beside me? This morning, every forehead was heavy with sleep and stuck fast to the tabletops; deaf and slow, a snore rose from this vast Gethsemane like a

---

Latin poem: "Devotional vessel / Mystical Rose / Tower of David, pray for us! / Heavenly portal / Ocean star"; Rimbaud's narrator is invoking Thimothina as one would the Virgin Mary in the liturgy.

Gethsemane like a trumpet's call on judgment day: Reference to the Gospel According to Matthew as Jesus and his disciples arrive in Gethsemane: "And he cometh unto the disciples, and findeth them asleep, and saith unto Peter, What, could ye not watch with me one hour? Watch and pray, that ye enter not into temptation: the spirit indeed is willing, but the flesh is weak."

trumpet's call on judgment day. I, stoic, serene, upright and rising above all those corpses like a palm above ruins, scorning incongruous smells and sounds, I hold my head in my hand, I listen to the beating of my Thimothina-gorged heart, and my eyes plunged into the azure sky, spied through the topmost windowpane!...

—18 May:

Gratitude to the Holy Spirit who inspired these charming lines: I will embed them in my heart: and when heaven permits me to see Thimothina again, I will offer them to her in exchange for the white socks!...

I have entitled it The Breeze:

In his cottony refuge
The zephyr sleeps with sweet breath:
In his nest of silk and wool
The zephyr sleeps, with gay chin!

When the zephyr lifts his wing
In his cottony refuge,
When he runs where flowers call him,
His sweet breath smells so good!

O quintessential breeze!
Quintessence of love!
When the dew has dried,
How good it smells all day!

Jesus! Joseph! Jesus! Mary!
It's like a condor's wing
Lulling those at prayer!
Penetrating and putting us to sleep!

. . . .

The ending is too personal and sweet: I will preserve it in the tabernacle of my soul. On my next day off, I will read it to my divine and fragrant Thimothina.

We wait in peaceful contemplation.

. . . .

Date unknown. We wait!...

16 June!—

Thy will be done, my Lord: I put no obstacle in your path! If you would have Thimothina's love steer clear of your servant, it is doubtless your choice to make: but, Lord Jesus, have you not loved yourself, have you not known the lance of love and because of it how to condescend to the suffering of the wicked! Pray for me!

Oh! I have been waiting forever for June 15th and these two hours: I held my soul in check with these words: On June 15th, you will be free: that day, I combed my few modest strands of hair, and with a fragrant rose pomade, plastered them to my forehead, just like Thimothina's braids; I pomaded my eyebrows; I scrupulously brushed my black clothes, made up for a few of my physical shortcomings, and arrived at the long looked-forward-to doorbell of Césarin Labinette. After a rather long wait, he arrived, skullcap gallantly askew over an ear, a heavily pomaded strand of hair lashing his face like a scar, one hand in his yellow-flowered dressing-gown pocket, the other on the latch... He offered a cursory hello, screwed up his nose as he glanced at my black-laced boots, and led me inside, hands in his pockets, drawing his dressing-gown before him just like Abbot ____ does with his cassock, thus offering me a topographical survey of his inferior region.

So I followed him.

He crossed the kitchen, and I followed him into his sitting room. Oh that sitting room! I have fixed it in my mind with the pins of memory! The walls were covered in brown flowers; the mantel bore an enormous black wood clock with columns; two blue vases full of roses; a painting of the

Battle of Inkerman hung on the walls; as well as a drawing by one of Césarin's friends, of a windmill whose grindstone slaps a little stream that looks like spittle, the sort of scene with which every beginner blackens his first pages. Poetry is unquestionably preferable!...

In the center of the sitting room, at a table with a blue cloth, around which my heart saw only Thimothina, no matter that several friends of Monsieur Césarin's sat with her—the former executor of the sacristy of ____ parish and his wife Madame Riflandouille—both joined my Monsieur Césarin himself who sat down the moment I entered the room. I sat in an overstuffed chair, thinking that a part of me was pressed against upholstery doubtless woven by Thimothina; I greeted everyone, and, with my black hat settled on the table like a shield, I listened...

I didn't speak, but my heart spoke! The men continued a game of cards they had begun before I arrived: I noticed that each was cheating more than the next, a realization of considerable sorrow to me. When the game was done, they gathered around the empty fireplace; I was at one corner of the semi-circle, nearly hidden by Césarin's enormous friend, whose chair was the only barrier between Thimothina and myself: I was pleased with how little attention was being paid me; relegated to sit behind the honorary sacristan, I could let my heart's emotions play freely upon my face without fear of discovery; I gave myself over to sweet abandon; and I let the conversation rise and fall between the three of them; for Thimothina spoke only rarely; she cast loving glances at her seminarian, and not daring to stare straight at him, she directed her bright eyes towards my impeccably shined shoes!... I, behind the fat sacristan, I gave myself over to my heart.

Initially, I leaned towards her with my eyes raised to the heavens. Her back was to me. So I sat up straighter, and, my head bowed to my chest, released a sigh; she didn't budge. I fingered my buttons, moved my lips, made the sign of the cross; she didn't see a thing. And so, carried away, insane with love, I bent deeply towards her, holding my hands as though I

Battle of Inkerman: A battle of the Crimean War that took place during the Siege of Sebastopol, on November 5, 1854.

were taking communion, and then released a lengthy, dolorous *ah!* Misery! For as I gesticulated, in prayer, I fell from my chair with a dull thump, and the fat sacristan turned towards me, snickering, and Thimothina said to her father:

—Gracious, Monsieur Léonard has fallen to the floor!

Her father snickered! Misery!

The sacristan made room and helped me back onto my overstuffed chair where I sat, red with shame and weak with love. But I lowered my eyes: I wanted to sleep! Their company was unpleasant, unaware as it was of the love that suffered in the shadows: I wanted to sleep! But the conversation had turned towards me!...

I feebly reopened my eyes...

Césarin and the sacristan each smoked slender cigars with affectations of every possible permutation, making them seem ridiculous: the sacristan's wife sat on the edge of her seat, her hollow chest bent forward, smoothing the ruffs of her yellow dress piled behind her and rising to her neck, while delicately plucking the petals from a rose: a horrible smile parted her lips and revealed two black and yellow teeth settled in her narrow gums like battered crockery on an old stove,—You, Thimothina, you are beautiful, with your white collarlet, your lowered gaze, and your flat braids.

—This young man has a future; his present bespeaks of what will come, said the sacristan while releasing a wave of gray smoke...

—Oh yes! Monsieur Léonard will be a credit to the cloth, said the sacristan's wife, nasally: her two teeth were revealed!

I, I blushed like a good boy; I saw that their chairs were slowly creeping away from my own, and that they were whispering about me...

Thimothina kept staring at my shoes; the two dirty teeth frightened me... The sacristan laughed ironically: my head was still bowed!...

—Lamartine is dead, exclaimed Thimothina suddenly.

Dear Thimothina! You threw the name Lamartine into the conversation for your idolater, your poor poet, Léonard; so I raised my forehead sensing that only the thought of poetry would restore these sinners to a state of virginity; I felt my wings beginning to beat, and beaming, my gaze fixed on Thimothina, I said:

—The author of *Poetic Meditations* wore a wreath of laurel!

—The swan of poetry has expired! said the sacristan's wife.

—Yes, but he sang his funeral dirge, I enthusiastically replied.

—Well, she cried, Monsieur Léonard is a poet in his own right! Last year his mother showed me some of the work of his muse . . .

Then, emboldened, I ventured:

—Oh Madame! I have neither lyre nor kithara with me . . .

—Oh do bring it another day!

—Nonetheless, should it not displease such honorable company—and at this point I withdrew a piece of paper from my pocket—I should like to read a few lines . . . dedicated to Mademoiselle Thimothina.

—Yes yes! Very good, young man! Recite, recite! Take your place at the front of the room . . .

I stood . . . Thimothina still staring at my shoes . . . The sacristan's wife made like a Madonna; the two men leaned towards each other . . . I blushed; I coughed, and I spoke, singing tenderly:

In his cottony refuge
The zephyr sleeps with sweet breath:
In his nest of silk and wool
The zephyr sleeps, with gay chin!

The room exploded with laughter: the men leaned nearer to each other and made disgusting puns; worst of all was the sacristan's wife who, her gaze directed heavenward, made like a mystic, and smiled broadly, baring her horrible teeth! Thimothina, Thimothina was doubled over with laughter! This was the coup de grâce: she was clutching her sides!

—A sweet zephyr settled in cotton, remarkable, remarkable! Said Césarin *père* with a snort. I thought I began to get wind of something . . . But the burst of laughter only lasted a second: everyone attempted to regain their composure, faltering only occasionally thereafter . . .

—Please continue young man, it's very good, continue!

When the zephyr lifts his wing
In his cottony refuge,
When he runs where flowers call him,
His sweet breath smells so good!

This time, a giant guffaw shook my listeners; Thimothina was looking at my shoes: I was hot, my feet were burning beneath her gaze, swimming in sweat; I kept telling myself: I've worn these socks for a month, this gift of her love; and these looks that she casts upon my feet are further testimony of her love: she adores me!

And then, it seemed to me that the slightest scent rose from my shoes: And then I understood the horrible laughter of all assembled! I understood that Thimothina Labinette, lost within this mean-spirited bunch, could never give free rein to her passions! I understood that I too would have to swallow this dolorous love hatched in my heart one afternoon in May in the Labinettes' kitchen before the writhing posterior of the Virgin with Bowl!

At four in the afternoon, the hour we were due back, the sitting room clock rang; overcome, burning with love, mad with sorrow, I grabbed my hat and fled, upending a chair as I ran down the hallway murmuring: I adore Thimothina, and I ran straight to the seminary . . .

My habit's black tails flew behind me in the wind like sinister birds! . . .

. . . .

30 June.

From now on, I leave the care of my sorrow to the divine muse; martyr to love at eighteen, and, in my affliction, I think about another martyr of the sex responsible for all our joy and happiness: denied the one I love, I will love the cloth! May Christ and Mary hold me to their breasts; I will follow them; I'm not worthy of untying Jesus' shoelaces. Such sorrow! Such suffering! At eighteen years and seven months, I too bear a cross, a crown of thorns! And rather than a reed in my hands, I carry a kithara! It will be the balm for my wound!

. . . .

—One year later,
—August 1.—

Today, I donned the sacred robes; I will serve God; I will be given a vicarage and a humble servant in some wealthy village. I have faith; I shall meet my salvation, without extravagance, living the life of a wholesome servant of God, with his servant. My mother the holy Church will warm me at her breast: Blessed be her name! Blessed be the Lord our God!

. . . And as for that cruelly cherished passion that I banished to the very bottom of my heart, I'll carry its weight: without exactly reliving it, I can draw upon its memory; how sweet such things are! I was born for love, and faith!—Maybe one day, upon returning to this city, perhaps I'll have the fortune to take Thimothina's confession. And I still have a souvenir of her: for the last year, I haven't changed the socks she gave me . . .

These socks—my God! I won't take them off until I reach your blessed Paradise!

III. 1871

Deserts of Love

"Deserts of Love" is a prose experiment of unknown context.

DESERTS OF LOVE

Note

What follows is the work of a young—very young—*man,* whose life came together by hook and by crook; motherless, landless, heedless of everything already too well known, fleeing the threat of any moral impingement, like many sorry young men before him. But so annoyed and troubled was he that he made for death like it was some sort of terrible, fatal shame. Never having known a woman's love—however hot-blooded—his heart and soul and all his strength had their origins in strange, sad missteps. The following dreams—his loves!—that came to him in beds or along streets, can, as they play out, perhaps be seen as having religious connotations; perhaps they will remind readers of the endless sleep of the fabled Mohammedan—brave, and circumcised! But this strange suffering holds an uncomfortable authority: one can't help but sincerely desire that this Soul—lost in our midst and wishing death, or so it seems—find true comfort at that ultimate instant and, then, find itself worthy.

A. Rimbaud

Deserts of Love (I)

This is certainly the same countryside. The same rustic house that belonged to my parents: the very room where above the doors reside red-

---

Mohammedan: According to Michelet in his *Histoire de France,* the Mohammedans to whom R. refers belonged to an eleventh-century sect known for their assassinational prowess. Leaders of the sect, to instill members with the necessary courage, would have them drink potions that would put them to sleep: while they slept, they would be conveyed to some pleasure palace. Upon awakening, the members would be convinced that this was the first taste of the paradise guaranteed them for their murderous efforts.

dening pastoral scenes, coats of arms, lions. One dines in a hall filled with candles and wines and rustic wainscoting. The table is very large. And the servants! There were many, as many as I had recalled. —And there was even one of my old friends who'd stopped by, a priest, and dressed like one: it allowed him greater freedom. I remember his crimson room, with yellow paper windowpanes: and his books, all hidden away, that had been soaked by the sea.

I was abandoned, in this endless country house; I read in the kitchen, drying my muddy clothes in front of my hosts' parlor conversations: moved to death by morning's murmuring milk and the late century's night.

I was in a very dark room: what was I doing? A servant drew close: I can tell you she was a little dog, however pretty, and, it seemed to me, possessing an inexpressible maternal nobility: pure, familiar, utterly charming! She pinched my arm.

I don't even remember her face very well anymore: this isn't so that I might manage to remember her arm, whose skin I rolled between my fingers; nor her mouth, which my own seized upon like a desperate little wave, endlessly digging for something within. I backed her into a basket filled with cushions and boat canvas in a dark corner. All I remember now are her white lace panties.

Then, such despair! The barrier shifted, somehow became the shadows of trees, and I sank beneath the amorous sadness of night.

Deserts of Love (II)

This time, it's the Woman I saw in the city, and to whom I spoke, and who speaks to me.

I was in a lightless room. I was told she was there: and I saw her in my bed, all for me, lightlessly! I was very emotional, not least because this was happening in my family home: and so an unease took hold of me! I was dressed in rags, while she, clearly a woman of the world who was giving herself to me: she had to leave! With a nameless unease, I took her, letting her fall off the bed, nearly naked; and, in my unspeakable weakness, I fell upon her and dragged us through the dark rugs! The family lamp reddened the neighboring rooms one after the next. And then the woman disappeared. I shed more tears than God could ever have asked.

I went out into the endless city. O fatigue! Drowning in the deaf night and in the flight of joy. It was like a winter night, with snow that would snuff out the world once and for all. Friends to whom I cried out *where is she* responded falsely. I went to the windows where she stands each night: I ran to the buried garden. I was cast out. I cried endlessly, because of all this. Finally, I went down into a place filled with dust, and, sitting on some sort of frame, I let my body cry itself dry of every tear. —Nonetheless, my exhaustion returned over and over.

I understood that she had gone back to her daily life; and that this kind turn and the possibility of its recurrence was now more distant than a star. She didn't return, and never will, this Adorable who paid me a visit—something I never could have foreseen. Unquestionably, this time I cried more than all the world's children.

IV. 1872

Gospels

Rimbaud's versions of the Gospels, drawn primarily from John IV and V, though with touches of John II, Mark II, and Luke V. What larger possible work these traces might have been a part of is uncertain. As the third "[III]" was discovered on the backside of "False Conversion," an early draft (see p. 345) of "Night in Hell," some have supposed it might have been part of R.'s original conception of Season, *but that is so much speculation.*

FROM THE GOSPELS

[I]

In Samaria, many had shown their faith in him. Them he did not see. Samaria the upstart, the egoist, the most rigid observer of its protestant laws since Judaea and its ancient tablets; there, universal wealth obviated enlightened discussion. Sophistry—slave and soldier of routine—had already slit the throats of more than one prophet whom it had flattered first.

The words of the woman at the fountain were therefore sinister: "You're a prophet. You know what I've done."

Women and men once believed in prophets. Now they believe in politicians.

A few paces from the foreign village, were he taken for a prophet (since he had appeared so odd to them, though incapable of proving any sort of physical threat), what would he do?

Jesus couldn't say a word to Samaria.

[II]

The light sweet air of Galilee: its inhabitants received them with curious joy: They had seen him, shaking with righteous fury, whipping the temple's moneychangers and gamesellers. A miracle of pale and furious youth, they believed.

He felt his hand held in hands heavy with rings and at the mouth of an officer. The officer was on his knees in the dust: and his head was attractive enough, though half bald.

Carriages streamed through the narrow streets; quite a commotion for such a town; all seemed it should have been well that night.

Jesus withdrew his hand: a gesture of childish, feminine pride. "The rest of you, if you don't see miracles, you don't believe a thing."

Jesus had yet to perform any miracles. He had, at a wedding, in a green and pink dining room, raised his voice to the Holy Virgin. And no one had mentioned the wine of Cana at Capernaum, neither at the market, nor along the docks. Perhaps among the bourgeois.

Jesus said: "Go: your son is fine." The officer left, as one might with a mild medicine, and Jesus continued along less traveled streets. Bindweed and borage revealed their magical gleam from between the cobbles. At last in the distance he saw the dusty prairie, and the buttercups and daisies begging mercy of daylight.

[III]

Bethesda, a pool of five porches, was a spot of contention. It seemed to me to be a sort of sinister bathhouse, forever weighed down in rain and darkness, and beggars stirring on its steps illuminated by flashes of approaching hellish storms of lightning, joking about their blind blue eyes or their stumps they'd wrapped in blue or white cloths. O military watering hole, O public bathhouse! The water was always black, and nary a cripple ever fell in, even in dream.

It was there that Jesus made his first serious move: with these unspeakable cripples. There was a day in February, March, or April, when the sun—at 2 in the afternoon—left a great scythe of light upon the interred surface of the water; and there, well behind the cripples, I would have been able to see this solitary beam awakening buds and crystals and worms, in which reflection, equivalent to a white angel sleeping on his side, all these infinitely pale reflections began to stir.

And so all the sinners, slender tenacious sons of the demon, who, to sensitive hearts, made these men seem more terrifying than monsters, now wanted to throw themselves into this water. The infirm—scoffing no more—made their way down with desire.

The first entrants left cured, it was said. No. The sins abandoned them on the steps, and forced them to find other purchase: for their Demon could only remain in places where alms were assured.

After noon, Jesus too entered. No one washed, nor brought animals to drink. The light in the pool was yellow like the last leaves on the vines. The divine master leaned against a column: he watched the sons of Sin; the demon stuck out his tongue at their tongues; and laughed at them, or denied them.

The Paralytic, who had long lain on his side, rose, and the Damned watched him cross through the crowd with a strangely confident stride and disappear into the city.

The first . . . were assured: In the manuscript, this paragraph is followed by an aborted section that begins, "Some sign, o divine will; and every obedience is assured nearly before your . . . ," which R. crossed out before continuing.

V. 1873

A Season in Hell

A. RIMBAUD

UNE

SAISON EN ENFER

PRIX : UN FRANC

BRUXELLES
ALLIANCE TYPOGRAPHIQUE (M.-J. POOT ET COMPAGNIE)
37, rue aux Choux, 37

1873

★ ★ ★ ★

Long ago, if my memory serves, life was a feast where every heart was open, where every wine flowed.

One night, I sat Beauty on my knee. —And I found her bitter. —And I hurt her.

I took arms against justice.

I fled, entrusting my treasure to you, o witches, o misery, o hate.

I snuffed any hint of human hope from my consciousness. I made the muffled leap of a wild beast onto any hint of joy, to strangle it.

Dying, I called my executioners over so I could bite the butts of their rifles. I called plagues to suffocate me with sand, blood. Misfortune was my god. I lay in the mud. I withered in criminal air. And I even tricked madness more than once.

And spring left me with an idiot's unbearable laughter.

Just now, having nearly reached death's door, I thought about seeking the key to the old feast, through which, perhaps, I might regain my appetite.

Charity is the key. —Such an inspiration proves I was dreaming!

"A hyena you'll remain, etc. . . ." cries the demon that crowns me with merry poppies. "Make for death with every appetite intact, with your egotism, and every capital sin."

Ah. It seems I have too many already: —But, dear Satan, I beg you not to look at me that way, and while you await a few belated cowardices—you who so delight in a writer's inability to describe or inform—watch me tear a few terrible leaves from my book of the damned.

OPPOSITE: Cover of the first edition of *Une saison en enfer.*

BAD BLOOD

My Gallic forebears gave me pale blue eyes, a narrow skull, and bad reflexes in a fight. I dress as barbarically as they. But I don't butter my hair.

The Gauls were the most inept animal-skinners and grass-burners of their day.

They gave me: idolatry, a love of sacrilege, and every vice: anger, lust—glorious lust—but above all, deceit and sloth.

I find even the thought of work unbearable. Masters and workers both are peasants. There's no difference between a hand holding a pen and a hand pushing a plow. An age of hands! —I'll have no part in it. Domesticity goes too far too fast. Begging—despite its inherent decency—pains me. Criminals are as bad as eunuchs: so what if I'm whole.

But. Who made my tongue so truthless that it has shepherded and safeguarded my sloth this far? Lazier than a toad, I've gotten by without lifting a finger: I've lived everywhere. There isn't a family in Europe I don't know. —Which is to say families like mine which owe everything to the Declaration of the Rights of Man. —I've known every young man of means.

If only I had one predecessor in French history!

But no, none.

It's clear to me that I belong to a lesser race. I have no concept of rebellion. The only time my race ever rose up was to pillage: like wolves on carcasses they didn't even kill.

I know French history, know the Church's eldest daughter. Had I been born a boor, I would have journeyed to the holy land; in my head are roads through Swabian plains, views of Byzantium, ramparts of Jerusalem; the cult of Mary and of pity on the cross comingle amidst a thousand profane visions. —I sit like a leper on broken pots and nettles, at the foot of walls eaten away by sun. —Later, I would have been a mercenary bivouacking beneath German nights.

But there's more! I dance on the sabbath, in a red clearing with old women and children.

I don't remember anything prior to this earth and this Christianity. I don't see myself anywhere but in that past. And always alone; without family, speaking what language? I never see myself in Christ's councils; nor in the councils of Lords—Christ's delegates.

What was I last century? I only see myself now. No more vagabonds or nebulous wars. The inferior race has spread, everywhere—people or, as we now say, reason: nationality and science.

Oh, science! We've remade the world. For body and soul—as viaticum—we have medicine and philosophy—home remedies and cover-versions of popular songs. Princely amusements and the games they forbade. Geography, cosmography, mechanics, chemistry . . . !

Science, the new nobility. Progress. The world turns. Why wouldn't it?

Numerical visions. We close in upon the *Animus.* What I say is irrefutable, oracular. I understand, and not knowing how to explain myself except in pagan words, I'm better off shutting my mouth.

Pagan blood returns! The *Animus* nears, why won't Christ help me, grace my soul with nobility and liberty. But the Gospel is gone. The Gospel! The Gospel.

I await God, hungrily. I am an eternal member of an inferior race.

There I am on the beaches of Brittany. Cities blaze in the night. My day is done: I'm leaving Europe. The marine air will burn my lungs; unknown climates will tan my skin. To swim, trample grass, hunt, and above all, smoke; drink liquors as strong as molten metal—like our cherished ancestors around their fires.

I'll return with iron limbs, dark skin, an imperious gaze: my mask will mark me as member of a powerful race. I'll have gold: be lazy and merciless. Women pamper fierce invalids returned from hot countries. I'll enter politics. Saved.

Now, though, I'm cursed: I can't stand my country. The best I can hope for is drunken sleep, by the shore.

But we don't leave. —We take the same roads, burdened with my vice, vice that since the age of reason has sunk its roots right into my side—climbing skyward, beating me, toppling me, dragging me along.

The final innocence and the final humility. That does it. I won't hump my disgusts and deceits across the world.

We're off! The march, the burden, the desert, the boredom, the anger.

What flag will I bear? What beast worship? What shrine besiege? What hearts break? What lies tell? —And walk through whose blood?

Better yet: steer well clear of Justice. —The hard life, simple brutishness—lift the coffin's lid with a withered fist, sit inside, suffocate. Neither old age, nor danger: fear isn't French.

I feel so forsaken I orient my instinct for perfection on any sacred image. O self-sacrifice; o magnanimous charity! All for me, of course! *De profundis Domine*—what a fool I am!

When I was very young, I admired hardened criminals locked behind prison doors; I visited inns and taverns they frequented; *with their eyes,* I saw the blue sky and the blossoming work of the fields; I tracked their scent through cities. They were more powerful than saints, more prudent than explorers—and they, they alone, were witnesses to glory and reason!

On the roads, through winter nights, without a home, without habits, without bread, a voice strangled my frozen heart: "Weakness or strength: Those are your options, so strength it is. You know neither where you're going, nor why you're going, entering anywhere, answering anyone. You're no more likely to be killed than a corpse." By morning, I had developed such a lost, dead expression that those I met *may not have even seen me.*

In cities, mud suddenly seemed red and black, like a mirror when a lamp is moved through an adjoining room, like treasure found in a forest. Good luck, I cried, and I saw a sky flooded with smoke and flame; and to my left, to my right, all the world's riches burned like a billion thunderbolts.

But orgies and womanly companionship were denied me. Not one friend. I saw myself in front of an angry mob, facing a firing squad, weeping incomprehensible sorrows and forgiving them, like Joan of Arc: "Priests, professors, masters: you falter bringing me to justice. I was never one of you; I was never Christian; my race *sang* upon the rack; I don't understand your laws; I have no moral compass, I'm a beast: you falter..."

Yes, my eyes are shut to your light. I'm an animal, a nigger. But I can be saved. You're all fake niggers, you brutal, greedy maniacs. Merchant? No: nigger. Magistrate? Nigger. General? Nigger. Emperor—you itchy old scab—nigger. You drank Satan's duty-free booze. —Fever and cancer thrill you. Cripples and codgers are so decent they *ask* to be boiled. —The wisest move would be to leave this continent, creeping with madness, a madness that seeks hostages for lost souls. I set out in search of the true kingdom of the children of Ham.

Do I really know nature? Do I know myself?—*No more words.* I bury the dead in my belly. Shouts, drums, dance, dance, dance, dance! I can't imagine a moment when whites will arrive and I'll tumble into the void.

Hunger, thirst, shouts, dance, dance, dance, dance!

Whites arrive. A cannon! I submit to baptism, dress, work.

My heart is struck by grace. And I never saw it coming!

I've done nothing wrong. My days bring no burden, I'll be spared repentance. I won't have to suffer the torments of a soul dead to decency, whose harsh light rises as if from funeral tapers. The fate of the favorite son: an early grave, blanketed with limpid tears. Of course debauchery is as stupid as vice. Cast rot aside. But no clock will ever do more than merely mark our hours of purest pain! Will I be carried off, like a child, to play in paradise, forgetting all my misfortune!

Quick: are there other lives? —It's impossible to sleep surrounded by riches. Riches are supremely public. Only divine love grants the keys to science. I see that nature is only a spectacle of goodness. Farewell chimeras, ideals, mistakes.

The angels' prudent songs rise from the ship of souls: divine love. — Two loves! I may die of earthly love, or of devotion. I've left souls behind whose suffering will swell with my departure! You pluck me from the shipwreck; are those who remain not my friends?

Save them!

Reason is born within me. The world is good. I bless life. I will love my brothers. These are no longer idle promises of youth, nor a hope of evading old age and death. God is my strength. I praise God.

Boredom is no longer my bride. I know these passions and disasters too well—the rages, the debauches, the madness—my burden lifts. Let us soberly consider the depth of my innocence.

I can no longer find consolation in being beaten. There is no chance of a honeymoon when Jesus Christ is your father-in-law.

I'm no prisoner of reason. I said: God. I want salvation to bring freedom: what do I do? I've lost my taste for frivolity. Nor do I need devotion or divine love. I don't repent the age of sensitive hearts. Contempt and charity have their place: I reserve mine for the top of this angelic ladder of common sense.

As for pre-existing happiness, whether domestic or not . . . no: I just can't. I'm too exhausted, too weak. Life blossoms with work, an old truth: my life isn't sufficiently substantial, it flies away, floats far above the bustle, over the focal point of the world.

What an old maid I'm becoming, not even courageous enough to love death!

If only God gave me heavenly, aerial calm, and the power of prayer—like ancient saints. —Saints! What strength! The anchorites were artists abandoned by the world.

Unending farce! My innocence leaves me in tears. Life is the farce we lead.

Enough! Here's punishment! —*March!*

Ah! How my lungs burn, how my temples stew! Night rolls in my eyes from all this sun! The heart . . . The limbs . . .

Where are we going? To war? I'm weak! The troops advance. Tools, weapons… Time…!

Shoot! Shoot me! I'm over here! Or I'll surrender…—Cowards! —I'll kill myself! I'll throw myself under a horse!

Ah…!

—I'll get used to it.

That's the French thing to do. That's the path of honor.

NIGHT IN HELL

I swallowed a gollup of poison. —May the advice I received be thrice blessed! —My gut burned. The violence of the venom wracked my limbs, left me deformed, threw me to the ground. I die of thirst, suffocate, can't even cry out. It's hell: eternal suffering! The flames rise! I burn, as you'd expect. Demon, do your worst!

I once got a glimpse of conversion to goodness and happiness, of salvation. Can I describe what I saw, here in this hymn-deaf hell? There were millions of enchanting creatures, harmonious spiritual song, peace and power, noble ambitions: what else can I say?

Noble ambitions!

Yet, I'm still here, still alive. So what if damnation is eternal! Any man who would destroy himself is damned, isn't he? I believe I'm in hell, therefore I am. Catechism in action. I'm the slave of my baptism. O parents, you guaranteed my suffering and you guaranteed your own. Poor innocent! —Hell has no purchase on pagans. —Still alive! Later, the delights of damnation deepen. Crime, quick: so I can fall into the void, as human law assures.

Shut up! Just shut up! It's all just shame and blame, look: Satan himself says that fire is vulgar, that anger is pathetic, absurd. —Enough...! Enough of errors whispered my way, of magics, fake perfumes, childish music! —And to think I already possess the truth, that I can discern justice: my judgment is sound and sure, I'm prepared for perfection... Pride. —The skin on my scalp dries to dust. Pity! I'm afraid, O Lord! I thirst; such thirst! Ah: Childhood, grass, rain, the stony lake, *moonlight when the clock strikes twelve*... the hour when the devil waits at the belfry. Mary! Holy Virgin! —The shame of my stupidity.

Up above, are there no honest souls who wish me well...? Come... There's a pillow pressed to my lips, they can't hear me, these ghosts. And no one ever thinks of anyone else. Better they steer clear. Surely I smell like I'm burning.

Hallucinations come, are without number. As before: I have no faith in history, no memory of principles. But I'll shut up about all this: poets and visionaries would be jealous. I'm a thousand times richer, and I'll be miserly as the sea. Look—life's clock just stopped. I'm no longer of this earth. —Theology is serious business: hell is absolutely *down below*—and heaven on high. —Ecstasy, nightmare, sleep in a nest of flame.

Nature's attentions only bring mischief... Satan and Ferdinand run through wild wheat... Jesus walks on crimson thorns that do not bend beneath him... Jesus once walked on troubled waters. The lamp showed him standing before us, white, with brown hair, by an emerald wave...

I will unveil every mystery: whether religious or natural, death, birth, the future, the past, cosmogony, the void. I have mastered phantasmagoria.

Listen...!

I possess every talent! —No one is here, and yet someone is: I won't squander my treasure. Shall I offer you African chants? Houri dances? Shall I disappear? Make my plunge in search of the *ring?* Shall I? I'll forge gold, and cures.

Then put your faith in me; faith relieves; directs; cures. Everyone, come—even the littlest children—let me console you, let the heart spread wide—the miraculous heart!—Poor mankind, a race of laborers! I don't ask for prayers; your faith is my reward.

—And think of me. It's worth the loss of the world. I'm lucky to see my suffering ended. Alas: my life was little more than a few mild madnesses.

Fine. Make any face you want.

Unquestionably, we are beyond the world. Not a single sound. My sense of touch is gone. My château, my Saxony, my willow grove. Evenings, mornings, nights, days... How weary I am!

There should be a hell for my anger, a hell for my pride—and a hell for every caress: a satanic symphony.

I die of weariness. Here is my tomb, I join the worms—horror of horrors! Satan, you joker: you would see me consumed by your charms. I protest! I protest! Give me the pitchfork's sting, the fire's flame.

Ah, to rise back to life! To look once again upon our deformities. And this poison, this kiss countlessly cursed! My weakness; worldly cruelty! O God have pity, hide me, I am wicked!—I am hidden and I am not.

Flames rise again, bearing the damned.

DELIRIA

I
FOOLISH VIRGIN
Hellish Husband

Hear a hellmate's confession:

"O heavenly Husband, O Lord, do not refuse this confession from the saddest of your servants. I am lost. I am drunk. I am impure. O this life!

"Forgive, heavenly Lord, forgive! Ah! Forgive. Too many tears! And, I hope, too many tears to come.

"Later, I'll meet my heavenly Husband. I was born beneath His yoke. But now, I'm someone else's whipping boy!

"Now I'm at the bottom of the world. O the women I call my friends... No, not my friends... I've never known such delirium and torture... It's ridiculous!

"How I suffer, how I scream: I truly suffer. There's nothing I wouldn't contemplate doing now, burdened as I am with the contempt of the most contemptible of hearts.

"So enough, let's confess, even if it means repeating it twenty times over—however dreary and insignificant.

"I am the slave of a hellish Husband, to him who undid foolish virgins. There's no doubt he's the same demon. He's no ghost, no phantom. But I, whose wisdom has been squandered, who is damned and dead to the world—I won't be killed! —How can I explain all of this? I barely know how to talk anymore. I'm in mourning; I weep; I'm afraid. A breath of fresh air, O Lord, if you would, if you would please!

"I am widowed...—I was widowed...but yes, I was, once, very proper, and I wasn't born simply to become bones! —He was very nearly a child... His mysterious ways seduced me. I forgot all my earthly duties in order to follow him. O this life! Real life is elsewhere. We aren't of this earth. I go where he goes, how can't I? And yet he blows up at me all the time, *me—poor soul.* That demon! —He's doubtless a demon, *for he is certainly not a man.*

"He says: 'I don't like women. Love must be reinvented, that much is clear. Women want security. And once they get it, goodness and beauty are out the window: cold disdain is the meat of marriage. Or I'll see women who seem happy, who even I could befriend, and I see them devoured by brutes as sensitive as butchers . . .'

"I listen to him turning infamy into glory, cruelty into charm. 'I am a member of a long-lost race: my forefathers were Scandinavian: they pierced their own sides, drank their own blood. —I'll gash myself everywhere, tattoo myself, make myself as grotesque as a Mongol: you'll see: I'll be screaming in the streets. I want to go mad with rage. Don't show me jewels; I'll cringe and writhe on the rug. I'd stain any wealth that came my way with blood. I'll never work . . .' Many nights, this demon would grab me, and we would wrestle and fight! —Nights, usually drunk, he'd wait in the street or a house, waiting to frighten me to death. —'You'll see: I'll get my throat cut. It'll be disgusting.' By day, he struts around like he's some sort of criminal!

"And then, occasionally, he'd speak a tender kind of talk, about remorse engendered by death; about miserable wretches who are everywhere; about backbreaking toil; about farewells that break hearts. In the dives where we'd drink, he'd cry while watching the people around us: misery's cattle. He'd prop up drunks in dark streets. He had compassion for the little children of mean mothers. —He'd conduct himself with all the kindness of a girl going to Sunday school. He'd pretend to be enlightened about everything—business, art, medicine. —I followed him, how couldn't I?

"I learned the spiritual landscape he surrounded himself with: clothes, drapes, furniture: I lent him weapons . . . and a second face. I saw everything that moved him, exactly as he did. Whenever he grew dissipated, I followed him nonetheless, me, executing strange tasks, far away, good or bad: I knew I would never really become a part of his world. Next to his sweetly sleeping body, I spent so many sleepless hours trying to figure out why he wanted to escape from reality. No man before him had wished for such a thing. I was aware—without being afraid of him—that he could be a menace to society. Maybe he had found a way *to change life as we know it?* No, he was only searching, or so he said. His charity is bewitching, and I am its prisoner. No other soul was strong enough—the strength of despair!—to have withstood his protection and love. And anyway, I couldn't imagine him with anyone else: we know only the Angel we're given, never another, or so I believe. I inhabited his heart as one might a palace: it was empty, precisely so no one would learn that a person as ignoble as you were there: and there it is. Alas! I needed him. But what did he want with me, drab and lifeless as I was? He didn't make me a better person, and he didn't manage to kill me! Sad, angry, I would occasionally say, 'I understand you.' He'd just shrug his shoulders.

"And so my sorrow was endlessly renewed, and seeing myself drifting further out to sea—as anyone would have noticed, had I not already been condemned to be forgotten by everyone—I grew more and more hungry for some measure of kindness from him. His kisses and his warm embraces were a heaven, a dark heaven, into which I had entered, and where I would have preferred to have remained: poor, deaf, mute, blind. I got used to it. I saw us as two good children, free to stroll through Heavenly sadness. We got along perfectly. We worked side by side, filled with emotion. But, after a penetrating caress, he said: 'How ridiculous all you've been through will seem when I'm no longer here. When you no longer have my arms beneath your neck, nor my heart to lie upon, nor my mouth upon your eyes. Because one day, I'll go far away. I must make myself useful to others, too: it's my duty. However unsavory this seems... dear heart...' Immediately, in the wake of his absence, I felt both gripped by vertigo and thrown into the most unbearable darkness: death. I made him swear he wouldn't leave me. He swore a lover's promise twenty times over. It was as meaningless as when I said, 'I understand you.'

"Oh, but I was never jealous of him! I don't think he'll ever really leave me. What would become of him? He hasn't a friend in the world: and he won't take a job. He wants to live the life of a sleepwalker. Can goodness and charity by themselves find him a place in the world? From time to time, I forget my pitiful circumstances and think: he'll make me strong, we'll explore together, we'll hunt in deserts, we'll sleep on the sidewalks of unknown cities, without worries, without sorrow. Or I'll awake and find that his magical powers will have transformed all laws and customs, leaving the world intact; I'll be left with my desires, joys, insouciance. Oh, give me this life of innocent adventure in return for the suffering I've endured. But he won't. I can't appreciate his ideals. He told me he has regrets, hopes: but they don't concern me. Does he speak of God? Perhaps I should. I'm at the very bottom of the abyss, and I've forgotten how to pray.

"Were he to explain his sorrows, would I understand them better than his derision? He attacks me, spending hours making me feel guilty for everything that has ever meant anything to me in this life, and yet, he takes umbrage when I cry.

" '—Do you see that dapper fellow, going into that lovely, little house: his name is Duval, Dufour, Armand, Maurice, something. And inside, some woman has devoted her life to loving that idiot: she's probably dead, doubtless a saint in heaven. You'll kill me as surely as he killed that woman. That's what happens to people like us, we who are kind-hearted…' Alas! There were days when he believed all mankind's motions were dictated by some wholesale, grotesque delirium: and he'd laugh wretchedly, at length. —Then, like some sweet sister, his maternal impulses would return. Were he less of a savage, we'd be saved! But even his sweetness is mortal. Surrendered, I follow. —I'm insane!

"Perhaps one day he'll miraculously disappear; but were he returned to heaven, I would need to know that I might glimpse my darling's assumption."

One strange couple.

DELIRIA

II

ALCHEMY OF THE WORD

My turn. A tale of one of my follies.

For some time, I'd boasted a mastery of every arena, and had found famous painters and poets ridiculous.

I preferred bad paintings: hanging above doors, on sets or carnival backdrops, billboards, cheap prints; and unfashionable literature, church Latin, barely literate erotica, novels beloved by grannies, fairy tales, children's books, old operas, silly songs, simple scansions.

I dreamed crusades, unimagined journeys of discovery, invisible republics, failed religious wars, moral revolutions, racial and continental drift: I believed in every enchantment.

I invented colors for vowels! —Black *A,* white *E,* red *I,* blue *O,* green *U.* —I regulated the shape and movement of every consonant, and, based on an inner scansion, flattered myself with the belief I had invented a poetic language that, one day or another, would be understood by everyone, and that I alone would translate.

It started out as an exercise. I wrote silences; nights; I recorded the unnameable. I found the still point of the turning Earth.

Far from birds, herds, and village girls,
What did I drink, on my knees, in this heath
Surrounded by delicate hazelnut trees,
And warm green afternoon mist!

What of this budding brook could I have drunk,
—Voiceless elms, flowerless grass, cloudy sky!—
Drunk from these yellow gourds, far from my beloved
Cabin? A golden liquor that makes you sweat.

I made a suspect sign for an inn.
A storm came, chased the sky. At night,
Water from forests disappeared on virgin sands,
Godly wind tossed ice upon ponds;

Crying, I saw gold—but could not drink.—*

At four in the morning, in summer,
Love's sleep lives.
Beneath the bowers, dawn stirs
        The scent of evening's celebrations.

But there, under the great oak
Near the Hesperidean sun,
Carpenters in shirtsleeves
        Are already busy

In their mossy Desert, peacefully,
They prepare precious woodwork
On which the town
        Will paint fake skies.

O Venus! For these charming workers' sakes
Subjects of some Babylonian king
Leave these Lovers be
        Leave their souls entwined.

                O Queen of Shepherds,
        Bring drink to these workmen,

*A different version of this poem, "Tear," appears on p. 112.

So their vigor is restored
While waiting to swim in the noontime sea.*

Worn-out poetical fashions played a healthy part in my alchemy of the word.

I settled into run-of-the-mill hallucinations: I very clearly saw a mosque in place of a factory, a group of drummers consisting of angels, carriages on the heavenly highways, a sitting room at the bottom of a lake; monsters, mysteries; the title of a vaudeville could conjure anything.

Then, I explained my magical sophisms with hallucinations of words!

I ended up believing my spiritual disorder sacred. I was lazy, proof of my fever: I envied the happiness of animals—caterpillars, symbolic of the innocence of limbo; moles, virginity's sleep!

I grew bitter. I said farewell to the world in a ballad:

SONG FROM THE TALLEST TOWER

May it come, may it come,
The age when we'll be one.

I've been so patient
I nearly forgot.
Fear and suffering
Have taken wing.
Unwholesome thirst
Stains my veins.

May it come, may it come,
The age when we'll be one.

So the meadow
Surrendered,

*A different version of this poem, "Good Morning Thoughts," appears on p. 110.

Lush and blossoming
With incense and weeds,
And the fierce buzzing
Of filthy flies.

May it come, may it come,
The age when we'll be one.

I loved desert, scorched orchards, sun-bleached shops, warm drinks. I dragged myself through stinking streets and, eyes closed, offered myself to the sun, god of fire.

"General, if upon your ruined ramparts a single cannon yet remains, bombard us with clods of earth. Strike shop mirrors! Sitting rooms! Feed our cities dust. Coat gargoyles in rust. Fill boudoirs with fiery, ruby ash . . ."

Oh! The drunken gnat in the urinal of an inn, smitten with borage, dissolved by a shaft of light!

HUNGER

If I have taste, it's for
Earth and stone,
I feast on air,
Rock, iron, coal.

Turn, my hungers. Graze
    A field of sounds.
Sample bindwood's poison;
    It merrily abounds.

A very different version of "Song from the Tallest Tower" appears on p. 114, and of "Hunger" on p. 121.

Eat rocks we crack,
Old church stones,
Pebbles floods attack
Loaves in valleys sown.

———

The wolf howls beneath the leaves
While spitting out pretty plumes
From his feast of fowl:
I, like him, myself consume.

Salad and fruit
Are waiting to be picked;
But the spider in the hedge
Eats only violets.

Let me sleep! Let me boil
On Solomon's altars.
The brew bubbles up and spills
Merging with the Kidron.

O happiness, o reason: I finally chased the blue from the sky, this blue that's really black; and I lived, a golden spark, forged from *natural* light.

Full of joy, I expressed myself as ridiculously and strangely as possible.

Rediscovered!
What? —Eternity.
Sea and sun
As one.

My eternal soul,
Heed you vow
Despite empty night
And fiery day.

Break
From earthly approval,
And common urges!
And soar, accordingly . . .

—No hope.
Nul orietur.
Knowledge through patience,
Suffering is certain.

No more tomorrow,
Your silken embers,
    Your duty,
    Is ardor.

Rediscovered.
What? —Eternity.
Sea and sun
As one.

I became opera: I saw that all living things were doomed, to bliss: that's not living; it's just a way to waste what we have, a drain. Morality is a weakness of mind.

It seemed to me we were owed *other* lives. One fellow knows not what he does: he's an angel. Another family is a litter of puppies. I argued with countless men, using examples drawn from their other lives. —That's how I fell in love with a pig.

Madness—the kind you lock away—breeds sophistries, and I haven't missed a single one. I could list them all: I've got them down.

My health suffered. Terror struck. I'd sleep for days, and, risen, such sad dreams would stay with me. I was ripe for death, and down a dangerous road my weakness drew me to the edges of the earth and on to Cimmeria, that dark country of winds.

I sought voyages, to disperse enchantments that had colonized my mind. Above a sea I came to love as if it were rinsing me of stain, I watched a consoling cross rise. Damnation, in the shape of a rainbow. Bliss was my undoing, my remorse, my worm: my life would always be too ungovernable to devote to strength and beauty.

Bliss! Her tooth, sweet as death, bit, every time a cock crowed in the darkest cities—*ad matutinum,* when *Christus venit:*

O seasons, o châteaux!
Who possesses a perfect soul?

I made a magical study
Of inescapable bliss

Think of Bliss each time you hear
The rooster's call, far or near.

Bliss has finally set me free
From desire's tyranny.

Its spell took soul and shape
Letting every goal escape.

O seasons, o châteaux!

When Bliss departs at last
Death takes us each, alas.

O seasons, o châteaux!

But that's over with. Now I know how to greet beauty.

ad matutinum... Christus venit: "In the morning... when Christ comes."

THE IMPOSSIBLE

My high youth! The great roads in every weather, a supernatural sobriety, a disinterest matched only by the most accomplished beggars, and such pride at having no country, no friends—what idiocy that all was! And I'm only realizing it now!

—I was right to scorn men who never miss a kiss, parasites on the propriety and health of our women who, as a result, have been left so little in common with us.

All my disdain was on the mark: after all, I'm still leaving.

Leaving!

Let me explain.

Even yesterday, I sighed: "For God's sake! I think there are enough damned souls down here! I've had plenty: I know them all. We always recognize each other; and drive each other nuts. We see charity as a foreign concept. But we're polite about it; our interactions with the world exhibit every propriety." Is this so shocking? The world: businessmen and simpletons! —We're hardly embarrassing ourselves.

But how will the elect receive us? Many of them are insincere, given, to approach them, we muster stores of courage or humility. But they're all we have. So count your blessings!

Since I seem to have rediscovered my two cents' worth of reason—it doesn't go far! —I see that my discomfort comes from not having realized sooner that we're in the West. Western swamps! Not that I believe that all light has been spoiled, all forms exhausted, all movements misdirected . . . It's nonetheless clear that my animus has every desire to adopt the latest advances in cruelty, developed since the East fell. Every desire indeed!

Well . . . that about does it for my two cents! The soul knows best, wants me to head East. I'll have to shut it up if I want to end up as I'd hoped.

I cursed the hands of saints, and with them any glimmers of art, pride of inventors, enthusiasm of pillorers; I returned to the East and to its early, eternal wisdom. —However, it seems now it too has been a fetid, vulgar dream!

Nonetheless, I never really let myself dream of the joy of escaping modernity's tortures. I never had the Koran's bastard wisdom in mind. —Isn't it torture to realize that since the advent of science and Christianity, man has been *playing with himself,* proving facts, puffing with pride every time he repeats his proofs, and acting like this is some sort of life! What subtle, idiotic torture; and the source of my spiritual wanderings. Perhaps even nature grows tired of itself! M. Prudhomme was born at Christ's side.

We're brewing all this fog! We eat fever with our watery vegetables. Drunkenness! Tobacco! Ignorance! Worship! —What does it have to do with the thinking and wisdom of the East, that primitive homeland? Why bother with a modern world, if the same poisons spread?

Men of the Church say: Understood. But you mean to say Eden. There's nothing to learn in the history of the Eastern peoples. —True enough; I was dreaming of Eden! What does the purity of ancient races have to do with my dream!

Philosophers: The world is ageless. Humanity moves where it will. You're in the West, but free to live in an East of your imagining, however ancient as fits your needs—and to live well there. Be not among the defeated. Philosophers, you're from your West!

Take heed, soul. Don't fall prey to sudden salvation. Get ready! Science never moves fast enough for us!

—But it seems my soul sleeps.

Were it truly awake from this moment forward, we would be approaching a truth that, even now, may be encircling us with her weeping angels! —Had it been awake, I wouldn't have succumbed to injurious instincts, to an immemorial age…! —If it had never been awakened, I would be drifting through purest wisdom…!

O purity!

This instant of awakening has conjured a vision of purity! The spirit leads us to God!

Bitter misfortune!

LIGHTNING

Man's labors! Explosions that, from time to time, illuminate my abyss.

"Nothing is vanity; to knowledge, and beyond!" cries the modern Ecclesiastes, which is to say *Everyone.* And yet, the cadavers of the wicked and idle fall upon the hearts of everyone else... Oh hurry up, hurry up; below, beyond the night, will we miss the eternal rewards that await...?

—What can I do? I know work: and science is too slow. How prayer gallops, how light rumbles... I see it all. It's too clear, too hot; you'll make do without me. I have my task, and I'll be as proud as anyone else, when I set it aside.

My life has been worn away. So come! Let's pretend, let's sit idly by... O how pitiful! And we'll go on living our lives of simple amusement, dreaming of grotesque loves and fantastic worlds, complaining and arguing over the shape and appearance of the earth, acrobat, beggar, artist, bandit—priest! In my hospital bed, the stench of incense suddenly returned; guardian of sacred scents, confessor, martyr...

Then and there, I admitted my filthy upbringing. Who cares! Twenty years is plenty, if it's plenty for everyone else...

No! No! Now is too soon: to hell with death! My pride won't settle for something as insubstantial as work: my betrayal of the world is too brief a torture. At the last possible moment, I'll lash out to the right... to the left...!

And then—oh my soul—we'll have lost any hope of eternity!

MORNING

Once upon a time, wasn't my childhood pleasant, heroic, fabulous, worthy of being written on golden leaves—what luck! What crime or error left me deserving my present weakness? Those of you who believe that animals cry tears of sorrow, that the sick suffer, that the dead have nightmares, try to explain my fall, and my sleep. I can now no longer explain myself any better than a beggar mumbling his *Pater* and *Ave Maria. I no longer know how to speak!*

And yet, today, I believe I've finished speaking of my hell. It was truly hell; the real thing, whose doors were swung open by the son of man.

Out of the same desert, on the same night, my weary eyes forever stare at—a silver star, but without setting life's Kings in motion, the three magi—heart, soul, spirit. When, beyond mountains and rivers, will we embrace the birth of new endeavors, new wisdom, the departure of tyrants and demons, the end of superstition, and be the first to worship Christmas all across the earth!

The song of heaven, the progress of nations! Slaves, curse not this life.

FAREWELL

Autumn already! —But if we're seeking divine clarity there's no point in bemoaning an everlasting sun, far from those who die with the seasons.

Autumn. Our boat, risen through the moveless fogs, turns towards misery's port, an enormous city whose sky is stained with fire and mud. Ah... the rotting rags, rain-soaked bread, drunkenness, a thousand crucifying loves! This ghoulish queen will never relent, queen of millions of dead souls and bodies *that will be judged!* And there I see myself again, skin eaten away by mud and plague, my hair full of worms, my armpits too, and my heart full of fatter worms, just lying there beside ageless, loveless unknowns... I could have died there... Unbearable. I hate poverty.

And I fear winter, the season of comfort!

—Sometimes, I'll see endless beaches in the skies above, filled with pale rejoicing nations. A great golden vessel, high above me, flutters varicolored flags in the morning breeze. I invented every celebration, every victory, every drama. I tried to invent new flowers, new stars, new flesh, new tongues. I thought I had acquired supernatural powers. Well then! The time has come to bury my imagination and my memories! A fitting end for an artist and teller of tales!

Free from all morality, I who called himself magus and angel, surrender to the earth in search of duty, ready to embrace life's rough road. Peasant!

Am I wrong? Will charity be a sister of death?

Finally, I ask forgiveness for feeding on lies. Okay: let's go.

And not even one friendly hand! And where can help be found?

Yes: the dawn is harsh, to say the least.

But victory is mine: everything moderates, the grinding teeth, the hissing fires, the putrid sighs. The filthy memories are wiped away. My final regrets flee—my jealousy of beggars, brigands, friends of death, rejects of every stripe. Were I to enact vengeance against all the damned!

One must be absolutely modern.

No more hymns: remain on the road you've chosen. Brutal night! Dried blood burns on my face, and nothing is near me, only that unbearable bush... Spiritual combat is as brutal as battle between men; but the vision of justice is God's pleasure alone.

Nonetheless, the eve is here. We welcome an infusion of true strength, and affection. And at dawn, armed with fiery patience, we'll at last enter glorious cities.

Why was I seeking a friendly hand? I have an advantage now: I can laugh off truthless loves, and strike down duplicitous couples with shame—down below, I experienced a hell women know well—and now I'll be able to *possess truth in a single body and soul.*

April–August 1873

VI. 1872–1874
Illuminations

N° 5. — 13 *Mai* 1886

LA VOGUE

LES ILLUMINATIONS

APRÈS LE DÉLUGE

Aussitôt que l'idée du Déluge se fut rassise,

Un lièvre s'arrêta dans les sainfoins et les clochettes mouvantes, et dit sa prière à l'arc-en-ciel, à travers la toile de l'araignée.

Oh ! les pierres précieuses qui se cachaient, — les fleurs qui regardaient déjà.

Dans la grande rue sale, les étals se dressèrent, et l'on tira les barques vers la mer étagée là-haut comme sur les gravures.

Le sang coula, chez Barbe-Bleue, — aux abattoirs, dans les cirques, où le sceau de Dieu blêmit les fenêtres. Le sang et le lait coulèrent.

Les castors bâtirent. Les « mazagrans » fumèrent dans les estaminets.

AFTER THE FLOOD

After the idea of the Flood had receded,

A rabbit rested within swaying clover and bellflowers, saying his prayers to a rainbow spied through a spider's web.

Oh what precious stones sunk out of sight, what flowers suddenly stared.

On the dirty main drag it was back to business; ships went to sea, piled on the water like a postcard.

Blood flowed—at Bluebeard's, in slaughterhouses, in circuses—wherever God's mark marred windows. Milk and blood flowed.

Beavers dammed. Steam rose from coffee cups in small cafés.

The mansion's windows were still streaming, mourning children within contemplating amazing scenes.

A door slammed, and the child whirled his arms through the town square, movements understood by weathervanes and weathercocks everywhere, beneath a tumultuous downpour.

Madame ★★★ put a piano in the Alps. Mass and First Communion were given at the hundred thousand altars of the cathedral.

Caravans left. The Hotel Splendide was built atop a chaos of ice in the polar night.

Ever since, the Moon has heard jackals whimpering in thyme-strewn deserts, and club-footed eclogues growling in orchards. At last, in a violet, blooming stand, Eucharis said: Spring Is Here.

Rise, waters. —Foam; roll over the bridge and through the woods—black veils and organ strains—lightning, thunder—rise and roam. Waters and sorrows, step forward and reveal the Floods.

For since they relented—what precious stones have sunk—what flowers have bloomed—who cares! And the Queen, the Witch who sparks her blaze in a bowl of Earth, never tells us what she knows, and what we do not.

OPPOSITE: First page of the first printing of *Illuminations* in *La Vogue.*

CHILDHOOD

I

This idol, black-eyed and blonde-topped, without parents or playground, and nobler than Fables, whether Aztec or Flemish: his domain of insolent blues and greens borders beaches named by shipless waves, names ferociously Greek, Slav, Celt.

At the edge of the forest—dream flowers chime, brighten to bursting—an orange-lipped girl, cross-legged in a flood of light soaking the fields, her nakedness shaded, crossed, and clothed by rainbows, blossoms, sea.

Ladies promenading on terraces by the sea; toddlers and giants, gorgeous black women garbed in gray moss-green, jewels set just so into the rich ground of the groves, the unfrozen gardens—young mothers and elder sisters, faces flushed with pilgrimage, sultanas, princesses pacing in lordly gowns, girls from abroad, and sweetly melancholy souls.

What a bore, to say "dearest body" and "dearest heart."

II

There: the little dead girl, behind the rosebushes. —The dead young mother comes down the steps. The cousin's carriage creaks on the sand. —The little brother—(off in India!) in a field of carnations at sunset. —Old men buried upright in a rampart of wallflowers.

A swarm of golden leaves surrounds the general's house. We're in the south. You follow the red road to reach the empty inn. The château is for sale; its shutters have fallen off. —The priest must have fled with the key to the church. —All around the park, groundskeepers' cabins stand empty... The fences are so high you only see the tips of trees rustling above them. But there's nothing inside to see.

Meadows reach across to roosterless villages and blacksmithless towns.

Floodgates are wide open. O the calvaries and windmills in the wilderness, the islands and millstones.

Magic flowers buzzed. Hillsides cradled *him*. Beasts of fabulous elegance made rounds. Clouds gathered on a rising sea, filled by an eternity of hot tears.

III

A bird is in these woods, its song stops you, makes you blush.

And here's a clock that will not chime.

And here's a pit with a nest of white beasts.

And here's a cathedral that sinks, and a lake that rises.

And here's a little carriage abandoned in a thicket, or that rolls beribboned down the road.

And here's a troupe of little actors in costume, spied on the edge of the woods.

And when you're hungry and thirsty, here's someone to chase you away.

IV

I'm the saint praying on a balcony—like peaceful beasts grazing along the Sea of Palestine.

I'm the scholar in a plain reading chair. Branches and rain beat the library windows.

I'm the pedestrian on the high road through the stunted woods; the sound of floodgates drowns out my footsteps. I stare at the melancholy wash of another golden sunset.

Or I could be the child abandoned on a high seas jetty, a bumpkin along a lane that butts the sky.

The path is harsh. The hillocks are weed. The air is still. How far we are from birds and streams. The end of the world must be just ahead.

V

So rent me a tomb whose cinderblocks peek through their whitewash—deep below ground.

I rest my elbows on the table, the lamp brightly illuminates newspapers and boring books I'm dumb enough to reread.

Far, far above my subterranean sitting room, houses settle and spread, fog gathers. Mud is red or black. Monstrous city, endless night!

Nearer are the sewers. At my flanks, the width of the world. Or perhaps azure abysses, pits of fire. Perhaps moons and comets collide at these depths, seas and stories.

In these bitter hours, I imagine spheres of sapphire and steel. I have mastered silence. So what's that vent doing, up there, illuminating a corner of my ceiling?

TALE

A Prince was troubled by his tendency to act on only his most obvious impulses. He could imagine a sort of revolutionary love, and suspected his wives capable of more than mere complaisance embellished with blue skies and riches. He wanted truth, hours of complete desire and satisfaction. Whether an aberration of piety or no, he wanted it all the same. At the very least, he was willing to find out.

—All the women who had been with him were put to death. Slaughter in Beauty's garden. They blessed him beneath the blade. He sought no replacements. —Yet the women reappeared.

He killed all his followers, after hunting or drinking. —None ceased to follow him.

He took pleasure slitting the throats of rare beasts. He torched palaces. He pounced on people and tore them apart. —Yet the crowd, the golden roofs, the beautiful beasts: all remained.

Can one rejoice in destruction, be rejuvenated by cruelty? His people didn't grumble. None objected.

One night, he galloped high in his saddle. A Genie appeared, of ineffable, inexpressible beauty. His face and bearing suggested a complex, multifaceted love; unspeakable—even unbearable—happiness! The Prince and the Genie vanished into each other, completely. How could they not have died of it? They died together.

But the Prince passed away in his palace, at a routine age. The Prince was the Genie. The Genie was the Prince.

Our desires lack an inner music.

SIDESHOW

Muscle-bound goons. The kind that rape the world. Self-satisfied, in no hurry to devote their remarkable faculties to understanding another's mind. Such wise men. Stares as blank as summer nights, red and black, tricolored, golden star-stung steel: twisted features, leaden, pale, inflamed; hoarse guffaws. A grim onslaught of pretense. To hear what these kids would say about Cherubino in their rough voices and violent ways. They're heading to town to get it from behind, all decked out in sickening *luxury*.

A violent Paradise of runaway sneers! But no match for your Fakirs and hackneyed theatrics. In costumes sewn together with all the taste of a nightmare, they strut through assorted laments, tragedies filled with all every brigand and demigod missing from religion and history. Chinese, Hottentots, bohemians, fools, hyenas, Molochs, ancient lunacies, sinister demons—they slip savage slaps and tickles into your mother's old chestnuts. A little avant-guarde here, some three-hankie stuff there. Master jugglers who use riveting comedy to transform players and scenes. Eyes ignite, blood sings, bones stretch, tears and red rivulets run. Their clowning can last minutes, or months.

Only I have the key to this savage sideshow.

ANTIQUE

Graceful son of Pan! Beneath your flower- and berry-crowned brow, the precious spheres of your eyes revolve. Your wine-stained cheeks seem hollow. Your fangs gleam. Your chest is a lyre, music flows from your pale arms. Your heart beats in a belly where two sexes sleep. At night, wander, softly moving this thigh, then this other thigh, and this left leg.

BEING BEAUTEOUS

Out of the snow rises a Beautiful Being. Whisperings of death and rounds of unheard music lift this worshipped shape, make it expand and tremble like a ghost; black and scarlet wounds colonize immaculate flesh. Life's colors deepen, dance, and radiate from this Vision fresh off the blocks. Tremors rise and rumble, and the wild flavor of these effects is outdone by mortal whisperings and raucous music that the distant world hurls upon our mother of beauty: she pulls back, she rears. Oh! Our bones are draped in amorous new flesh.

★ ★ ★ ★

O the ashen face, the coarse thatch, the crystal arms! The cannon I collapse upon, through a topple of trees and soft air.

Being Beauteous: Rimbaud's title for this poem was in English, as given.

LIVES

I

O the vast avenues of the holy land, the terraces of the temple. What became of the Brahman who taught me the Proverbs? From then, from there, I still see images, even of old women. I remember hours of silver and sun along rivers, the hand of the land upon my shoulder, and our caresses in the fragrant fields. A rising flock of scarlet pigeons thunders through my thoughts. —In exile, life was a stage where literature's masterpieces were played out. I could share untold riches that remain unknown. I watch you unearth your discoveries. I know what will be! My wisdom? You disdain it like chaos. What is my nothingness, in the face of the stupor awaiting you?

II

I'm an inventor unique among my predecessors; think of me as a musician who has discovered the key of love. For now, a gentleman from a barren land and a sober sky, I try to stir myself with memories of a beggar's boyhood; my apprenticeship, days in wooden shoes, arguments, five or six unimaginable losses, and a few wild nights where my stubbornness kept me from losing it completely. I don't regret my earlier allotment of divine joy: the sobriety of this desolate landscape nourishes my wild skepticism. But because this skepticism no longer has its place, and since I'm consumed with a brand-new mess—I'm destined to become a miserable kook.

III

I met the world, in an attic I was confined to at twelve. There, I furnished illustrations to the human comedy. I learned history, in a cellar. At some nocturnal celebration in a northern city, I met women who modeled for the old masters. I was schooled in the sciences in a Paris back alley. I made my own masterpieces and retired to an appropriately magnificent Oriental retreat. I brewed my blood. My burden was lifted. My brooding was over. I am beyond all parting, and past persuading.

DEPARTURE

Seen enough. Visions confronted in every weather.
Had enough. Urban tumult, by night and day, forever.
Known enough. Life's still-points. —O tumult and Visions!
Departure for fresh affection and noise!

ROYALTY

One fine morning, in a land of very decent people, a gorgeous man and woman were shouting in the town square:

"Friends, I want her to be queen!"

"I want to be queen!" She laughed, and trembled.

He spoke to his friends of revelation, of an ordeal undergone. They swooned, one against the other.

And so they ruled all morning, as crimson curtains blazed from windows, and then all afternoon, as they strolled the palm gardens.

FOR A REASON

Striking your finger on a drum discharges all sound and begins a new harmony.

Taking a single step suggests the advent and advance of new men.

Your head turns away: new love! Your head turns back—new love!

All the children sing: "Change our fates, hobble the plague, start with time." They beg: "Elevate anywhere our fortunes and hopes."

Arrival from always, for departure to everywhere.

DRUNKEN MORNING

Goodness and Beauty, and they're *mine*! The noise is unbearable but it won't faze me! Storybook tortures! Hurray (for once) for great work and bodily miracles! Children's laughter marks both beginning and end. This poison lingers in our veins even when we withdraw to the silence of prior discord. Now that we warrant such torture, let's make good on the superhuman promise our bodies and souls deserve: this promise, this madness! Elegance, science, violence! They promised to bury the tree of good and evil in the shadows, and cast off tyrannical shackles of decency, so we could cultivate true love. The beginning was begun on the border with disgust, and the end—unable to seize eternity while on the run—the end unfolds with a stampede of perfume.

Children's laughter, sobriety of slaves, austerity of virgins, fear of faces and forms from this place—be blessed by the memory of this night. In the beginning there was hooliganism, in the end angels of ice and fire.

Sacred drunken night! Sacred if only for the mask you grant us. Fair enough! We won't forget how you blessed our hours. We put faith in poison. We know how to live completely, every day.

Behold an age of *Assassins.*

LINES

When the world is no more than a lone dark wood before our four astonished eyes—a beach for two faithful children—a musical house for our bright liking—I will find you.

Even if only one old man remains, peaceful and beautiful, steeped in "unbelievable luxury"—I'll be at your feet.

Even if I create all of your memories—even if I know how to control you—I'll suffocate you.

When we are strong—who retreats? When happy, who feels ridiculous? When cruel, what could be done with us?

Dress up, dance, laugh. —I could never toss Love out the window.

My companion, my beggar, my monstrous girl! You care so little about these miserable women, their schemes—my discomfort. Seize us with your unearthly voice! Your voice: the only antidote to this vile despair.

UNTITLED FRAGMENTS

A cloudy morning in July. The taste of ash floats in the air; the smell of sweating wood in a hearth—flowers rotting in water—havoc along walkways—drizzle of canals moving across fields—and why stop there—why not add toys, and incense?

I ran ropes from spire to spire; garlands from window to window; gold chains from star to star; and I dance.

The mountain pond smokes endlessly. What witch will rise against the whitening sunset? What violet foliage will fall?

While public funds are spent on brotherly bacchanals, a bell of rosefire rings in the clouds.

A black powder rains gently on my evening, kindling an agreeable taste for India ink. —I lower the gas-jets, throw myself on the bed, and, turned towards the shadows, I see you: my daughters—my queens!

WORKERS

O the warm February morning. How the sudden South rekindled our memories of unbearable poverty, of youthful miseries.

Henrika had on a brown-and-white-checkered cotton skirt straight out of the last century, a ribboned bonnet, and a silk scarf. It looked sadder than mourning. We took a walk in the suburbs. It was overcast, and the South wind stirred rank smells of ravaged gardens and starched fields.

All this couldn't have wearied my wife as much as it did me. Along a high path, in a puddle left by the previous month's flood, she pointed to some tiny fish.

The city, its smoke and noise, pursued us down the roads. O better world, a habitation blessed only by sky and shade! The South only reminds me of miserable childhood moments, summer despairs, the awful glut of strength and knowledge that fate has always denied me. No: we won't spend summer in this cheap country where we'll be little more than orphans betrothed. I won't let these hardened arms drag *a beloved image* after them.

BRIDGES

Crystal gray skies. A strange pattern of bridges, some straight, some arched, others falling at oblique angles to the first, their shapes repeating in the illuminated curves of the canal, all of them so long and light that the banks, heavily canopied, sink and shrink. A few of these bridges are still freighted with hovels. Others sport masts, flags, fragile parapets. Minor chords crisscross as ropes rise from shore. You can make out a red coat, maybe some other outfits, and musical instruments. Are the tunes familiar, bits of chamber music, remnants of national anthems? The water is gray and blue, broad as an arm of the sea. —Falling from the top of the sky, a white beam of light obliterates this comedy.

CITY

I am a transient, and not altogether unhappy, citizen of a metropolis considered modern, given every conceivable standard of taste has been avoided, in both interior decoration and exterior architecture, and even in the plan of the city itself. You'd be hard-pressed to find the barest trace of a monument to superstition here. Morality and Language have finally been refined to their purest forms! These millions of people who have no need to know one another conduct their educations, professions, and retirements with such similarity as to suppose that the length of their lives must be several times shorter than statistics would indicate for continentals. Moreover, from my window, I see new ghosts rolling through unwaveringly thick coal-smoke—our dark woods, our summer night! —a new batch of Furies approaching a cottage that is both my country and my fullest heart, as everything resembles it here. Death without tears, a diligent servant girl, a desperate Love, and a perfect Crime, whimpering in the muddy street.

RUTS

On the right, the summer dawn stirs the leaves and mists and noises of this corner of the park, while on the left, embankments paint the wet road's thousand little ruts in violet shadow. A stream of enchantments: Wagons filled with gilded wooden animals, poles, and motley tenting, drawn at full gallop by twenty dappled circus horses, and children and men riding amazing beasts: twenty gilded conveyances, flagged and flowered like ancient coaches, like something from a fairy tale, filled with children dressed for a country fair. There are even coffins, sporting ebony plumes, beneath night-dark canopies, behind the trot of massive blue-black mares.

CITIES [I]

Such cities! Alleghenies and Lebanons out of a dream, staged and scaled for a people their equal. Chalets of crystal and wood move on invisible pulleys and rails. Bordered by colossi and copper palms, ancient craters bellow melodiously through flames. Feasts of love ring out across canals strung behind the chalets. A pack of pealing bells calls from the gorges. Guilds of gigantic singers gather, wearing clothes and bearing banners as dazzling as light from the summits. On platforms in passes, Rolands sound their valor. On footbridges spanning abysses and rooftops of inns, the ardent sky ignites flagpoles. The collapse of old apotheoses joins heaven to earth, fields where seraphic centauresses gambol and dance between avalanches. A sea freighted with orphic fleets and rumbling pearls and precious conches unfolds above the highest peaks, disturbed by Venus' perpetual birth—a sea that sometimes darkens with fatal flashes. Harvested flowers as big as guns and goblets are lowing on the hillsides. Parades of Mabs climb the ravine in red and opaline dresses. Up above, their feet in the falls and brambles, stags suckle Diana's breasts. Suburban Bacchantes sob, the moon burns and bawls. Venus visits the caves of blacksmiths and hermits. Groups of belfries sing the people's ideas. Unfamiliar music escapes from castles of bone. All the old mythologies gambol and dance, and urges, like elk, stampede through the streets. The Paradise of storms collapses. Savages dance ceaselessly at the feast of night. And, once, I even descended into the flow of a Baghdad boulevard where groups were singing joyously of new work, blown by a thick breeze, moving around but unable to elude the fabulous ghosts of the mountains where we must have met.

What fine arms and hour will return this region to me, whence my slumbers and slightest movements come?

VAGABONDS

Pathetic brother! What wretched sleepless nights he caused! "I had little passion for this undertaking. I played to his weaknesses. If we returned to exile, to slavery, I would be to blame." He believed, strangely, I was both jinxed and innocent. His reasons were disturbing.

I responded by snickering at this satanic doctor, and fleeing out the window. Beyond a countryside singing with strains of singular music, I created ghosts of future, nocturnal luxury.

After this vaguely hygienic distraction, I would relax on my pallet. And, nearly every night, just as I had fallen asleep, this poor brother would rise, mouth dry, eyes bulging—just as he'd dreamed—and drag me into the next room while screaming his idiotic sorrowful dream.

Essentially, sincerely, I had taken it upon myself to return him to his primitive, sun-worshipping state—and we wandered, sustained by wine from cellars and the road's dry bread—as I impatiently sought means and ends.

CITIES [II]

The official acropolis surpasses our most colossal conceptions of modern barbarity. Impossible to adequately describe the flat daylight produced by this immutably gray sky, the imperial sheen of the edifices, and the eternal snow on the ground. With a singular taste for enormity, they reproduced all the marvels of classical architecture. I attend painting expositions in places twenty times larger than Hampton Court. And what paintings! A Norwegian Nebuchadnezzar built the staircases of the government buildings; the underlings I was able to see are already haughtier than Brahmins, and I trembled as guards and construction foremen passed outside the colossi. As the buildings were sited along squares, closed courtyards and terraces within, traffic has been shut out. The parks are displays of nature at its most primitive, artfully laid out. Some of the upper parts of town are inexplicable: a boatless arm of the sea unrolls its blue sleeve of delicate hail between piers loaded with giant candelabras. A short bridge leads to a postern directly beneath the dome of Sainte-Chapelle. This dome is an artistic steel frame roughly fifteen thousand feet wide.

From certain points on the copper footbridges, platforms, and staircases that wind through the markets and around pillars, I thought I could judge the depth of the city! One marvel I couldn't reconcile: are the city's other regions above or beneath the level of the acropolis? Reconnaissance is impossible for the tourist of today. The commercial quarter is a circus in a single style: arcaded galleries. You can't see shops, but the snow on sidewalks is trampled; a few nabobs—as rare as pedestrians on a London Sunday morning—make their way towards a diamond diligence. A few red velvet divans: ice cold drinks are served, running eight hundred to eight thousand rupees. I start to look for a theater in this circus, but I realize that the shops fill with dark dramas all their own. There must be a police presence. But the law must be sufficiently strange here that I abandon imagining what local adventurers are like.

The suburb, as elegant as a beautiful Paris street, enjoys luminous light. The local democrats number a few hundred souls. Here, again, the houses aren't in rows; the suburb loses itself strangely in the countryside, the "Country" that fills the eternal West with forests and endless plantations where savage gentlemen seek distraction beneath the light they made.

VIGILS

I

Enlightened leisure, neither fever nor languor, in a meadow or a bed.
A friend neither ardent nor weak. A friend.
A love neither tormenting nor tormented. A love.
The air and the world, unsought. A life.
—Was this it?
—And the dream grows cool.

II

Lightning returns to the branches of the building. From opposite ends of the room, whatever the setting, harmonic elevations merge. The wall before the watcher is a psychological succession of parts of friezes, atmospheric sections, and geological strata. —A dream, intense and swift, of sentimental groups, people of every possible character amidst every possible appearance.

III

At night, the lamps and rugs of the vigil make the sounds of waves along keel and steerage.

The sea of the vigil, like Amélie's breasts.

The tapestries hang halfway up, the doves of the vigil plunge into a thicket of emerald lace.

. . . .

The back of black hearth, real suns from shorelines: Ah! magical wells; only a glimpse of dawn, this time.

MYSTIC

On the hillside, angels twirl their wool dresses through pastures of emerald and steel.

Meadows of flame leap to the hillock's crest. On the left, its humus has been trampled by murders and battles, disastrous noises etch a map of the terrain. Behind the crest to the right is a line leading to the Orient, to progress.

And while the band running across the top of the image is made by the spinning and leaping sound heard in conches and human nights . . .

The blossoming sweetness of stars and sky and all the rest falls in front of the hillside before us like a basket—and turns the abyss below to blossom and blue.

DAWN

I held the summer dawn in my arms.

Nothing stirred in front of the palaces. The water was dead. Camps of shadows rested on the road through the woods. I walked, awakening live warm breaths as precious stones looked on and wings soundlessly rose.

The first undertaking, in a path already filled with cool pale glimmers of light, was a flower that told me its name.

I laughed at a blonde *wasserfall* whose tresses streamed between firs; at the silvered summit I recognized the goddess.

So, one by one, I lifted her veils. In a lane, whirling my arms. In a field, shouting to a rooster. Into the city she fled, between steeples and domes, and I gave chase, running like a beggar on marble docks.

At the crest of the road, near a stand of laurels, I enveloped her in her gathered veils, and felt something of her boundless shape. Dawn and the child fell to the forest floor.

It was noon when I awoke.

FLOWERS

From a golden slope—among silk ropes, gray veils, green velvets, and crystal discs that blacken like the bronze of the sun—I watch the foxglove open on a carpet of silver filigree, eyes and hair.

Pieces of yellow gold scattered over agate, mahogany pillars supporting an emerald dome, bouquets of white satin and delicate sprays of rubies surround the water-rose.

Like some god's enormous blue eyes staring from within a silhouette of snow, sea and sky attract a crowd of strong young roses to the marble steps.

COMMON NOCTURNE

A breath of air opens operatic breaches in walls—rotten rooftops reel—hearths are sundered—casements covered. —One foot braced on a gargoyle, I cut through the vineyard in a carriage whose age is fixed by its convex mirrors, its curved woodwork, and contoured seats. A cloistered hearse of sleep, a cabin for my nonsense, the carriage veers onto the grass, away from the highway: and through an imperfection, high in the window on the right, spin pale lunar forms, leaves, breasts; —A deep green and blue invade the scene.

Unharnessing by a gravel patch.

—Here we'll whistle for the storm, for Sodoms—for Solymas—for wild beasts and armies,

(—Will coachmen and animals from some dream exit the airless woods to thrust me, up to my eyes, beneath the surface of a silken source?)

—And send us off, whipped by lapping waters and spilled drinks, to the howls of mastiffs…

—A breath of air, and hearths are sundered.

SEASCAPE

Chariots of silver and copper—
Prows of silver and steel—
Beat foam—
Stirring stumps of bramble—
Currents from the moor,
And the vast ruts of the tidal ebb
Flow eastward, circularly,
Towards the pillars of the forest—
Towards the pilings of the pier,
Whose corner is struck
By whirlwinds of light.

WINTER CELEBRATED

The waterfall sings behind opera-buffa shacks. Girandoles prolong sunset's greens and reds across orchards and paths by the river Meander. Nymphs out of Horace with First Empire coifs—Siberian dances, Chinese ladies out of Boucher.

ANGUISH

Might it be She could forgive my eternally dashed ambitions; in the end, can wealth make up for ages of indigence; can a day of success absolve the shame of my fatal incompetence?

(O palms and diamonds! —Love and strength! Greatest joys and glories! Of every type and place—demon, god—this being's youth: myself!)

Can accidents of scientific fantasy and organizations of social brotherhood be cherished as the progressive restitution of our earliest liberty?

But the Vampire who keeps us in line decrees we must amuse ourselves with what she leaves—that or start telling jokes.

So let me wallow in my wounds, in heavy air and sea; tormented by watery silence and murderous air; tortures that jeer at me, atrociously, in stormy silence.

METROPOLITAN

From indigo straights to Ossian seas, on pink and orange sands bathed by a wine-dark sky, crystal boulevards have sprung up and intersected, settled soon after by poor young families who buy food from street vendors. Nothing fancy.

—Cities!

Helmets, wheels, barges, buttocks—all flee the asphalt desert in a ragtag line, sheets of fog paper the sky with unbearable layers, curving, withdrawing, falling, made of the most sinister black smoke the mourning sea could muster.

—Battles!

Look up: the arched wooden bridge; Samaria's last vegetable gardens; masks lit by the lantern whipped by the cold night; a stupid water nymph in an ugly dress, at the bottom of the river; luminous skulls in the rows of peas—other phantasmagoria.

—Country.

Roads lined with fences, and walls barely containing their copses, brutal flowers called *hearts and sisters,* Damascus languidly damned, property belonging to fairy-tale aristocracies straight out of the Rhineland, Japan, Guarani, still attuned to ancient musics—inns never to open again—and princesses, and if you aren't too overcome, stars for you to study.

—Sky.

The morning when you struggled through the snow-glare with Her: green lips, ice, black flags, blue beams of light, purple perfumes of polar sun.

—Your strength.

BARBARIAN

Long after the seasons and days, the living and land,

A flag of flesh, bleeding over silken seas and arctic flowers (they do not exist).

Surviving old heroic fanfares still assaulting hearts and heads, far from earlier assassins.

A flag of flesh, bleeding over silken seas and arctic flowers (they do not exist).

Such sweetness!

Infernos hailing frosty gusts—such sweetness! Fires in a rain of diamond wind, tossed by an earthly heart, endlessly burned to black, for us.

—O world!

(Far from the old retreats and fires we hear and smell.)

Infernos and seafoam. Music, drifting abysses, icicles clashing with stars.

O Sweetness; O world; O music! And look: shapes; hair and eyes, floating. And white tears, boiling. O sweetness! And a feminine voice at volcanic depths, in arctic caves.

A flag . . .

FAIRY

In starry silence, virgin shadow, and impassive light, ornamental saps conspired for Hélène. Summer's ardor was entrusted to songless birds, and the predictable languor to a priceless funeral barge adrift in coves of dead loves and sunken scents.

—After the time when lumberwomen sang to the torrent's rumblings under the forest's ruins, after beastly bells rang, in valleys, and after cries from the steppes.

Fur and shadow shook, for Hélène's childhood—along with the breasts of the poor and the legends of the sky.

And her eyes and her dancing were better still than bursts of precious light, convincing cold, and even the pleasure of the singular setting and time.

Fairy: Rimbaud's title for this poem was in English, as given.

WAR

As a child, certain skies sharpened my sight: their varied temperaments refined my face. Phenomena awoke. —Now, the endless rise of moments and mathematical infinities chase me through a world where I suffer every civil success, respected by strange children and subjected to limitless affection. —I dream of war, of might and right, of utterly unforeseeable logic.

It's as simple as a musical phrase.

ADVT.

For sale: what the Jews haven't sold, what neither nobles nor criminals have dared, what remains unknown to both wicked love and society's infernal probity: what neither time nor science need notice:

Reconditioned Voices; the brotherly awakening of all choral and orchestral energies and their instantaneous outcry; rare opportunity to liberate our senses!

For sale: priceless Bodies—ignore race, world, sex, lineage! Riches rising to meet every step! A flood of diamonds, undammed.

For sale: anarchy for everyone, satisfaction guaranteed to those with irreproachable taste; gruesome death guaranteed for lovers and zealots!

For sale: living places and leaving places, sports, extravaganzas and creature comforts, and all the noise, movement, and hope they foment!

For sale: mathematical certainties and astonishing harmonic leaps. Unimaginable discoveries and terminologies—available now.

Wild, tireless bounds towards invisible splendor, intangible delight—alarming secrets for every vice—and the frightening gaiety of crowds.

For sale: Bodies; voices; incalculable, inarguable riches—that will never be sold. Vendors keep selling! Salesmen have nothing but time.

YOUTH

I
Sunday

Beneath the sky's unalterable collapse, memories and rhythms fill house, head, and spirit, as soon as all the number crunching is set aside.

—A horse bolts across the suburban earth, through gardens and lumberyards, stabbed by carbonic plague. Somewhere in the world, a histrionic woman sighs after unforeseen abandonment. Desperadoes pine for storm, injury, and debauch. Along rivers, little children choke down curses.

Let us return to our studies, despite the clamor of all-consuming work that collects and mounts in the masses.

II
Sonnet

Man of ordinary make, flesh
was it not once a fruit hanging in the orchard—o
days of youth! the body a treasure to squander—o
to love, a peril or power of the Psyche? Earth
had slopes fertile with princes and artists,
and your descendants and race drove you
to crimes and to mourning: the world, your fortune
and your peril. But now, this work done, you, your calculations,
—you, your impatience—are but dance and
voice, neither fixed nor forced, whether season
for a double event: invention and success
—a humanity both brotherly and singular, throughout a universe

without a face—might and right reflecting both dance
and voice, a voice we're only beginning to hear.

III

At Twenty

Instructive voices exiled... Naïve body bitterly sober...—Adagio.

Ah the infinite egotism of adolescence! The studious optimism: that summer, the world was filled with flowers! Dying airs and dying shapes... A choir to soothe impotence and absence! A choir of glasses, of nocturnal melodies... Now nerves begin the hunt.

IV

Enough of this temptation of St. Anthony. The struggle against failing zeal, tics of puerile pride, terror, and collapse.

But you'll return to the task: every harmonic and architectural possibility will stir within you. Unbidden, perfect creatures will present themselves for your use. As if a dream, the curiosity of old crowds and idle luxuries will collect around you. Your memory and your senses will be nourishment for your creativity. What will become of the world when you leave? No matter what happens, no trace of now will remain.

PROMONTORY

Golden dawn and shivering night find our brig along the coast of this villa and its grounds that form a promontory as vast as Epirus and the Peloponnesus or the great islands of Japan or Arabia! Temples illuminated by the return of processions; sweeping views of coastal fortifications; dunes inscribed with the hot flowers of bacchanal; Carthaginian canals and embankments of a degenerate Venice; faint eruptions of Etnas, crevasses of flowers and glacial waters, washhouses settled in stands of German poplars; strange parks, hillsides hung with heads of Japanese trees, and circular facades of Scarborough or Brooklyn, the "Royal" or the "Grand"; their railways flank, plumb, and overhang a Hotel plucked from the history of the biggest, most ornate buildings in Italy, America, and Asia, whose windows and terraces are now brimming with lights, drinks, and heavy breezes, are wide open to souls of travelers and nobles alike—who permit, by day, the varied tarantellas of the shores—and even the ritornellos of art's storied valleys, to miraculously decorate the Promontory Palace facades.

DEVOTION

To my Sister Louise Vanaen de Voringhem: her blue habit turned towards the North Sea. —For the shipwrecked.

To my Sister Léonie Aubois d'Asby: *hooooo;* humming, stinking summer grass. —For fevers inflicting mothers and children.

To Lulu—that demon—who has retained a taste for oratories from the time of girlfriends and grammar school. For the Men! For Madame ★★★.

To the adolescent I was. To that holy old codger, hermitage or mission.

To the spirit of the poor. And to an exalted clergy.

Just as to any cult, in any place that memorializes a cult, amid whatever events wherever we wander, subject to a moment's inspiration or the most serious vices.

Tonight, in the towering icy mirrors of Circeto, fat as fish, and illuminated like the ten months of the red night—(the fire of her amber heart)—my only prayer, as mute as these nocturnal regions, precedes gallantries more violent than this polar chaos.

At any price and in any place, even on metaphysical journeys.

—But no more *then*.

DEMOCRACY

"The flag fits the filthy land, and our argot drowns the drum.

"In cities, we nourish the most cynical prostitution. We slaughter logical revolts.

"To fragrant republics in flood! To serve the most monstrous military-industrial exploitations.

"Goodbye *here,* no matter where. Goodwill recruits, understand: our philosophy will be ferocity; ignorant of science, cads for comfort; to hell with the sputtering world. This road is real.

"Forward, march!"

STAGES

The comedy of old perpetuates itself while divvying up its idylls:

A street strewn with stages.

A long wooden pier running from one end of a rocky field to the other where barbarian hoards roam beneath bare trees.

Through corridors of black gauze following footsteps of passersby amidst lanterns and leaves.

Birds straight out of medieval mystery plays swoop down onto the masonry of floating stages stirred by a canopied archipelago of spectators' boats.

Lyrical scenes, accompanied by fife and drum, bow beneath nooks nestled near ceilings of lounges in modern clubs and oriental halls of yore.

The extravaganza moves to the top of an amphitheater crowned by a copse—or, instead, fidgets and warbles for the Boeotians, in the shadow of swaying trees on the fields' ridge.

On stage, the *opéra-comique* is divided at the intersection of ten partitions built between the gallery and the footlights.

HISTORIC EVENING

For example: an evening when a humble traveler withdraws from within earshot of impending economic doom, a master's hands may awaken a pastoral harpsichord; they play cards at the bottom of a pond, a mirror that conjures queens' and kings' favorites; there are saints, veils, threads of harmony, and chromatic strains at sunset.

He shudders at the approach of hunts and hordes. Comedy drips onto the grassy stage. Only then are the poor and weak ashamed, because of their stupid plans!

In his captive sight—Germany builds its way to the moon; Tatar deserts shine—old conflicts endure amidst a Celestial Empire; over stairways and armchairs of stone—a little world, pale and flat, Africa and Occident, rises. Then, a ballet of known nights and seas, a worthless chemistry, impossible melodies.

The same bourgeois magic wherever the mail train leaves us! The least sophisticated physicist feels it's no longer possible to endure this intimate atmosphere, a fog of physical remorse whose manifestation is disease enough.

No! The rise of heat, of sundered seas, of subterranean fires, of the planet's untethering and its resultant exterminations—facts from the Bible and the Nornes, presented without the least malice, and to which serious people will bear witness. —And yet, hardly the stuff of legend.

BOTTOM

Reality always too troublesome for my exalted character—I nonetheless found myself chez Madame, transformed into a big, blue-gray bird, soaring near the ceiling's moldings, trailing my wings through evening shadows.

At the foot of the baldachino that held her beloved jewels and bodily charms, I became a giant bear with purple gums and thick, miserable fur, eyes fixed on the crystal and silver on the sideboard.

Shadows swam, a torrid aquarium. In the morning—pugnacious June dawn—I ran to the fields, an ass, braying and brandishing my grief, until Sabines from the suburbs threw themselves upon my breast.

Bottom: Rimbaud's title for this poem was in English, as given.

H

Hortense's every gesture is violated by every atrocity. Her solitude, the mechanics of eroticism; her lassitude, the dynamics of love. Under childhood's watchful eye, she served, for countless years, as the fiery hygiene of races. Her door is open to misery. There, the morality of contemporary peoples is disembodied by her passion, or her action. —O the bitter shudder of young loves seen by gaslight on the bloody ground: Find Hortense!

MOVEMENT

The wagging movement along the banks of the river's falls,
The gulf at stern,
The slope's speed,
The current's pull
Flows through unimaginable lights
And new elements
Travelers enveloped in a valley of waterspouts
And *strom.*

These are the world's conquerors
Seeking their own elemental fortunes;
Sport and comfort travel with them;
They bring knowledge
Of race, classes, animals.
Aboard this Vessel.
Rest and restlessness
Under a flood of light
During terrible evenings of study.

Because from the banter around the instruments—blood, flowers, fire,
jewels—
From the uneasy accountings aboard this fugitive craft,
We see, rolling like seawalls past a motorized hydraulic road:
Their monstrous store of studies, illuminated endlessly—
They are driven into harmonic ecstasy,
And heroics of discovery.
Beneath astonishing atmospheric accidents
A young couple remains alone on the ark
—Can ancient savageries be absolved?—
And sings, standing watch.

GENIUS

Because he has opened the house to foaming winter and to noisy summer, he is affection, he is now, he who purified what we drink, what we eat, he who is the charm of brief visits and the unearthly delight of destinations. He is affection, he is the future, strength, and love that we, standing in furious boredom, watch, passing through tempestuous skies, flying flags of ecstasy.

He is love, reinvented in perfect measure, reason both marvelous and unforeseen, and eternity: an instrument adored for its fatality. We have all known the terror of his sacrifice and of our own: Let us delight in our health, in the vigor of our faculties, in selfish affection and passion for him who loves us throughout his infinite days...

And we remember, and he embarks... And if Adoration goes away, and nonetheless rings, his promise rings: "Enough of these superstitions, these old bodies, these houses and days. Our time has fallen away!"

He will not depart, he will not descend from a heaven once again, he will not manage to redeem women's anger, and men's laughter, and all our sin: for it is already done, by his being, and being loved.

O his breaths, his faces, his flights; the terrible speed of formal perfection and action.

O fertile mind, boundless universe!

His body! Long-dreamt release and shattering grace meet new violence!

The sight of him, his sight! All old genuflections and sorrows are *lifted* in his wake.

His day! The abolition of all streaming, echoing sufferings through a music more intense.

His stride! Migration is more momentous than ancient invasions.

O he, and we! Old charities pale before such benevolent pride.

O world! And the clear song of new sorrows!

He knew us all and loved us all. This winter night, from cape to cape, from farthest pole to nearest château, from crowd to beach, from face to face, with weary emotions and waning strength, let us hail him, and see him, and send him forth, and down beneath the tides and up in snowy deserts, let us seek his sight, his breath, his body, his day.

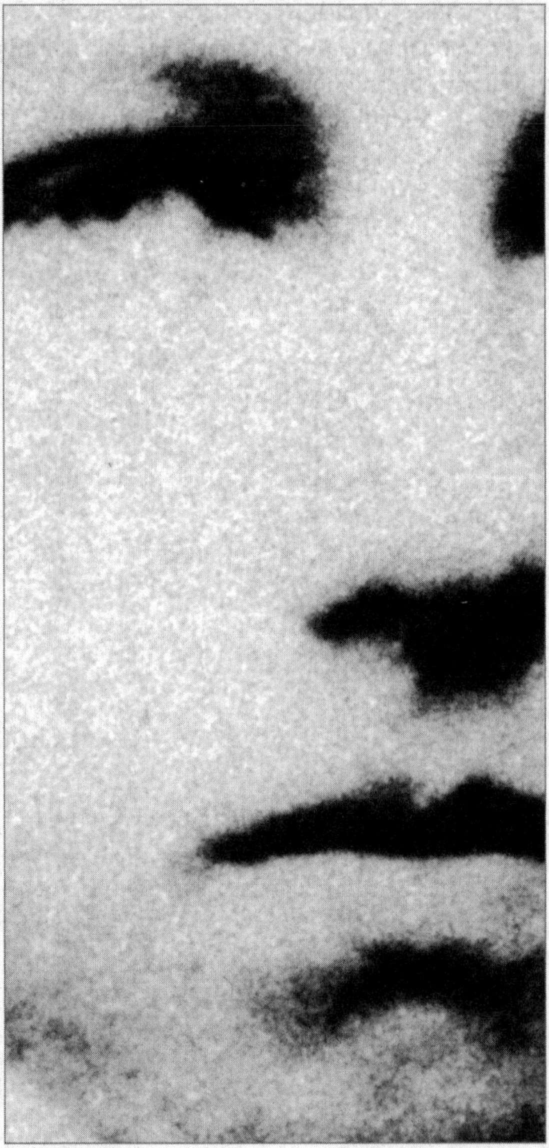

UNCOLLECTED WRITINGS

I. SCHOOLWORK

The following represents a sampling of works from Rimbaud's brief but high-flying academic career. Of the eight pieces, written while he was a day student at the Collège de Charleville, four are variations and expansions in Latin on themes supplied by his teachers; two are fairly straightforward translations from French into Latin; one is a translation from Latin into French that represents a solitary example in Rimbaud's oeuvre of Eliot's maxim that good poets borrow, great poets steal: a moment of plagiarism that went undetected for half a century. The last is a pastiche of the French of François Villon. We have them today because of their appearance in regional publications of the day that honored outstanding examples of student writing throughout France.

"Ver erat..." ("It was spring...") was written in Latin, in three hours, on November 6, 1868, two weeks after Rimbaud's fourteenth birthday. Rimbaud's assignment was to improvise a composition from lines by Horace from his Odes: *Book III, Number IV, "Descende caelo...." The lines were:* "Me fabulosa Vulture in Apulo/ Altricis extra limen Apuliae,/Ludo fatigatumque somno/Fronde nova puerum palumbres/Texere.... /.... Ut premer sacra/Lauroque collataque myrto/Nonsine Dis...." *("In my youth, on a day when I was sick of playing on the banks of the river Vultur in Apulia, not far from my native home therein, marvelous doves covered me in new leaves... I was crowned in Laurel and Myrrh, but clearly not without divine instigation...") The composition was deemed so extraordinary by his teacher, M. Duprez, that he sent it to* Le Moniteur de l'Enseignement secondaire, spécial et classique, Bulletin officiel de l'Académie de Douai, *a regional educational bulletin in which the finest examples of student work appeared, conferring prestige on school and child. "Ver erat..." appeared on January 15, 1869. For this and other translations from Rimbaud's Latin, I have used the French translations of Jules Mouquet from his* OC, *of Pierre Brunel in his* OC, *and of Marc Ascione in Alain Borer's* O/V.

"IT WAS SPRING..."

It was spring; illness kept Orbilius immobilized in Rome.
My barbarous teacher's tendencies were silenced.
The sound of his blows was far from my ears,
And my arms no longer ached from the rod.
I seized the opportunity: I made for the beckoning hills
Leaving everything behind; far from my studies and
Delivered from cares, simple pleasures remade my tired spirit.
My heart overflowing with incomprehensible contentment,
I never once thought about my unbearable school
Or the black boredom of my teacher's words;
Instead I relished contemplating the endless landscape
Lest I miss the happy miracles of the earth in spring.

My boyish heart didn't loll around in the grass:
It aspired to greater things:
I don't know what divine inspiration gave wing
to my exalted feelings: As if struck with stupor
I remained silent, eyes absorbed
In contemplation. I felt the hot love of the land
Insinuating itself within me: just as an iron
Ring attracted by the secret force of a Magnesium stone
Soundlessly attaches itself as if by invisible hooks.

Nevertheless, resting limbs worn out from
Wandering, I reclined on the river's green bank,
Lulled to sleep by its low murmur; I prolonged my repose,
Cradled by the concert of birdsong and of the zephyr's breath.
And then through the airy valley came doves
In a white band, bearing garlands of fragrant flowers in their beaks
Gathered by Venus in her Cyprian gardens.
Their swarm gently reached the grass
Where I reclined, then, beating their wings
They ringed my head and bound my hands
With a chain of leaves; crowning my temples
With fragrant myrrh, they lifted me, lighter than air,
Into it. Their flock bore me up to the high clouds
Half dozing under a bower of roses: the wind's breath
Caressed my gently swaying bed.
Once the doves had returned home,
At the foot of a mountain whose summit was invisible,
They rapidly reached their nests above
Depositing me, awake, before departing.
O sweet nests!... A blinding white light
Blossomed around my shoulders,
And covered my body with its rays:
And this light was nothing like that darker light which,
Mixed with shadow, obscures our sight:

A light foreign to the earth, a celestial light!
Through my chest, a celestial current
Flowed, like a divine river, undammed.

Nevertheless, the birds returned; in their beaks
They carried crowns of laurel like Apollo's,
Apollo whose fingers fed his lyre's voice.
But when they crowned my brow with laurel,
The heavens parted above me and before my
Amazed eyes, flying on a golden cloud, was Phoebus
Himself whose godly hand extended
A sweet voiced plectrum to my own.
And upon my head he wrote these words with a heavenly flame:
YOU WILL BE A POET . . . An extraordinary heat suddenly flowed
Through my limbs, like a limpid fountain
Of brilliant flowing crystal igniting with rays of sunlight.
Even the doves changed shape:
The choir of muses appeared, singing sweet
Melodious songs, they took me in their tender arms
And held me on the air while thrice repeating the omen,
And thrice crowning me with laurel.

Rimbaud Arthur.

Day student at le Collège de Charleville.

Born in Charleville on 20 October 1854.

"Jamque novus..." ("And the new year...") is another Latin effort, whose date of composition is unknown. It also appeared in Le Moniteur de l'Enseignement secondaire, *on June 1, 1869. This time, rather than having the class improvise a composition using lines from Horace, M. Duprez assigned the class a poem by Jean Reboul of Nîmes (1796–1864), "L'Ange et l'enfant" ("Angel and Child"). It might interest readers to consider this piece with Rimbaud's "The Orphans' New Year's Gifts," his first published poem, which was composed around the same time as "Jamque novus...," and appeared in January 1870 in the* Revue pour tous.

"AND THE NEW YEAR HAD ALREADY BEGUN..."

And the new year had already begun,
A fine day for children, a day so long awaited
And so quickly forgotten! Snuggled in a smiling sleep,
The drowsy child is silent... He is tucked into his cradle
Of feathers; his rattle falls with a grumble to the ground
As he enjoys untroubled sleep, and dreaming first
Of his mother's gifts, he soon receives those
Of the inhabitants of the sky. His smiling lips part; barely
They seem to mouth god's name. Sitting near his head, an angel
Leans towards him, spying the minute murmurs of an
Innocent heart and, himself transfixed by the image of the child,
Contemplates this heavenly face; he admires the joys
Written on the serene brow, the joys of his soul,
This flower as yet untouched by the South wind:
"Child like me,
Come, let us climb into the heavens together! Enter the celestial
Kingdom; live in the palace you have seen in sleep,
You are worthy of it! Earth can't bear a child of heaven!
Here, you can't trust anyone; mortals never cherish

Real bliss; even from the scent of flowers rises
Something bitter, and heavy hearts never know
Joys sorrow-tinged; pleasure never unencumbered
By cloud, and tears always glimmer
Through ambiguous laughter. And to what end?
Seeing your brow withered by bitter life,
And worries troubling your blue eyes with tears?
No, no: a God breaks the binds that tie you to life.
May your mother not wear mourning veils!
May she see your coffin no differently from your cradle!
May she forgo her heavy brow, and may your funeral not
Weigh upon her face but fill her hands with lilies:
For a pure heart, its final hours are its most beautiful!"

And he then brought his wing delicately to his rosy lips,
And harvested the child without him feeling a thing, and took
Upon his wings the soul of the harvested child, and carried him
To higher places while gently beating his wings... Now the cradle holds
Only paling limbs, which still have their beauty,
But the vivifying breath now neither nourishes nor gives life.
He is dead... But upon his lips still sweet with kisses
Laughter dies and his mother's name roams,
And as he dies he still remembers the gifts of New Year's Day.
You would think his heavy eyes were shut with tranquil sleep.
But this sleep, more than some new mortal reward,
What heavenly light rings his brow;
A child of earth no longer, a son of heaven instead.

Oh! What tears his mother cries for her departed child,
And how she showers his cherished tomb with streams of tears!
But each time she closes her eyes to enjoy sweet sleep,
A little angel appears to her on the rosy threshold
Of the sky and calls, softly: Maman.
She smiles at his smile: Soon, gliding on air,

He flies with snow white wings around his astonished mother
And to her maternal lips joins his lips divine.

Rimbaud Arthur.

Born on 20 October 1854 in Charville

"Nascitur arabis..." ("A very big baby was born...") was written in Latin on July 2, 1869, between 6 A.M. and noon, in a regional competition for which Rimbaud won first prize. The subject of the composition was merely "Jugurtha," a Numidian king of the second century A.D. The grandson of Jugurtha would have been Abd el-Kader.

"A VERY BIG BABY WAS BORN..."

Providence sometimes makes the same man
reappear in different centuries.
BALZAC, *Letters*

I

A very big baby was born in the mountains of Arabia
And a light breeze said: "He is the grandson of Jugurtha..."

Little time had passed when he—who would soon be
The Great Jugurtha of the Arab country and people—
Had risen into the air, and when his parents saw
The child's shadow they were amazed: for it was
The shadow of the Great Jugurtha, speaking,
Telling of his life and offering this augury:
"O my country! O land that I defended with my blood!"
And he paused a breath at the zephyr's interruption...
"Rome, previously the dark den of countless bandits,
Broke apart its confining walls and spilled through them
And—the blackguard—annexed its neighboring lands.
Endlessly spilled their blood without success

Balzac: Not Honoré, but *Guez* de Balzac, a seventeenth-century epistolarian.

For the sake of their liberty: Rome, more powerful
Than its rivals, crushed them, when they resisted alliance."

A very big baby was born in the mountains of Arabia
And a light breeze said: "He is the grandson of Jugurtha..."

"Even I, for a very long time, had believed that this people
Possessed a noble soul; but when I became a man, I was allowed
To see this country nose to nose, and I saw a great wound
Across its broad chest! —A low poison had insinuated
Its way into its limbs: a fatal golden thirst... apparently
It afflicted all our soldiers... —This prostituted city reigned the earth:
I decided to see how I stacked up against that queen—Rome;
I scorned that people whom the universe obeys...!"

A very big baby was born in the mountains of Arabia
And a light breeze said: "He is the grandson of Jugurtha..."

"For when Rome decided to meddle
In Jugurtha's affairs and bit by bit take hold
Of my country, I was fully aware, and heard
The rattling of threatening chains, and resolved
To resist Rome, knowing the pain of a wounded soul!
O sublime countrymen! Warriors! Holy brethren!
This earth—regina of the clouds, mother of heaven—
This earth will crumble, crumble down drunk on my memories.
How we Numidians laughed off this city, this Rome!
The barbarian from Jugurtha roamed like wildfire:
No one could oppose the Numidians!"

A very big baby was born in the mountains of Arabia
And a light breeze said: "He is the grandson of Jugurtha..."

"Heeding the call, I had the gumption to brave Roman territory
And make straight for their city— O Numidians! We stood

Face to face, and I struck her, scorning her mercenary army.
—Our people rose and took up arms long forgotten:
I didn't lower my sword: I had no hope
Of triumph: at least I could give them a good fight!
So I set rivers against each other, rocks against
Roman battalions: sometimes they fought in Libyan sands,
Sometimes they retreated to mountaintop hideouts:
Often their blood tinted the hills of my country...
And they were stunned by our sudden tenacity!"

A very big baby was born in the mountains of Arabia
And a light breeze said: "He is the grandson of Jugurtha..."

"Perhaps I would have ended up defeating the enemy troops...
But for Bocchus' duplicity... But what more can be said on that account?
Satisfied, I abandoned my country and my royal honors,
Satisfied to have thrown the rebellious gauntlet at Rome's feet.
—But now there is a new conqueror of the Arab peoples,
France!... You, my son, if you bend steely destiny,
You will be your country's redeemer... You the downtrodden, to war!
May you in your broken hearts find the courage of yore!
Brandish your swords once again! And as you remember Jugurtha,
Repel the conquerors, spill your blood for the motherland!
O may Arab lions rise for war,
And rip rival troops apart with their teeth!
—And you! Grow, child! Fortune smiles on you.
May the French no longer dishonor Arab shores!"

—And the child laughed as it played with its curved sword!

II

Napoleon! Oh Napoleon! This new Jugurtha
Has been vanquished: it rots, in chains, in some low gaol...

See Jugurtha turn in the shadow to face another warrior
And with a calming voice murmur these words to him:
"Give yourself, my son, to the new God! Abandon your woes!
Witness the dawn of a better day... France will break
Your chains... And you will see Algeria, under French dominion,
Prosper: You will accept the treaty of a generous nation,
And soon be made great by a great country, a priest
Of justice and sworn faith... Love your father Jugurtha
With all your heart... And always remember his destiny!

III

"For the Genius of Arab shores will be revealed!"

Rimbaud Jean-Nicolas-Arthur.
Day Student at le Collège de Charleville

"Olim inflatus . . ." ("Long ago . . .") also ran in Le Moniteur de l'Enseignement secondaire, *on April 15, 1870. Composed during the prior academic year, though at an unknown date, this composition represents a more straightforward example of translation, though with some expansion. Rimbaud was given a text by the abbé Delille in French detailing the fight between Hercules and the river Achelous, who had lost out to Hercules for the hand of Deianira, whom Achelous had loved. Rimbaud translated Delille's version into Latin. Delille's version in turn was a translation into French of Ovid's Latin telling (*Metamorphoses, *IX), which was doubtless a translation and expansion from Hesiod's Greek.*

"LONG AGO . . ."

Long ago, Achelous' swollen waters rose from his broad bed,
A tumult that irrupted across sloping valleys, over rolling
Herds and through the yellowing harvest's waves.
Men's houses perished while fields flourished, reaching to
Faraway deserts. The Nymph abandoned her valley,
The choruses of Fauns fell silent: all watched
The fury of the flood. Hercules, hearing their pleas,
Compassion's waters rose within him: so he tried to brake
The river's fury, throwing his gigantic body
Into the greater waves, his powerful arms driving back
The foaming breakers, taming them to their beds.
From the beaten river rose a wrathful murmuring wave.
And in a flash, the river god took a serpent's shape:
He hissed and gnashed, buckled his blue back,
And beat the trembling banks with his furious tail.
So: Hercules leapt; his meaty arms wound
Around the writhing neck, tightening; and despite resistance,
Hercules crushed it, whipping a tree trunk
Across its tired back, laying the river god half-dead upon the black sand.

Hercules turned towards him, fiercely, shaking: "Impudent beast, you dare Defy the
Arms of Hercules? My arms were made for this,
A lesson first learned in my crib—surely you must have heard—
Where and when these arms undid two dragons . . . !"

Shame stirred the river god to rebellion, his heart
Heavy, sorrowing the sullied honor of his name;
His ferocious eyes burned with ardor like two fires.
Horns rose from his terrible brow and winds awoke.
Horribly he lowed, and the air shuddered with his lowing.
But Alcmena's son wasn't impressed . . . and struck:
Leaping, grabbing, shaking, and upending
Its flailing body once again onto the ground: Hercules pressed his knee to its neck
Which cracked; and, tightening his powerful grip around its gasping mouth,
He crushed and squashed it with all his power, until it groaned its last.
From the dead beast's bleeding brow, magnificent Hercules rent
A horn—memento of his mettle. Then the Fauns
And the choruses of Dryads and their sister Nymphs,
Whose lands and wealth the victor had avenged,
Approached the hero slumbering beneath a tree
Reliving all his ancient exploits in joyful sleep.
Their merry band surrounded him: they decked his brow
With a crown of flowers and decorated it in garlands of green.
And all of them seized the horn that lay next to him
With a single hand, and filled this bloody trophy
To overflowing with fruits and fragrant flowers.

Rimbaud

Day Student, Collège de Charleville

"Tempus erat..." ("In those days...") was written in Latin for Rimbaud's professor George Izambard, and translated and augmented here and there from a French original. The piece ran in Le Moniteur de l'Enseignement secondaire *on April 15, 1870.*

"IN THOSE DAYS ..."

In those days, Jesus lived in Nazareth.
The child grew in virtue as he grew in age.
One morning, when the roofs of the houses had just begun to blush,
Jesus rose from bed, the others still preyed upon by sleep,
So that when Joseph awoke the work would be completed.
Leaning on the work in progress, face serene,
Jesus pushed a huge saw forward and back
Cutting board after board with his boyish arm.
In the distance, the sun shone on high mountains,
And a silver beam entered through low windows.
See the cowhands leading their herds through the pastures,
Vying with each other in admiration for the young worker
And the sounds of morning work.
"Who is this child?" they asked. His face contained
Both gravity and beauty; strength shook from his arms.
This young laborer worked the cedar artfully, like a seasoned laborer;
Long ago, Hiram himself hadn't worked with any greater ardor
When, in the presence of Salomon, he cut cedars and girders
For the temple with powerful, able hands.
Yet the body of the boy bent with greater suppleness
Like a delicate reed; and his axe rose to his shoulder and fell true,
Over and again.

But, his mother, hearing the grumbling of saw and blade,
Had left her bed, and in silence entering softly

Anxiously observed her child hard at work
Moving all that wood…; lips clenched,
She watched and although she held him gently in
Her peaceful gaze, unsaid words trembled on her lips.
Laughter danced in her tears… But suddenly the saw
Buckled and cut the fingers of the unsuspecting child.
His white shirt stained with crimson blood,
And a mild cry escaped his lips… but suddenly sensing
His mother, he hid his reddening fingers beneath his clothes;
And, pretending to smile, he greeted his mother.
But she, throwing herself at her son's feet, alas,
Caressed his fingers in her fingers and lowered gentle hands
While weeping and wetting her face with tears.
But the child, stoic: "Why, my foolish mother, are you crying!
Because the saw's edge grazed my finger!
The time for tears is yet to come!"
And then he returned to work; and his mother, silent
And pale, turned her white face to the ground,
Deep in thought, and once again with her son's face before her eyes
And with sad eyes, said: "Oh Great God, may your holy will be done!"

A. Rimbaud

"Verba apollonii de Marco Cicerone" is another performance by Rimbaud once again saved from obliteration by Le Moniteur de l'Enseignement secondaire, *appearing in its April 15, 1870, issue. This piece, Rimbaud's longest Latin work, takes a five-point Latin outline and makes it breathe with the blood of Apollonius Molo, the Greek orator who opened schools of rhetoric in Rhodes and Rome, and whose pupils included Julius Caesar and Cicero. We imagine Cicero has just finished his presentation, and the teacher takes the floor, to gush.*

APOLLONIUS THE GREEK SPEAKS OF MARCUS CICERO

You have heard, my disciples, Cicero's speech in which he seemed convincingly Greek during a speech in Greek, truthful in making fiction seem fact, and not a bit like a boy in a schoolboy exercise. And such penetrating argumentation, such acuity and discernment in his articulation of the facts, such force and heartbreaking peroration! And above all such elegance and abundance in shape of expression! How magnificently the periods fall into place, one upon the next! It's no accident that nature wished to decorate Cicero with every gift: Rome needs him to hearken back to the eloquence of the Gracchi, the eloquence of Brutus; real trials demand his attentions, real thieves deserve denunciation in the name of innocence and of art itself. Courage then, young man: you who make your voice heard today in this scholarly vault will soon utter harangues in the forum, before an audience that will applaud you no less than I do today, I am sure. May I not be proud that such an orator has emerged from my class? It will be my greatest glory to have shaped your study of the art of words, or rather to have grown old as I witnessed the blossoming of your abilities: what greater or sweeter reward than to be known as Cicero's old teacher? Perhaps this glory will have its own posterity. But you, my students, I think are able to recognize the superiority of Cicero's unrivaled gifts. Praise him as I do, and surely imitate him: one day you will be proud to say that you studied with Cicero.

But even in so great a joy lurks sadness and regret; for though I do not hesitate an instant in praising the intelligence and eloquence of Marcus Tullius Cicero, I cannot forget that he is Roman. You, Cicero, who best all my other pupils, are Roman, a Roman I shaped and taught! All of Greece has been overrun by Rome; it consoles itself, perhaps, over the loss of its liberty, with the thought that though its might holds no dominion over the earth, its genius still does. You Romans envy us this unassailable empire; you would see us dethroned from dominion over the kingdom of words that you might appropriate the one thing you do not own! After Corinth and the other Greek cities, Rome took all our wealth, moving our paintings to Rome, as well as the gold and silver that now decorates their temples and public buildings: soon Rome will seek to rend the last remaining glory from our ruined country that still survives intact in our crumbled cities! We prefer to think that our writers are beyond imitation, that the age of Pericles is unique in history. And then this Roman age rises, measuring itself against its ancestor, claiming itself capable of birthing poets worthy of Sophocles and Euripides, poets of our unrivaled Periclean age; claiming itself capable of birthing orators worthy of Lysias and Isocrates, philosophers worthy of Plato and Xenophon, and greater minds still whose wisdom is beyond imagining. It is not unlikely that Rome will soon have triumphed over even the art of Greece: already they rival us, with Plautus Rudius as their Aristophanes and Terence for our Menander. For Terence is already a household name even to the Greeks. Some call him half-Menander, and would place him at the top of the heap and could not be considered inferior to the Greeks... if he had been able to unite his comic drive to a pure and elegant style. Better yet, the Romans are pioneering their own genres: they believe satire is their creation; Lucilus was essentially the first to explore this form of moral rectitude, and doubtless poets to come will honor this form through their inventions. What can I say of the orators? Surely you've already heard about the eloquence of the Gracchi, and about famous Brutus's oratorical verve? And you, Marcus Tullius, do you not rival our orators? Is that the reason why so many young Romans find themselves in our schools, where we teach them by the example of our illustrious forebears? For if the gods themselves decided that we would shape our own conquerors, this itself comes from Greek literature: in essence, the Romans greet this fight renewed; on the contrary, we come to it as schoolmasters and decadents; who but the ancients do we heap with praise? There are no more orators or poets burgeoning in Greece; but Rome is bursting with new and imminent writers, while the Greek genius seems to have been completely snuffed out. Essentially, how could it have been otherwise? How can I stand before you today and bemoan your looming victory without acknowledging a loss of eloquence equal to our loss of liberty? Eloquence was in full bloom when we were free to lead our land; now that our liberty has been crushed and trampled underfoot, we're little but an instrument in the hands of a governor installed to oversee Rome's holdings: we remember how Pericles praised our citizens fallen in defense of our country: but will we praise those of our citizens carried off and conscripted into the service of the Roman empire, falling under the sword at the distant ends of the earth? Demosthenes, we know, attacked Philipus in stinging speeches and shamed the traitors to his city. But today would we attack our enemy, given how we handed the country over to him? Eloquence flourished when the laws were born in the agora, when our orators, throughout their harangues, addressed themselves to the gods of the country, its people, its statues of great men. Now laws are imposed upon us by a Roman governor and we haven't the wherewithal to oppose them or him. Like liberty, eloquence has perished beneath the lictor's rod: ever since, all we've been able to do is flip though the pages of the ancients and find those speeches they once spoke in public squares. We no longer debate what matters; we bat around empty, abstract notions to ensure that our conquerors find nothing criminal in our actions. One day in Rome, Tullius too will be missed, when some tyrant once again herds eloquence from the forum and into the schools: for eloquence is the voice of liberty; how then could it ever suffer the untimely yoke of tyranny?

Nonetheless my students, may none of this deter you in your studies, and may all those whom I have already known to be studious remain for-

---

Philipus: Of Macedonia, in the *Philipics.*

ever faithful to themselves; of course this is no consolation to us for the loss of glory, we who've lost everything but the images of our heroes; if we were remembering the mark of those days when we blossomed in the midst of all the good that coursed over the earth, covering it with fountains, cities, colonies; if we were remembering our conquest of all of Asia and nearly all of Italy, what feeling could we have but regret in remembering our glory and prosperity, what sentiments but anger and sorrow when we consider the destiny that awaits our Gaul. But since the ineluctable law of the gods has decided that it will be conquered and scorned as Greece was before it, this mother, this wet nurse of warriors, all thoughts or ideas of glory are driven from our minds. All that remains to us is the consolation of the arts, of study and thought, for it is the joy that remains within our sorrow, some shade of liberty within servitude; we turn our gaze away from our present humiliation and instead towards the dignity of our ancient authors, and we rejoice at the sweet dialogue mined from within their books, between Homer and Plato and the like, not about public matters that aren't ours to decide any longer, but instead about poetry, the immortal gods, and all the subjects about which these great men so admirably spoke. And if the gods permit it, you as well, Tullius, whom I found gifted with so brilliant a spirit, will not betray me or my hopes as you return to your land; and in the middle of the applause of the people, do not forget this Greek, Apollonious, who shaped you through study and verbal discipline, and always believe that the applause that doubtless will greet you will bring you no greater joy and pride than it gives me to hear you have.

Rimbaud

"Invocation à Vénus" ("Invocation to Venus") appeared in Le Moniteur de l'Enseignement secondaire *on April 15, 1870. The assignment was to translate the first twenty-seven lines of Lucretius'* De rerum natura *into French. Rimbaud did this with customary facility and flair, though the means to his ends were entirely new to him: he plagiarized most of it, but it still won him honors, as the theft was not discovered until 1922 when Jules Mouquet compared Rimbaud's work to a translation by Parnassian Sully-Prudhomme that had appeared in May 1869, a few months before the supposed composition of Rimbaud's "translation." Rimbaud's is twenty-six lines whereas Prudhomme's was twenty-four; thus Rimbaud added a few words, made some changes that most critics consider tasteful improvements. Thus it was a creative endeavor for Rimbaud, although chiefly editorial. It is interesting to note that this piece made the fourth work of Rimbaud's to appear in the April 15* Moniteur, *making it very nearly a de facto chapbook.*

INVOCATION TO VENUS

O godly delights, mortal delights,
Beneath the sky's stars, you, Venus,
Mother of Aeneas' sons, inhabit everything.
Waves alive with scudding ships, and fecund soil:
Through you, every being breathes, grows,
Turns, sees the luminous sun. You appear . . .
The sight of your radiant brow dispels
Winds and dark clouds. The Ocean
Smiles; fertile with its makings,
The Earth conjures flowers beneath your steps;
Bright day shines purer still beneath the azure heavens.
As April reappears and swells with youth,
Ready to convey sweet tenderness to all.
The Zephyr's breath has breached its prison,
The aerial world announces your season;

Charmed, the birds submit to your will, o Goddess;
The wild herd leaps into the thick grass
And swimming splits the wave, and every living thing
Is slave to your grace, burning in your pursuit.
Through seas and storms and mountain ranges
Nesting woods and greening hills, you spill
Enduring love into every heart that carries
Each and all from age to age to propagate the race.
The world knows nothing, Venus, but your empire.
Nothing wakes without you; neither inspiration
Nor love: to your work my own aspires.

A. Rimbaud.

Day Student at le Collège de Charleville.

This piece is also known in French by the title "From Charles d'Orléans to Louis XI." This assignment was written for Rimbaud's teacher George Izambard, and the English title has been ascribed to it by editors, rather than being penned by Rimbaud. This homework assignment was different from the others in this section in that it was not a translation but a literary research project, which required Rimbaud to steep himself in the language of other writers, particularly that of François Villon (his Petit Testament *and* Grand Testament*) and Charles d'Orléans. This type of assignment was known, during the period, as a* devoir de discours français, *a study in French discourse.*

"SIRE, TIME HAS ABANDONED HIS RAINCOAT . . ."

Sire, time has abandoned his raincoat; the harbingers of summer are here: we slam the door in Mérencolie's face! Long lives ballads and lays! Morality plays and farces! May the clerics of the secret society of Basoche mount them for our pleasure: let us hear of the Wiseman and the Fool; of the conversion of Theophilus the cleric; of how Saints Peter and Paul went to Rome and were martyred! Long live ladies in doubled collars and embroidered finery! Is it not excellent, Sire, when beneath the trees and blue-robed skies, when the bright sun gleams, to voice sweet rondos and ballads sung bright and clear? *There's a tree in the forest of love* or *Say yes but once, sweet lady* or *Rich in love is always better* . . . Well Sire . . . you see I've gotten all riled up, but you too will end up like me: Master François Villon, happy as the day is long, who gently jeers life into rhyme, like a cricket caught indoors, feeding on peasant bread and water, crying and bemoaning his condition at the foot of Châtelet! You shall be hung! So he was informed before the notary: and chilled to the bone the poor mischief-maker made an epitaph for himself and his companions: and the gracious gallants whose rhymes you love so well wait to dance at Montfaulcon, more pecked by birds than thimbles, in drizzle and sun!

Oh Sire! Villon isn't some sort of joke! Those poor dusters have their own problems. Clerics await appointments to the university; idlers, monkey-peddlers, rebec players who pay their way in song, stable-jockeys, two-penny kings, roughneck soldiers hiding their noses in pewter pots more than in war helmets:* all these poor kids—dirty and dry as cannon mops, whose only glimpse of bread is in shop windows, numb fingers bundled up in winter—picked master François as their wet nurse! But necessity often leads to misunderstanding, and hunger makes the wolf leap from the woods: perhaps Escollier, one hungry day, took tripe from butchers' vats to make a fricassee at Popin's watering hole or Pestel's tavern? Maybe he snagged a dozen loaves from the baker, or switched a bottle of water with one of Baigneux wine over at the *Pomme du Pin*? Maybe one wild night on the Plat d'Étain, he outfoxed an ambush upon his arrival; or did they surprise him, near Montfaulcon, during a querulous supper with a dozen whores? These are the misfits of master François! He sketches a portly clergyman lolling in bed with a dame; says the chaplain can't trifle right now with taking confession... except from chambermaids... and ladies. To mock his flock, he suggests contemplation while under house arrest, contemplation while peering up at that particular necklace, so jolly and charming, beautiful as a birds, all this while they tremble beneath the claws of their judges, those terrifying black birds who rule in the wakes of magpies and crows! He and his companions, such a poor, pitiful bunch, add a new string of hanged men to the arms of the forest: the wind turns them into smoldering stews in the soft, sonorous leaves; and you, Sire, and everyone who loves the poet, can't help but laugh and cry while reading his joyous ballads: they dream they left the singing cleric to die, and can't hunt Mérencolie!

Piper and thief, master François is nonetheless the earth's best son: he scoffs at plump Jacobean stews: but he honors the church of Christ, and Mother Mary, and the very Holy Trinity! He honors the house of Parliament, mother of all that's good, and sister of the blessed angels; to the nay-sayers of the kingdom of France, he would wish as much evil upon them as—By God!—tavern-keepers who boil their wine. He knows all too well that he was but bile in his mad youth! Winter, foodless nights

*Olivier Basselin, *Vaux-de-Vire*. [Rimbaud's note.]

around the Maubuay fountain or in some ruined pool, crouching before a hemp fire reddening his gaunt face, he dreams of having a house and a soft bed, had he only studied . . . ! Often as black and hot as a sorcerer on horseback, he stares through mortises into houses: "Oh those savory, delicate morsels: tarts, flans, fat golden gelatins! I'm hungrier than Tantalus! Roast! Roast! —It smells sweeter than amber, than rodents! Wine from the Beaune in great silver vessels! It burns my throat! Oh if I had only studied! —And my chausses make me thirsty, and my threadbare cape, and my hat's saw-toothed brim! Would that I came upon some sad Alexander who would welcome me warmly however inappropriately I was attired— and to him I could sing as I wished like that sweet fiddler Orpheus! Would I could live honorably, once, before I died!" So that's it: living on rondos, the reflection of moonlight on old rooftops, lantern-light on the ground: slim pickings indeed; then, all decked out, little cuties pass by wearing next to nothing, as if in promise of a decent lay; then, the memory of wild taverns, filled with shouts of drinkers tossing tin pots and sometimes swords, snickering laughter; voices of beggars' rebecs; the memory of old black roads where the floors and girders of houses jut madly into the road as if to kiss; or, during the thick dark night, passing with the sounds of rapiers dragged along, laughter and horrible howls . . . And the bird returns nest near taverns and girls!

Oh Sire! We can't raise our rudders to the wind in this time of joy! The hangman's rope droops in May, when everything sings and laughs, when the sun shines on even the most leprous walls! There will be hanged men to celebrate! Villon is in parliamentary hands: the executioner won't listen to some little bird! Sire, it would be wrong to hang these gentle clerics: these poets, you see, are not from down here: let them live their strange lives, let them go hungry and grow cold. Let them run, love and sing: these mad children are as rich as Jacques Cœur; rhyme fills their souls, rhymes that laugh and cry, that make us laugh and cry: let them live. God blesses the merciful: let the world bless the poets.

A. Rimbaud

Jacques Cœur: Fourteenth-century merchant of extraordinary wealth.

II. FROM A SCHOOL NOTEBOOK

Less a notebook than a coverless collection of unlined pages, the following document has proved a source of debate within the French scholarly community for over a century. What has been called the "Prologue" (reproduced in the Prose section, page 159, with regularized spelling and punctuation), is presented in many editions as Rimbaud's earliest surviving work, while it is actually an excerpt from this notebook, never before presented in its entirety in English. The excerpt was first published in 1897, but the complete text of the notebook did not appear in French print until 1956 in Suzanne Briet's RNP. *She gave it the title "Notebook, age 10," offering the scholarly surmise debated ever since: was he ten, or eleven, when he wrote it? The possibility that the entire notebook could have been written by Rimbaud at ten, no matter how precocious he doubtless was, is made problematic by a familiarity with Greek and Latin forms that he would have been less likely to have known that scholastic year. Regardless, the precise date of its composition must remain speculative. The notebook consists principally of Rimbaud's paraphrases and translations of classical texts, only some of which are known, and offers readers insight into the rigors of his early education. I have reproduced the text with the line breaks as they appear in the notebook. Their brevity is due to Rimbaud's having written two columns of text to a page. There are numerous errors of spelling and grammar in the several languages employed, and I have elected not to reproduce those errors (when he misspells his own name, I leave it, for fun). Lastly, I have omitted those sections that are in a Latin incomprehensible even to classicists, such as Rimbaud's thorny paraphrases of the Vulgate Bible. The ●'s represent ink spots Rimbaud left on the page.*

FROM A SCHOOL NOTEBOOK

P.1, c.1

Aristomanes lifted himself up, extended
his hand and met the hairy
skin of a very large
animal. Attracted
by the scent of the cadavers
it was a fox who frequently
fed upon unfortunates
fallen into the abyss. so a
glimmer of hope, however slight it
was, shined for Aristomanes[.] he decided
that this animal had known
a way out and that he could manage to leave
this horrible place. he straightaway grabbed
the fox's tail as he was turning to
bite him but Aristomanes presented him
with the backside of his left arm
covered in a scrap of fabric that he
had ● collected to use as blankets at
night. The fox, desperate to
best his enemy, that couldn' . . . ●
stop the contusions caused
by the crevices in the rocks, nor
the horrible rips they made upon him. . . .
the bramble and thorns, he finally noticed
an opening hidden by where the
light came through and through which penetrat . . . doubtless

---

P.1, c.1: "P" designates the original page of the notebook, "c" the column on that page. *Aristomanes:* A general of Messenia dating from the seventh century before Christ who fought a thirty-year struggle against the Lacedaemonians, whom he eventually vanquished.

the foxes: so Aristomanes let go and

tried to flee but at the same time
he dragged behind him

reaching the opening, he widened it
with all possible effort. For
the spirit of life and love and
liberty, he would soon meet up again with

P.1, c.2

[the] Lacedaemonians, throwing all he had...
at them once again, and seeming to
the Lacedaemonians as a vision of vengeance,
escaped to punish them for
their unspeakable cowardice ____

Croesus

Croesus, who doesn't dare buck the recommendations
of the oracle, no matter how much he might believe
that with his forces alone he would be in
good shape to best Cyrus, cautiously sent
ambassadors to Sparta, to convince
the Lacedaemonians to ally with them
they said the following: "Croesus, Lydia's king,
would have us tell you in his voice: o Lacedaemonians,
The God of Delphi ordered me to make
peace with the Greeks, and I speak to you
because I have learned that you are the 1st
people of Greece. I want us to

Croesus: According to Pierre Brunel, the story paraphrased by Rimbaud comes from Herodotus's *Histories, Book I,* in which Herodotus tells of Croesus, King of Lydia (from 563–548 B.C.), last of the Mermnadae, who made peace with Greece so they might crush Cyrus of Persia, who had invaded Lydia.

ally honestly, without treachery: nothing
stood in the way of the Lacedaemonians,
hungry for glory, to accept the proposition
of the Lydian king; and they had heard
the oracle's response, and they were very
flattered that the Lydians had come
to them so it wasn't difficult to
persuade them to enter into friendship
with Croesus, and the promis . . . to send
him deputies for a start, and soon
after an army corps . . .
[. . .]
But Cyrus didn't wait for them to have
received reinforcements,

P.2, c.1

Pretty little flies that the desire
overcame me to describe them. the next day
I saw another kind that I descr[ibed]
I so observed over the course of three week[s]
thirty-seven radically
different species but in
end there were so
many and of such variety,
that I abandoned these studies
however interesting, because
I needed a rest, or, to
tell the truth, I didn't have the words. the
flies I had observed
were easily distinguished from
one another by their colors,

Pretty little flies that the desire: Suzanne Briet in her *RNP* (p. 47) notes that Rimbaud is leapfrogging roughly through a section of Bernardin de Saint-Pierre's *Studies of Nature.*

their shapes and their attrac[tiveness]
some were golden,
some green, or bronze,
or tiger-striped, or striped
with blue, or brown
or cloudy and glistening[.]
some had heads
rounded like a turban
while others stretched to points
and a few seemed
as dark as
a corner of black velvet
and it sparked ●
others like ●
rubies there wasn't any less
variety to their wings
A few were
long and shiny
like mother-of-pearl blades
others, short and fat
that resembled reticula
of the finest gauze, some

P.2, c.2

glided whirling
while others rose while
heading against the wind,
by a mechanism very
nearly the same as those of
paper kites
that rise, at
an angle to the axis
of the wind
[…]

P.4, c.1

there is no animal with the exception of man ● which has some
notion of god but among men there is no
nation so savage as that it doesn't believe in a
god but because in all things ● consent of
nations on must avow that some sort of divine power exists
disputing with the gods is a bad habit
and is iniquitous should that be done seriously either as
a joke which is why the greatest sophist of his time
Protagoras denied at the beginning of a book that the gods
existed, and was run from the city under order of the Athenians
and his books were burned on the public squares. It
is further told that a talent of silver was to be given to him
who killed him as [?] doubt over the existence of the gods
avoid his punishment which is so intense that him who,
when he would have seen heaven would not have known there was a
god.
the beauty of the world the order of things and the revolutions of
sun and moon and all the stars indic[ates] enough by their
appearance that aren't the result of chance and proves to us that some
sort some sort of superior and eternal order exists
that but be ● admired by the human type
rimbaud arthur *deinde pendata gens indica nonne petebent* A
rimbaud arthur *deinde pendata gens indica nonne petebent* A
deinde
deinde Secur quod est preciperam
deinde Secur quod est preciperam
deinde Secur quod est preciperam
deinde Secur quod est preciperam

P.4, c.1: In all likelihood a translation or paraphrase of an unidentified Latin text, not precocious religio-philosophical reflections.

deinde Secur quod est preciperam
deinde Secur quod est preciperam
deinde Secur quod est preciperam

P.5, c.1

When the roman republic was administered
By those to whom in had been confided, Cicero brought
Him all his thoughts and cares and he
Took great pains to act rather than write
When the power fell into the hands
of Julius Caesar he didn't give in
to the worries that weighed upon him,
nor to the pleasures of a worthless sort of man

Arthur
The infinitely little
However small these insects may have been, they
were worthy of my attention, since they
had been worthy of that the creator. Therefore
I continued my observations, however inexact they
must have been; for I must always ignore
that the insects which frequented my
rosebushes during the night, perhaps attracted
by phosphorescent light we do not see.
while examining the leaves of
● my plant close up under a micro
scope, I found them divided into compartments
bristling with tiny hairs and separated by canals......
to me these compartments seemed identical
to the great green floors and their hairy
plants, among which there were
forked threads of gold, nature having done nothing

---

deinde Secur quod est preciperam: The one person who might have some insight into precisely what this means is long gone. It is, apparently, the verbal equivalent of an abstract doodle.

in vain. When she makes use of places ready
to be inhabited, she puts animals there.
you never see her limit the growth
of a region; one may therefore believe, without
f●hypothesis that there are animals

P.5, c.2

That weigh upon the leaves of Art
Plants like the animals
In our fields; that
Sleep in the shadow of their
[...] imperceptible and which
find in the plains
of a few millimeters
spectacles which we don...
no idea the yellow anthers
of flowers, suspended.... Upon
white swaths, presenting them
with double golden joists in
perfect balance on columns
more beautiful than polished ivory;
the corollas of the canopies, ruby
and topaz, of incommensurable
grandeur; the nectars
of the sugary rivers; the other parts
of the blossoming cups,
urns, pavilions, domes that
neither man's architects nor silversmiths......
have managed to imitate.
In Cato's discourse
Invenitur in virtutes

Cato's: Marcus Porcius Cato, also known as Censorious, a Roman warrior and statesman who became censor of Rome and later wrote a treatise on farming, *De Re Rustica. Invenitur in virtutes:* "The virtue of invention."

we find all the qualities
Catoni omes qualitates
of the orator. It is said that the bees
have a king. When one serves the laws
one serves God, it is said
that the lion fears
the cock's crow. When
one loves others one has suf
ficient virtue.
when one gives to a beggar,
one gives to God himself.

P.6, c.1

one sells one's liberty when one
accepts a kindness. When
one interrogates with treachery,
one does not deserve to hear
the truth. One can barely
change the opinion of the
people when one wishes peace,
one prepares for war while
never ceasing to regret having
kept silent. with those things great
enough and worthy of being remembered,
one looks at the plans first, and then
what was actually accomplished

—Arthur

P.7, c.1

when Aesop was the slave of a tyrant,
he was ordered to prepare dinner.

Catoni[s] om[n]es qualitates: "All of Cato's qualities." *when Aesop… his lantern:* Brunel locates this story in Phaedrus's *Fables,* the Latin "*Aesopus ad garrulum,*" "Aesop to the Chatterbox."

needing fire, he left the house....
to house. At last he found where
to rest his lantern
●
could you think yourself my equal, you and I
● have very different
Destinies, I spend my
life in the temples and palaces
of kings, as it pleases me. I do 14
nothing, and enjoy the finest things 13
whereas you work 2
ceaselessly and lead a very hard 2
life." The ant responded: "you 3
do nothing, it is true, and now en —
joy many advantages; but 34
when the more difficult season comes,
your destiny will change with the weather
cold and hunger will soon carry you off
I on the other hand will find a house
well in advance and will spend the winter
securely. it is glorious, you say, to
live among kings and gods; there's more
enterprise in work."

P.7, c.2

what is the area of a piece of land whose length
Is 252m 80 and whose width is 78m 600 at the end and 84m 20 at the

if 20 liters cost 3250 what is the price of 7 [...]
if 2 cubic meters of wood cost

"The ant... enterprise in work": More Phaedrus, c.f. Brunel. This time his *Formica et musca,* "The Ant and the Fly," a story more familiar to us in the version by La Fontaine (1621–95) in his "La Cigale et la Fourmi," popularly known as "The Ant and the Grasshopper," an instance of translation in which the staid "cicada" was replaced by the apparently more appealing grasshopper.

[…]

Aesop (continued
so, because it had had been so long
that he had been on the road, he hurried
back to the square when a chatterbox

from the crowd he spoke to him: Aesop, what are you doing in daylight
with a lantern
I am looking for a man, he said and he hurried back to the house

P.8, c.1

If 2 cubic meters of wood cost 32f
how much would 7 decimeters cost

32	2		1 f 60
12	16	10	7
00	60	1 f 60	11,20
000			

inasmuch as man approaches
elements of matter, the principles
of its science disappear and
when he looks to advance in ——
infinite space, his frustrated intel
ligence is lost in the face
of so many greater marvels.
in essence, grab a magnifying glass,
and watch matter multiply, so
to speak, with attention to the extent that
his works diminish in volume
look at the gold, the crimson, the azure, the mother-of-pearl
and all the [wrongs?] with which she occasionally

embellishes the cuirass of the ugliest
insect. Look at the gleaming network
she spreads across the wing of a mite
look at that multitude of eyes, these
clear-sighted crowns which she
rings around the heads of
flies it seems to……
contemplate creation, which
tenderly tries to prevail
over magnificence. Upon examination
the eye of a whale or elephant

P.8, c.2

reveal details whose tininess
hides them from our eyes; and these
details aren't, seen close up,
aren't the last nor where the work ends
art

In genesis, the begin
nings of the world were first
recounted by Moses. the light,
he said comma, the firmament
the earth the plants, the sun,
the fish, the birds and
all the animals were suc
cessively created by God
then man was made.
Adam, the first man,
and eve, the first woman,
were put in a delicious
garden, there they were free……
and happy. By this bliss
wasn't to last long.

Eve was seduced by the serpent,
Adam was led by Eve
to evil; guilty, husband and wife
were chased from paradise by the lord......
annoyed and since then work......
sorrow, illness, the ter......
and every misery
came to them
        Prejudice
the Athenians were brought together in
a theater, called to judge a
celebrated historian who had
already come to possess a great renown
in the varied cities of Greece,
with the skill he used
to imitate the calls

P.9, c.1

of animals, I attempted in vain to
portray the level of enthusiasm with which
they greeted they greeted his presence
applause, stamping of feet, and laughter
to which all the world would have given way:
the most morose of men would have had
to laugh and applaud
like all the rest. Nevertheless, amidst
such general satisfaction, a farmer
too was there and elected to
complain about all the admiration that
he held was unmerited I predict,
he said, to prove to you that this man
is not worth all the praise you lavish upon him, nor
that you so cherish.

Maxims

fili mi ne judicas homines
quun vides illorum conspectun
nam saepe, si divites sunt, mali
sunt. Rimbaud athur [*sic*] de Charville
n° loqueris hominis impis nam
mox illi similis eris
volo tibi fabulam narrare
ut conservas præceptum
discipulus posuerat malum ma
lam in mensà et circum mi
serat aliorum malorum
bonarum mox illæ malæ
fient. Est sic hominis
frequentas impias. arthur……

[…]

The stag and the bull….
A stag chased from forests
he had been using as a hideout
ran in blind fear into
a neighboring farm to avoid
imminent death with which
the hunters had him threatened
and hid himself in a stable full
of cattle that presented itself
at the perfect moment. Rimbaud arthur

---

fili mi…mali sunt: "My son, do not judge men on their looks, for often, if they are rich, they are evil." *n° loqueris…frequentas impias:* "Speak not of the sinner, for soon you will be just as he. I should tell you a fable to instill this precept. A student set a rotten apple on a table beside some bad apples [*sic*], and soon the good apples will too be bad. So it is the same if you spend time among sinners." *The stag and the bull:* Phaedrus, *Fables,* "*Cervus et boves.*"

Charleville *illusar ipse ab illud isp......*
iniqui serius aut ocius dant pœmas
malifici.

P.10, c.1

I.

Prologue

The sun was still hot;
nonetheless now it barely illuminated
the earth; just like
a torch placed before
gigantic vaults doesn't
cast much more than a
weak glimmer so the
sun earthly torch
is snuffed out while
a final weak glimmer escapes
from its fiery body
nonetheless allowing one to
see the green leaves of the
trees the little flowers that
wilt and the gigantic
summits of the pines,
poplars and age-old oaks.
the refreshing wind, meaning
a cool breeze stirs
the leaves of the trees with a rustling
nearly the same as the noise
from silver streams which

---

illusar... malifici: "Wrongful damage brings punishment sooner or later." *Prologue:* The original home of "The sun was still hot..." (see p. 159).

flow at my feet. the ferns
bend their green foreheads to...
the wind, I went to sleep but
not before having drunk water
from the stream.
I dreamt that . . . .
. . . .

... I was born in Reims in 1503
Reims was then a little town
or better said a village
nonetheless known because of
its beautiful cathedral, witness
to the coronation of king Clovis.

P.10, c.2

My parents weren't very rich
but very honest; they had
nothing but a little
house that had always
belonged to them and which was
in their possession twenty
years before I was
born and also a few thousand francs
to which we should add the
few louis d'or whose provenance
was my mother's thrift......
my father was an officer* in
the king's army, he was a
tall man, thin,
black hair, beard, eyes, skin
all the same color...... although

**colonel des cent-gardes.* [Rimbaud's footnote.]

when I was born he was only
48 or fifty one would
have said he was easily
60 or...... 58 he was
brusque, hotheaded,
often angry and never willing
to suffer what displeased him
my mother was very dif
ferent sweet woman, calm,
easily startled, and
nonetheless kept the house in
perfect order... she was
so calm, that my father
entertained her like
a little girl. they loved me
best my brothers were less
courageous than I though
taller: I didn't like
studying meaning learning
to read, write, and count......

P.11, c.1

but fixing up a
house or gardening, or
running errands, that's fine, I
like doing all that.
I still remember a day
my father promised me twenty
sous if I did a division
problem properly; I started; but I
couldn't finish. ah! how many times
had he promised me... sous
toys treats even

five francs one time if I could
. . . read . . . something to him . . . des
pite that my father put me in
school as soon as I turned ten.
Why, I asked myself, learn
Greek and Latin? I don't know. really
who needs it what do I care
if I pass . . . . . . what does it matter
if I pass, right? Sure they say that
you won't get a job if you don't pass I
don't want a job I'll be independently wealthy anyway why learn latin
even if you want one; no one
even speaks it sometimes
I see it in newspapers but
thank God I'll never be a journalist
why learn history and geography? Sure
you need to know that Paris is in France
but no one ever asks what latitude learning about the lives of
Chinaldon of
Nabopolassar of Darius of Cyrus and of Alexander

P.11, c.2

and their other historical pals with
diabolical names, it's tor
ture? ——————————
What do I care if Alexander
was famous? Who cares . . .
who knows if the Latins even existed?
maybe it's some sort of made up language
and even if they had existed then
why can't they just leave me to be
independently wealthy and keeping
their language to themselves what

did I—ever do to them that they
lead me to this torture. and Greek.....
that dirty language isn't spoken
by a single soul in the world!......
ah *saperlipotte de saperlopopette* ●
sapristi I'll be independently wealthy
it's a waste to wear out the seat
of your pants on the benches.....
saperlipopettouille!
to be a shoeshine to get a job as
a shoeshine you have to take a test
because the jobs you are offered are
either shoeshine or swineherd or cattlehand
thank god none of that's for me
saperlipouille!
you get paid with slaps
in the face they call you an
animal which isn't true
little fella etc
More soon
ah *saperpopuillotte!*"
Arth.......

[...]

P.12, c.2

III

Post vivenda res, expectas finem.
The pact
there are a few more things for me to

---

saperlipotte...: See footnote on p. 160.

write but I'm stopping
intentionally 1st out of fear that I would
seem importunate whosoever occupies
[himself with] the range of your affairs
to come, if someone wants to try,
perhaps the same thing,
he [will] find examples in the
body of the work for nature
is in such abundance that it's
more likely that the artisan is insufficient for the task than the task for the artisan....

[....]

III. FRAGMENTS AND RECONSTRUCTIONS

A. VIA RIMBAUD

"Credo in unam" was an early draft of "Sun and Flesh." The chief difference between the two versions is the inclusion in the former of a long section between parts three and four that was ultimately cut, and reproduced below.

From CREDO IN UNAM

Free and proud, Man raised his head!
And the first glimmer of original beauty
Shook the god in the altar of flesh!
Happy with the present good, sad for sufferings past,
Man would sound the depths—would know!
Thought—a mare long stabled and broken
Leaps from his brow! She must learn *Why . . . !*
Let her leap, let Man find Faith!
—Why this azure silence, this unsoundable space?
Why these gold stars streaming like sand?
Were one to climb the skies
Forever, what would one find?
Does some shepherd guide this great flock
Of worlds, wandering through the horror of space?
And these worlds that the great ether embraces,
Do they tremble at the sound of an eternal voice?
—And Man, can he see? Can he say: I believe?
Is the voice of thought more than a dream?
If man is so recently born, and life is so short,
Where does he spring from? Does he sink
Into the deep seas of Germs, Fetuses, Embryos,
To the bottom of a vast Crucible where
Mother Nature revives him—a living thing—
To love amidst roses and to grow with the wheat . . . ?

We cannot know! —Our shoulders bear
A cloak of ignorance and confining chimeras!
Men are monkeys fallen from their mothers' wombs,
Our pale reason hides any answers!
We try to look: —Doubt punishes us!
Doubt, doleful bird, beats us with its wings…
—And the horizon flees in perpetual flight…!

. . . .

The heavens are wide open! All mysteries are dead
In Man's eye, who stands, crossing his strong arms
Within the endless splendor of nature's bounty!
He sings… and the woods with him, and the rivers
Murmur a jubilant song that rises into the light!…
—It is Redemption! It is love! It is love!

This poem is in the same parodic mode and time frame as poems in the Album Zutique, *though not a part of that manuscript.*

"THE CHILD WHO GATHERED BULLETS ..."

The child who gathered bullets, the Pubescent Boy
Whose veins contain an exile's blood and an
Illustrious Father's blent, hears life burgeoning
Within him, and longs to take his place elsewhere,
Beyond the curtains of Crib and Throne. But:
His delicate features aren't longing for the Future:
—He's set all that aside. He has sweet dreams,
And fine Enghiens within reach.* His eyes
Are bottomless pools of icy solitude;
"Clearly, the poor boy's in the grip of The Habit."

François Coppée
†

**because "Enghiens, at home."* [A.R.'s note, Ed.] Rimbaud is referring to the advertising slogan of Enghiens, a brand of gargling liquids.

This short fragment from a letter Rimbaud wrote to Ernest Delahaye on October 14, 1875, has proven a source of debate. Some consider this Rimbaud's last poem, calling it "Dream." André Breton considered it to be a great poem, representing "... the absolute triumph of pantheistic delirium." Others, like scholar Steve Murphy, think very little of it, going so far as to assert, "It isn't a poem ... [and] referring to it as 'Dream' is wrongheaded." Rimbaud's letter presents the fragment much as he had his earlier poems in letters, leading some to believe it is written in all seriousness. Murphy believes the lines are presented as a parody of Rimbaud's youthful presentations. "Dream," though it does precede the lines, seems like a deliberately incongruous name, harkening back to his ambitious titles past, though not borne out in the lines that follow.

FROM A LETTER TO ERNEST DELAHAYE, OCTOBER 14, 1875

THE BARRACKS AT NIGHT: "DREAM"

In the barracks, hunger finds you
    It's true . . .
Outpourings and explosions. The ingenuity
    Of the engineer: "That's me, Gruyère!"
Lefêvbre: "Keller!"
The ingenious engineer: "I'm Brie!"
Soldiers cut their bread: "C'est la vie!"
The ingenious engineer: "I'm Roquefort!"
                    —"We're done for . . . !"
                    —"That's me, Gruyère!"
                        And Brie . . . ! etc.
                    —Waltz—
Lefêvbre and I are one . . .   etc . . .

Lefêvbre: the son of Rimbaud's mother's landlord at the time. *Keller:* wine cellar, in German. Also the name of a bureaucrat who established longer terms for mandatory French military service. *The ingenious engineer:* the word in French is "*génie*," which can mean genius (in the *Illumination* so named) or genie (in the *Illumination* "Tale") or military engineer. Here, context seems to dictate an amalgam.

B. VIA PAUL VERLAINE

Verlaine first transcribed these quatrains on the back of the letter of October 14, 1883, that Ernest Delahaye had sent him, which included two sonnets by Rimbaud that Verlaine called the "filths" (see Section C). His scatological memory jogged by the reappearance of the poems, Verlaine jotted down these two shorts that, he later explained in a letter to Charles Morice on December 20 of the same year, had been written by Rimbaud on a wall of a hotel bathroom at 100 rue du café de Cluny. Rimbaud had signed them "Albert Mérat," a forgotten contemporary of his and Verlaine's who, upon arrival for the famous group portrait by Henri de Fantin-Latour, refused to be depicted in the company of "pimps and thieves," and was replaced, as Graham Robb writes, "like a modern-day Daphne, with a vase of flowers." Rimbaud, in these verses, suggested a location more appropriate for Mérat's exalted presence. The verses have previously appeared together as though constituting a single poem, but the evidence of Verlaine's letter to Morice in which they are set down as they are below indicates that they were independent bits of whimsy, though united by a common toilet.

VERSES FOR BATHROOM WALLS

The hole of this seat so poorly made
That it ties our guts in knots
Should be bricked over
By real bastards.

—Albert Mérat
Paris, 1872

When the famous Tropmann destroyed Henri Kink,
That assassin should have had to sit on this seat,
Because Badingue's cunt and Henri V's cunt
Are truly worthy of this besieged throne.

Paris, 1872

Attributed to Rimbaud by Verlaine in his Romances sans paroles. *Epigraph to his "Ariettes oubliées."*

"IT RAINED SOFTLY …"

It rained softly on the city.

Tropmann: (the name was actually spelled Troppmann) was a nineteenth-century serial killer who obliterated eight members of the Kink family, in September 1869. *Henri Kink:* One of the six Kink children killed. He was ten. *Badingue:* The nickname by which Napoleon III was known. *Henri V:* The count of Chambourd, aspirant to the throne.

C. VIA ERNEST DELAHAYE

These two sonnets—originally published in 1923 along with the "Sonnet to an Asshole" from the Album Zutique *under the editorial title "Les Stupra" (L. Obscenities)—come to us from Rimbaud's friend Ernest Delahaye, who claimed to know them by heart. No manuscript in Rimbaud's hand exists. Delahaye wrote to Verlaine on October 14, 1883, with the transcriptions, to which Verlaine made a few minor adjustments. Verlaine called the trio of sonnets "immondes," or "filths." For this edition, "Sonnet to an Asshole" appears with the rest of the* Album *from which it was drawn, while the two below are relegated to this section with the rest of Delahaye's rememberings.*

TWO SONNETS

1.

"ANCIENT ANIMALS SULLIED THEMSELVES . . ."

Ancient animals sullied themselves, even on the run
Their glans coated in blood and excrement.
Our fathers flaunted their members proudly
By the shape of the shaft and the seed of the sac.

For females of the middle ages, whether angels or sows,
A stud with ample rigging was required;
Even a Kléber, judging by breeches that perhaps
Exaggerate a little, wasn't lacking in resources.

Besides, man is the equal of the proudest animal;
The enormity of their members shouldn't surprise us;
But a sterile hour has struck: the horse

And the bull have bridled their ardor,
And no one dares erect his genital pride
In woods teeming with foolish children.

2.

"OUR ASSES AREN'T LIKE THEIRS."

Our asses aren't like theirs. I've often seen
Men unbuttoned behind hedges,
Or, during unembarrassed childhood dips,
Have observed form and function of our asses.

Firmer, generally pale, and featuring
Clearly defined planes covered by a screen
Of hair; whereas for women, only in charming
Furrows does their long, tufted satin bloom.

Touching and miraculously clever,
Like a cheek creased by a smile found
Only on angels from sacred paintings.

Oh to be so naked! Seeking joy and repose,
Our fronts turned to our allotted backs, each
Free to whisper glorious sobs.

"Oh if the bells are bronze!" was written, according to Delahaye, on an outing taken by him and Rimbaud in Charleville that ended in the infiltration of an unlocked steeple door.

Jean Baudry is the pseudonym Rimbaud chose for an essay he sent to a publication called Progrès des Ardennes. *Jean Balouche is presumably Delahaye's nom de guerre for this adventure, but he claims he chose Charles Dhayle. Desdouets, not surprisingly, is the principal of their school.*

"OH IF THE BELLS ARE BRONZE!"

Oh if the bells are bronze!
Our hearts are full of despair!
In June of eighteen-hundred seventy-one,
Massacred by a black being,
We Jean Baudry and Jean Balouche,
Having done as we wished,
Died in this spooky steeple
While cursing Desdouets!...

"At the feet of dark walls..." is a fragment Delahaye claimed was part of an early satire Rimbaud shared with him at school that showcased the acid satire of the style later found in "To Music" and "Sitting Men."

"AT THE FEET OF DARK WALLS..."

At the feet of dark walls, beating skinny dogs...

"In back, the porter leapt..." is a squib of verse Delahaye claimed memorialized a porter at their school always seen with a flower in his mouth. It is supposed to be exemplary of a humorous style of schoolboy verse which Rimbaud wrote during this period.

"IN BACK, THE PORTER LEAPT..."

In back, the porter leapt in grotesque hiccups,
Having swallowed a rose...

"A brunette, just sixteen . . ." represents the first and last lines, writes Delahaye, of a twenty- or thirty-line poem from the spring of 1871, on a theme involving "an Andomache" in a tight spot.

"A BRUNETTE, JUST SIXTEEN . . ."

A brunette, just sixteen when she was married
. . . .

. . . .

For she loved her son of seventeen.

Delahaye claims "You lied . . ." was part of a satirical screed Rimbaud sent to Henri Perrin, the editor-in-chief of the Nord-Est, *Charleville's Republican newspaper, in hopes of publication, which were not fulfilled. As the* Nord-Est *only commenced publication as of July 1, 1871, it would have had to have been sent some time thereafter. In French, it has long been referred to under the rubric "La Plainte du vieillard monarchiste" ("Gripes of the Old Monarchist") which, according to Steve Murphy, is erroneous, as Delahaye never mentioned such a title in his memoir* Souvenirs familiers, *the fragment's only source.*

"YOU LIED . . ."

. . . . You
Lied, on my femur, you lied, musky
Apostle! Do you want to see us ruined?
Would you care to peel our bald heads?
But I, I have two femurs, hobbled and cut!
. . . .

Because you ooze sweat every day in school
Onto the collars of your habits as though

We could make donuts from them, or
You're a dental mask, or at riding school
You're a plucked horse drooling into a cone,
You think you can wipe out my forty years of office?

. . . .

I have my femur! I have my femur! I have my femur!
For forty years I've hobbled on the edge
Of my beloved solid walnut chair;
The impression of the wood forever remains;
And when I glimpse, I, your impure organ,
Of all you subscribers, clown, you subscribers,
Withdrawing that limp organ with their hands, [...]
I will touch over and again, during every tomorrow,
This femur worked for forty years!

[Grocers' Gripes] is another fragment, part of a larger satirical whole, Delahaye claims was also sent to Perrin at the Nord-Est. *The subject is an excoriation of pro-monarchist grocers.*

[GROCERS' GRIPES]

Let him enter the store, when the moon reflects
        Off its blue vitrines,
Let him grab the boxes of endive while we watch.

D. VIA LABARRIÈRE

The following fragments stem from the memory of one of Rimbaud's less intimate schoolmates, Paul Labarrière, and are therefore deeply suspect, but fun. When interviewed by Jules Moquet in 1933, Labarrière confessed to having lost a forty-page notebook containing "50 or 60 poems" that Rimbaud had given him in the winter of 1870–1871. Labarrière claims to have misplaced the notebook in 1885, during a move. The second fragment was said to be the first line of a poem concerning "geese and ducks splashing around on a pond." In a letter Rimbaud sent to Delahaye on June 10, 1871, he told his friend they would go "Wherever vignettes are perennial / Wherever verses are sweet!" The last fragment seems to be the last line of the notebook, from a poem reportedly forty or fifty lines long, describing the bank of a river.

. . . . Are these
. . . . [barrels?] . . . that we burst?
. . . . No!
It's a head chef snoring like a bassoon.

Oh the perennial vignettes!

. . . Among the gold, the quartz the porcelain
. . . . a banal chamberpot,
An indecent reliquary for old courtesans,
Bends his shameful flanks over the royal mahogany.

And the drunken poet tells off the Universe!

E. VIA P. ARNOULT AND JEAN RICHEPIN

In Arnoult's Rimbaud *(1943) he tells of a conversation in 1924 with Jean Richepin, who read him a yellowed sheet in Rimbaud's hand, the text below.*

[...] When the Iranian caravan stopped at the fountain of Ctésiphon, they were upset to see it had run dry. Some accused the magi, others the imams. In unison, the camel drivers shouted curses [...] They had been on the road for many moons with [...] loaded with incense, myrrh, and gold. Their chief cried out [...] decided to suppress [...] Some accepted.

F. ERRANT MANUSCRIPT PHRASES

Phrase on the back of the first draft manuscript of "Fêtes de la Patience" ("Patience Celebrated") of "Bannières de Mai" ("May Banners").

Take heed, o absent life of mine!

G. FRAGMENTS FROM THE *ALBUM ZUTIQUE*

This first fragment derived from a game common to the period, bouts-rimés, *in which the final words of the lines of a poem are given by one person to another, who is then charged with completing the poem. Here, Rimbaud's Zutist friends supplied the words in italics, to which he provided lines that precede them. The manuscript of the poem, however, is badly damaged, missing nearly all of Rimbaud's contribution, thus we only have a tantalizingly limited view (nine complete words) of Rimbaud's capacity for spontaneous whimsy.*

The second fragment reproduces the left half of a poem. It is all that remains of a badly damaged manuscript page.

BOUTS-RIMÉS (POEM IN SET RHYMES)

[ ] *leviticus,*
[ ] tawny *buttock,*
[ ]-*matic,*
[ ]-nee*crude.*

[ ] *apoplectic,*
[ ]-*niverous,*
[ ]-*nastics,*
[ ]-ux member of *steel.*

[ ] and painted with *bile,*
[ ] *small wooden bowl.*
[ ]-*an.*

[ ] fruit of *Asia.*
[ ] *seized,*
[ ] of *bronze.*

—A.R.

"BUT . . ."

But, it [ ]
Having [ ]
I may [ ]
And of my [ ]
Dream the [ ]
The painting [ ]
Of animals [ ]
And, far from [ ]
The elaborat . . . [ ]
Of a *Choler* . . . [ ]

IV. A DRAFT OF *A SEASON IN HELL*

The following fragmentary draft of A Season in Hell *was discovered in three pieces over the course of fifty years, beginning in 1897. Numerous transcriptions of the very fragile manuscript, which is difficult to read, exist. The translation is based on my collation of various transcriptions, principally those of Henri de Bouillane de Lacoste and Pierre Brunel, versions which differ considerably. Anything that appears within brackets is editorial. Interlineated text should be read as Rimbaud's alternatives to or replacements of the text immediately below it.*

[*FROM* BAD BLOOD]

Yes it's one of my vices, which stops and which ~~resumes~~ walks with me again, and, my chest open, I would see a horrible, sickly heart. During my childhood, I felt ~~the~~ its roots

grew

of suffering hurled at my side: today, it ~~climbs~~ to the sky, it ~~felt to me~~ is stronger than I am, it beats me, drags me, throws me to the ground.

it's said

So ^ renounce joy, avoid work, don't ~~play~~

my hope[?] and my higher treasons and my

in the world, ^the last innocence, the last timidity.

blows

We're off. March! the desert. the burden. ^ misfortune. boredom. anger.—hell, science and spiritual delight etc.

I'll fight for

Under ^ which demon's flag will I fight? What beast will I worship? through whose blood will I walk? What will I have to scream? What lies will I have to uphold? ~~At~~ what shrine will I have to attack which hearts have to break?

Better yet, ~~to avoid the bruta~~[l] ~~hand~~ to suffer[?] death's dumb justice, I will hear complaints sung ~~today, on the steps~~

the hard life

Justice endures[?]. Popular point. pure exhaustion—to lift the lid of the coffin with a withered fist, sit inside, and suffocate. ~~I won't grow old~~ No old age. Nor any dangers, terror isn't French.

Ah! I feel so forsaken, that I direct my instincts for perfection at any sacred image: another raw deal.

~~To what end~~ O my curtailment, ~~and~~ o my unbelievable charity ~~my~~ *De profunidis, domine!* ~~How~~ I am a fool?

Enough. Here's the punishment! No more talk of innocence. March Oh! My loins transplant themselves, the heart [illegible word], the chest burns, the head is battered, night rolls in the eyes, in the Sun ~~Do I know where, I go~~ Where will we fight?

Ah! My friend! My filthy youth! Go…go as the others advance ~~they move~~ altars and arms

Oh! Oh. It's weakness, foolishness, me!

Let's go, fire upon me or I'll give up! ~~The packsaddle~~ May someone wound me, I throw myself on my belly, trampled beneath the hooves of a horse.

Ah!

I'll get used to it.

Oh that, I would lead a French life, and I would follow the path of honor.

FALSE CONVERSION

Unhappy day! I swallowed a great ~~glass~~ gulp of poison. The rage of despair made me blow up against nature objects, me, which I would tear apart. May the advice I received be thrice blessed! ~~My~~ My gut burned the violence of the venom contorted by limbs, left me deformed. I die of thirst. I suffocate. I can't even cry out. This is hell eternal suffering. Look how ~~the~~ the flames rise! Demon, do your worst ~~devil,~~

As one should
It's
a handsome and good

~~Satan~~ stir it up. I burn ~~well~~ ^ a good hell.

I once glimpsed ~~salvation~~ conversion, goodness, happiness, salvation. Can I even describe what I saw no one is a poet in hell ~~As soon as~~ it was ~~the apparition of thousands of charming people~~ an admirable spiritual song, strength and peace, noble ambitions, what else can I say!

Ah! noble ambitions! my hate. ~~I'll rebegin~~ Rebegin furious

~~The misfortune o my misfortune and the misfortune of others~~ which matters little to me

existence: fury in the blood ~~animal life~~ the stupefaction ^ and its still life: if damnation is eternal. Its ~~still life still~~. The enactment of religious law why it was once sewn similarly in my spirit. ~~We had The~~ My parents caused my misfortune, and their own, which matters little to me. They took advantage of my innocence. Oh! The very idea of baptism. There are those who have lived badly, who live badly, and who feel nothing! It's my baptism and ~~the~~ my weakness to which I am a slave. Still alive! Later the delights of damnation will deepen. I recognize ~~the demon~~ damnation. ~~When~~ A man who wishes to

I believe in hell so here I am

mutilate himself is assuredly damned. ^ Some crime, quick, so that I can fall into the void, in accordance with the law of man.

Shut up! Just shut up! This is all just shame and blame next to me; it's Satan who Satan himself says that his fire is lowly, idiotic, that my anger is horribly ugly.—Enough . . . ! Shut up! These are errors whispered in my ear ~~the~~ magics, ~~th~~

the.

alchemies, mysticisms, fake perfumes, childish music, Satan

So the poets are damned. No, that's not it.

takes care of all that.

And to think that I possess the truth. That I possess judgment both sound and sure on any subject, that I am prepared for perfection ~~Shut up, it's~~ pride! Now. I'm just a babe in the woods the skin on my scalp dries to dust. Pity! I am afraid, O Lord! my Lord! my lord. I am afraid, pity. Ah I'm thirsty, o my childhood, my village, the fields, the lake on the strand the moonlight when the clock strikes twelve. Satan is in the clock so that I'll go mad. O Mary, Holy Virgin false feeling, false prayer.

[*FROM* DELIRIA II: ALCHEMY OF THE WORD]

At last my spirit becomes[ ]
~~From London or Peking, or Ber~~[ ]
Which ~~disappear~~ we ~~joke on~~ [ ]
of general celebration. ~~Look~~ [ ]
the ~~little [illegible]~~ [ ]
I would have ~~wanted the chalky desert of~~ [ ]

I loved ward drinks, sunbleached shops, scorched orchards. I spent many hours with my tongue hanging out, like an exhausted animal: I dragged myself through the stinking streets, and eyes closed, I ~~prayed to~~ offered myself to the sun. God of fire, may he upend me, ~~and,~~ General, king, I say, if you still have an old cannons [*sic*] on your collapsing ramparts, bombarding man with ~~pieces~~ lumps of dry earth. Strike splendid shop mirrors! Cool sitting rooms! May ~~spiders And~~ [illegible word] Make cities eat their dust! Coat gargoyles in

quickly burning boudoirs

rust. On time toss ruby sand the

~~I wore clothing made of~~ canvas. I [four illegible words] I broke stones on roads forever swept clean. ~~The sun set towards the shit, at the center of the earth~~ [three illegible words] a shit in

convulsion

the valley a the drunken gnat in the urinal of an isolated inn,

dissolves in a sunbeam

smitten with the borage ~~and which will wilt in the sun~~

HUNGER

~~I think about~~ I thought about ~~about animals~~ the happiness of animals, caterpillars were the crowd [illegible word], ~~little~~

innocent

~~bodies~~ white bodies limbs: ~~the romantic spider made a romantic shadow invaded by the opal dawn~~; the brown bug

[illegible word]

person, waited ~~for us to~~ [illegible word] impassioned. Happy The mole, all virginity's sleep!

I withdrew ~~from contact~~ Shocking virginity, ~~which I try~~ to describe with a sort of romance Song from the tallest tower.

I believed I had found

~~I~~ [several illegible words, crossed out] reason and happiness. I listened ~~from~~ the sky, the blue, which is black, and I lived, a spark of gold struck from the *natural* light. It's very

I expressed ~~the most~~ stupidly.

serious.

ETERNITY

And ~~the crowning blow~~ Out of joy, I became a fabulous opera.

GOLDEN AGE

In this ~~period it was~~ it was my eternal life, unwritten, unsung,

worldly laws

—something like Providence in which one believes and which do not sing.

After these noble minutes, ~~came~~ utter stupidity. I ~~myse~~ see a propensity for being undone by bliss in everyone: the action

not life bad

wasn't but a ~~instinctive~~ means of wasting a belly full of life: ~~only, me I leave with the knowledge~~, a sweet and sinister risk, ~~an~~ disturbance, ~~deviation~~ bad habits. The moral ~~genius~~ was the weakness of the brain
[ ]beings and everything seemed to me
[ ]other lives around them. This monsieur
[ ]an angel. This family isn't
[ ]With many men
[ ]moment from one of their other lives
[ ]history no more principles. Nor another sophism of

I could repeat them all and others

imprisoned madness. I no longer felt a thing. The ~~hallucinations~~

and many others and others
I know how to do it

~~were~~ [several illegible crossed-out words] But now I would not try to make myself heard.

I believed

A month of this. My sanity ~~fled~~ was threatened. I had more to do than merely live. The hallucinations were more alive ~~more~~

sadder and more remote

~~horrifying~~ the terror ~~no longer~~ came! I dreamt everywhere.

MEMORY

I found myself ripe for ~~demise~~, death and my weakness drew me to the edges of the earth and to a life where the whirlwind [...] in dark Cimmeria, country of the dead, where a great [...] took a dangerous route left nearly the whole soul with a [...] on a skiff coursed for dread.

ENDS OF THE EARTH

will shut my

I traveled a bit. I went North: I ~~will remember in~~ brain all

wanted to recognize the

the feudal odors, shepherdesses, primitive sources. I loved the sea [illegible phrase] ~~the magic ting in the luminous water illuminated~~ as if it was for her to wash me ~~clean of these aberrations~~ of a stain. I saw the consoling cross. I had been damned by the rainbow and religious; and thanks to Bliss,

magics

~~my remorse~~ my fate, my worm, and who ~~I~~ however ~~the world seems brand new, to me who had~~ raised every ~~the possible impressions~~; making my life too immense drained even after

only

my [illegible crossed-out word] to sincerely love strength and

very truly

beauty.

matutinum

In the biggest cities, at dawn, *ad diluculum,* when *Christus venit* ~~when for the strong among us Christ comes~~ her tooth, sweet as ~~the~~ death, warning me with the cock's crow.

---

ad diluculum: Dawn.

BL[IS]S

So weak I no longer thought society could bear my

Pity

Such misfortune

presence, except out of ^ What possible pasture for this beautiful disgust? Benevol[ence].

[Illegible phrase] Little by little it passed.

Now I can't stand mystical leaps and stylistic strangenesses.

My beauty[?]

Now I can say that art is folly. Our great poets just as easily: art is folly.

Hail beauty.

V. FOUR SEASONS

Although multiple manuscript versions of many of Rimbaud's poems exist, in most instances the differences are illustrative of ambivalence over issues of capitalization or punctuation. The case of "O saisons, ô chateaux" is very different, as the four versions we possess differ in substantial ways. They offer a partial view of Rimbaud leaping from an interesting, if messy, series of possibilities to a beautiful certainty, or certainties. The first two versions have never been translated into English before. The third is available everywhere, and the fourth is Rimbaud's final refinement printed in A Season in Hell.

In versions 1 and 2, my translations gloze the originals line by line. Version 3 is identical to its twin on page 132 of the Poetry *section. Version 4 is based on the French text of the poem as it appears in* A Season in Hell; *however, the translation reproduced here differs considerably from the one on page 214. I reproduce these alternate solutions to offer a glimpse at the sorts of decisions faced by a translator of poetry.*

VERSION 1

~~c'est pour dire que ce n'est rien, la vie~~	~~which is to say that life is nothing~~
~~voilà donc les saisons~~	~~so here are the seasons~~
O les saisons et châteaux	O the seasons and châteaux
~~Où court où vole où coule~~	~~Where runs where flies or flows~~
L'âme n'est pas sans défauts	The soul isn't without flaws
J'ai fait la magique étude	I made a magical study
Du Bonheur que nul n'élude	Of Bliss, which no one escapes
~~Chaque [...] son coq gaulouis~~	~~Each [...] his Gallic cock~~
Je suis à lui, chaque fois	I follow him, every time
Si chante son coq gaulois	If his Gallic cock sings
~~Puis~~ J[...]rai rien: plus d'envie	~~Then~~ I [...] nothing: no more desire
Il s'est chargé de ma vie	It has taken control of my life
Ce Charme! il prit âme et corps	This charm! It takes soul and body
Et dispersa mes efforts	And disperses my efforts
Quoi comprendre à ma parole	What is to be understood from my words
Il fait qu'elle fuie et vole	The result is that they flee and fly
Eh! si le malheur m'entraîne	If misfortune conditions me
Sa disgrâce m'est certaine	My disgrace is assured at its hands
~~C'est pour moi~~	~~It's for me~~
Il faut que son dédain, las!	Alas his disdain
~~Soit pour moi~~	~~Either for me~~
Me livre ay plus prompt trép[as]	Delivers me directly to death[.]

VERSION 2

O saison O châteaux	O season O châteaux
Quelle L'âme n'est pas sans défauts	What The soul isn't without flaws
J'ai fait la magique étude	I made a magical study
Du Bonheur que nul n'élude	Of Bliss, which no one escapes
Je suis à lui, chaque fois	I follow him, every time
Si chante son coq gaulois	If his Gallic cock sings
[...] rien: plus d'envie	[...] nothing: no more desire
Il s'est chargé de ma vie	It has taken control of my life.
Ce Charme! il prit âme et corps	This charm! It takes soul and body
Je me crois libre d'efforts	I think I'm freed from exertions
Quoi comprendre à ma parole	What is to be understood from my words
Il fait qu'elle fuie et vole	The result is that they flee and fly
Oh! si ce malheur m'entraîne	Oh! If this misfortune conditions me
Sa disgrâce m'est certaine	My disgrace is assured at its hands
Il faut que son dédain, las!	Alas his disdain
Me livre au plus prompt trép[as]	Delivers me directly to death[.]

VERSION 3

O saisons, ô châteaux Quelle âme est sans défauts?	O seasons, o châteaux Who possesses a perfect soul?
O saisons, ô châteaux!	O seasons, o châteaux!
J'ai fait la magique étude Du Bonheur, que nul n'élude.	I made a magical study Of inescapable Bliss.
O vive lui, chaque fois Que chante son coq Gaulois.	All hail Bliss, throughout Gaul When you hear the rooster's call.
Mais! je n'aurai plus d'envie, Il s'est chargé de ma vie.	Bliss has finally set me free From desire's tyranny.
Ce Charme! il prit âme et corps. Et dispersa tous efforts.	Its spell took soul and shape, Letting every goal escape.
Que comprendre à ma parole? Il fait qu'elle fuie et vole!	What do my words mean? Meaning flees, takes wing!
o saisons, ô châteaux	o seasons, o châteaux

This version is from *Poetry, V 1872,* p. 132.

VERSION 4

O saisons, ô châteaux! Quelle âme est sans défauts?	O seasons, o châteaux! Weakness visits every soul.
J'ai fait la magique étude Du bonheur, qu'aucun n'élude.	I made a magical exegesis Of this Bliss that won't release us.
Salut à lui, chaque fois Que chante le coq gaulois.	Think of Bliss each time you hear The rooster's call, far or near.
Ah! je n'aurai plus d'envie: Il s'est chargé de ma vie.	I've been unburdened of desire: Bliss is all I now require.
Ce charme a pris âme et corps Et dispersé les efforts.	Its spell took shape and soul, Eradicating every goal.
O saisons, ô châteaux!	O seasons, o châteaux!
L'heure de sa fuite, hélas! Sera l'heure du trépas.	When Bliss departs at last Death takes us each, alas.
O saisons, ô châteaux!	O seasons, o châteaux!

VI. LETTERS

"The Artist as Critic"

While a great many of Rimbaud's letters to various correspondents have survived, very few of them are devoted to discussion of his literary pursuits. Those that do treat the subject of words and his use of them are significant not just for their relative scarcity. They were often our only source for the poems Rimbaud sent with them.

For generations, scholars and readers have depended upon these letters as windows into Rimbaud's evolving creative method, particularly the letters of spring 1871 to Paul Demeny, a poet, and George Izambard, one of Rimbaud's instructors and his chief mentor of the period, in which Rimbaud outlines his views on poetry. Editors have come to call these letters the "lettres du voyant," or "The Seer Letters," for in them, Rimbaud refers to the desire to become a seer (or visionary), incorporating that capacity or tendency into his definition of The Poet. While Rimbaud is unambiguous in his statement and restatement of this ambition, he frequently undercuts his didactic, mandarin tone with withering irony, particularly in the segues to the poems sent with the letters. It is for the reader to decide whether it is appropriate or advisable to see the poet through the prism of seerdom, or, at the very least, only through such a prism. Much of Rimbaud's work, early and late, can be seen in a very different, and less restrictive, sense.

Not to be neglected, too, are the letters that bookend this section: missives to the poet Banville, in which the neophyte came knocking at the doors of the established, in hopes of being shown in. In the first, he comes with hat in hand; in the last, fly unzipped.

LETTER TO THÉODORE DE BANVILLE

Charleville (Ardennes), May 24, 1870

Cher Maître,

These are the months of love; I'm seventeen, the time of hope and chimeras, as they say, and so, a child blessed by the hand of the Muse (how trivial that must seem), I've set out to express my good thoughts, my hopes, my feelings, the provinces of poets—I call all of this Spring.

For if I have decided to send you a few poems—via the hands of Alp. Lemerre, that excellent editor—it is because I love all poets, all the good Parnassians—since the poet is inherently Parnassian—taken with ideal beauty; that is what draws me to you, however naïvely, your relation to Ronsard, a brother of the masters of 1830, a true romantic, a true poet. That is why. Silly, isn't it? But there it is.

In two years, perhaps one, I will have made my way to Paris.—*Anch'io*, gentlemen of the press, I will be a Parnassian! Something within me... wants to break free... I swear, Master, to eternally adore the two goddesses, Muse and Liberty.

Try to keep a straight face while reading my poems:

You would make me ridiculously happy and hopeful were you, *Maître*, to see if a little room were found for "*Credo in Unam*" among the Parnassians...

I could appear in the final issue of *le Parnasse:* it would be a Credo for poets!

Ambition! Such madness!

Arthur Rimbaud

Théodore de Banville: a Parnassian poet of the day of no small reputation, and whose posterity today rests chiefly on the collection *Odes funambulesques.* Rimbaud's letter was sent to him care of his publisher, Alphonse Lemerre. In as brazen a cold-letter as one finds in literature, the "seventeen"-year-old Rimbaud (who, at writing, was actually fifteen and a half) asked to be admitted to the big leagues, and made it clear, despite the self-effacement, that he believed himself more than ready, an assessment that Banville must not have shared, as he offered Rimbaud no help at all. *Anch'io:* an allusion to the famous remark by Coreggio, who as he stood before Raphael's canvas of Saint Cecilia said, "*Anch'io son pittore*": "I too will be a painter." "*Credo in Unam*": an earlier, longer version of "Sun and Flesh."

“Sensation” [p. 11]
“Ophelia” [p. 17]
“Credo in Unam” [p. 12 and p. 325]

Were these poems to find a place in *le Parnasse,* wouldn’t they sing the poet’s creed?

I am unknown: so what? Poets are brothers. These verses believe; they love; they hope: that’s enough.

Help me, *Maître:* help me find my footing: I am young: give me your hand…

LETTER TO GEORGE IZAMBARD
Charleville, May 13, 1871

And so you’re a professor again. You’ve said before that we owe something to Society; you’re a member of the brotherhood of teachers; you’re on track. —I’m all for your principles: I cynically keep myself alive; I dig up old dolts from school: I throw anything stupid, dirty, or plain wrong at them I can come up with: beer and wine are my reward. *Stat mater dolorosa, dum pendet filius.* I owe society something, doubtless—and I’m right. You are too, for now. Fundamentally, you see your principles as an argument for subjective poetry: your will to return to the university trough—

“Sensation,” “Ophelia,” “Credo in Unam”: These poems originally accompanied the letter. *Wine:* The word here in French is *filles,* which would make the most contextual sense as *girls.* However, the translation of the word as *wine* is justified: in the slang of the region and the era, *filles* did mean small glasses of wine. As Rimbaud could well have written an unambiguous word for wine (*du vin*), it seems advisable to alert the reader to the possibility that Rimbaud meant both, despite the current vogue for assuming that Rimbaud couldn’t possibly have had any interest in girls. *Stat mater dolorosa, dum pendet filius:* The Catholic liturgy for September 15 reads, in part, “*Stabat mater dolorosa, / Juxta crucem lacrimosa / Dum pende bat Filius*” (which has its source in John 19:25). Rimbaud is being cheeky. *Subjective poetry:* Rimbaud means a poetry that refers too directly to oneself, whereas *objective poetry* is a poetry that looks beyond self to other objects, including other people. It is important to keep in mind how inherently subjective these distinctions are.

sorry!—proves it! But you will end up an accomplished complacent who accomplishes nothing of any worth. That's without even beginning to discuss your dry-as-dust subjective poetry. One day, I hope—as do countless others—I'll see the possibility for objective poetry in your principles, said with more sincerity than you can imagine! I will be a worker: it's this idea that keeps me alive, when my mad fury would have me leap into the midst of Paris' battles—where how many other workers die as I write these words? To work now? Never, never: I'm on strike.

Right now, I'm beshitting myself as much as possible. Why? I want to be a poet, and I'm working to turn myself into a *seer:* you won't understand at all, and it's unlikely that I'll be able to explain it to you. It has to do with making your way towards the unknown by a derangement of *all the senses.* The suffering is tremendous, but one must bear up against it, to be born a poet, and I know that's what I am. It's not at all my fault. It's wrong to say *I think:* one should say *I am thought.* Forgive the pun.

I is someone else. Tough luck to the wood that becomes a violin, and to hell with the unaware who *quibble* over what they're completely missing anyway!

You aren't my *teacher.* I'll give you this much: is it satire, as you'd say? Is it poetry? It's fantasy, always.—But, I beg you, don't underline any of this, either with pencil, or—at least not too much—with thought.

"STOLEN HEART" [p. 55]

Which isn't to say it means nothing.—WRITE BACK.

With affection, AR. Rimbaud

LETTER TO PAUL DEMENY

Charleville, May 15, 1871

I resolved to provide you with an hour of new literature;

I'll jump right in with a psalm on current events:

"THE BATTLE SONG OF PARIS" [p. 56]

Now, prose on the future of poetry.

All ancient poetry culminated with Greek poetry—Harmonious Life. From Greece to the romantic movement—the Middle Ages—there are writers and versifiers. From Ennius to Theroldus, from Theroldus to Casimir Delavigne, it's all rhymed prose, a game, the sloppiness and glory of innumerable ridiculous generations: Racine is the standout, pure, strong, great. Had his rhymes been ruined and his hemistiches muddled, the Divine Dunderhead would be as forgotten today as the next author of the *Origins.*—After Racine, the game got old. It kept going for two thousand years!

Neither joke nor paradox. Reason fills me with more certainty about all this than a Young France would have been with fury. So the *neophytes* are free to curse their forebears: it's their party and the night is young.

Romanticism has never been fairly appraised; who would have? Critics!! The romantics, who so clearly prove that the song is infrequently the work of a singer, which is to say rarely is its thought both sung and *understood* by its singer.

For I is someone else. If the brass awakes as horn, it can't be to blame. This much is clear: I'm around for the hatching of my thought: I watch it, I listen to it: I release a stroke from the bow: the symphony makes its rumblings in the depths, or leaps fully-formed onto the stage.

If old fools hadn't completely misunderstood the nature of the Ego, we wouldn't be constantly sweeping up these millions of skeletons which,

---

Origins: A work that was a buzzword for banality in the nineteenth century. *Young France:* The *Jeunes-France* were a group of pro-romanticists about whom Théophile Gautier wrote.

since time immemorial, have hoarded products of their monocular intellects, a blindness of which they claim authorship!

In Greece, as I mentioned, poems and lyres turned *Action into Rhythm.* Later, music and rhyme became games, mere pastimes. The study of this past proves precious to the curious: many get a kick out of reworking these antiquities: let them. The universal intelligence has, of course, always shed ideas; man harvests a portion of these mental fruits: they measured themselves against them, wrote books about them: so things progressed, man not working to develop himself, not yet awake, or not yet enveloped in the fullness of the dream. Functionaries, writers: author, creator, poet—such a man never existed.

The first task of any man who would be a poet is to know himself completely; he seeks his soul, inspects it, tests it, learns it. And he must develop it as soon as he's come to know it; this seems straightforward: a natural evolution of the mind; so many *egoists* call themselves authors; still others believe their intellectual growth is entirely self-induced! But all this is really about making one's soul into a monster: like some *comprachico!* Like some man sewing his face with a crop of warts.

I mean that you have to be a *seer,* mold oneself into a *seer.*

The Poet makes himself into a *seer* by a long, involved and logical *derangement of all the senses.* Every kind of love, of suffering, of madness; he searches himself; he exhausts every possible poison so that only essence remains. He undergoes unspeakable tortures that require complete faith and superhuman strength, rendering him the ultimate Invalid among men, the master criminal, the first among the damned—and the supreme Savant! For he arrives at the *unknown!* For, unlike everyone else, he has developed an already rich soul! He arrives at the unknown, and when, bewildered, he ends up losing his understanding of his visions, he has, at least, seen them! It doesn't matter if these leaps into the unknown kill

---

Comprachico: from Victor Hugo's *L'Homme qui rit* (1869): "*Comprachicos* trafficked in children. They bought and sold them. They didn't strip them: that's another industry. What *did* they do with them? They turned them into monsters. Why monsters? For the fun of it... to degrade man by remaking him, degrading the whole by disfiguring it. Some vivisectionists of the era succeeded in wiping human faces clean of any hint of the divine."

him: other awful workers will follow him; they'll start at the horizons where the other has fallen!

—more in six minutes—

At this point I'll insert another psalm from *off book:* lend a forgiving ear—and everyone will be delighted.—Bow in hand, I begin:

"MY LITTLE LOVES" [p. 58]

There it is. And please be aware that were it not for fear of making you spend 60 centimes on postage—I who, frozen in fear, have been broke for seven months—would be sending you, Monsieur, my one hundred hexameter "Lovers of Paris," and my two hundred hexameter "Death of Paris"!—But I digress:

The poet is really a thief of fire. Humanity, and even the *animals,* are his burden; he must make sure his inventions live and breathe; if what he finds *down below* has a form, he offers form: if it is formless, he offers formlessness. Find the words;

—What's more, given every word is an idea, the day of a single universal language will dawn! Only an academic deader than a fossil could compile a dictionary no matter what the language. Just thinking about the first letter of the alphabet would drive the weak to the brink!

This language will be of the soul, for the soul, encompassing everything, scents, sounds, colors, thought mounting thought. The poet will define the unknown quantity awaking in his era's universal soul: he would offer more than merely formalized thought or evidence *of his march on* Progress! He will become *a propagator of progress* who renders enormity a norm to be absorbed by everyone!

This will be a materialistic future, you'll see. These poems will be built to last, brimming with *Number* and *Harmony.* At its root, there will be

---

"Lovers of Paris"... "Death of Paris": These two poems no longer exist, though it's more likely they never did. Rimbaud is making fun of poems of that length and style, as he is of the idea of speaking about poems quantitatively (if you liked my 100 hexameter poem, you'll surely love my 200 hexameter poem twice as much). *Thief of fire:* C.f. Prometheus.

something of Greek Poetry to them. Eternal art would have its place; poets are citizens too, after all. Poetry will no longer beat *within* action; it *will be before* it.

Poets like this will arrive! When woman will be freed from unending servitude, when she too will live for and by her *self,* man—so abominable up until now—having given her freedom, will see her become a poet as well! Women will discover the unknown! Will her world of ideas differ from ours? She will find strange, unfathomable, repugnant, delicious things; we will take them in, we will understand.

In the interim, we require new ideas and forms of our *poets.* All the hacks will soon think they've managed this.—Don't bet on it!

The first romantics were *seers* without even really realizing it: their soul's education began by accident: abandoned trains still smoking, occasionally taking to the tracks. Lamartine was a seer now and again, but strangling on old forms. Hugo, too pigheaded, certainly *saw* in his most recent works: *Les Misérables* is really a *poem.* I've got *Les Chatiments* with me; *Stella* gives some sense of Hugo's vision. Too much Belmontet and Lamennais with their Jehovahs and colonnades, massive crumbling edifices.

For us, a sorrowful generation consumed by visions and insulted by his angelic sloth, Musset is fourteen times worse! O the tedious tales and proverbs! O his *Nuits!* His *Rolla, Namouna, La Coupe.* It's all so French, which is to say unbearable to the nth degree; French, but not Parisian. Another work by that odious genius who inspired Rabelais, Voltaire and Jean La Fontaine, with notes by M. Taine! How vernal, Musset's mind! And how delightful, his love! Like paint on enamel, his dense poetry! We will savor *French* poetry endlessly, in France. Every grocer's son can reel off something Rollaesque, every seminarian has five hundred rhymes hidden in his notebook. At fifteen, these passionate impulses give boys boners; at sixteen, they've already resolved to recite their lines *with feeling;* at eighteen, even seventeen, every schoolboy who can write a *Rolla,* does—and they all

---

Les Chatiments . . . Stella: Hugo's *Les Chatiments. Stella:* from Book VI thereof. *Belmontet:* Louis Belmontet (1799–1879), poet parodied in the *Album Zutique* (see p. 150).

do! Some may even still die from it. Musset couldn't do anything: there mere visions behind the gauze curtains: he closed his eyes. French, half-dead, dragged from tavern to schooldesk, the beautiful corpse has died, and, ever since, we needn't waste our time trying to rouse him with our abominations!

The second romantics are true *seers;* Th. Gautier, Lec. de Lisle, Th. de Banville. But to explore the invisible and to hear the unheard are very different from reviving the dead: Baudelaire is therefore first among seers, the king of poets, *a true God.* And yet even he lived in too aestheticized a world; and the forms for which he is praised are really quite trite: the inventions of the unknown demand new forms.

In the rut of old forms, among innocents, A. Renaud did a *Rolla;* L. Grandet did his; the Gauls and Mussets; G. Lafenestre, Coran, Cl. Popelin, Soulary, L. Salles; schoolboys Marc, Aicard, Theuriet; the dead and the dumb, Autran, Barbier, L. Pichat, Lemoyne, the Deschamps, the Desessarts; the journalists, L. Cladel, Robert Luzarches, X. de Ricard; the fantasists, C. Mendes; the bohemians; the women; the prodigies, Leon Dierx, Sully Prudhomme, Coppée; the new so-called Parnassian school, has two seers, Albert Mérat and Paul Verlaine, a true poet.—There it is.

So I work to turn myself into a *seer.* And conclude with a pious song.

"SQUATTING" [p. 60]

You'd be a son-of-a-bitch not to respond: quickly: in a week I'll be in Paris, maybe.

Au revoir, A. Rimbaud

The second romantics: Whereas in Rimbaud's worldview the first romantics were the *Jeunes-France,* these second romantics were part of the "Art for Art's Sake" ideal, in France the Parnassian Poets, Pater and Wilde in England, etc. They are generally called, in French literary history, Neo-Romantics.

LETTER TO PAUL DEMENY
Charleville, June 10, 1871

"POETS, AGE SEVEN" [p. 65]
"THE POOR AT CHURCH" [p. 68]

Look—don't be mad—at these notions for some funny doodles: an antidote to those perennially sweet sketches of frolicking cupids, where hearts ringed in flames take flight, green flowers, drenched birds, Leucadian promontories, etc...—These triolets are also as good as gone...

Perennially sweet sketches
And sweet verse.

Look—don't be mad—

"STOLEN HEART" [p. 55]

So that's what I've been up to.

I have three requests:

Burn, *I'm not kidding,* and I hope you will respect my wishes as you would a man on his deathbed, burn *all the poems I was dumb enough to send you* when I was in Douai: be so kind as to send me, if you can and if you want to, a copy of your *Glaneuses,* which I want to reread and is impossible for me to buy since my mother hasn't given me a penny in six months—*oh too bad!* Finally, please respond, anything at all, to this and my previous letter.

I wish you a good day, which is something.

A. Rimbaud.

LETTER TO THÉODORE DE BANVILLE

Charleville, Ardennes, August 15, 1871

"ON THE SUBJECT OF FLOWERS: REMARKS, ADDRESSED TO THE POET" [p. 78]

Monsieur and Maître,

Perhaps you recall, in June of 1870, having received a hundred or a hundred and fifty mythological hexameters for the provinces entitled *Credo in Unam?* You were so good to respond!

The same idiot is sending you more of his stuff, this time signed Alcide Bava—Sorry.

I'm eighteen. —I still admire Banville's poetry.

Last year I was only seventeen!

Am I progressing?

Alcide Bava

A.R.

I'm eighteen: Actually, only seventeen at the time.

ŒUVRES COMPLÈTES

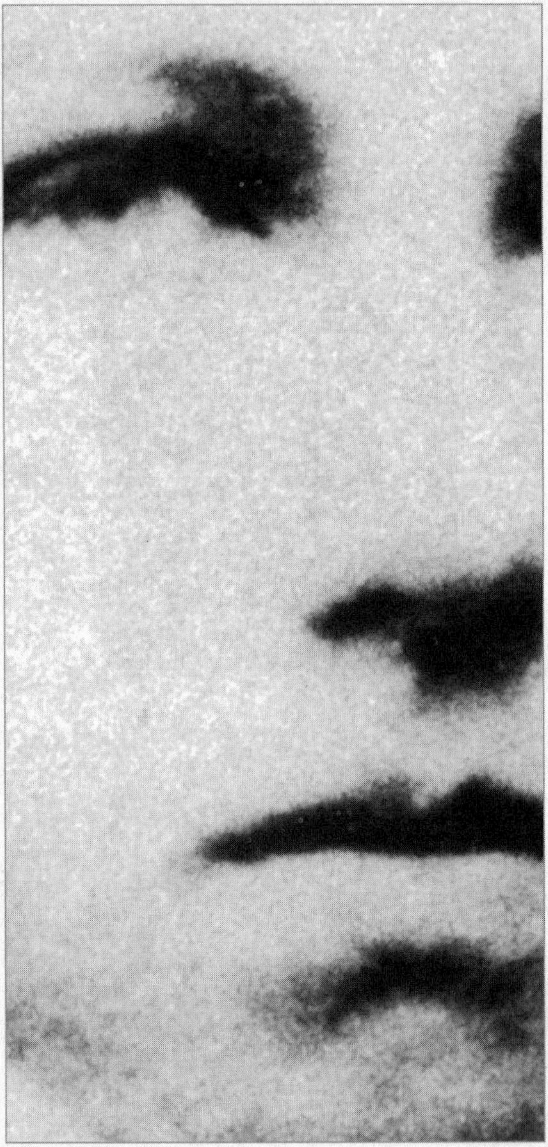

POÉSIES

I. 1869

LES ÉTRENNES DES ORPHELINS

I

La chambre est pleine d'ombre; on entend vaguement
De deux enfants le triste et doux chuchotement.
Leur front se penche, encore alourdi par le rêve,
Sous le long rideau blanc qui tremble et se soulève...
—Au dehors les oiseaux se rapprochent frileux;
Leur aile s'engourdit sous le ton gris des cieux;
Et la nouvelle Année, à la suite brumeuse,
Laissant traîner les plis de sa robe neigeuse,
Sourit avec des pleurs, et chante en grelottant...

II

Or les petits enfants, sous le rideau flottant,
Parlent bas comme on fait dans une nuit obscure.
Ils écoutent, pensifs, comme un lointain murmure...
Ils tressaillent souvent à la claire voix d'or
Du timbre matinal, qui frappe et frappe encor
Son refrain métallique en son globe de verre...
—Puis, la chambre est glacée... on voit traîner à terre,
Épars autour des lits, des vêtements de deuil:
L'âpre bise d'hiver qui se lamente au seuil
Souffle dans le logis son haleine morose!
On sent, dans tout cela, qu'il manque quelque chose...
—Il n'est donc point de mère à ces petits enfants,
De mère au frais sourire, aux regards triomphants?
Elle a donc oublié, le soir, seule et penchée,
D'exciter une flamme à la cendre arrachée,
D'amonceler sur eux la laine et l'édredon
Avant de les quitter en leur criant: pardon.
Elle n'a point prévu la froideur matinale,
Ni bien fermé le seuil à la bise hivernale?...

—Le rêve maternel, c'est le tiède tapis,
C'est le nid cotonneux où les enfants tapis,
Comme de beaux oiseaux que balancent les branches,
Dorment leur doux sommeil plein de visions blanches!…
—Et là,—c'est comme un nid sans plumes, sans chaleur,
Où les petits ont froid, ne dorment pas, ont peur;
Un nid que doit avoir glacé la bise amère…

III

Votre cœur l'a compris:—ces enfants sont sans mère.
Plus de mère au logis!—et le père est bien loin!…
—Une vieille servante, alors, en a pris soin.
Les petits sont tout seuls en la maison glacée;
Orphelins de quatre ans, voilà qu'en leur pensée
S'éveille, par degrés, un souvenir riant…
C'est comme un chapelet qu'on égrène en priant:
—Ah! quel beau matin, que ce matin des étrennes!
Chacun, pendant la nuit, avait rêvé des siennes
Dans quelque songe étrange où l'on voyait joujoux,
Bonbons habillés d'or, étincelants bijoux,
Tourbillonner, danser une danse sonore,
Puis fuir sous les rideaux, puis reparaître encore!
On s'éveillait matin, on se levait joyeux,
La lèvre affriandée, en se frottant les yeux…
On allait, les cheveux emmêlés sur la tête,
Les yeux tout rayonnants, comme aux grands jours de fête,
Et les petits pieds nus effleurant le plancher,
Aux portes des parents tout doucement toucher…
On entrait!… Puis alors les souhaits… en chemise,
Les baisers répétés, et la gaîté permise!

IV

Ah! c'était si charmant, ces mots dits tant de fois!
—Mais comme il est changé, le logis d'autrefois:
Un grand feu pétillait, clair, dans la cheminée,
Toute la vieille chambre était illuminée;
Et les reflets vermeils, sortis du grand foyer,
Sur les meubles vernis aimaient à tournoyer…
—L'armoire était sans clefs!… sans clefs, la grande armoire!
On regardait souvent sa porte brune et noire…
Sans clefs!… c'était étrange!… on rêvait bien des fois
Aux mystères dormant entre ses flancs de bois,

Et l'on croyait ouïr, au fond de la serrure
Béante, un bruit lointain, vague et joyeux murmure…
—La chambre des parents est bien vide, aujourd'hui:
Aucun reflet vermeil sous la porte n'a lui;
Il n'est point de parents, de foyer, de clefs prises:
Partant, point de baisers, point de douces surprises!
Oh! que le jour de l'an sera triste pour eux!
—Et, tout pensifs, tandis que de leurs grands yeux bleus
Silencieusement tombe une larme amère,
Ils murmurent: «Quand donc reviendra notre mère?»
. . . .

V

Maintenant, les petits sommeillent tristement:
Vous diriez, à les voir, qu'ils pleurent en dormant,
Tant leurs yeux sont gonflés et leur souffle pénible!
Les tout petits enfants ont le cœur si sensible!
—Mais l'ange des berceaux vient essuyer leurs yeux,
Et dans ce lourd sommeil met un rêve joyeux,
Un rêve si joyeux, que leur lèvre mi-close,
Souriante, semblait murmurer quelque chose…
—Ils rêvent que, penchés sur leur petit bras rond,
Doux geste du réveil, ils avancent le front,
Et leur vague regard tout autour d'eux se pose…
Ils se croient endormis dans un paradis rose…
Au foyer plein d'éclairs chante gaîment le feu…
Par la fenêtre on voit là-bas un beau ciel bleu;
La nature s'éveille et de rayons s'enivre…
La terre, demi-nue, heureuse de revivre,
A des frissons de joie aux baisers du soleil…
Et dans le vieux logis tout est tiède et vermeil:
Les sombres vêtements ne jonchent plus la terre,
La bise sous le seuil a fini par se taire…
On dirait qu'une fée a passé dans cela!…
—Les enfants, tout joyeux, ont jeté deux cris… Là,
Près du lit maternel, sous un beau rayon rose,
Là, sur le grand tapis, resplendit quelque chose…
Ce sont des médaillons argentés, noirs et blancs,
De la nacre et du jais aux reflets scintillants;
Des petits cadres noirs, des couronnes de verre,
Avant trois mots gravés en or: «À NOTRE MÈRE!»
. . . .

II. 1870

SENSATION

Par les soirs bleus d'été, j'irai dans les sentiers,
Picoté par les blés, fouler l'herbe menue:
Rêveur, j'en sentirai la fraîcheur à mes pieds.
Je laisserai le vent baigner ma tête nue.

Je ne parlerai pas, je ne penserai rien:
Mais l'amour infini me montera dans l'âme,
Et j'irai loin, bien loin, comme un bohémien,
Par la Nature,—heureux comme avec une femme.

Mars 1870.

SOLEIL ET CHAIR

I
Le Soleil, le foyer de tendresse et de vie,
Verse l'amour brûlant à la terre ravie,
Et, quand on est couché sur la vallée, on sent
Que la terre est nubile et déborde de sang;
Que son immense sein, soulevé par une âme,
Est d'amour comme dieu, de chair comme la femme,
Et qu'il renferme, gros de sève et de rayons,
Le grand fourmillement de tous les embryons!

Et tout croît, et tout monte!

—Ô Vénus, ô Déesse!
Je regrette les temps de l'antique jeunesse,
Des satyres lascifs, des faunes animaux,

Dieux qui mordaient d'amour l'écorce des rameaux
Et dans les nénufars baisaient la Nymphe blonde!
Je regrette les temps où la sève du monde,
L'eau du fleuve, le sang rose des arbres verts
Dans les veines de Pan mettaient un univers!
Où le sol palpitait, vert, sous ses pieds de chèvre;
Où, baisant mollement le clair syrinx, sa lèvre
Modulait sous le ciel le grand hymne d'amour;
Où, debout sur la plaine, il entendait autour
Répondre à son appel la Nature vivante;
Où les arbres muets, berçant l'oiseau qui chante,
La terre berçant l'homme, et tout l'Océan bleu
Et tous les animaux aimaient, aimaient en Dieu!
Je regrette les temps de la grande Cybèle
Qu'on disait parcourir, gigantesquement belle,
Sur un grand char d'airain, les splendides cités;
Son double sein versait dans les immensités
Le pur ruissellement de la vie infinie.
L'Homme suçait, heureux, sa mamelle bénie,
Comme un petit enfant, jouant sur ses genoux.
—Parce qu'il était fort, l'Homme était chaste et doux.

Misère! Maintenant il dit: Je sais les choses,
Et va, les yeux fermés et les oreilles closes.
—Et pourtant, plus de dieux! plus de dieux! l'Homme est Roi,
L'Homme est Dieu! Mais l'Amour, voilà la grande Foi!
Oh! si l'homme puisait encore à ta mamelle,
Grande mère des dieux et des hommes, Cybèle;
S'il n'avait pas laissé l'immortelle Astarté
Qui jadis, émergeant dans l'immense clarté
Des flots bleus, fleur de chair que la vague parfume,
Montra son nombril rose où vint neiger l'écume,
Et fit chanter, Déesse aux grands yeux noirs vainqueurs,
Le rossignol aux bois et l'amour dans les cœurs!

II
Je crois en toi! je crois en toi! Divine mère,
Aphrodité marine!—Oh! la route est amère
Depuis que l'autre Dieu nous attelle à sa croix;
Chair, Marbre, Fleur, Vénus, c'est en toi que je crois!
—Oui, l'Homme est triste et laid, triste sous le ciel vaste,
Il a des vêtements, parce qu'il n'est plus chaste,
Parce qu'il a sali son fier buste de dieu,

Et qu'il a rabougri, comme une idole au feu,
Son corps Olympien aux servitudes sales!
Oui, même après la mort, dans les squelettes pâles
Il veut vivre, insultant la première beauté!
—Et l'Idole où tu mis tant de virginité,
Où tu divinisas notre argile, la Femme,
Afin que l'Homme pût éclairer sa pauvre âme
Et monter lentement, dans un immense amour,
De la prison terrestre à la beauté du jour,
La Femme ne sait plus même être Courtisane!
—C'est une bonne farce! et le monde ricane
Au nom doux et sacré de la grande Vénus!

III

Si les temps revenaient, les temps qui sont venus!
—Car l'Homme a fini! l'Homme a joué tous les rôles!
Au grand jour, fatigué de briser des idoles
Il ressuscitera, libre de tous ses Dieux,
Et, comme il est du ciel, il scrutera les cieux!
L'Idéal, la pensée invincible, éternelle,
Tout le dieu qui vit, sous son argile charnelle,
Montera, montera, brûlera sous son front!
Et quand tu le verras sonder tout l'horizon,
Contempteur des vieux jougs, libre de toute crainte,
Tu viendras lui donner la Rédemption sainte!
—Splendide, radieuse, au sein des grandes mers
Tu surgiras, jetant sur le vaste Univers
L'Amour infini dans un infini sourire!
Le Monde vibrera comme une immense lyre
Dans le frémissement d'un immense baiser!

—Le Monde a soif d'amour: tu viendras l'apaiser.

IV

Ô splendeur de la chair! ô splendeur idéale!
Ô renouveau d'amour, aurore triomphale
Où, courbant à leurs pieds les Dieux et les Héros,
Kallipige la blanche et le petit Éros
Effleureront, couverts de la neige des roses,
Les femmes et les fleurs sous leurs beaux pieds écloses!
Ô grande Ariadné, qui jettes tes sanglots
Sur la rive, en voyant fuir là-bas sur les flots,
Blanche sous le soleil, la voile de Thésée,

Ô douce vierge enfant qu'une nuit a brisée,
Tais-toi! Sur son char d'or brodé de noirs raisins,
Lysios, promené dans les champs Phrygiens
Par les tigres lascifs et les panthères rousses,
Le long des fleuves bleus rougit les sombres mousses.
Zeus, Taureau, sur son cou berce comme une enfant
Le corps nu d'Europé, qui jette son bras blanc
Au cou nerveux du Dieu frissonnant dans la vague,
Il tourne lentement vers elle son œil vague;
Elle, laisse traîner sa pâle joue en fleur
Au front de Zeus; ses yeux sont fermés; elle meurt
Dans un divin baiser, et le flot qui murmure
De son écume d'or fleurit sa chevelure.
—Entre le laurier-rose et le lotus jaseur
Glisse amoureusement le grand Cygne rêveur
Embrassant la Léda des blancheurs de son aile;
—Et tandis que Cypris passe, étrangement belle,
Et, cambrant les rondeurs splendides de ses reins,
Étale fièrement l'or de ses larges seins
Et son ventre neigeux brodé de mousse noire,
—Héraclès, le Dompteur, qui, comme d'une gloire,
Fort, ceint son vaste corps de la peau du lion,
S'avance, front terrible et doux, à l'horizon!

Par la lune d'été vaguement éclairée,
Debout, nue, et rêvant dans sa pâleur dorée
Que tache le flot lourd de ses longs cheveux bleus,
Dans la clairière sombre où la mousse s'étoile,
La Dryade regarde au ciel silencieux...
—La blanche Séléné laisse flotter son voile,
Craintive, sur les pieds du bel Endymion,
Et lui jette un baiser dans un pâle rayon...
—La Source pleure au loin dans une longue extase...
C'est la Nymphe qui rêve, un coude sur son vase,
Au beau jeune homme blanc que son onde a pressé.
—Une brise d'amour dans la nuit a passé,
Et, dans les bois sacrés, dans l'horreur des grands arbres,
Majestueusement debout, les sombres Marbres,
Les Dieux, au front desquels le Bouvreuil fait son nid,
—Les Dieux écoutent l'Homme et le Monde infini!

Mai [18]70.

OPHÉLIE

I

Sur l'onde calme et noire où dorment les étoiles
La blanche Ophélia flotte comme un grand lys,
Flotte très lentement, couchée en ses longs voiles…
—On entend dans les bois lointains des hallalis.

Voici plus de mille ans que la triste Ophélie
Passe, fantôme blanc, sur le long fleuve noir;
Voici plus de mille ans que sa douce folie
Murmure sa romance à la brise du soir.

Le vent baise ses seins et déploie en corolle
Ses grands voiles bercés mollement par les eaux;
Les saules frissonnants pleurent sur son épaule,
Sur son grand front rêveur s'inclinent les roseaux.

Les nénuphars froissés soupirent autour d'elle;
Elle éveille parfois, dans un aune qui dort,
Quelque nid, d'où s'échappe un petit frisson d'aile:
—Un chant mystérieux tombe des astres d'or.

II

Ô pâle Ophélia! belle comme la neige!
Oui tu mourus, enfant, par un fleuve emporté!
—C'est que les vents tombant des grands monts de Norwège
T'avaient parlé tout bas de l'âpre liberté;

C'est qu'un souffle, tordant ta grande chevelure,
À ton esprit rêveur portait d'étranges bruits;
Que ton cœur écoutait le chant de la Nature
Dans les plaintes de l'arbre et les soupirs des nuits;

C'est que la voix des mers folles, immense râle,
Brisait ton sein d'enfant, trop humain et trop doux;
C'est qu'un matin d'avril, un beau cavalier pâle,
Un pauvre fou, s'assit muet à tes genoux!

Ciel! Amour! Liberté! Quel rêve, ô pauvre Folle!
Tu te fondais à lui comme une neige au feu:

Tes grandes visions étranglaient ta parole
—Et l'Infini terrible effara ton œil bleu!

III
—Et le Poète dit qu'aux rayons des étoiles
Tu viens chercher, la nuit, les fleurs que tu cueillis,
Et qu'il a vu sur l'eau, couchée en ses longs voiles,
La blanche Ophélia flotter, comme un grand lys.

VÉNUS ANADYOMÈNE

Comme d'un cercueil vert en fer blanc, une tête
De femme à cheveux bruns fortement pommadés
D'une vieille baignoire émerge, lente et bête,
Avec des déficits assez mal ravaudés;

Puis le col gras et gris, les larges omoplates
Qui saillent; le dos court qui rentre et qui ressort;
Puis les rondeurs des reins semblent prendre l'essor;
La graisse sous la peau paraît en feuilles plates;

L'échine est un peu rouge, et le tout sent un goût
Horrible étrangement; on remarque surtout
Des singularités qu'il faut voir à la loupe...

Les reins portent deux mots gravés: *Clara Venus;*
—Et tout ce corps remue et tend sa large croupe
Belle hideusement d'un ulcère à l'anus.

PREMIÈRE SOIRÉE

—Elle était fort déshabillée
Et de grands arbres indiscrets
Aux vitres jetaient leur feuillée
Malinement, tout près, tout près.

Assise sur ma grande chaise,
Mi-nue, elle joignait les mains.

Sur le plancher frissonnaient d'aise
Ses petits pieds si fins, si fins.

—Je regardai, couleur de cire,
Un petit rayon buissonnier
Papillonner dans son sourire
Et sur son sein,—mouche au rosier.

—Je baisai ses fines chevilles.
Elle eut un doux rire brutal
Qui s'égrenait en claires trilles,
Un joli rire de cristal.

Les petits pieds sous la chemise
Se sauvèrent: «Veux-tu finir!»
—La première audace permise,
Le rire feignait de punir!

—Pauvrets palpitants sous ma lèvre,
Je baisai doucement ses yeux:
—Elle jeta sa tête mièvre
En arrière: «Oh! c'est encor mieux!...

Monsieur, j'ai deux mots à te dire...»
—Je lui jetai le reste au sein
Dans un baiser, qui la fit rire
D'un bon rire qui voulait bien...

—Elle était fort déshabillée
Et de grands arbres indiscrets
Aux vitres jetaient leur feuillée
Malinement, tout près, tout près.

LES REPARTIES DE NINA

LUI. —Ta poitrine sur ma poitrine,
Hein? nous irions,
Ayant de l'air plein la narine,
Aux frais rayons

Du bon matin bleu, qui vous baigne
Du vin de jour?…
Quand tout le bois frissonnant saigne
Muet d'amour

De chaque branche, gouttes vertes,
Des bourgeons clairs,
On sent dans les choses ouvertes
Frémir des chairs:

Tu plongerais dans la luzerne
Ton blanc peignoir,
Rosant à l'air ce bleu qui cerne
Ton grand œil noir,

Amoureuse de la campagne,
Semant partout,
Comme une mousse de champagne,
Ton rire fou:

Riant à moi, brutal d'ivresse,
Qui te prendrais.
Comme cela,—la belle tresse,
Oh!—qui boirais

Ton goût de framboise et de fraise,
Ô chair de fleur!
Riant au vent vif qui te baise
Comme un voleur,

Au rose églantier qui t'embête
Aimablement:
Riant surtout, ô folle tête,
À ton amant!…

. . . .

Dix-sept ans! Tu seras heureuse!
Oh! les grands prés!
La grande campagne amoureuse!
—Dis, viens plus près!…

—Ta poitrine sur ma poitrine,
Mêlant nos voix,
Lents, nous gagnerions la ravine,
Puis les grands bois!...

Puis, comme une petite morte,
Le cœur pâmé,
Tu me dirais que je te porte,
L'œil mi-fermé...

Je te porterais, palpitante,
Dans le sentier:
L'oiseau filerait son andante:
Au Noisetier...

Je te parlerais dans ta bouche:
J'irais, pressant
Ton corps, comme une enfant qu'on couche,
Ivre du sang

Qui coule, bleu, sous ta peau blanche
Aux tons rosés:
Et te parlant la langue franche...
Tiens!...—que tu sais...

Nos grands bois sentiraient la sève
Et le soleil
Sablerait d'or fin leur grand rêve
Vert et vermeil.

. . . .

Le soir?...Nous reprendrons la route
Blanche qui court
Flânant, comme un troupeau qui broute,
Tout à l'entour

Les bons vergers à l'herbe bleue
Aux pommiers tors!
Comme on les sent toute une lieue
Leurs parfums forts!

Nous regagnerons le village
        Au ciel mi-noir;
Et ça sentira le laitage
        Dans l'air du soir;

Ça sentira l'étable, pleine
        De fumiers chauds,
Pleine d'un lent rythme d'haleine,
        Et de grands dos

Blanchissant sous quelque lumière;
        Et, tout là-bas,
Une vache fientera, fière,
        À chaque pas...

—Les lunettes de la grand-mère
        Et son nez long
Dans son missel; le pot de bière
        Cerclé de plomb,

Moussant entre les larges pipes
        Qui, crânement,
Fument: les effroyables lippes
        Qui, tout fumant,

Happent le jambon aux fourchettes
        Tant, tant et plus:
Le feu qui claire les couchettes
        Et les bahuts.

Les fesses luisantes et grasses
        D'un gros enfant
Qui fourre, à genoux, dans les tasses,
        Son museau blanc

Frôlé par un mufle qui gronde
        D'un ton gentil,
Et pourlèche la face ronde
        Du cher petit...

Noire, rogue au bord de sa chaise,
        Affreux profil,

Une vieille devant la braise
Qui fait du fil;

Que de choses verrons-nous, chère,
Dans ces taudis,
Quand la flamme illumine, claire,
Les carreaux gris!...

—Puis, petite et toute nichée
Dans les lilas
Noirs et frais: la vitre cachée,
Qui rit là-bas...

Tu viendras, tu viendras, je t'aime!
Ce sera beau.
Tu viendras, n'est-ce pas, et même...

ELLE. —*Et mon bureau?*

«MORTS DE QUATRE-VINGT-DOUZE [...]»

«... Français de soixante-dix, bonapartistes,
républicains, souvenez-vous de vos pères en 92, etc.;»
—PAUL DE CASSAGNAC
—*Le Pays*—

Morts de Quatre-vingt-douze et de Quatre-vingt-treize,
Qui, pâles du baiser fort de la liberté,
Calmes, sous vos sabots, brisiez le joug qui pèse
Sur l'âme et sur le front de toute humanité;

Hommes extasiés et grands dans la tourmente,
Vous dont les cœurs sautaient d'amour sous les haillons,
Ô Soldats que la Mort a semés, noble Amante,
Pour les régénérer, dans tous les vieux sillons;

Vous dont le sang lavait toute grandeur salie,
Morts de Valmy, Morts de Fleurus, Morts d'Italie,
Ô million de Christs aux yeux sombres et doux;

Nous vous laissions dormir avec la République,
Nous, courbés sous les rois comme sous une trique:
—Messieurs de Cassagnac nous reparlent de vous!

Fait à Mazas, 3 septembre 1870.

LES EFFARÉS

Noirs dans la neige et dans la brume
Au grand soupirail qui s'allume
        Leurs culs en rond

A genoux, cinq petits—misère!—
Regardent le Boulanger faire
        Le lourd pain blond

Ils voient le fort bras blanc qui tourne
La pâte grise et qui l'enfourne
        Dans un trou clair.

Ils écoutent le bon pain cuire.
Le Boulanger au gras sourire
        Grogne un vieil air.

Ils sont blottis, pas un ne bouge,
Au souffle du soupirail rouge
        Chaud comme un sein.

Quand pour quelque médianoche,
Façonné comme une brioche
        On sort le pain,

Quand, sous les poutres enfumées,
Chantent les croûtes parfumées
        Et les grillons,

Que ce trou chaud souffle la vie
Ils ont leur âme si ravie
        Sous leurs haillons,

Ils se ressentent si bien vivre
Les pauvres Jésus pleins de givre
Qu'ils sont là tous,

Collant leurs petits museaux roses
Au treillage, grognant des choses
Entre les trous,

Tout bêtes, faisant leurs prières
Et repliés vers ces lumières
Du ciel rouvert,

Si fort, qu'ils crèvent leur culotte
Et que leur chemise tremblotte
Au vent d'hiver.

ROMAN

I
On n'est pas sérieux, quand on a dix-sept ans.
—Un beau soir, foin des bocks et de la limonade,
Des cafés tapageurs aux lustres éclatants!
—On va sous les tilleuls verts de la promenade

Les tilleuls sentent bon dans les bons soirs de juin!
L'air est parfois si doux, qu'on ferme la paupière;
Le vent chargé de bruits,—la ville n'est pas loin,—
A des parfums de vigne et des parfums de bière....

II
—Voilà qu'on aperçoit un tout petit chiffon
D'azur sombre, encadré d'une petite branche,
Piqué d'une mauvaise étoile, qui se fond
Avec de doux frissons, petite et toute blanche...

Nuit de juin! Dix-sept ans!—On se laisse griser.
La sève est du champagne et vous monte à la tête...
On divague; on se sent aux lèvres un baiser
Qui palpite là, comme une petite bête....

III

Le cœur fou Robinsonne à travers les romans,
—Lorsque, dans la clarté d'un pâle réverbère,
Passe une demoiselle aux petits airs charmants,
Sous l'ombre du faux-col effrayant de son père…

Et, comme elle vous trouve immensément naïf,
Tout en faisant trotter ses petites bottines,
Elle se tourne, alerte et d'un mouvement vif….
—Sur vos lèvres alors meurent les cavatines…

IV

Vous êtes amoureux. Loué jusqu'au mois d'août.
Vous êtes amoureux—Vos sonnets La font rire.
Tous vos amis s'en vont, vous êtes mauvais goût.
—Puis l'adorée, un soir, a daigné vous écrire….!

—Ce soir-là,…—vous rentrez aux cafés éclatants,
Vous demandez des bocks ou de la limonade…
—On n'est pas sérieux, quand on a dix-sept ans
Et qu'on a des tilleuls verts sur la promenade.

29 sept. 70

RÊVÉ POUR L'HIVER

À xxx Elle.

L'hiver, nous irons dans un petit wagon rose
Avec des coussins bleus.
Nous serons bien. Un nid de baisers fous repose
Dans chaque coin moelleux.

Tu fermeras l'œil, pour ne point voir, par la glace,
Grimacer les ombres des soirs,
Ces monstruosités hargneuses, populace
De démons noirs et de loups noirs.

Puis tu te sentiras la joue égratignée…
Un petit baiser, comme une folle araignée,
Te courra par le cou…

Et tu me diras: «Cherche!», en inclinant la tête;
—Et nous prendrons du temps à trouver cette bête
—Qui voyage beaucoup...

En Wagon, le 7 octobre 70

LE BUFFET

C'est un large buffet sculpté; le chêne sombre,
Très vieux, a pris cet air si bon des vieilles gens;
Le buffet est ouvert, et verse dans son ombre
Comme un flot de vin vieux, des parfums engageants;

Tout plein, c'est un fouillis de vieilles vieilleries,
De linges odorants et jaunes, de chiffons
De femmes ou d'enfants, de dentelles flétries,
De fichus de grand-mère où sont peints des griffons;

—C'est là qu'on trouverait les médaillons, les mèches
De cheveux blancs ou blonds, les portraits, les fleurs sèches
Dont le parfum se mêle à des parfums de fruits.

—Ô buffet du vieux temps, tu sais bien des histoires,
Et tu voudrais conter tes contes, et tu bruis
Quand s'ouvrent lentement tes grandes portes noires.

octobre 70

L'ÉCLATANTE VICTOIRE DE SAAREBRÜCK,—

remportée aux cris de vive l'Empereur! Gravure belge brillamment coloriée, se vend à Charleroi, 35 centimes.

Au milieu, l'Empereur, dans une apothéose
Bleue et jaune, s'en va, raide, sur son dada
Flamboyant; très heureux,—car il voit tout en rose,
Féroce comme Zeus et doux comme un papa;

En bas, les bons Pioupious qui faisaient la sieste
Près des tambours dorés et des rouges canons,

Se lèvent gentiment. Pitou remet sa veste,
Et, tourné vers le Chef, s'étourdit de grands noms!

À droite, Dumanet, appuyé sur la crosse
De son chassepot, sent frémir sa nuque en brosse,
Et: «Vive l'Empereur!!»—Son voisin reste coi...

Un schako surgit, comme un soleil noir...—Au centre,
Boquillon rouge et bleu, très naïf, sur son ventre
Se dresse, et,—présentant ses derrières—: «De quoi?..»

octobre 70

LA MALINE

Dans la salle à manger brune, que parfumait
Une odeur de vernis et de fruits, à mon aise
Je ramassais un plat de je ne sais quel met
Belge, et je m'épatais dans mon immense chaise.

En mangeant, j'écoutais l'horloge,—heureux et coi.
La cuisine s'ouvrit avec une bouffée
—Et la servante vint, je ne sais pas pourquoi,
Fichu moitié défait, malinement coiffée

Et, tout en promenant son petit doigt tremblant
Sur sa joue, un velours de pêche rose et blanc,
En faisant, de sa lèvre enfantine, une moue,

Elle arrangeait les plats, près de moi, pour m'aiser;
—Puis, comme ça,—bien sûr pour avoir un baiser,—
Tout bas: «Sens donc: j'ai pris *une* froid sur la joue...»

Charleroi, octobre 70

AU CABARET-VERT, CINQ HEURES DU SOIR

Depuis huit jours, j'avais déchiré mes bottines
Aux cailloux des chemins. J'entrais à Charleroi.

—*Au Cabaret-Vert:* je demandai des tartines
De beurre et du jambon qui fût à moitié froid.

Bienheureux, j'allongeai les jambes sous la table
Verte: je contemplai les sujets très naïfs
De la tapisserie.—Et ce fut adorable,
Quand la fille aux tétons énormes, aux yeux vifs,

—Celle-là, ce n'est pas un baiser qui l'épeure!—
Rieuse, m'apporta des tartines de beurre,
Du jambon tiède, dans un plat colorié,

Du jambon rose et blanc parfumé d'une gousse
D'ail,—et m'emplit la chope immense, avec sa mousse
Que dorait un rayon de soleil arriéré

Octobre 70

LE DORMEUR DU VAL

C'est un trou de verdure où chante une rivière
Accrochant follement aux herbes des haillons
D'argent; où le soleil, de la montagne fière,
Luit: c'est un petit val qui mousse de rayons.

Un soldat jeune, bouche ouverte, tête nue,
Et la nuque baignant dans le frais cresson bleu,
Dort; il est étendu dans l'herbe, sous la nue,
Pâle dans son lit vert où la lumière pleut.

Les pieds dans les glaïeuls, il dort. Souriant comme
Sourirait un enfant malade, il fait un somme:
Nature, berce-le chaudement: il a froid.

Les parfums ne font pas frissonner sa narine;
Il dort dans le soleil, la main sur sa poitrine
Tranquille. Il a deux trous rouges au côté droit.

Octobre 1870

À LA MUSIQUE

Place de la gare, à Charleville

Sur la place taillée en mesquines pelouses,
Square où tout est correct, les arbres et les fleurs,
Tous les bourgeois poussifs qu'étranglent les chaleurs
Portent, les jeudis soirs, leurs bêtises jalouses

—L'orchestre militaire, au milieu du jardin,
Balance ses schakos dans la Valse des fifres:
—Autour, aux premiers rangs, parade le gandin;
Le notaire pend à ses breloques à chiffres

Des rentiers à lorgnons soulignent tous les couacs:
Les gros bureaux bouffis traînent leurs grosses dames
Auprès desquelles vont, officieux cornacs,
Celles dont les volants ont des airs de réclames;

Sur les bancs verts, des clubs d'épiciers retraités
Qui tisonnent le sable avec leur canne à pomme,
Fort sérieusement discutent les traités,
Puis prisent en argent, et reprennent: «En somme!...»

Épatant sur son banc les rondeurs de ses reins,
Un bourgeois à boutons clairs, bedaine flamande,
Savoure son onnaing d'où le tabac par brins
Déborde—vous savez, c'est de la contrebande;—

Le long des gazons verts ricanent les voyous;
Et, rendus amoureux par le chant des trombones,
Très naïfs, et fumant des roses, les pioupious
Caressent les bébés pour enjôler les bonnes...

—Moi, je suis, débraillé comme un étudiant
Sous les marronniers verts les alertes fillettes:
Elles le savent bien; et tournent en riant,
Vers moi, leurs yeux tout pleins de choses indiscrètes

Je ne dis pas un mot: je regarde toujours
La chair de leurs cous blancs brodés de mèches folles:
Je suis, sous le corsage et les frêles atours,
Le dos divin après la courbe des épaules

J'ai bientôt déniché la bottine, le bas...
—Je reconstruis les corps, brûlé de belles fièvres.
Elles me trouvent drôle et se parlent tout bas...
—Et je sens les baisers qui me viennent aux lèvres...

BAL DES PENDUS

Au gibet noir, manchot aimable,
Dansent, dansent les paladins
Les maigres paladins du diable
Les squelettes de Saladins.

Messire Belzebuth tire par la cravate
Ses petits pantins noirs grimaçant sur le ciel,
Et, leur claquant au front un revers de savate,
Les fait danser, danser aux sons d'un vieux Noël!

Et les pantins choqués enlacent leurs bras grêles:
Comme des orgues noirs, les poitrines à jour
Que serraient autrefois les gentes damoiselles,
Se heurtent longuement dans un hideux amour.

Hurrah! les gais danseurs, qui n'avez plus de panse!
On peut cabrioler, les tréteaux sont si longs!
Hop! qu'on ne sache plus si c'est bataille ou danse!
Belzebuth enragé râcle ses violons!

Ô durs talons, jamais on n'use sa sandale!
Presque tous ont quitté la chemise de peau:
Le reste est peu gênant et se voit sans scandale.
Sur les crânes, la neige applique un blanc chapeau:

Le corbeau fait panache à ces têtes fêlées,
Un morceau de chair tremble à leur maigre menton:
On dirait, tournoyant dans les sombres mêlées,
Des preux, raides, heurtant armures de carton.

Hurrah! la bise siffle au grand bal des squelettes!
Le gibet noir mugit comme un orgue de fer!
Les loups vont répondant des forêts violettes:
À l'horizon, le ciel est d'un rouge d'enfer...

Holà, secouez-moi ces capitans funèbres
Qui défilent, sournois, de leurs gros doigts cassés
Un chapelet d'amour sur leurs pâles vertèbres:
Ce n'est pas un moustier ici, les trépassés!

Oh! voilà qu'au milieu de la danse macabre
Bondit dans le ciel rouge un grand squelette fou
Emporté par l'élan, comme un cheval se cabre:
Et, se sentant encor la corde raide au cou,

Crispe ses petits doigts sur son fémur qui craque
Avec des cris pareils à des ricanements,
Et, comme un baladin rentre dans la baraque,
Rebondit dans le bal au chant des ossements.

Au gibet noir, manchot aimable,
Dansent dansent les paladins
Les maigres paladins du diable,
Les squelettes de Saladins.

LE CHÂTIMENT DE TARTUFE

Tisonnant, tisonnant son cœur amoureux sous
Sa chaste robe noire, heureux, la main gantée,
Un jour qu'il s'en allait, effroyablement doux,
Jaune, bavant la foi de sa bouche édentée,

Un jour qu'il s'en allait,—«Oremus,»—un Méchant
Le prit rudement par son oreille benoîte
Et lui jeta des mots affreux, en arrachant
Sa chaste robe noire autour de sa peau moite!

Châtiment! . . . Ses habits étaient déboutonnés,
Et le long chapelet des péchés pardonnés
S'égrenant dans son cœur, Saint Tartufe était pâle!..

Donc, il se confessait, priait, avec un râle!
L'homme se contenta d'emporter ses rabats . . .
—Peuh! Tartufe était nu du haut jusques en bas!

LE FORGERON

Palais des Tuileries,
vers le 10 août 92

Le bras sur un marteau gigantesque, effrayant
D'ivresse et de grandeur, le front vaste, riant
Comme un clairon d'airain, avec toute sa bouche,
Et prenant ce gros-là dans son regard farouche,
Le Forgeron parlait à Louis Seize, un jour
Que le Peuple était là, se tordant tout autour,
Et sur les lambris d'or traînant sa veste sale.
Or le bon roi, debout sur son ventre, était pâle
Pâle comme un vaincu qu'on prend pour le gibet,
Et, soumis comme un chien, jamais ne regimbait
Car ce maraud de forge aux énormes épaules
Lui disait de vieux mots et des choses si drôles,
Que cela l'empoignait au front, comme cela!

«Or, tu sais bien, Monsieur, nous chantions tra la la
Et nous piquions les bœufs vers les sillons des autres:
Le Chanoine au soleil filait des patenôtres
Sur des chapelets clairs grenés de pièces d'or
Le Seigneur, à cheval, passait, sonnant du cor
Et l'un avec la hart, l'autre avec la cravache
Nous fouaillaient—Hébétés comme des yeux de vache,
Nos yeux ne pleuraient plus; nous allions, nous allions,
Et quand nous avions mis le pays en sillons,
Quand nous avions laissé dans cette terre noire
Un peu de notre chair... nous avions un pourboire
On nous faisait flamber nos taudis dans la nuit
Nos petits y faisaient un gâteau fort bien cuit

... «Oh! je ne me plains pas. Je te dis mes bêtises,
C'est entre nous. J'admets que tu me contredises.
Or, n'est-ce pas joyeux de voir, au mois de juin
Dans les granges entrer des voitures de foin
Enormes? De sentir l'odeur de ce qui pousse,
Des vergers quand il pleut un peu, de l'herbe rousse?
De voir des blés, des blés, des épis pleins de grain,
De penser que cela prépare bien du pain?...
Oh! plus fort, on irait, au fourneau qui s'allume,
Chanter joyeusement en martelant l'enclume,
Si l'on était certain de pouvoir prendre un peu,

Etant homme, à la fin!, de ce que donne Dieu!
—Mais voilà, c'est toujours la même vieille histoire!…

«Mais je sais, maintenant! Moi, je ne peux plus croire,
Quand j'ai deux bonnes mains, mon front et mon marteau,
Qu'un homme vienne là, dague sur le manteau,
Et me dise: Mon gars, ensemence ma terre;
Que l'on arrive encor, quand ce serait la guerre,
Me prendre mon garçon comme cela, chez moi!
—Moi, je serais un homme, et toi, tu serais roi,
Tu me dirais: Je veux!..—Tu vois bien, c'est stupide.
Tu crois que j'aime voir ta baraque splendide,
Tes officiers dorés, tes mille chenapans,
Tes palsembleu bâtards tournant comme des paons:
Ils ont rempli ton nid de l'odeur de nos filles
Et de petits billets pour nous mettre aux Bastilles
Et nous dirons: C'est bien: les pauvres à genoux!
Nous dorerons ton Louvre en donnant nos gros sous!
Et tu te soûleras, tu feras belle fête
—Et ces Messieurs riront, les reins sur notre tête!

«Non. Ces saletés-là datent de nos papas!
Oh! Le Peuple n'est plus une putain. Trois pas
Et, tous, nous avons mis ta Bastille en poussière
Cette bête suait du sang à chaque pierre
Et c'était dégoûtant, la Bastille debout
Avec ses murs lépreux qui nous racontaient tout
Et, toujours, nous tenaient enfermés dans leur ombre!
—Citoyen! citoyen! c'était le passé sombre
Qui croulait, qui râlait, quand nous prîmes la tour!
Nous avions quelque chose au cœur comme l'amour.
Nous avions embrassé nos fils sur nos poitrines.
Et, comme des chevaux, en soufflant des narines
Nous allions, fiers et forts, et ça nous battait là….
Nous marchions au soleil, front haut,—comme cela—,
Dans Paris! On venait devant nos vestes sales.
Enfin! Nous nous sentions Hommes! Nous étions pâles,
Sire, nous étions soûls de terribles espoirs:
Et quand nous fûmes là, devant les donjons noirs,
Agitant nos clairons et nos feuilles de chêne,
Les piques à la main; nous n'eûmes pas de haine,
—Nous nous sentions si forts, nous voulions être doux!

. . . .

. . . .

«Et depuis ce jour-là, nous sommes comme fous!
Le tas des ouvriers a monté dans la rue,
Et ces maudits s'en vont, foule toujours accrue
De sombres revenants, aux portes des richards.
Moi, je cours avec eux assommer les mouchards:
Et je vais dans Paris, noir, marteau sur l'épaule,
Farouche, à chaque coin balayant quelque drôle,
Et, si tu me riais au nez, je te tuerais!
—Puis, tu peux y compter, tu te feras des frais
Avec tes hommes noirs, qui prennent nos requêtes
Pour se les renvoyer comme sur des raquettes
Et, tout bas, les malins! se disent: «Qu'ils sont sots!»
Pour mitonner des lois, coller de petits pots
Pleins de jolis décrets roses et de droguailles
S'amuser à couper proprement quelques tailles,
Puis se boucher le nez quand nous marchons près d'eux,
—Nos doux représentants qui nous trouvent crasseux!—
Pour ne rien redouter, rien, que les baïonnettes . . . ,
C'est très bien. Foin de leur tabatière à sornettes!
Nous en avons assez, là, de ces cerveaux plats
Et de ces ventres-dieux. Ah! ce sont là les plats
Que tu nous sers, bourgeois, quand nous sommes féroces,
Quand nous brisons déjà les sceptres et les crosses!..»

. . . .

Il le prend par le bras, arrache le velours
Des rideaux, et lui montre en bas les larges cours
Où fourmille, où fourmille, où se lève la foule,
La foule épouvantable avec des bruits de houle,
Hurlant comme une chienne, hurlant comme une mer,
Avec ses bâtons forts et ses piques de fer,
Ses tambours, ses grands cris de halles et de bouges,
Tas sombre de haillons saignant de bonnets rouges:
L'Homme, par la fenêtre ouverte, montre tout
Au roi pâle et suant qui chancelle debout,
Malade à regarder cela!

«C'est la Crapule,
Sire. Ça bave aux murs, ça monte, ça pullule:
—Puisqu'ils ne mangent pas, Sire, ce sont des gueux!
Je suis un forgeron: ma femme, est avec eux,
Folle! Elle croit trouver du pain aux Tuileries!
—On ne veut pas de nous dans les boulangeries.
J'ai trois petits. Je suis crapule.—Je connais

Des vieilles qui s'en vont pleurant sous leurs bonnets
Parce qu'on leur a pris leur garçon ou leur fille:
C'est la crapule.—Un homme était à la bastille,
Un autre était forçat: et tous deux, citoyens
Honnêtes. Libérés, ils sont comme des chiens:
On les insulte! Alors, ils ont là quelque chose
Qui leur fait mal, allez! C'est terrible, et c'est cause
Que se sentant brisés, que, se sentant damnés,
Ils sont là, maintenant, hurlant sous votre nez!
Crapule.—Là-dedans sont des filles, infâmes
Parce que,—vous saviez que c'est faible, les femmes,—
Messeigneurs de la cour,—que ça veut toujours bien,—
Vous [leur] avez craché sur l'âme, comme rien!
Vos belles, aujourd'hui, sont là. C'est la crapule.

. . . .

«Oh! tous les Malheureux, tous ceux dont le dos brûle
Sous le soleil féroce, et qui vont, et qui vont,
Qui dans ce travail-là sentent crever leur front
Chapeau bas, mes bourgeois! Oh! ceux-là, sont les Hommes!
Nous sommes Ouvriers, Sire! Ouvriers! Nous sommes
Pour les grands temps nouveaux où l'on voudra savoir,
Où l'Homme forgera du matin jusqu'au soir,
Chasseur des grands effets, chasseur des grandes causes;
Où, lentement vainqueur, il domptera les choses
Et montera sur Tout, comme sur un cheval!
Oh! splendides lueurs des forges! Plus de mal,
Plus!—Ce qu'on ne sait pas, c'est peut-être terrible:
Nous saurons!—Nos marteaux en main; passons au crible
Tout ce que nous savons: puis, Frères, en avant!
Nous faisons quelquefois ce grand rêve émouvant
De vivre simplement, ardemment, sans rien dire
De mauvais, travaillant sous l'auguste sourire
D'une femme qu'on aime avec un noble amour:
Et l'on travaillerait fièrement tout le jour,
Ecoutant le devoir comme un clairon qui sonne:
Et l'on se sentirait très heureux: et personne
Oh! personne, surtout, ne vous ferait ployer!
On aurait un fusil au-dessus du foyer. . . .

. . . .

«Oh! mais l'air est tout plein d'une odeur de bataille!
Que te disais-je donc? Je suis de la canaille!
Il reste des mouchards et des accapareurs.

Nous sommes libres, nous! Nous avons des terreurs
Où nous nous sentons grands, oh! si grands! Tout à l'heure
Je parlais de devoir calme, d'une demeure....
Regarde donc le ciel!—C'est trop petit pour nous,
Nous crèverions de chaud, nous serions à genoux!
Regarde donc le ciel!—Je rentre dans la foule
Dans la grande canaille effroyable, qui roule,
Sire, tes vieux canons sur les sales pavés:
—Oh! quand nous serons morts, nous les aurons lavés
—Et si, devant nos cris, devant notre vengeance,
Les pattes des vieux rois mordorés, sur la France
Poussent leurs régiments en habits de gala
Eh bien, n'est-ce pas, vous tous? Merde à ces chiens-là!»
. . . .

—Il reprit son marteau sur l'épaule.
La foule
Près de cet homme-là se sentait l'âme soûle,
Et, dans la grande cour, dans les appartements,
Où Paris haletait avec des hurlements,
Un frisson secoua l'immense populace
Alors, de sa main large et superbe de crasse
Bien que le roi ventru suât, le Forgeron,
Terrible, lui jeta le bonnet rouge au front!

MA BOHÊME (FANTAISIE)

Je m'en allais, les poings dans mes poches crevées;
Mon paletot aussi devenait idéal;
J'allais sous le ciel, Muse! et j'étais ton féal;
Oh! là là! que d'amours splendides j'ai rêvées!

Mon unique culotte avait un large trou.
—Petit-Poucet rêveur, j'égrenais dans ma course
Des rimes. Mon auberge était à la Grande-Ourse.
—Mes étoiles au ciel avaient un doux frou-frou

Et je les écoutais, assis au bord des routes,
Ces bons soirs de septembre où je sentais des gouttes
De rosée à mon front, comme un vin de vigueur;

Où, rimant au milieu des ombres fantastiques,
Comme des lyres, je tirais les élastiques
De mes souliers blessés, un pied près de mon cœur!

LE MAL

Tandis que les crachats rouges de la mitraille
Sifflent tout le jour par l'infini du ciel bleu;
Qu'écarlates ou verts, près du Roi qui les raille,
Croulent les bataillons en masse dans le feu;

Tandis qu'une folie épouvantable, broie
Et fait de cent milliers d'hommes un tas fumant;
—Pauvres morts! dans l'été, dans l'herbe, dans ta joie,
Nature! ô toi qui fis ces hommes saintement! . .—

—Il est un Dieu, qui rit aux nappes damassées
Des autels, à l'encens, aux grands calices d'or;
Qui dans le bercement des hosannah s'endort;

Et se réveille, quand des mères, ramassées
Dans l'angoisse, et pleurant sous leur vieux bonnet noir,
Lui donnent un gros sou lié dans leur mouchoir!

RAGES DE CÉSARS

L'homme pâle, le long des pelouses fleuries,
Chemine, en habit noir, et le cigare aux dents:
L'Homme pâle repense aux fleurs des Tuileries
—Et parfois son œil terne a des regards ardents…

Car l'Empereur est soûl de ses vingt ans d'orgie!
Il s'était dit: «Je vais souffler la Liberté
Bien délicatement, ainsi qu'une bougie!»
La Liberté revit! Il se sent éreinté!

Il est pris.—Oh! quel nom sur ses lèvres muettes
Tressàille? Quel regret implacable le mord?
On ne le saura pas. L'Empereur a l'œil mort.

Il repense peut-être au Compère en lunettes…
—Et regarde filer de son cigare en feu,
Comme aux soirs de Saint-Cloud, un fin nuage bleu.

III. 1871

LE CŒUR VOLÉ

Mon triste cœur bave à la poupe,
Mon cœur couvert de caporal:
Ils y lancent des jets de soupe,
Mon triste cœur bave à la poupe:
Sous les quolibets de la troupe
Qui pousse un rire général,
Mon triste cœur bave à la poupe
Mon cœur couvert de caporal!

Ithyphalliques et pioupiesques
Leurs quolibets l'ont dépravé!
Au gouvernail on voit des fresques
Ithyphalliques et pioupiesques
Ô flots abracadabrantesques
Prenez mon cœur, qu'il soit lavé:
Ithyphalliques et pioupiesques
Leurs quolibets l'ont dépravé!

Quand ils auront tari leurs chiques
Comment agir, ô cœur volé?
Ce seront des hoquets bachiques
Quand ils auront tari leurs chiques
J'aurai des sursauts stomachiques
Moi, si mon cœur est ravalé:
Quand ils auront tari leurs chiques
Comment agir, ô cœur volé?

Mai 1871

CHANT DE GUERRE PARISIEN

Le Printemps est évident, car
Du cœur des Propriétés vertes,
Le vol de Thiers et de Picard
Tient ses splendeurs grandes ouvertes!

Ô Mai! quels délirants culs-nus!
Sèvres, Meudon, Bagneux, Asnières,
Ecoutez donc les bienvenus
Semer les choses printanières!

Ils ont schako, sabre et tam-tam
Non la vieille boîte à bougies
Et des yoles qui n'ont jam, jam . . .
Fendent le lac aux eaux rougies!

Plus que jamais nous bambochons
Quand arrivent sur nos tanières
Crouler les jaunes cabochons
Dans des aubes particulières!

Thiers et Picard sont des Eros,
Des enleveurs d'héliotropes,
Au pétrole ils font des Corots:
Voici hannetonner leurs tropes. . . .

Ils sont familiers du Grand Truc!..
Et couché dans les glaïeuls, Favre
Fait son cillement aqueduc,
Et ses reniflements à poivre!

La Grand ville a le pavé chaud,
Malgré vos douches de pétrole,
Et décidément, il nous faut
Vous secouer dans votre rôle . . .

Et les Ruraux qui se prélassent
Dans de longs accroupissements,
Entendront les rameaux qui cassent
Parmi les rouges froissements!

MES PETITES AMOUREUSES

Un hydrolat lacrymal lave
Les cieux vert-chou:
Sous l'arbre tendronnier qui bave,
Vos caoutchoucs

Blancs de lunes particulières
Aux pialats ronds,
Entrechoquez vos genouillères
Mes laiderons!

Nous nous aimions à cette époque,
Bleu laideron!
On mangeait des œufs à la coque
Et du mouron!

Un soir, tu me sacras poète,
Blond laideron:
Descends ici, que je te fouette
En mon giron;

J'ai dégueulé ta bandoline,
Noir laideron;
Tu couperais ma mandoline
Au fil du front

Pouah! mes salives desséchées,
Roux laideron
Infectent encor les tranchées
De ton sein rond!

Ô mes petites amoureuses,
Que je vous hais!
Plaquez de fouffes douloureuses
Vos tétons laids!

Piétinez mes vieilles terrines
De sentiment;
—Hop donc! Soyez-moi ballerines
Pour un moment! . .

Vos omoplates se déboîtent,
Ô mes amours!
Une étoile à vos reins qui boitent,
Tournez vos tours!

Et c'est pourtant pour ces éclanches
Que j'ai rimé!
Je voudrais vous casser les hanches
D'avoir aimé!

Fade amas d'étoiles ratées,
Comblez les coins!
—Vous crèverez en Dieu, bâtées
D'ignobles soins!

Sous les lunes particulières
Aux pialats ronds,
Entrechoquez vos genouillères,
Mes laiderons!

ACCROUPISSEMENTS

Bien tard, quand il se sent l'estomac écœuré,
Le frère Milotus, un œil à la lucarne
D'où le soleil, clair comme un chaudron récuré,
Lui darde une migraine et fait son regard darne,
Déplace dans les draps son ventre de curé

Il se démène sous sa couverture grise
Et descend, ses genoux à son ventre tremblant,
Effaré comme un vieux qui mangerait sa prise,
Car il lui faut, le poing à l'anse d'un pot blanc,
À ses reins largement retrousser sa chemise!

Or, il s'est accroupi, frileux, les doigts de pied
Repliés, grelottant au clair soleil qui plaque
Des jaunes de brioche aux vitres de papier;
Et le nez du bonhomme où s'allume la laque
Renifle aux rayons, tel qu'un charnel polypier.

. . . .

Le bonhomme mijote au feu, bras tordus, lippe
Au ventre: il sent glisser ses cuisses dans le feu,
Et ses chausses roussir, et s'éteindre sa pipe;
Quelque chose comme un oiseau remue un peu
À son ventre serein comme un monceau de tripe!

Autour, dort un fouillis de meubles abrutis
Dans des haillons de crasse et sur de sales ventres;
Des escabeaux, crapauds étranges, sont blottis
Aux coins noirs: des buffets ont des gueules de chantres
Qu'entrouvre un sommeil plein d'horribles appétits

L'écœurante chaleur gorge la chambre étroite;
Le cerveau du bonhomme est bourré de chiffons:
Il écoute les poils pousser dans sa peau moite,
Et parfois, en hoquets fort gravement bouffons
S'échappe, secouant son escabeau qui boite...

. . . .

Et le soir, aux rayons de lune, qui lui font
Aux contours du cul des bavures de lumière,
Une ombre avec détails s'accroupit, sur un fond
De neige rose ainsi qu'une rose trémière....
Fantasque, un nez poursuit Venus au ciel profond.

L'ORGIE PARISIENNE ou PARIS SE REPEUPLE

Ô lâches, la voilà! Dégorgez dans les gares!
Le soleil essuya de ses poumons ardents
Les boulevards qu'un soir comblèrent les Barbares.
Voilà la Cité sainte, assise à l'occident!

Allez! on préviendra les reflux d'incendie,
Voilà les quais, voilà les boulevards, voilà
Les maisons sur l'azur léger qui s'irradie
Et qu'un soir la rougeur des bombes étoila!

Cachez les palais morts dans des niches de planches!
L'ancien jour effaré rafraîchit vos regards.
Voici le troupeau roux des tordeuses de hanches:
Soyez fous, vous serez drôles, étant hagards!

Tas de chiennes en rut mangeant des cataplasmes,
Le cri des maisons d'or vous réclame. Volez!
Mangez! Voici la nuit de joie aux profonds spasmes
Qui descend dans la rue. Ô buveurs désolés,

Buvez! Quand la lumière arrive intense et folle,
Fouillant à vos côtés les luxes ruisselants,
Vous n'allez pas baver, sans geste, sans parole,
Dans vos verres, les yeux perdus aux lointains blancs?

Avalez, pour la Reine aux fesses cascadantes!
Écoutez l'action des stupides hoquets
Déchirants! Écoutez sauter aux nuits ardentes
Les idiots râleux, vieillards, pantins, laquais!

Ô cœurs de saleté, bouches épouvantables,
Fonctionnez plus fort, bouches de puanteurs!
Un vin pour ces torpeurs ignobles, sur ces tables…
Vos ventres sont fondus de hontes, ô Vainqueurs!

Ouvrez votre narine aux superbes nausées!
Trempez de poisons forts les cordes de vos cous!
Sur vos nuques d'enfants baissant ses mains croisées
Le Poète vous dit: «Ô lâches, soyez fous!

Parce que vous fouillez le ventre de la Femme,
Vous craignez d'elle encore une convulsion
Qui crie, asphyxiant votre nichée infâme
Sur sa poitrine, en une horrible pression.

Syphilitiques, fous, rois, pantins, ventriloques,
Qu'est-ce que ça peut faire à la putain Paris,
Vos âmes et vos corps, vos poisons et vos loques?
Elle se secouera de vous, hargneux pourris!

Et quand vous serez bas, geignant sur vos entrailles,
Les flancs morts, réclamant votre argent, éperdus,
La rouge courtisane aux seins gros de batailles
Loin de votre stupeur tordra ses poings ardus!

Quand tes pieds ont dansé si fort dans les colères,
Paris! quand tu reçus tant de coups de couteau,

Quand tu gis, retenant dans tes prunelles claires
Un peu de la bonté du fauve renouveau,

Ô cité douloureuse, ô cité quasi morte,
La tête et les deux seins jetés vers l'Avenir
Ouvrant sur ta pâleur ses milliards de portes,
Cité que le Passé sombre pourrait bénir:

Corps remagnétisé pour les énormes peines,
Tu rebois donc la vie effroyable! tu sens
Sourdre le flux des vers livides en tes veines,
Et sur ton clair amour rôder les doigts glaçants!

Et ce n'est pas mauvais. Les vers, les vers livides
Ne gêneront pas plus ton souffle de Progrès
Que les Stryx n'éteignaient l'œil des Cariatides
Où des pleurs d'or astral tombaient des bleus degrés.»

Quoique ce soit affreux de te revoir couverte
Ainsi; quoiqu'on n'ait fait jamais d'une cité
Ulcère plus puant à la Nature verte,
Le Poète te dit: «Splendide est ta Beauté!»

L'orage te sacra suprême poésie;
L'immense remuement des forces te secourt;
Ton œuvre bout, la mort gronde, Cité choisie!
Amasse les strideurs au cœur du clairon sourd.

Le Poète prendra le sanglot des Infâmes,
La haine des Forçats, la clameur des Maudits;
Et ses rayons d'amour flagelleront les Femmes.
Ses strophes bondiront: Voilà! voilà! bandits!

—Société, tout est rétabli:—les orgies
Pleurent leur ancien râle aux anciens lupanars:
Et les gaz en délire, aux murailles rougies,
Flambent sinistrement vers les azurs blafards!

Mai 1871.

LES POÈTES DE SEPT ANS

Et la Mère, fermant le livre du devoir,
S'en allait satisfaite et très-fière, sans voir,
Dans les yeux bleus et sous le front plein d'éminences
L'âme de son enfant livrée aux répugnances.

Tout le jour il suait d'obéissance; très
Intelligent; pourtant des tics noirs, quelques traits,
Semblaient prouver en lui d'âcres hypocrisies.
Dans l'ombre des couloirs aux tentures moisies,
En passant il tirait la langue, les deux poings
À l'aine, et dans ses yeux fermés voyait des points.
Une porte s'ouvrait sur le soir: à la lampe
On le voyait, là-haut, qui râlait sur la rampe,
Sous un golfe de jour pendant du toit. L'été
Surtout, vaincu, stupide, il était entêté
À se renfermer dans la fraîcheur des latrines:
Il pensait là, tranquille et livrant ses narines.
Quand, lavé des odeurs du jour, le jardinet
Derrière la maison, en hiver, s'illunait,
Gisant au pied d'un mur, enterré dans la marne
Et pour des visions écrasant son œil darne,
Il écoutait grouiller les galeux espaliers.
Pitié! ces enfants seuls étaient ses familiers
Qui, chétifs, fronts nus, œil déteignant sur la joue,
Cachant de maigres doigts jaunes et noirs de boue
Sous des habits puant la foire et tout vieillots,
Conversaient avec la douceur des idiots!
Et si, l'ayant surpris à des pitiés immondes,
La mère s'effrayait; les tendresses, profondes,
De l'enfant se jetaient sur cet étonnement.
C'était bon. Elle avait le bleu regard,—qui ment!

À sept ans, il faisait des romans, sur la vie
Du grand désert, où luit la Liberté ravie,
Forêts, soleils, rios, savanes!—Il s'aidait
De journaux illustrés où, rouge, il regardait
Des Espagnoles rire et des Italiennes.
Quand venait, l'œil brun, folle, en robes d'indiennes,
—Huit ans,—la fille des ouvriers d'à côté,
La petite brutale, et qu'elle avait sauté,

Dans un coin, sur son dos, en secouant ses tresses,
Et qu'il était sous elle, il lui mordait les fesses,
Car elle ne portait jamais de pantalons;
—Et, par elle meurtri des poings et des talons,
Remportait la saveur de sa peau dans sa chambre.

Il craignait les blafards dimanches de décembre,
Où, pommadé, sur un guéridon d'acajou,
Il lisait une Bible à la tranche vert-chou;
Des rêves l'oppressaient chaque nuit dans l'alcôve.
Il n'aimait pas Dieu; mais les hommes, qu'au soir fauve,
Noirs, en blouse, il voyait rentrer dans le faubourg
Où les crieurs, en trois roulements de tambour
Font autour des édits rire et gronder les foules.
—Il rêvait la prairie amoureuse, où des houles
Lumineuses, parfums sains, pubescences d'or,
Font leur remuement calme et prennent leur essor!

Et comme il savourait surtout les sombres choses,
Quand, dans la chambre nue aux persiennes closes,
Haute et bleue, âcrement prise d'humidité,
Il lisait son roman sans cesse médité,
Plein de lourds ciels ocreux et de forêts noyées,
De fleurs de chair aux bois sidérals déployées,
Vertige, écroulements, déroutes et pitié!
—Tandis que se faisait la rumeur du quartier,
En bas,—seul, et couché sur des pièces de toile
Ecrue, et pressentant violemment la voile!

26 Mai 1871

LES PAUVRES À L'ÉGLISE

Parqués entre des bancs de chêne, aux coins d'église
Qu'attiédit puamment leur souffle, tous leurs yeux
Vers le chœur ruisselant d'orrie et la maîtrise
Aux vingt gueules gueulant les cantiques pieux;

Comme un parfum de pain humant l'odeur de cire,
Heureux, humiliés comme des chiens battus,

Les Pauvres au bon Dieu, le patron et le sire,
Tendent leurs oremus risibles et têtus.

Aux femmes, c'est bien bon de faire des bancs lisses,
Après les six jours noirs où Dieu les fait souffrir!
Elles bercent, tordus dans d'étranges pelisses,
Des espèces d'enfants qui pleurent à mourir;

Leurs seins crasseux dehors, ces mangeuses de soupe,
Une prière aux yeux et ne priant jamais,
Regardent parader mauvaisement un groupe
De gamines avec leurs chapeaux déformés

Dehors, le froid, la faim, l'homme en ribotte:
C'est bon. Encore une heure; après, les maux sans noms!
—Cependant, alentour, geint, nasille, chuchote
Une collection de vieilles à fanons:

Ces effarés y sont et ces épileptiques
Dont on se détournait hier aux carrefours;
Et, fringalant du nez dans des missels antiques
Ces aveugles qu'un chien introduit dans les cours.

Et tous, bavant la foi mendiante et stupide,
Récitent la complainte infinie à Jésus
Qui rêve en haut, jauni par le vitrail livide,
Loin des maigres mauvais et des méchants pansus,

Loin des senteurs de viande et d'étoffes moisies,
Farce prostrée et sombre aux gestes repoussants;
—Et l'oraison fleurit d'expressions choisies,
Et les mysticités prennent des tons pressants,

Quand, des nefs où périt le soleil, plis de soie
Banals, sourires verts, les Dames des quartiers
Distingués,—ô Jésus!—les malades du foie
Font baiser leurs longs doigts jaunes aux bénitiers.

Juin 1871

LES SŒURS DE CHARITÉ

Le jeune homme dont l'œil est brillant, la peau brune,
Le beau corps de vingt ans qui devrait aller nu,
Et qu'eût, le front cerclé de cuivre, sous la lune
Adoré, dans la Perse un Génie inconnu,

Impétueux avec des douceurs virginales
Et noires, fier de ses premiers entêtements,
Pareil aux jeunes mers, pleurs de nuits estivales
Qui se retournent sur des lits de diamants;

Le jeune homme, devant les laideurs de ce monde
Tressaille dans son cœur largement irrité
Et plein de la blessure éternelle et profonde,
Se prend à désirer sa sœur de charité.

Mais, ô Femme, monceau d'entrailles, pitié douce,
Tu n'es jamais la Sœur de charité, jamais,
Ni regard noir, ni ventre où dort une ombre rousse
Ni doigts légers, ni seins splendidement formés.

Aveugle irréveillée aux immenses prunelles
Tout notre embrassement n'est qu'une question:
C'est toi qui pends à nous, porteuse de mamelles;
Nous te berçons, charmante et grave Passion.

Tes haines, tes torpeurs fixes, tes défaillances
Et les brutalités souffertes autrefois
Tu nous rends tout, ô Nuit pourtant sans malveillances
Comme un excès de sang épanché tous les mois

—Quand la femme, portée un instant, l'épouvante,
Amour, appel de vie et chanson d'action
Viennent la Muse verte et la Justice ardente
Le déchirer de leur auguste obsession.

Ah! sans cesse altéré des splendeurs et des calmes,
Délaissé des deux Sœurs implacables, geignant
Avec tendresse après la science aux bras almes
Il porte à la nature en fleur son front saignant.

Mais la noire alchimie et les saintes études
Répugnent au blessé, sombre savant d'orgueil;
Il sent marcher sur lui d'atroces solitudes
Alors, et toujours beau, sans dégoût du cercueil,

Qu'il croie aux vastes fins, Rêves ou Promenades
Immenses, à travers les nuits de Vérité
Et t'appelle en son âme et ses membres malades
O Mort mystérieuse, ô sœur de charité.

Juin 1871

LES PREMIÈRES COMMUNIONS

I

Vraiment, c'est bête, ces églises des villages
Où quinze laids marmots, encrassant les piliers
Ecoutent, grasseyant les divins babillages,
Un noir grotesque dont fermentent les souliers:
Mais le soleil éveille, à travers des feuillages
Les vieilles couleurs des vitraux irréguliers.

La pierre sent toujours la terre maternelle
Vous verrez des monceaux de ces cailloux terreux
Dans la campagne en rut qui frémit solennelle
Portant près des blés lourds, dans les sentiers ocreux,
Ces arbrisseaux brûlés où bleuit la prunelle,
Des nœuds de mûriers noirs et de rosiers fuireux.

Tous les cent ans on rend ces granges respectables
Par un badigeon d'eau bleue et de lait caillé:
Si des mysticités grotesques sont notables
Près de la Notre-Dame ou du Saint empaillé,
Des mouches sentant bon l'auberge et les étables
Se gorgent de cire au plancher ensoleillé.

L'enfant se doit surtout à la maison, famille
Des soins naïfs, des bons travaux abrutissants;
Ils sortent, oubliant que la peau leur fourmille
Où le Prêtre du Christ plaqua ses doigts puissants.

On paie au Prêtre un toit ombré d'une charmille
Pour qu'il laisse au soleil tous ces fronts brunissants

Le premier habit noir, le plus beau jour de tartes
Sous le Napoléon ou le Petit Tambour
Quelque enluminure où les Josephs et les Marthes
Tirent la langue avec un excessif amour
Et que joindront, au jour de science, deux cartes,
Ces seuls doux souvenirs lui restent du grand Jour.

Les filles vont toujours à l'église, contentes
De s'entendre appeler garces par les garçons
Qui font du genre après messe ou vêpres chantantes.
Eux qui sont destinés au chic des garnisons
Ils narguent au café les maisons importantes
Blousés neuf, et gueulant d'effroyables chansons.

Cependant le Curé choisit pour les enfances
Des dessins; dans son clos, les vêpres dites, quand
L'air s'emplit du lointain nasillement des danses
Il se sent, en dépit des célestes défenses,
Les doigts de pied ravis et le mollet marquant.

—La Nuit vient, noir pirate aux cieux d'or débarquant.

II
Le Prêtre a distingué parmi les catéchistes,
Congrégés des Faubourgs ou des Riches Quartiers,
Cette petite fille inconnue, aux yeux tristes,
Front jaune. Les parents semblent de doux portiers
«Au grand Jour, le marquant parmi les Catéchistes,
Dieu fera sur ce front neiger ses bénitiers»

III
La veille du grand Jour, l'enfant se fait malade.
Mieux qu'à l'Eglise haute aux funèbres rumeurs,
D'abord le frisson vient,—le lit n'étant pas fade—
Un frisson surhumain qui retourne: «Je meurs…»

Et, comme un vol d'amour fait à ses sœurs stupides,
Elle compte, abattue et les mains sur son cœur,
Les Anges, les Jésus et ses Vierges nitides
Et, calmement, son âme a bu tout son vainqueur.

Adonaï!...—Dans les terminaisons latines,
Des cieux moirés de vert baignent les Fronts vermeils
Et tachés du sang pur des célestes poitrines
De grands linges neigeux tombent sur les soleils!

—Pour ses virginités présentes et futures
Elle mord aux fraîcheurs de ta Rémission,
Mais plus que les lys d'eau, plus que les confitures
Tes pardons sont glacés, ô Reine de Sion!

IV
Puis la Vierge n'est plus que la vierge du livre
Les mystiques élans se cassent quelquefois....
Et vient la pauvreté des images, que cuivre
L'ennui, l'enluminure atroce et les vieux bois;

Des curiosités vaguement impudiques
Epouvantent le rêve aux chastes bleuités
Qui s'est surpris autour des célestes tuniques,
Du linge dont Jésus voile ses nudités.

Elle veut, elle veut, pourtant, l'âme en détresse,
Le front dans l'oreiller creusé par les cris sourds
Prolonger les éclairs suprêmes de tendresse,
Et bave...—L'ombre emplit les maisons et les cours.

Et l'enfant ne peut plus. Elle s'agite, cambre
Les reins et d'une main ouvre le rideau bleu
Pour amener un peu la fraîcheur de la chambre
Sous le drap, vers son ventre et sa poitrine en feu...

V
A son réveil,—minuit,—la fenêtre était blanche.
Devant le sommeil bleu des rideaux illunés,
La vision la prit des candeurs du dimanche,
Elle avait rêvé rouge. Elle saigna du nez.

Et se sentant bien chaste et pleine de faiblesse
Pour savourer en Dieu son amour revenant
Elle eut soif de la nuit où s'exalte et s'abaisse
Le cœur, sous l'œil des cieux doux, en les devinant,

De la nuit, Vierge-Mère impalpable, qui baigne
Tous les jeunes émois de ses silences gris;
Elle eut soif de la nuit forte où le cœur qui saigne
Ecoule sans témoin sa révolte sans cris.

Et faisant la Victime et la petite épouse,
Son étoile la vit, une chandelle aux doigts
Descendre dans la cour où séchait une blouse,
Spectre blanc, et lever les spectres noirs des toits...

VI
Elle passa sa nuit sainte dans des latrines.
Vers la chandelle, aux trous du toit coulait l'air blanc,
Et quelque vigne folle aux noirceurs purpurines,
En deçà d'une cour voisine s'écroulant.

La lucarne faisait un cœur de lueur vive
Dans la cour où les cieux bas plaquaient d'ors vermeils
Les vitres; les pavés puant l'eau de lessive
Souffraient l'ombre des murs bondés de noirs sommeils
. . . .

VII
Qui dira ces langueurs et ces pitiés immondes,
Et ce qu'il lui viendra de haine, ô sales fous
Dont le travail divin déforme encor les mondes,
Quand la lèpre à la fin mangera ce corps doux?
. . . .

VIII
Et quand, ayant rentré tous ses nœuds d'hystéries
Elle verra, sous les tristesses du bonheur,
L'amant rêver au blanc million des Maries,
Au matin de la nuit d'amour, avec douleur:

«Sais-tu que je t'ai fait mourir? J'ai pris ta bouche,
Ton cœur, tout ce qu'on a, tout ce que vous avez;
Et moi, je suis malade: Oh! je veux qu'on me [couche]
Parmi les Morts des eaux nocturnes abreuvés

«J'étais bien jeune, et Christ a souillé mes haleines
Il me bonda jusqu'à la gorge de dégoûts!

Tu baisais mes cheveux profonds comme les laines
Et je me laissais faire:... ah! va, c'est bon pour vous,

Hommes! qui songez peu que la plus amoureuse
Est, sous sa conscience aux ignobles terreurs
La plus prostituée et la plus douloureuse,
Et que tous nos élans vers Vous sont des erreurs!

Car ma Communion première est bien passée
Tes baisers, je ne puis jamais les avoir sus:
Et mon cœur et ma chair par ta chair embrassée
Fourmillent du baiser putride de Jésus!»

IX

Alors l'âme pourrie et l'âme désolée
Sentiront ruisseler tes malédictions
—Ils auront couché sur ta Haine inviolée,
Echappés, pour la mort, des justes passions.

Christ! ô Christ, éternel voleur des énergies
Dieu qui pour deux mille ans vouas à ta pâleur
Cloués au sol, de honte et de céphalalgies
Ou renversés les fronts des femmes de douleur.

Juillet 1871

CE QU'ON DIT AU POÈTE À PROPOS DE FLEURS

I

À Monsieur Théodore de Banville.

Ainsi, toujours, vers l'azur noir
Où tremble la mer des topazes,
Fonctionneront dans ton soir
Les Lys, ces clystères d'extases!

À notre époque de sagous,
Quand les Plantes sont travailleuses,
Le Lys boira les bleus dégoûts
Dans tes Proses religieuses!

—Le lys de monsieur de Kerdrel,
Le Sonnet de mil huit cent trente,
Le Lys qu'on donne au Ménestrel
Avec l'œillet et l'amarante!

Des lys! Des lys! On n'en voit pas!
Et dans ton Vers, tel que les manches
Des Pécheresses aux doux pas,
Toujours frissonnent ces fleurs blanches!

Toujours, Cher, quand tu prends un bain,
Ta chemise aux aisselles blondes
Se gonfle aux brises du matin
Sur les myosotis immondes!

L'amour ne passe à tes octrois
Que les Lilas,—ô balançoires!
Et les Violettes du Bois,
Crachats sucrés des Nymphes noires!...

II

Ô Poètes, quand vous auriez
Les Roses, les Roses soufflées,
Rouges sur tiges de lauriers,
Et de mille octaves enflées!

Quand BANVILLE en ferait neiger,
Sanguinolentes, tournoyantes,
Pochant l'œil fou de l'étranger
Aux lectures mal bienveillantes!

De vos forêts et de vos prés,
Ô très paisibles photographes!
La Flore est diverse à peu près
Comme des bouchons de carafes!

Toujours les végétaux Français,
Hargneux, phtisiques, ridicules,
Où le ventre des chiens bassets
Navigue en paix, aux crépuscules;

Toujours, après d'affreux dessins
De Lotos bleus ou d'Hélianthes,

Estampes roses, sujets saints
Pour de jeunes communiantes!

L'Ode Açoka cadre avec la
Strophe en fenêtre de lorette;
Et de lourds papillons d'éclat
Fientent sur la Pâquerette.

Vieilles verdures, vieux galons!
Ô croquignoles végétales!
Fleurs fantasques des vieux Salons!
—Aux hannetons, pas aux crotales,

Ces poupards végétaux en pleurs
Que Grandville eût mis aux lisières,
Et qu'allaitèrent de couleurs
De méchants astres à visières!

Oui, vos bavures de pipeaux
Font de précieuses glucoses!
—Tas d'œufs frits dans de vieux chapeaux,
Lys, Açokas, Lilas et Roses!...

III
Ô blanc Chasseur, qui cours sans bas
À travers le Pâtis panique,
Ne peux-tu pas, ne dois-tu pas
Connaître un peu ta botanique?

Tu ferais succéder, je crains,
Aux Grillons roux les Cantharides,
L'or des Rios au bleu des Rhins,—
Bref, aux Norwèges les Florides:

Mais, Cher, l'Art n'est plus, maintenant,
—C'est la vérité,—de permettre
À l'Eucalyptus étonnant
Des constrictors d'un hexamètre;

Là!... Comme si les Acajous
Ne servaient, même en nos Guyanes,
Qu'aux cascades des sapajous,
Au lourd délire des lianes!

—En somme, une Fleur, Romarin
Ou Lys, vive ou morte, vaut-elle
Un excrément d'oiseau marin?
Vaut-elle un seul pleur de chandelle?

—Et j'ai dit ce que je voulais!
Toi, même assis là-bas, dans une
Cabane de bambous,—volets
Clos, tentures de perse brune,—

Tu torcherais des floraisons
Dignes d'Oises extravagantes!...
—Poète! ce sont des raisons
Non moins risibles qu'arrogantes!...

IV

Dis, non les pampas printaniers
Noirs d'épouvantables révoltes,
Mais les tabacs, les cotonniers!
Dis les exotiques récoltes!

Dis, front blanc que Phébus tanna,
De combien de dollars se rente
Pedro Velasquez, Habana;
Incague la mer de Sorrente

Où vont les Cygnes par milliers;
Que tes strophes soient des réclames
Pour l'abatis des mangliers
Fouillés des hydres et des lames!

Ton quatrain plonge aux bois sanglants
Et revient proposer aux Hommes
Divers sujets de sucres blancs,
De pectoraires et de gommes!

Sachons par Toi si les blondeurs
Des Pics neigeux, vers les Tropiques,
Sont ou des insectes pondeurs
Ou des lichens microscopiques!

Trouve, ô Chasseur, nous le voulons,
Quelques garances parfumées

Que la Nature en pantalons
Fasse éclore!—pour nos Armées!

Trouve, aux abords du Bois qui dort,
Les fleurs, pareilles à des mufles,
D'où bavent des pommades d'or
Sur les cheveux sombres des Buffles!

Trouve, aux prés fous, où sur le Bleu
Tremble l'argent des pubescences,
Des calices pleins d'Œufs de feu
Qui cuisent parmi les essences!

Trouve des Chardons cotonneux
Dont dix ânes aux yeux de braises
Travaillent à filer les nœuds!
Trouve des Fleurs qui soient des chaises!

Oui, trouve au cœur des noirs filons
Des fleurs presque pierres,—fameuses!—
Qui vers leurs durs ovaires blonds
Aient des amygdales gemmeuses!

Sers-nous, ô Farceur, tu le peux,
Sur un plat de vermeil splendide
Des ragoûts de Lys sirupeux
Mordant nos cuillers Alfénide!

V
Quelqu'un dira le grand Amour,
Voleur des sombres Indulgences:
Mais ni Renan, ni le chat Murr
N'ont vu les Bleus Thyrses immenses!

Toi, fais jouer dans nos torpeurs,
Par les parfums les hystéries;
Exalte-nous vers des candeurs
Plus candides que les Maries...

Commerçant! colon! médium!
Ta Rime sourdra, rose ou blanche,
Comme un rayon de sodium,
Comme un caoutchouc qui s'épanche!

De tes noirs Poèmes,—Jongleur!
Blancs, verts, et rouges dioptriques,
Que s'évadent d'étranges fleurs
Et des papillons électriques!

Voilà! c'est le Siècle d'enfer!
Et les poteaux télégraphiques
Vont orner,—lyre aux chants de fer,
Tes omoplates magnifiques!

Surtout, rime une version
Sur le mal des pommes de terre!
—Et, pour la composition
De Poèmes pleins de mystère

Qu'on doive lire de Tréguier
À Paramaribo, rachète
Des Tomes de Monsieur Figuier,
—Illustrés!—chez Monsieur Hachette!

Alcide Bava
A. R.
14 juillet 1871

LE BATEAU IVRE

Comme je descendais des Fleuves impassibles,
Je ne me sentis plus guidé par les haleurs:
Des Peaux-Rouges criards les avaient pris pour cibles
Les ayant cloués nus aux poteaux de couleurs.

J'étais insoucieux de tous les équipages,
Porteur de blés flamands ou de cotons anglais.
Quand avec mes haleurs ont fini ces tapages
Les Fleuves m'ont laissé descendre où je voulais.

Dans les clapotements furieux des marées,
Moi, l'autre hiver, plus sourd que les cerveaux d'enfants,
Je courus! Et les Péninsules démarrées
N'ont pas subi tohu-bohus plus triomphants.

La tempête a béni mes éveils maritimes.
Plus léger qu'un bouchon j'ai dansé sur les flots
Qu'on appelle rouleurs éternels de victimes,
Dix nuits, sans regretter l'œil niais des falots!

Plus douce qu'aux enfants la chair des pommes sures,
L'eau verte pénétra ma coque de sapin
Et des taches de vins bleus et des vomissures
Me lava, dispersant gouvernail et grappin.

Et dès lors, je me suis baigné dans le Poème
De la Mer, infusé d'astres, et lactescent,
Dévorant les azurs verts; où, flottaison blême
Et ravie, un noyé pensif parfois descend;

Où, teignant tout à coup les bleuités, délires
Et rhythmes lents sous les rutilements du jour,
Plus fortes que l'alcool, plus vastes que nos lyres,
Fermentent les rousseurs amères de l'amour!

Je sais les cieux crevant en éclairs, et les trombes
Et les ressacs et les courants: je sais le soir,
L'Aube exaltée ainsi qu'un peuple de colombes,
Et j'ai vu quelquefois ce que l'homme a cru voir!

J'ai vu le soleil bas, taché d'horreurs mystiques,
Illuminant de longs figements violets,
Pareils à des acteurs de drames très-antiques
Les flots roulant au loin leurs frissons de volets!

J'ai rêvé la nuit verte aux neiges éblouies,
Baiser montant aux yeux des mers avec lenteurs,
La circulation des sèves inouïes,
Et l'éveil jaune et bleu des phosphores chanteurs!

J'ai suivi, des mois pleins, pareille aux vacheries
Hystériques, la houle à l'assaut des récifs,
Sans songer que les pieds lumineux des Maries
Pussent forcer le mufle aux Océans poussifs!

J'ai heurté, savez-vous, d'incroyables Florides
Mêlant aux fleurs des yeux de panthères à peaux

D'hommes! Des arcs-en-ciel tendus comme des brides
Sous l'horizon des mers, à de glauques troupeaux!

J'ai vu fermenter les marais énormes, nasses
Où pourrit dans les joncs tout un Léviathan!
Des écroulements d'eaux au milieu des bonaces,
Et les lointains vers les gouffres cataractant!

Glaciers, soleils d'argent, flots nacreux, cieux de braises!
Échouages hideux au fond des golfes bruns
Où les serpents géants dévorés des punaises
Choient, des arbres tordus, avec de noirs parfums!

J'aurais voulu montrer aux enfants ces dorades
Du flot bleu, ces poissons d'or, ces poissons chantants.
—Des écumes de fleurs ont bercé mes dérades
Et d'ineffables vents m'ont ailé par instants.

Parfois, martyr lassé des pôles et des zones,
La mer dont le sanglot faisait mon roulis doux
Montait vers moi ses fleurs d'ombre aux ventouses jaunes
Et je restais, ainsi qu'une femme à genoux...

Presque île, ballottant sur mes bords les querelles
Et les fientes d'oiseaux clabaudeurs aux yeux blonds.
Et je voguais, lorsqu'à travers mes liens frêles
Des noyés descendaient dormir, à reculons!

Or moi, bateau perdu sous les cheveux des anses,
Jeté par l'ouragan dans l'éther sans oiseau,
Moi dont les Monitors et les voiliers des Hanses
N'auraient pas repêché la carcasse ivre d'eau;

Libre, fumant, monté de brumes violettes,
Moi qui trouais le ciel rougeoyant comme un mur
Qui porte, confiture exquise aux bons poètes,
Des lichens de soleil et des morves d'azur,

Qui courais, taché de lunules électriques,
Planche folle, escorté des hippocampes noirs,
Quand les juillets faisaient crouler à coups de triques
Les cieux ultramarins aux ardents entonnoirs;

Moi qui tremblais, sentant geindre à cinquante lieues
Le rut des Béhémots et les Maelstroms épais,
Fileur éternel des immobilités bleues,
Je regrette l'Europe aux anciens parapets!

J'ai vu des archipels sidéraux! et des îles
Dont les cieux délirants sont ouverts au vogueur:
—Est-ce en ces nuits sans fond que tu dors et t'exiles,
Million d'oiseaux d'or, ô future Vigueur?—

Mais, vrai, j'ai trop pleuré! Les Aubes sont navrantes.
Toute lune est atroce et tout soleil amer:
L'âcre amour m'a gonflé de torpeurs enivrantes.
Ô que ma quille éclate! Ô que j'aille à la mer!

Si je désire une eau d'Europe, c'est la flache
Noire et froide où vers le crépuscule embaumé
Un enfant accroupi plein de tristesses, lâche
Un bateau frêle comme un papillon de mai.

Je ne puis plus, baigné de vos langueurs, ô lames,
Enlever leur sillage aux porteurs de cotons,
Ni traverser l'orgueil des drapeaux et des flammes,
Ni nager sous les yeux horribles des pontons.

L'HOMME JUSTE

[. . . . .]
Le Juste restait droit sur ses hanches solides:
Un rayon lui dorait l'épaule; des sueurs
Me prirent: «Tu veux voir rutiler les bolides?
Et, debout, écouter bourdonner les flueurs
D'astres lactés, et les essaims d'astéroïdes?

«Par des farces de nuit ton front est épié,
Ô Juste! Il faut gagner un toit. Dis ta prière,
La bouche dans ton drap doucement expié;
Et si quelque égaré choque ton ostiaire,
Dis: Frère, va plus loin, je suis estropié!»

Et le Juste restait debout, dans l'épouvante
Bleuâtre des gazons après le soleil mort:
«Alors, mettrais-tu tes genouillères en vente,
Ô vieillard? Pèlerin sacré! Barde d'Armor!
Pleureur des Oliviers! Main que la pitié gante!

«Barbe de la famille et poing de la cité,
Croyant très doux: ô cœur tombé dans les calices,
Majestés et vertus, amour et cécité,
Juste! plus bête et plus dégoûtant que les lices!
Je suis celui qui souffre et qui s'est révolté!

«Et ça me fait pleurer sur mon ventre, ô stupide,
Et bien rire, l'espoir fameux de ton pardon!
Je suis maudit, tu sais! Je suis soûl, fou, livide,
Ce que tu veux! Mais va te coucher, voyons donc,
Juste! Je ne veux rien à ton cerveau torpide!

«C'est toi le Juste, enfin, le Juste! C'est assez!
C'est vrai que ta tendresse et ta raison sereines
Reniflent dans la nuit comme des cétacés!
Que tu te fais proscrire, et dégoises des thrènes
Sur d'effroyables becs de canne fracassés!

«Et c'est toi l'œil de Dieu! le lâche! quand les plantes
Froides des pieds divins passeraient sur mon cou,
Tu es lâche! Ô ton front qui fourmille de lentes!
Socrates et Jésus, Saints et Justes, dégoût,
Respectez le Maudit suprême aux nuits sanglantes!»

J'avais crié cela sur la terre, et la nuit
Calme et blanche occupait les Cieux pendant ma fièvre
Je relevai mon front: le fantôme avait fui,
Emportant l'ironie atroce de ma lèvre. . . .
—Vents nocturnes! venez au Maudit! Parlez-lui!

Cependant que, silencieux sous les pilastres
D'azur, allongeant les comètes et les nœuds
D'univers, remuement énorme sans désastres,
L'ordre, éternel veilleur, rame aux cieux lumineux
Et de sa drague en feu laisse filer des astres!

Ah qu'il s'en aille, lui, la gorge cravatée
De honte, ruminant toujours mon ennui, doux
Comme le sucre sur la denture gâtée
—Tel que la chienne après l'assaut des fiers toutous,
Léchant son flanc d'où pend une entraille emportée

Qu'il dise charités crasseuses et progrès...
—J'exècre tous ces yeux de Chinois [...]aines,
[...] qui chante: nana, comme un tas d'enfants près
De mourir, idiots doux aux chansons soudaines:
O Justes, nous chierons dans vos ventres de grés

LES MAINS DE JEANNE-MARIE

Jeanne-Marie a des mains fortes,
Mains sombres que l'été tanna,
Mains pâles comme des mains mortes.
—Sont-ce des mains de Juana?

Ont-elles pris les crèmes brunes
Sur les mares des voluptés?
Ont-elles trempé dans des lunes
Aux étangs de sérénités?

Ont-elles bu des cieux barbares,
Calmes sur les genoux charmants?
Ont-elles roulé des cigares
Ou trafiqué des diamants?

Sur les pieds ardents des Madones
Ont-elles fané des fleurs d'or?
C'est le sang noir des belladones
Qui dans leur paume éclate et dort.

Mains chasseresses des diptères
Dont bombinent les bleuisons
Aurorales, vers les nectaires?
Mains décanteuses de poisons?

Oh! quel Rêve les a saisies
Dans les pandiculations?

Un rêve inouï des Asies,
Des Khengavars ou des Sions?

—Ces mains n'ont pas vendu d'oranges,
Ni bruni sur les pieds des dieux:
Ces mains n'ont pas lavé les langes
Des lourds petits enfants sans yeux.

Ce ne sont pas mains de cousine
Ni d'ouvrières aux gros fronts
Que brûle, aux bois puant l'usine
Un soleil ivre de goudrons

Ce sont des casseuses d'échines
Des mains qui ne font jamais mal
Plus fatales que des machines,
Plus fortes que tout un cheval!

Remuant comme des fournaises,
Et secouant tous ses frissons
Leur chair chante des Marseillaises
Et jamais les Eleisons!

Ça serrerait vos cous, ô femmes
Mauvaises, ça broierait vos mains
Femmes nobles, vos mains infâmes
Pleines de blancs et de carmins

L'éclat de ces mains amoureuses
Tourne le crâne des brebis!
Dans leurs phalanges savoureuses
Le grand soleil met un rubis!

Une tache de populace
Les brunit comme un sein d'hier:
Le dos de ces Mains est la place
Qu'en baisa tout Révolté fier!

Elles ont pâli, merveilleuses,
Au grand soleil d'amour chargé
Sur le bronze des mitrailleuses
À travers Paris insurgé!

Ah! quelquefois, ô Mains sacrées,
À vos poings, Mains où tremblent nos
Lèvres jamais désenivrées,
Crie une chaîne aux clairs anneaux!

Et c'est un Soubresaut étrange
Dans nos êtres, quand, quelquefois
On veut vous déhâler, Mains d'ange,
En vous faisant saigner les doigts!

Fév. 72

IV. POEMES NON DATÉS, c. 1870–1872

LES ASSIS

Noirs de loupes, grêlés, les yeux cerclés de bagues
Vertes, leurs doigts boulus crispés à leurs fémurs
Le sinciput plaqué de hargnosités vagues
Comme les floraisons lépreuses des vieux murs;

Ils ont greffé dans des amours épileptiques
Leur fantasque ossature aux grands squelettes noirs
De leurs chaises; leurs pieds aux barreaux rachitiques
S'entrelacent pour les matins et pour les soirs!

Ces vieillards ont toujours fait tresse avec leurs sièges,
Sentant les soleils vifs percaliser leur peau,
Ou, les yeux à la vitre où se fanent les neiges,
Tremblant du tremblement douloureux du crapaud.

Et les Sièges leur ont des bontés: culottée
De brun, la paille cède aux angles de leurs reins;
L'âme des vieux soleils s'allume emmaillottée
Dans ces tresses d'épis où fermentaient les grains.

Et les Assis, genoux aux dents, verts pianistes
Les dix doigts sous leur siège aux rumeurs de tambour
S'écoutent clapoter des barcarolles tristes,
Et leurs caboches vont dans des roulis d'amour.

—Oh! ne les faites pas lever! C'est le naufrage....
Ils surgissent, grondant comme des chats giflés,
Ouvrant lentement leurs omoplates, ô rage!
Tout leur pantalon bouffe à leurs reins boursouflés

Et vous les écoutez, cognant leurs têtes chauves
Aux murs sombres, plaquant et plaquant leurs pieds tors

Et leurs boutons d'habit sont des prunelles fauves
Qui vous accrochent l'œil du fond des corridors!

Puis ils ont une main invisible qui tue:
Au retour, leur regard filtre ce venin noir
Qui charge l'œil souffrant de la chienne battue
Et vous suez pris dans un atroce entonnoir.

Rassis, les poings noyés dans des manchettes sales
Ils songent à ceux-là qui les ont fait lever
Et, de l'aurore au soir, des grappes d'amygdales
Sous leurs mentons chétifs s'agitent à crever

Quand l'austère sommeil a baissé leurs visières
Ils rêvent sur leur bras de sièges fécondés,
De vrais petits amours de chaises en lisière
Par lesquelles de fiers bureaux seront bordés;

Des fleurs d'encre crachant des pollens en virgule
Les bercent, le long des calices accroupis
Tels qu'au fil des glaïeuls le vol des libellules
—Et leur membre s'agace à des barbes d'épis.

LES CHERCHEUSES DE POUX

Quand le front de l'enfant, plein de rouges tourmentes,
Implore l'essaim blanc des rêves indistincts,
Il vient près de son lit deux grandes sœurs charmantes
Avec de frêles doigts aux ongles argentins.

Elles assoient l'enfant devant une croisée
Grande ouverte où l'air bleu baigne un fouillis de fleurs
Et dans ses lourds cheveux où tombe la rosée
Promènent leurs doigts fins, terribles et charmeurs.

Il écoute chanter leurs haleines craintives
Qui fleurent de longs miels végétaux et rosés
Et qu'interrompt parfois un sifflement, salives
Reprises sur la lèvre ou désirs de baisers.

Il entend leurs cils noirs battant sous les silences
Parfumés; et leurs doigts électriques et doux
Font crépiter parmi ses grises indolences
Sous leurs ongles royaux la mort des petits poux.

Voilà que monte en lui le vin de la Paresse,
Soupir d'harmonica qui pourrait délirer;
L'enfant se sent, selon la lenteur des caresses
Sourdre et mourir sans cesse un désir de pleurer.

LES DOUANIERS

Ceux qui disent: Cré Nom, ceux qui disent macache,
Soldats, marins, débris d'Empire, retraités
Sont nuls, très nuls, devant les Soldats des Traités
Qui tailladent l'azur frontière à grands coups d'hache

Pipe aux dents, lame en main, profonds, pas embêtés
Quand l'ombre bave aux bois comme un mufle de vache
Ils s'en vont, amenant leurs dogues à l'attache,
Exercer nuitamment leurs terribles gaîtés!

Ils signalent aux lois modernes les faunesses
Ils empoignent les Fausts et les Diavolos
«Pas de ça, les anciens! Déposez les ballots!»

Quand sa sérénité s'approche des jeunesses,
Le Douanier se tient aux appas contrôlés!
Enfer aux Délinquants que sa paume a frôlés!

"L'ÉTOILE A PLEURÉ ROSE . . ."

L'étoile a pleuré rose au cœur de tes oreilles,
L'infini roulé blanc de ta nuque à tes reins
La mer a perlé rousse à tes mammes vermeilles
Et l'Homme saigné noir à ton flanc souverain.

ORAISON DU SOIR

Je vis assis, tel qu'un ange aux mains d'un barbier,
Empoignant une chope à fortes cannelures,
L'hypogastre et le col cambrés, une Gambier
Aux dents, sous l'air gonflé d'impalpables voilures.

Tels que les excréments chauds d'un vieux colombier,
Mille Rêves en moi font de douces brûlures:
Puis par instants mon cœur triste est comme un aubier
Qu'ensanglante l'or jeune et sombre des coulures.

Puis, quand j'ai ravalé mes rêves avec soin,
Je me tourne, ayant bu trente ou quarante chopes,
Et me recueille, pour lâcher l'âcre besoin:

Doux comme le Seigneur du cèdre et des hysopes,
Je pisse vers les cieux bruns très haut et très loin,
Avec l'assentiment des grands héliotropes.

TÊTE DE FAUNE

Dans la feuillée, écrin vert taché d'or,
Dans la feuillée incertaine et fleurie,
D'énormes fleurs où l'âcre baiser dort
Vif et devant l'exquise broderie,

Le Faune affolé montre ses grands yeux
Et mord la fleur rouge avec ses dents blanches.
Brunie et sanglante ainsi qu'un vin vieux,
Sa lèvre éclate en rires par les branches;

Et quand il a fui, tel un écureuil,
Son rire perle encore à chaque feuille
Et l'on croit épeuré par un bouvreuil
Le baiser d'or du bois qui se recueille.

VOYELLES

A noir, E blanc, I rouge, U vert, O bleu: voyelles,
Je dirai quelque jour vos naissances latentes:
A, noir corset velu des mouches éclatantes
Qui bombinent autour des puanteurs cruelles,

Golfes d'ombre; E, candeurs des vapeurs et des tentes,
Lances des glaciers fiers, rois blancs, frissons d'ombelles;
I, pourpres, sang craché, rire des lèvres belles
Dans la colère ou les ivresses pénitentes;

U, cycles, vibrements divins des mers virides,
Paix des pâtis semés d'animaux, paix des rides
Que l'alchimie imprime aux grands fronts studieux;

O, Suprême Clairon plein des strideurs étranges,
Silences traversés des Mondes et des Anges:
—Ô l'Oméga, rayon violet de Ses Yeux!

V. 1872

COMÉDIE DE LA SOIF

1. LES PARENTS

Nous sommes tes Grands-Parents,
Les Grands!
Couverts des froides sueurs
De la lune et des verdures.
Nos vins secs avaient du cœur!
Au soleil sans imposture
Que faut-il à l'homme? boire.

MOI. —Mourir aux fleuves barbares.

Nous sommes tes Grands-Parents
Des champs.
L'eau est au fond des osiers:
Vois le courant du fossé
Autour du château mouillé.
Descendons en nos celliers;
Après, le cidre et le lait.

MOI. —Aller où boivent les vaches.

Nous sommes tes Grands-Parents;
Tiens, prends
Les liqueurs dans nos armoires
Le Thé, le Café, si rares,
Frémissent dans les bouilloires.
—Vois les images, les fleurs.
Nous rentrons du cimetière.

MOI. —Ah! tarir toutes les urnes!

2. L'ESPRIT

Éternelles Ondines
        Divisez l'eau fine.
Vénus, sœur de l'azur,
        Émeus le flot pur.

Juifs errants de Norwège
        Dites-moi la neige.
Anciens exilés chers,
        Dites-moi la mer.

MOI. —Non, plus ces boissons pures,
        Ces fleurs d'eau pour verres;
Légendes ni figures
        Ne me désaltèrent;

Chansonnier, ta filleule
        C'est ma soif si folle
Hydre intime sans gueules
        Qui mine et désole.

3. LES AMIS

Viens, les vins vont aux plages,
Et les flots par millions!
Vois le Bitter sauvage
Rouler du haut des monts!

Gagnons, pèlerins sages,
L'absinthe aux verts piliers...

MOI. —Plus ces paysages.
Qu'est l'ivresse, Amis?

J'aime autant, mieux, même,
Pourrir dans l'étang,
Sous l'affreuse crème,
Près des bois flottants.

4. LE PAUVRE SONGE

Peut-être un Soir m'attend
Où je boirai tranquille
En quelque vieille Ville,
Et mourrai plus content:
Puisque je suis patient!

Si mon mal se résigne,
Si j'ai jamais quelque or,
Choisirai-je le Nord
Ou le Pays des Vignes?...
—Ah! songer est indigne

Puisque c'est pure perte!
Et si je redeviens
Le voyageur ancien,
Jamais l'auberge verte
Ne peut bien m'être ouverte.

5. CONCLUSION

Les pigeons qui tremblent dans la prairie,
Le gibier, qui court et qui voit la nuit,
Les bêtes des eaux, la bête asservie,
Les derniers papillons!... ont soif aussi.

Mais fondre où fond ce nuage sans guide,
—Oh! favorisé de ce qui est frais!
Expirer en ces violettes humides
Dont les aurores chargent ces forêts?

Mai 1872

BONNE PENSÉE DU MATIN

À quatre heures du matin, l'été,
Le sommeil d'amour dure encore.
Sous les bosquets l'aube évapore
L'odeur du soir fêté.

Mais là-bas dans l'immense chantier
Vers le soleil des Hespérides,
En bras de chemise, les charpentiers
        Déjà s'agitent.

Dans leur désert de mousse, tranquilles,
Ils préparent les lambris précieux
Où la richesse de la ville
        Rira sous de faux cieux.

Ah! pour ces Ouvriers charmants
Sujets d'un roi de Babylone,
Vénus! laisse un peu les Amants,
        Dont l'âme est en couronne.

        Ô Reine des Bergers!
    Porte aux travailleurs l'eau-de-vie,
    Pour que leurs forces soient en paix
En attendant le bain dans la mer, à midi.

Mai 1872.

LA RIVIÈRE DE CASSIS

La Rivière de Cassis roule ignorée
        En des vaux étranges:
La voix de cent corbeaux l'accompagne, vraie
        Et bonne voix d'anges:
Avec les grands mouvements des sapinaies
        Quand plusieurs vents plongent.

Tout roule avec des mystères révoltants
        De campagnes d'anciens temps:
De donjons visités, de parcs importants:
        C'est en ces bords qu'on entend
Les passions mortes des chevaliers errants:
        Mais que salubre est le vent!

Que le piéton regarde à ces claires-voies:
        Il ira plus courageux.

Soldats des forêts que le Seigneur envoie,
        Chers corbeaux délicieux!
Faites fuir d'ici le paysan matois
        Qui trinque d'un moignon vieux.

Mai 1872

LARME

Loin des oiseaux, des troupeaux, des villageoises,
Je buvais, accroupi dans quelque bruyère
Entourée de tendres bois de noisetiers,
Par un brouillard d'après-midi tiède et vert.

Que pouvais-je boire dans cette jeune Oise,
Ormeaux sans voix, gazon sans fleurs, ciel couvert.
Que tirais-je à la gourde de colocase?
Quelque liqueur d'or, fade et qui fait suer.

Tel, j'eusse été mauvaise enseigne d'auberge.
Puis l'orage changea le ciel, jusqu'au soir.
Ce furent des pays noirs, des lacs, des perches,
Des colonnades sous la nuit bleue, des gares.

L'eau des bois se perdait sur des sables vierges.
Le vent, du ciel, jetait des glaçons aux mares…
Or! tel qu'un pêcheur d'or ou de coquillages,
Dire que je n'ai pas eu souci de boire!

Mai 1872

FÊTES DE LA PATIENCE

1. Bannières de mai
2. Chanson de la plus haute Tour
3. Éternité
4. Âge d'or

BANNIÈRES DE MAI

Aux branches claires des tilleuls
Meurt un maladif hallali.
Mais des chansons spirituelles
Voltigent parmi les groseilles.
Que notre sang rie en nos veines,
Voici s'enchevêtrer les vignes.
Le ciel est joli comme un ange.
L'azur et l'onde communient.
Je sors. Si un rayon me blesse
Je succomberai sur la mousse.

Qu'on patiente et qu'on s'ennuie
C'est trop simple. Fi de mes peines.
Je veux que l'été dramatique
Me lie à son char de fortune.
Que par toi beaucoup, ô Nature,
—Ah moins seul et moins nul!—je meure.
Au lieu que les Bergers, c'est drôle,
Meurent à peu près par le monde.

Je veux bien que les saisons m'usent.
À toi, Nature, je me rends;
Et ma faim et toute ma soif.
Et, s'il te plaît, nourris, abreuve.
Rien de rien ne m'illusionne;
C'est rire aux parents, qu'au soleil,
Mais moi je ne veux rire à rien;
Et libre soit cette infortune.

Mai 1872

CHANSON DE LA PLUS HAUTE TOUR

Oisive jeunesse
À tout asservie,
Par délicatesse
J'ai perdu ma vie.
Ah! Que le temps vienne
Où les cœurs s'éprennent.

Je me suis dit: laisse,
Et qu'on ne te voie:
Et sans la promesse
De plus hautes joies.
Que rien ne t'arrête
Auguste retraite.

J'ai tant fait patience
Qu'à jamais j'oublie;
Craintes et souffrances
Aux cieux sont parties.
Et la soif malsaine
Obscurcit mes veines.

Ainsi la Prairie
À l'oubli livrée,
Grandie, et fleurie
D'encens et d'ivraies
Au bourdon farouche
De cent sales mouches.

Ah! Mille veuvages
De la si pauvre âme
Qui n'a que l'image
De la Notre-Dame!
Est-ce que l'on prie
La Vierge Marie?

Oisive jeunesse
À tout asservie
Par délicatesse
J'ai perdu ma vie.
Ah! Que le temps vienne
Où les cœurs s'éprennent!

Mai 1872

L'ÉTERNITÉ

Elle est retrouvée.
Quoi?—L'Éternité.

C'est la mer allée
Avec le soleil.

Âme sentinelle,
Murmurons l'aveu
De la nuit si nulle
Et du jour en feu.

Des humains suffrages,
Des communs élans
Là tu te dégages
Et voles selon.

Puisque de vous seules,
Braises de satin,
Le Devoir s'exhale
Sans qu'on dise: enfin.

Là pas d'espérance,
Nul orietur.
Science avec patience,
Le supplice est sûr.

Elle est retrouvée.
Quoi?—L'Éternité.
C'est la mer allée
Avec le soleil.

Mai 1872

ÂGE D'OR

Quelqu'une des voix
Toujours angélique
—Il s'agit de moi,—
Vertement s'explique:

Ces mille questions
Qui se ramifient
N'amènent, au fond,
Qu'ivresse et folie;

Reconnais ce tour
Si gai, si facile:
Ce n'est qu'onde, flore,
Et c'est ta famille!

Puis elle chante. Ô
Si gai, si facile,
Et visible à l'œil nu...
—Je chante avec elle,—

Reconnais ce tour
Si gai, si facile,
Ce n'est qu'onde, flore,
Et c'est ta famille!... etc...

Et puis une voix
—Est-elle angélique!—
Il s'agit de moi,
Vertement s'explique;

Et chante à l'instant
En sœur des haleines:
D'un ton Allemand,
Mais ardente et pleine:

Le monde est vicieux;
Si cela t'étonne!
Vis et laisse au feu
L'obscure infortune.

Ô! joli château!
Que ta vie est claire!
De quel Âge es-tu,
Nature princière
De notre grand frère! etc...

Je chante aussi, moi:
Multiples sœurs! voix
Pas du tout publiques!
Environnez-moi
De gloire pudique... etc...

Juin 1872

JEUNE MÉNAGE

La chambre est ouverte au ciel bleu-turquin;
Pas de place: des coffrets et des huches!
Dehors le mur est plein d'aristoloches
Où vibrent les gencives des lutins.

Que ce sont bien intrigues de génies
Cette dépense et ces désordres vains!
C'est la fée africaine qui fournit
La mûre, et les résilles dans les coins.

Plusieurs entrent, marraines mécontentes,
En pans de lumière dans les buffets,
Puis y restent! le ménage s'absente
Peu sérieusement, et rien ne se fait.

Le marié a le vent qui le floue
Pendant son absence, ici, tout le temps.
Même des esprits des eaux, malfaisants
Entrent vaguer aux sphères de l'alcôve.

La nuit, l'amie oh! la lune de miel
Cueillera leur sourire et remplira
De mille bandeaux de cuivre le ciel.
Puis ils auront affaire au malin rat.

—S'il n'arrive pas un feu follet blême,
Comme un coup de fusil, après des vêpres.
—Ô spectres saints et blancs de Bethléem,
Charmez plutôt le bleu de leur fenêtre!

27 juin 1872

"EST-ELLE ALMÉE? . . ."

Est-elle almée? . . . aux premières heures bleues
Se détruira-t-elle comme les fleurs feues . . .
Devant la splendide étendue où l'on sente
Souffler la ville énormément florissante!

C'est trop beau! c'est trop beau! mais c'est nécessaire
—Pour la Pêcheuse et la chanson du Corsaire,
Et aussi puisque les derniers masques crurent
Encore aux fêtes de nuit sur la mer pure!

Juillet 1872

FÊTES DE LA FAIM

Ma faim, Anne, Anne,
Fuis sur ton âne.

Si j'ai du *goût,* ce n'est guères
Que pour la terre et les pierres
Dinn! dinn! dinn! dinn! Mangeons l'air,
Le roc, les charbons, le fer

Mes faims, tournez. Paissez, faims,
Le pré des sons!
Attirez le gai venin
Des liserons;

Les cailloux qu'un pauvre brise,
Les vieilles pierres d'églises,
Les galets, fils des déluges,
Pains couchés aux vallées grises!

Mes faims, c'est les bouts d'air noir;
L'azur sonneur;
—C'est l'estomac qui me tire.
C'est le malheur.

Sur terre ont paru les feuilles:
Je vais aux chairs de fruits blettes.
Au sein du sillon je cueille
La doucette et la violette.

Ma faim, Anne, Anne!
Fuis sur ton âne.

Août 1872

LES CORBEAUX

Seigneur, quand froide est la prairie,
Quand dans les hameaux abattus,
Les longs angelus se sont tus…
Sur la nature défleurie
Faites s'abattre des grands cieux
Les chers corbeaux délicieux.

Armée étrange aux cris sévères,
Les vents froids attaquent vos nids!
Vous, le long des fleuves jaunis,
Sur les routes aux vieux calvaires,
Sur les fossés et sur les trous
Dispersez-vous, ralliez-vous!

Par milliers, sur les champs de France,
Où dorment des morts d'avant-hier,
Tournoyez, n'est-ce pas, l'hiver,
Pour que chaque passant repense!
Sois donc le crieur du devoir,
O notre funèbre oiseau noir!

Mais, saints du ciel, en haut du chêne,
Mât perdu dans le soir charmé,
Laissez les fauvettes de mai
Pour ceux qu'au fond du bois enchaîne,
Dans l'herbe d'où l'on ne peut fuir,
La défaite sans avenir.

"QU'EST-CE POUR NOUS, MON CŒUR…"

Qu'est-ce pour nous, mon cœur, que les nappes de sang
Et de braise, et mille meurtres, et les longs cris
De rage, sanglots de tout enfer renversant
Tout ordre; et l'Aquilon encor sur les débris

Et toute vengeance? Rien!…—Mais si, tout encor,
Nous la voulons! Industriels, princes, sénats,
Périssez! puissance, justice, histoire, à bas!
Ça nous est dû. Le sang! le sang! la flamme d'or!

Tout à la guerre, à la vengeance, à la terreur,
Mon Esprit! Tournons dans la Morsure: Ah! passez,
Républiques de ce monde! Des empereurs,
Des régiments, des colons, des peuples, assez!

Qui remuerait les tourbillons de feu furieux,
Que nous et ceux que nous nous imaginons frères?
À nous! Romanesques amis: ça va nous plaire.
Jamais nous ne travaillerons, ô flots de feux!

Europe, Asie, Amérique, disparaissez.
Notre marche vengeresse a tout occupé,
Cités et campagnes!—Nous serons écrasés!
Les volcans sauteront! et l'océan frappé...

Oh! mes amis!—mon cœur, c'est sûr, ils sont des frères:
Noirs inconnus, si nous allions! allons! allons!
Ô malheur! je me sens frémir, la vieille terre,
Sur moi de plus en plus à vous! la terre fond,

Ce n'est rien! j'y suis! j'y suis toujours.

"PLATES-BANDES D'AMARANTES..."

Juillet. Bruxelles, Boulevart du Régent

Plates-bandes d'amarantes jusqu'à
L'agréable palais de Jupiter.
—Je sais que c'est Toi, qui, dans ces lieux,
Mêles ton Bleu presque de Sahara!

Puis, comme rose et sapin du soleil
Et liane ont ici leurs jeux enclos,
Cage de la petite veuve!...
        Quelles
Troupes d'oiseaux! o iaio, iaio!...

—Calmes maisons, anciennes passions!
Kiosque de la Folle par affection.
Après les fesses des rosiers, balcon
Ombreux et très-bas de la Juliette.

—La Juliette, ça rappelle l'Henriette,
Charmante station du chemin de fer
Au cœur d'un mont comme au fond d'un verger
Où mille diables bleus dansent dans l'air!

Banc vert où chante au paradis d'orage,
Sur la guitare, la blanche Irlandaise.
Puis de la salle à manger guyanaise
Bavardage des enfants et des cages.

Fenêtre du duc qui fais que je pense
Au poison des escargots et du buis
Qui dort ici-bas au soleil. Et puis
C'est trop beau! trop! Gardons notre silence.

—Boulevart sans mouvement ni commerce
Muet, tout drame et toute comédie,
Réunion des scènes infinie,
Je te connais et t'admire en silence.

"ENTENDS COMME BRAME ..."

Entends comme brame
près des acacias
en avril la rame
viride du pois!

Dans sa vapeur nette,
vers Phœbé! tu vois
s'agiter la tête
de saints d'autrefois...

Loin des claires meules
des caps, des beaux toits,
ces chers Anciens veulent
ce philtre sournois...

Or ni fériale
ni astrale! n'est
la brume qu'exhale
ce nocturne effet.

Néanmoins ils restent,
—Sicile, Allemagne,
dans ce brouillard triste
et blêmi, justement!

MICHEL ET CHRISTINE

Zut alors si le soleil quitte ces bords!
Fuis, clair déluge! Voici l'ombre des routes.
Dans les saules, dans la vieille cour d'honneur
L'orage d'abord jette ses larges gouttes.

O cent agneaux, de l'idylle soldats blonds,
Des aqueducs, des bruyères amaigries,
Fuyez! plaine, déserts, prairie, horizons
Sont à la toilette rouge de l'orage!

Chien noir, brun pasteur dont le manteau s'engouffre,
Fuyez l'heure des éclairs supérieurs;
Blond troupeau, quand voici nager ombre et soufre,
Tâchez de descendre à des retraits meilleurs.

Mais moi, Seigneur! voici que mon Esprit vole,
Après les cieux glacés de rouge, sous les
Nuages célestes qui courent et volent
Sur cent Solognes longues comme un railway.

Voilà mille loups, mille graines sauvages
Qu'emporte, non sans aimer les liserons,
Cette religieuse après-midi d'orage
Sur l'Europe ancienne où cent hordes iront!

Après, le clair de lune! partout la lande,
Rougissant leurs fronts aux cieux noirs, les guerriers
Chevauchent lentement leurs pâles coursiers!
Les cailloux sonnent sous cette fière bande!

—Et verrai-je le bois jaune et le val clair,
L'Epouse aux yeux bleus, l'homme au front rouge,—ô Gaule,
Et le blanc agneau Pascal, à leurs pieds chers,
—Michel et Christine,—et Christ!—fin de l'Idylle.

HONTE

Tant que la lame n'aura
Pas coupé cette cervelle,
Ce paquet blanc vert et gras
A vapeur jamais nouvelle,

(Ah! Lui, devrait couper son
Nez, sa lèvre, ses oreilles,
Son ventre! et faire abandon
De ses jambes! ô merveille!)

Mais, non, vrai, je crois que tant
Que pour sa tête la lame
Que les cailloux pour son flanc
Que pour ses boyaux la flamme

N'auront pas agi, l'enfant
Gêneur, la si sotte bête,
Ne doit cesser un instant
De ruser et d'être traître

Comme un chat des Monts-Rocheux;
D'empuantir toutes sphères!
Qu'à sa mort pourtant, ô mon Dieu!
S'élève quelque prière!

MÉMOIRE

I

L'eau claire; comme le sel des larmes d'enfance,
L'assaut au soleil des blancheurs des corps de femmes;
la soie, en foule et de lys pur, des oriflammes
sous les murs dont quelque pucelle eut la défense;

l'ébat des anges;—Non... le courant d'or en marche,
meut ses bras, noirs, et lourds, et frais surtout, d'herbe. Elle
sombre, ayant le Ciel bleu pour ciel-de-lit, appelle
pour rideaux l'ombre de la colline et de l'arche.

II

Eh! l'humide carreau tend ses bouillons limpides!
L'eau meuble d'or pâle et sans fond les couches prêtes.
Les robes vertes et déteintes des fillettes
font les saules, d'où sautent les oiseaux sans brides.

Plus pure qu'un louis, jaune et chaude paupière
le souci d'eau—ta foi conjugale, ô l'Épouse!—
au midi prompt, de son terne miroir, jalouse
au ciel gris de chaleur la Sphère rose et chère.

III

Madame se tient trop debout dans la prairie
prochaine où neigent les fils du travail; l'ombrelle
aux doigts; foulant l'ombelle; trop fière pour elle;
des enfants lisant dans la verdure fleurie

leur livre de maroquin rouge! Hélas, Lui, comme
mille anges blancs qui se séparent sur la route,
s'éloigne par delà la montagne! Elle, toute
froide, et noire, court! après le départ de l'homme!

IV

Regret des bras épais et jeunes d'herbe pure!
Or des lunes d'avril au cœur du saint lit! Joie
des chantiers riverains à l'abandon, en proie
aux soirs d'août qui faisaient germer ces pourritures!

Qu'elle pleure à présent sous les remparts! l'haleine
des peupliers d'en haut est pour la seule brise.
Puis, c'est la nappe, sans reflets, sans source, grise:
un vieux, dragueur, dans sa barque immobile, peine.

V

Jouet de cet œil d'eau morne, je n'y puis prendre,
ô canot immobile! oh! bras trop courts! ni l'une
ni l'autre fleur: ni la jaune qui m'importune,
là; ni la bleue, amie à l'eau couleur de cendre.

Ah! la poudre des saules qu'une aile secoue!
Les roses des roseaux dès longtemps dévorées!
Mon canot, toujours fixe; et sa chaîne tirée
Au fond de cet œil d'eau sans bords,—à quelle boue?

"O SAISONS, Ô CHÂTEAUX"

O saisons, ô châteaux
Quelle âme est sans défauts?

O saisons, ô châteaux!

J'ai fait la magique étude
Du Bonheur, que nul n'élude.

O vive lui, chaque fois
Que chante son coq Gaulois.

Mais! je n'aurai plus d'envie
Il s'est chargé de ma vie.

Ce Charme! il prit âme et corps
Et dispersa tous efforts.

Que comprendre à ma parole?
Il fait qu'elle fuie et vole!

ô saisons ô châteaux

VI. POEMES DE L'*ALBUM ZUTIQUE,* 1871–1872

L'IDOLE. SONNET DU TROU DU CUL

Obscur et froncé comme un œillet violet
Il respire, humblement tapi parmi la mousse
Humide encor d'amour qui suit la fuite douce
Des Fesses blanches jusqu'au cœur de son ourlet.

Des filaments pareils à des larmes de lait
Ont pleuré, sous le vent cruel qui les repousse,
À travers de petits caillots de marne rousse
Pour s'aller perdre où la pente les appelait.

Mon Rêve s'aboucha souvent à sa ventouse;
Mon âme, du coït matériel jalouse,
En fit son larmier fauve et son nid de sanglots.

C'est l'olive pâmée, et la flûte câline;
C'est le tube où descend la céleste praline:
Chanaan féminin dans les moiteurs enclos!

Albert Mérat.
P. V. - A. R.

LYS

O balançoirs! o lys! clysopompes d'argent!
Dédaigneux des travaux, dédaigneux des famines!
L'Aurore vous emplit d'un amour détergent!
Une douceur de ciel beurre vos étamines!

Armand Silvestre.
A. R.

VU À ROME

Il est, à Rome, à la Sixtine,
Couverte d'emblèmes chrétiens,
Une cassette écarlatine
Où sèchent des nez fort anciens:

Nez d'ascètes de Thébaïde,
Nez de chanoines du Saint Graal
Où se figea la nuit livide,
Et l'ancien plain-chant sépulcral.

Dans leur sécheresse mystique,
Tous les matins, on introduit
De l'immondice schismatique
Qu'en poudre fine on a réduit.

Léon Dierx.
A. R.

FÊTE GALANTE

Rêveur, Scapin
Gratte un lapin
Sous sa capote.

Colombina,
—Que l'on pina!—
—Do, mi,—tapote

L'œil du lapin
Qui tôt, tapin,
Est en ribote. . . .

Paul Verlaine
A. R.

"J'OCCUPAIS UN WAGON DE TROISIÈME..."

J'occupais un wagon de troisième: un vieux prêtre
Sortit son brûle-gueule et mit à la fenêtre,
Vers les brises, son front très calme aux poils pâlis.
Puis ce chrétien, bravant les brocarts impolis,
S'étant tourné, me fit la demande énergique
Et triste en même temps d'une petite chique
De caporal,—ayant été l'aumônier chef
D'un rejeton royal condamné derechef,—
Pour malaxer l'ennui d'un tunnel, sombre veine
Qui s'offre aux voyageurs, près Soissons, ville d'Aisne.

"JE PRÉFÈRE SANS DOUTE..."

Je préfère sans doute, au printemps, la guinguette
Où des marronniers nains bourgeonne la baguette,
Vers la prairie étroite et communale, au mois
De mai. Des jeunes chiens rabroués bien des fois
Viennent près des Buveurs triturer des jacinthes
De plate-bande. Et c'est, jusqu'aux soirs d'hyacinthe,
Sur la table d'ardoise où, l'an dix-sept cent vingt
Un diacre grava son sobriquet latin
Maigre comme une prose à des vitraux d'église
La toux des flacons noirs qui jamais ne les grise.

François Coppée.
A. R.

"L'HUMANITÉ CHAUSSAIT..."

L'Humanité chaussait le vaste enfant Progrès.

Louis-Xavier de Ricard
A. Rimbaud

CONNERIES—

I. Jeune goinfre.
Casquette
De moire,
Quéquette
D'ivoire,

Toilette
Très noire,
Paul guette
L'armoire,

Projette
Languette
Sur poire,

S'apprête
Baguette,
Et foire.
A. R.

II. Paris.
Al. Godillot, Gambier,
Galopeau, Volf-Pleyel,
—Ô Robinets!—Menier,
—O Christs!—Leperdriel!

Kinck, Jacob, Bonbonnel!
Veuillot, Tropmann, Augier!
Gill, Mendès, Manuel,
Guido Gonin!—Panier

Des Grâces! L'Hérissé!
Cirages onctueux!
Pains vieux, spiritueux!

Aveugles!—puis, qui sait?—
Sergents de ville, Enghiens
Chez soi!—soyons chrétiens!
A. R.

CONNERIES 2E SÉRIE

I. Cocher ivre.
Pouacre
Boit:
Nacre
Voit;

Âcre
Loi,
Fiacre
Choit!

Femme
Tombe:
Lombe

Saigne:
—Clame!
Geigne.
A.R.

VIEUX DE LA VIEILLE!

Aux paysans de l'empereur!
À l'empereur des paysans!
Au fils de Mars,
Au glorieux 18 *Mars!*
Où le Ciel d'Eugénie a béni les entrailles!

ETAT DE SIÈGE?

Le pauvre postillon, sous le dais de ferblanc,
Chauffant une engelure énorme sous son gant,
Suit son lourd omnibus parmi la rive gauche,
Et de son aine en flamme écarte la sacoche.
Et tandis que, douce ombre où des gendarmes sont,

L'honnête intérieur regarde au ciel profond
La lune se bercer parmi la verte ouate,
Malgré l'édit et l'heure encore délicate,
Et que l'omnibus rentre à l'Odéon, impur
Le débauché glapit au carrefour obscur!

François Coppée.
A. R.

LE BALAI

C'est un humble balai de chiendent, trop dur
Pour une chambre ou pour la peinture d'un mur.
L'usage en est navrant et ne vaut pas qu'on rie.
Racine prise à quelque ancienne prairie
Son crin inerte sèche: et son manche a blanchi.
Tel un bois d'île à la canicule rougi.
La cordelette semble une tresse gelée.
J'aime de cet objet la saveur désolée
Et j'en voudrais laver tes larges bords de lait,
O Lune où l'esprit de nos Sœurs mortes se plaît.

F. C.

EXIL

. . . .

Que l'on s'intéressa souvent, mon cher Conneau!.....
Plus qu'à l'Oncle Vainqueur, au Petit Ramponneau!..
Que tout honnête instinct sort du Peuple débile!. . . .
Hélas!! Et qui a fait tourner mal notre bile!. . . .
Et qu'il nous sied déjà de pousser le verrou
Au Vent que les enfants nomment Bari-barou!. . .
. . . .

Fragment d'une épître en Vers de Napoléon III, 1871.

L'ANGELOT MAUDIT

Toits bleuâtres et portes blanches
Comme en de nocturnes dimanches,

Au bout de la ville sans bruit,
La Rue est blanche, et c'est la nuit.

La Rue a des maisons étranges
Avec des persiennes d'Anges.

Mais, vers une borne, voici
Accourir, mauvais et transi,

Un noir Angelot qui titube
Ayant trop mangé de jujube.

Il fait caca: puis disparaît:
Mais son caca maudit paraît,

Sous la lune sainte qui vaque,
De sang sale un léger cloaque!

Louis Ratisbonne.
A. Rimbaud.

"LES SOIRS D'ÉTÉ ..."

Les soirs d'été, sous l'œil ardent des devantures,
Quand la sève frémit sous les grilles obscures
Irradiant au pied des grêles marronniers,
Hors de ces groupes noirs, joyeux ou casaniers,
Suceurs du brûle-gueule ou baiseurs du cigare,
Dans le kiosque mi-pierre étroit où je m'égare,
—Tandis qu'en haut rougeoie une annonce d'*Ibled,*—
Je songe que l'hiver figera le Filet
D'eau propre qui bruit, apaisant l'onde humaine,
—Et que l'âpre aquilon n'épargne aucune veine

Francis Coppée.
A. Rimbaud.

"AUX LIVRES DE CHEVET . . ."

Aux livres de chevet, livres de l'art serein,
Obermann et Genlis, Ver-vert et le Lutrin,
Blasé de nouveauté grisâtre et saugrenue,
J'espère, la vieillesse étant enfin venue,
Ajouter le Traité du Docteur Venetti.
Je saurai, revenu du public abêti,
Goûter le charme ancien des dessins nécessaires.
Ecrivain et graveur ont doré les misères
Sexuelles: et c'est, n'est-ce pas, cordial:
DR Venetti, Traité de l'Amour conjugal.

F. Coppée A.R

HYPOTYPOSES SATURNIENNES, EX BELMONTET

Quel est donc ce mystère impénétrable et sombre?
Pourquoi, sans projeter leur voile blanche, sombre
Tout jeune esquif royal gréé?

Renversons la douleur de nos lacrymatoires.
. . . .
L'amour veut vivre aux dépens de sa sœur,
L'amitié vit aux dépens de son frère.
. . . .
Le sceptre, qu'à peine on révère,
N'est que la croix d'un grand calvaire
Sur le volcan des nations!
. . . .
Oh! l'honneur ruisselait sur ta mâle moustache. Belmontet, archétype Parnassien.

LES REMEMBRANCES DU VIEILLARD IDIOT

Pardon, mon père!
Jeune, aux foires de campagne,
Je cherchais, non le tir banal où tout coup gagne,
Mais l'endroit plein de cris où les ân[es, le flan]c
Fatigué, déployaient ce long tu[be] sa[ng]lant

—Que je ne comprends pas encore!...
[Et puis] ma mère,
Dont la chemise avait une sente[ur amè]re
Quoique fripée au bas et jaune co[mme u]n fruit,
Ma mère qui montait au lit avec [un] bruit
—Fils du travail pourtant,—ma mè[re, a]vec sa cuisse
De femme mûre, avec ses reins très [g]ros où plisse
Le linge, me donna ces chaleurs q[ue] l'on tait!...

Une honte plus crue et plus calme, c'était
Quand ma petite sœur, au retour de la classe,
Ayant usé longtemps ses sabots sur la glace,
Pissait, et regardait s'échapper de sa lèvre
D'en bas serrée et rose, un fil d'urine mièvre!...

O pardon!
Je songeais à mon père parfois:
Le soir, le jeu de carte et les mots plus grivois,
Le voisin, et moi qu'on écartait, choses vues...
—Car un père est troublant!—et les choses conçues!..
Son genou, câlineur parfois; son pantalon
Dont mon doigt désirait ouvrir la fente,...—oh! non!—
Pour avoir le bout, gros, noir et dur, de mon père,
Dont la pileuse main me berçait!...
Je veux taire
Le pot, l'assiette à manche, entrevue au grenier,
Les almanachs couverts en rouge, et le panier
De charpie, et la Bible, et les lieux, et la bonne,
La Sainte-Vierge et le crucifix...
Oh! personne
Ne fut si fréquemment troublé, comme étonné!
Et maintenant, que le pardon me soit donné:
Puisque les sens infects m'ont mis de leurs victimes,
Je me confesse de l'aveu des jeunes crimes!...
. . . .

Puis!—qu'il me soit permis de parler au Seigneur!
Pourquoi la puberté tardive et le malheur
Du gland tenace et trop consulté? Pourquoi l'ombre
Si lente au bas du ventre? et ces terreurs sans nombre
Comblant toujours la joie ainsi qu'un gravier noir?
—Moi j'ai toujours été stupéfait. Quoi savoir?
. . . .

Pardonné?...
                    Reprenez la chancelière bleue,
Mon père.
          Ô cette enfance! . . . .
                              . . . .
          —et tirons-nous la queue! . . . .

François Coppée.
A. R.

RESSOUVENIR

Cette année où naquit le Prince impérial
Me laisse un souvenir largement cordial
D'un Paris limpide où des N d'or et de neige
Aux grilles du palais, aux gradins du manège,
Eclatent, tricolorement enrubannés.
Dans le remous public des grands chapeaux fanés,
Des chauds gilets à fleurs, des vieilles redingotes,
Et des chants d'ouvriers anciens dans les gargotes,
Sur des châles jonchés l'Empereur marche, noir
Et propre, avec la Sainte espagnole, le soir.

François Coppée

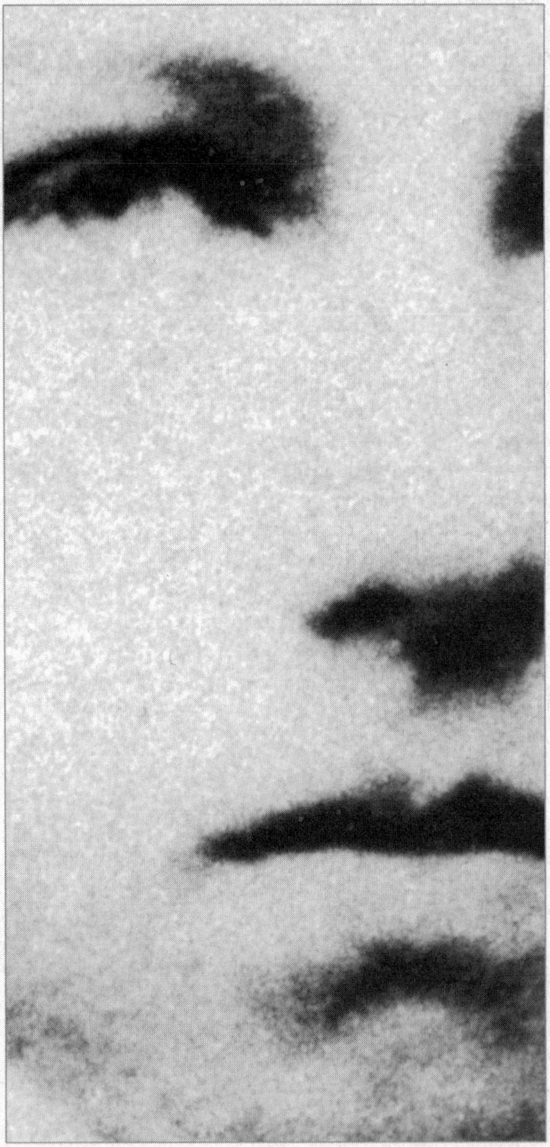

PROSES

I. 1866

"Le soleil était encore chaud..."

I

PROLOGUE

Le soleil était encore chaud; cependant il n'éclairait presque plus la terre; comme un flambeau placé devant les voûtes gigantesques ne les éclaire plus que par une faible lueur, ainsi le soleil, flambeau terrestre, s'éteignait en laissant échapper de son corps de feu une dernière et faible lueur, laissant encore cependant voir les feuilles vertes des arbres, les petites fleurs qui se flétrissaient, et le sommet gigantesque des pins, des peupliers et des chênes séculaires. Le vent rafraîchissant, c'est-à-dire une brise fraîche, agitait les feuilles des arbres avec un bruissement à peu près semblable à celui que faisait le bruit des eaux argentées du ruisseau qui coulait à mes pieds. Les fougères courbaient leur front vert devant le vent. Je m'endormis, non sans m'être abreuvé de l'eau du ruisseau.

II

Je rêvai que . . . .

. . . .

. . . . j'étais né à Reims, l'an 1503.

Reims était alors une petite ville ou, pour mieux dire, un bourg cependant renommé à cause de sa belle cathédrale, témoin du sacre du roi Clovis.

Mes parents étaient peu riches, mais très honnêtes: ils n'avaient pour tout bien qu'une petite maison qui leur avait toujours appartenu et qui était en leur possession vingt ans avant que je ne fus encore né en plus quelques mille francs auxquels il faut encore ajouter les petits louis provenant des économies de ma mère.

Mon père était officier, dans les armées du roi. C'était un homme grand, maigre, chevelure noire, barbe, yeux, peau de même couleur. Quoiqu'il n'eût guère, quand j'étais né, que 48 ou 50 ans, on lui en aurait certainement bien donné 60 ou 58. Il était d'un caractère vif, bouillant, souvent en colère, et ne voulant rien souffrir qui lui déplût.

Ma mère était bien différente: femme douce, calme, s'effrayant de peu de chose, et cependant tenant la maison dans un ordre parfait. Elle était si calme que mon père l'amusait comme une jeune demoiselle. J'étais le plus aimé. Mes frères étaient moins vaillants que moi et cependant plus grands. J'aimais peu l'étude, c'est-à-dire d'apprendre à lire, écrire et compter. Mais si c'était pour arranger une maison, cultiver un jardin, faire des commissions, à la bonne heure, je me plaisais à cela.

Je me rappelle qu'un jour mon père m'avait promis vingt sous, si je lui faisais bien une division; je commençai; mais je ne pus finir. Ah! combien de fois ne m'a-t-il pas promis des sous, des jouets, des friandises, même une fois cinq francs, si je pouvais lui lire quelque chose. Malgré cela, mon père me mit en classe dès que j'eus dix ans. Pourquoi—me disais-je—apprendre du grec, du latin? Je ne le sais. Enfin, on n'a pas besoin de cela. Que m'importe à moi que je sois reçu, à quoi cela sert-il d'être reçu, à rien, n'est-ce pas? Si, pourtant; on dit qu'on n'a une place que lorsqu'on est reçu. Moi, je ne veux pas de place; je serai rentier. Quand même on en voudrait une, pourquoi apprendre le latin? Personne ne parle cette langue. Quelquefois j'en vois sur les journaux; mais, dieu merci, je ne serai pas journaliste. Pourquoi apprendre et de l'histoire et de la géographie? On a, il est vrai, besoin de savoir que Paris est en France, mais on ne demande pas à quel degré de latitude. De l'histoire, apprendre la vie de Chinaldon, de Nabopolassar, de Darius, de Cyrus, et d'Alexandre, et de leurs autres compères remarquables par leurs noms diaboliques, est un supplice?

Que m'importe à moi qu'Alexandre ait été célèbre! Que m'importe... Que sait-on si les Latins ont existé? C'est peut-être quelque langue forgée; et quand même ils auraient existé, qu'ils me laissent rentier, et conservent leur langue pour eux. Quel mal leur ai-je fait pour qu'ils me flanquent au supplice? Passons au grec. Cette sale langue n'est parlée par personne, personne au monde!...

Ah! saperlipotte de saperlipopette! sapristi! moi je serai rentier; il ne fait pas si bon de s'user les culottes sur les bancs, saperlipopettouille!

Pour être décrotteur, gagner la place de décrotteur, il faut passer un examen; car les places qui vous sont accordées sont d'être ou décrotteur, ou porcher, ou bouvier. Dieu merci, je n'en veux pas, moi, saperlipouille! Avec ça des soufflets vous sont accordés pour récompense; on vous appelle animal, ce qui n'est pas vrai, bout d'homme, etc...

Ah! saperpouillotte!

La suite prochainement.
Arthur

II. 1870

Un Coeur sous une soutane

UN CŒUR SOUS UNE SOUTANE

—Intimités d'un Séminariste.—

...Ô Thimothina Labinette! Aujourd'hui que j'ai revêtu la robe sacrée, je puis rappeler la passion, maintenant refroidie et dormant sous la soutane, qui, l'an passé, fit battre mon cœur de jeune homme sous ma capote de séminariste!......

...Ier mai 18 . . . . .

...Voici le printemps. Le plant de vigne de l'abbé*** bourgeonne dans son pot de terre: l'arbre de la cour a de petites pousses tendres comme des gouttes vertes sur ses branches; l'autre jour, en sortant de l'étude, j'ai vu à la fenêtre du second quelque chose comme le champignon nasal du Sup***. Les Souliers de J*** sentent un peu; et j'ai remarqué que les élèves sortent fort souvent pour... dans la cour; eux qui vivaient à l'étude comme des taupes, rentassés, enfoncés dans leur ventre, tendant leur face rouge vers le poêle, avec une haleine épaisse et chaude comme celle des vaches! Ils restent fort longtemps à l'air, maintenant, et, quand ils reviennent, ricanent, et referment l'isthme de leur pantalon fort minutieusement,—non, je me trompe, fort lentement,—avec des manières, en semblant se complaire, machinalement, à cette opération qui n'a rien en soi que de très futile....

2 mai. Le Sup*** est descendu hier de sa chambre, et, en fermant les yeux, les mains cachées, craintif et frileux, il a traîné à quatre pas dans la cour ses pantoufles de chanoine!...

Voici mon cœur qui bat la mesure dans ma poitrine, et ma poitrine qui bat contre mon pupitre crasseux! Oh! je déteste maintenant le temps où les élèves étaient comme de grosses brebis suant dans leurs habits sales, et dormaient dans l'atmosphère empuanti[e] de l'étude, sous la lumière du gaz, dans la chaleur fade du poêle!...J'étends mes bras! je soupire, j'étends mes jambes...Je sens des choses dans ma tête, oh! des choses!...

...4 mai...

... Tenez, hier, je n'y tenais plus: j'ai étendu, comme l'ange Gabriel, les ailes de mon cœur. Le souffle de l'esprit sacré a parcouru mon être! J'ai pris ma lyre, et j'ai chanté:

Approchez-vous,
Grande Marie!
Mère chérie!
Du doux Jhésus!
Sanctus Christus!
Ô Vierge enceinte,
Ô mère sainte,
Exaucez-nous!

Ô! si vous saviez les effluves mystérieuses qui secouaient mon âme pendant que j'effeuillais cette rose poétique! Je pris ma cithare, et, comme le Psalmiste, j'élevai ma voix innocente et pure dans les célestes altitudes!!! O altitudo altitudinum!...

. . . .

... 7 mai.... Hélas! ma poésie a replié ses ailes, mais, comme Galilée, je dirai, accablé par l'outrage et le supplice: Et pourtant elle se meut!—lisez: elles se meuvent!—J'avais commis l'imprudence de laisser tomber la précédente confidence... J*** l'a ramassée, J***, le plus féroce des jansénistes, le plus rigoureux des séides du sup***, et l'a portée à son maître, en secret; mais le monstre, pour me faire sombrer sous l'insulte universelle, avait fait passer ma poésie dans les mains de tous ses amis!

Hier, le sup*** me mande; j'entre dans son appartement, je suis debout devant lui, fort de mon intérieur. Sur son front chauve frissonnait comme un éclair furtif son dernier cheveu roux; ses yeux émergeaient de sa graisse, mais calmes, paisibles; son nez, semblable à une batte, était mû par son branle habituel; il chuchotait un oremus; il mouilla l'extrémité de son pouce, tourna quelques feuilles de livre, et sortit un petit papier crasseux, plié...

Granananande Maarieie!...
Mèèèree Chééérieie!

Il ravalait ma poésie! il crachait sur ma rose! il faisait le Brid'oison, le Joseph, le bêtiot, pour salir, pour souiller ce chant virginal! Il bégayait et prolongeait chaque syllabe avec un ricanement de haine concentré et quand il fut arrivé au cinquième vers,... *Vierge enceinte!* il s'arrêta, contourna sa nasale, et! il—!! éclata: ... Vierge enceinte! Vierge enceinte! il disait cela avec un ton, en fronçant avec un frisson son abdomen proéminent, avec un ton si affreux, qu'une pudique rougeur couvrit mon front. Je tombai à genoux, les bras vers le plafond, et je m'écriai: Ô mon père!...

. . . .

—Votre lyyyre! votre cithâre! jeune homme! votre cithâre! des effluves mystérieuses! qui vous secouaient l'âme! J'aurais voulu voir! Jeune âme, je remarque là dedans, dans cette confession impie, quelque chose de mondain, un abandon dangereux, de l'entraînement, enfin!—

Il se tut, fit frissonner de haut en bas son abdomen: puis, solennel:

—Jeune homme, avez-vous la foi?...

—Mon père, pourquoi cette parole? Vos lèvres plaisantent-elles?... Oui, je crois à tout ce que dit ma mère... la Sainte Église!

—Mais... Vierge enceinte!... C'est la conception, ça, jeune homme; c'est la conception!...

—Mon père! je crois à la conception...

—Vous avez raison! jeune homme! C'est une chose...

... Il se tut...—Puis: Le jeune J*** m'a fait un rapport où il constate chez vous un écartement des jambes, de jour en jour plus notoire, dans votre tenue à l'étude; il affirme vous avoir vu vous étendre de tout votre long sous la table, à la façon d'un jeune homme... dégingandé. Ce sont des faits auxquels vous n'avez rien à répondre... Approchez-vous, à genoux, tout près de moi; je veux vous interroger avec douceur; répondez: vous écartez beaucoup vos jambes, à l'étude?

Puis il me mettait la main sur l'épaule, autour du cou, et ses yeux devenaient clairs, et il me faisait dire des choses sur cet écartement des jambes...... Tenez, j'aime mieux vous dire que ce fut dégoûtant, moi qui sais ce que cela veut dire, ces scènes-là!...

Ainsi, on m'avait mouchardé, on avait calomnié mon cœur et ma pudeur,—et je ne pouvais rien dire à cela, les rapports, les lettres anonymes des élèves les uns contre les autres, au Sup***, étant autorisées et commandées—, et je venais dans cette chambre, me f... sous la main de ce gros!... Oh! le séminaire!...

. . . .

10 mai.—Oh! mes condisciples sont effroyablement méchants et effroyablement lascifs. À l'étude, ils savent tous, ces profanes, l'histoire de mes vers et, aussitôt que je tourne la tête, je rencontre la face du poussif D***, qui me chuchote: Et ta cithare? et ta cithare? et ton journal? Puis, l'idiot L*** reprend: Et ta lyre? et ta cithare? Puis trois ou quatre chuchotent en chœur: Grande Marie... Grande Marie... Mère chérie!

Moi, je suis un grand benêt:—Jésus, je ne me donne pas de coups de pied!—Mais enfin, je ne moucharde pas, je n'écris pas d'ânonymes, et j'ai pour moi ma sainte poésie et ma pudeur!...

12 mai...

Ne devinez-vous pas pourquoi je meurs d'amour?
La fleur me dit: salut; l'oiseau me dit bonjour.
Salut: c'est le printemps! c'est l'ange de tendresse!

Ne devinez-vous pas pourquoi je bous d'ivresse!
Ange de ma grand'mère, ange de mon berceau,
Ne devinez-vous pas que je deviens oiseau,
Que ma lyre frissonne et que je bats de l'aile
    Comme hirondelle?......

J'ai fait ces vers-là hier, pendant la récréation; je suis entré dans la chapelle, je me suis enfermé dans un confessionnal, et là, ma jeune poésie a pu palpiter et s'envoler, dans le rêve et le silence, vers les sphères de l'amour. Puis, comme on vient m'enlever mes moindres papiers dans mes poches, la nuit et le jour, j'ai cousu ces vers en bas de mon dernier vêtement, celui qui touche immédiatement à ma peau, et, pendant l'étude, je tire, sous mes habits, ma poésie sur mon cœur, et je la presse longuement en rêvant.........

---

15 mai.—Les événements se sont bien pressés, depuis ma dernière confidence, et des événements bien solennels, des événements qui doivent influer sur ma vie future et intérieure d'une façon sans doute bien terrible!

Thimothina Labinette, je t'adore!

Thimothina Labinette, je t'adore! je t'adore! laisse-moi chanter sur mon luth, comme le divin Psalmiste sur son Psaltérion, comment je t'ai vue, et comment mon cœur a sauté sur le tien pour un éternel amour!

Jeudi, c'était jour de sortie: nous, nous sortons deux heures; je suis sorti: ma mère, dans sa dernière lettre, m'avait dit: «... tu iras, mon fils, occuper superficiellement ta sortie chez monsieur Césarin Labinette, un habitué à ton feu père, auquel il faut que tu sois présenté un jour ou l'autre avant ton ordination...»

...Je me présentai à monsieur Labinette, qui m'obligea beaucoup en me reléguant, sans mot dire, dans sa cuisine; sa fille, Thimothine, resta seule avec moi, saisit un linge, essuya un gros bol ventru en l'appuyant contre son cœur, et me dit tout à coup, après un long silence: Eh bien, Monsieur Léonard?...

Jusque-là, confondu de me voir avec cette jeune créature dans la solitude de cette cuisine, j'avais baissé les yeux et invoqué dans mon cœur le nom sacré de Marie: je relevai le front en rougissant, et, devant la beauté de mon interlocutrice, je ne pus que balbutier un faible: Mademoiselle?...

Thimothine! tu étais belle! Si j'étais peintre, je reproduirais sur la toile tes traits sacrés sous ce titre: La Vierge au bol! Mais je ne suis que poète, et ma langue ne peut te célébrer qu'incomplètement...

La cuisinière noire, avec ses trous où flamboyaient les braises comme des yeux rouges, laissait échapper, de ses casseroles à minces filets de fumée, une odeur céleste de soupe aux choux et de haricots; et devant elle, aspirant avec ton doux nez l'odeur de ces légumes, regardant ton gros chat avec tes beaux yeux gris, ô Vierge au bol, tu essuyais ton vase! Les bandeaux plats et clairs de tes cheveux se collaient pudiquement sur ton front jaune comme le soleil; de tes yeux courait un sillon bleuâtre jusqu'au milieu de ta joue, comme à Santa Teresa! ton nez, plein de l'odeur des haricots, soulevait ses narines délicates; un duvet léger, serpentant sur tes lèvres, ne contribuait pas peu à donner une belle énergie à ton visage; et, à ton menton, brillait un beau signe brun où frissonnaient de beaux poils follets: tes cheveux étaient sagement retenus à ton occiput par des épingles; mais une courte mèche s'en échappait... Je cherchai vainement tes seins; tu n'en as pas: tu dédaignes ces ornements mondains: ton cœur est tes seins!... quand tu te retournas pour frapper de ton pied large ton chat doré, je vis tes omoplates saillant et soulevant ta robe, et je fus percé d'amour, devant le tortillement gracieux des deux arcs prononcés de tes reins!...

Dès ce moment, je t'adorai: j'adorais, non pas tes cheveux, non pas tes omoplates, non pas ton tortillement inférieurement postérieur: ce que j'aime en une femme, en une vierge, c'est la modestie sainte; ce qui me fait bondir d'amour, c'est la pudeur et la piété; c'est ce que j'adorai en toi, jeune bergère!...

Je tâchais de lui faire voir ma passion, et, du reste, mon cœur, mon cœur me trahissait! Je ne répondais que par des paroles entrecoupées à ses interrogations; plusieurs fois, je lui dis Madame, au lieu de Mademoiselle, dans mon trouble! Peu à peu, aux accents magiques de sa voix, je me sentais succomber; enfin je résolus de m'abandonner, de lâcher tout: et, à je ne sais plus quelle question qu'elle m'adressa, je me renversai en arrière sur ma chaise, je mis une main sur mon cœur, de l'autre je saisis dans ma poche un chapelet dont je laissai passer la croix blanche, et, un œil vers Thimothine, l'autre au ciel, je répondis douloureusement et tendrement, comme un cerf à une biche:

—Oh! oui! Mademoiselle... Thimothina!!!

Miserere! miserere!—Dans mon œil ouvert délicieusement vers le plafond tombe tout à coup une goutte de saumure, dégouttant d'un jambon planant au-dessus de moi, et, lorsque, tout rouge de honte, réveillé dans ma passion, je baissais mon front, je m'aperçus que je n'avais dans ma main gauche, au lieu d'un chapelet, qu'un biberon brun;—ma mère me l'avait confié l'an passé pour le donner au petit de la mère chose!—De l'œil que je tendais au plafond découla la saumure amère:—mais, de l'œil qui te regardait, ô Thimothina, une larme coula, larme d'amour, et larme de douleur!.

. . . .

. . . .

Quelque temps, une heure après, quand Thimothina m'annonça une collation composée de haricots et d'une omelette au lard, tout ému de ses charmes, je répondis à mi-voix:

—J'ai le cœur si plein, voyez-vous, que cela me ruine l'estomac!—Et je me mis à table; oh! je le sens encore, son cœur avait répondu au mien dans son appel: pendant la courte collation, elle ne mangea pas:

—Ne trouves-tu pas qu'on sent un goût? répétait-elle; son père ne comprenait pas; mais mon cœur le comprit: c'était la Rose de David, la Rose de Jessé, la Rose mystique de l'écriture; c'était l'Amour!

Elle se leva brusquement, alla dans un coin de la cuisine et, me montrant la double fleur de ses reins, elle plongea son bras dans un tas informe de bottes, de chaussures diverses, d'où s'élança son gros chat; et jeta tout cela dans un vieux placard vide; puis elle retourna à sa place, et interrogea l'atmosphère d'une façon inquiète; tout à coup, elle fronça le front et s'écria:

—Cela sent encore!…

—Oui, cela sent, répondit son père assez bêtement: (il ne pouvait comprendre, lui, le profane!)

Je m'aperçus bien que tout cela n'était dans ma chair vierge que les mouvements intérieurs de sa passion! Je l'adorais et je savourais avec amour l'omelette dorée, et mes mains battaient la mesure avec la fourchette, et, sous la table, mes pieds frissonnaient d'aise dans mes chaussures!…

Mais, ce qui me fut un trait de lumière, ce qui me fut comme un gage d'amour éternel, comme un diamant de tendresse de la part de Thimothina, ce fut l'adorable obligeance qu'elle eut, à mon départ, de m'offrir une paire de chaussettes blanches, avec un sourire et ces paroles:

—Voulez-vous cela pour vos pieds, Monsieur Léonard?

. . . .

16 mai—Thimothina! Je t'adore, toi et ton père, toi et ton chat…

Thimothina, { Vas devotionis,
Rosa mystica,
Turris davidica, Ora pro nobis!
Cœli porta,
Stella maris,

17 mai—Que m'importent à présent les bruits du monde et les bruits de l'étude? Que m'importent ceux que la paresse et la langueur courbent à mes côtés? Ce matin, tous les fronts, appesantis par le sommeil, étaient collés aux tables; un ronflement, pareil au cri du clairon du jugement dernier, un ronflement sourd et lent s'élevait de ce vaste Gethsémani. Moi, stoïque, serein, droit et m'élevant au-dessus de tous ces morts comme un palmier au-dessus des ruines, méprisant les odeurs et les bruits incongrus, je portais ma tête dans ma main, j'écoutais battre mon cœur plein de Thimothina, et mes yeux se plongeaient dans l'azur du ciel, entrevu par la vitre supérieure de la fenêtre!…

—18 mai: Merci à l'Esprit Saint qui m'a inspiré ces vers charmants: ces vers, je vais les enchâsser dans mon cœur: et, quand le ciel me donnera de revoir Thimothina, je les lui donnerai, en échange de ses chaussettes!…

Je l'ai intitulée La Brise:

Dans sa retraite de coton
Dort le zéphyr à douce haleine:

Dans son nid de soie et de laine
Dort le zéphyr au gai menton!

Quand le zéphyr lève son aile
Dans sa retraite de coton,
Quand il court où la fleur l'appelle,
Sa douce haleine sent bien bon!

Ô brise quintessenciée!
Ô quintessence de l'amour!
Quand la rosée est essuyée,
Comme ça sent bon dans le jour!

Jésus! Joseph! Jésus! Marie!
C'est comme une aile de condor
Assoupissant celui qui prie!
Ça nous pénètre et nous endort!

. . . .

La fin est trop intérieure et trop suave: je la conserve dans le tabernacle de mon âme. À la prochaine sortie, je lirai cela à ma divine et odorante Thimothina.

Attendons dans le calme et le recueillement.

. . . .

Date incertaine. Attendons!…

16 juin!—Seigneur, que votre volonté se fasse: je n'y mettrai aucun obstacle! Si vous voulez détourner de votre serviteur l'amour de Thimothina, libre à vous, sans doute: mais, Seigneur Jésus, n'avez-vous pas aimé vous-même, et la lance de l'amour ne vous a-t-elle pas appris à condescendre aux souffrances des malheureux! Priez pour moi!

Oh! j'attendais depuis longtemps cette sortie de deux heures du 15 juin: j'avais contraint mon âme, en lui disant: Tu seras libre ce jour-là: le 15 juin, je m'étais peigné mes quelques cheveux modestes, et, usant d'une odorante pommade rose, je les avais collés sur mon front, comme les bandeaux de Thimothina; je m'étais pommadé les sourcils; j'avais minutieusement brossé mes habits noirs, comblé adroitement certains déficits fâcheux dans ma toilette, et je me présentai à la sonnette espérée de M. Césarin Labinette. Il arriva, après un assez long temps, la calotte un peu crânement sur l'oreille, une mèche de cheveux raide et fort pommadée lui cinglant la face comme une balafre, une main dans la poche de sa robe de chambre à fleurs jaunes, l'autre sur le loquet… Il me jeta un bonjour sec, fronça le nez en jetant un coup d'œil sur mes souliers à cordons noirs, et s'en alla devant moi, les mains dans ses deux poches, ramenant en devant sa robe de chambre, comme fait l'abbé*** avec sa soutane, et modelant ainsi à mes regards sa partie inférieure.

Je le suivis.

Il traversa la cuisine, et j'entrai après lui dans son salon. Oh! ce salon! je l'ai fixé dans ma mémoire avec les épingles du souvenir! La tapisserie était à fleurs brunes; sur la cheminée, une énorme pendule en bois noir, à colonnes; deux vases bleus avec des roses; sur les murs, une peinture de la bataille d'Inkermann; et un dessin au crayon, d'un ami de Césarin, représentant un moulin avec sa meule souffletant un petit ruisseau semblable à un crachat, dessin que charbonnent tous ceux qui commencent à dessiner. La poésie est bien préférable!...

Au milieu du salon, une table à tapis vert, autour de laquelle mon cœur ne vit que Thimothina, quoiqu'il s'y trouvât un ami de monsieur Césarin, ancien exécuteur des œuvres sacristaines dans la paroisse de ***, et son épouse, madame de Riflandouille, et que monsieur Césarin lui-même vînt s'y accouder de nouveau, aussitôt mon entrée.

Je pris une chaise rembourrée, songeant qu'une partie de moi-même allait s'appuyer sur une tapisserie faite sans doute par Thimothina, je saluai tout le monde, et, mon chapeau noir posé sur la table, devant moi, comme un rempart, j'écoutai...

Je ne parlais pas, mais mon cœur parlait! Les messieurs continuèrent la partie de cartes commencée: je remarquai qu'ils trichaient à qui mieux mieux, et cela me causa une surprise assez douloureuse. La partie terminée, ces personnes s'assirent en cercle autour de la cheminée vide; j'étais à un des coins, presque caché par l'énorme ami de Césarin, dont la chaise seule me séparait de Thimothina: je fus content en moi-même du peu d'attention que l'on faisait à ma personne; relégué derrière la chaise du sacristain honoraire, je pouvais laisser voir sur mon visage les mouvements de mon cœur sans être remarqué de personne; je me livrai donc à un doux abandon; et je laissai la conversation s'échauffer et s'engager entre ces trois personnes; car Thimothina ne parlait que rarement; elle jetait sur son séminariste des regards d'amour, et, n'osant le regarder en face, elle dirigeait ses yeux clairs vers mes souliers bien cirés!... Moi, derrière le gros sacristain, je me livrais à mon cœur.

Je commençai par me pencher du côté de Thimothina, en levant les yeux au ciel. Elle était retournée. Je me relevai, et, la tête baissée vers ma poitrine, je poussai un soupir; elle ne bougea pas. Je remis mes boutons, je fis aller mes lèvres, je fis un léger signe de croix; elle ne vit rien. Alors, transporté, furieux d'amour, je me baissai très fort vers elle, en tenant mes mains comme à la communion, et en poussant un ah!... prolongé et douloureux; Miserere! tandis que je gesticulais, que je priais, je tombai de ma chaise avec un bruit sourd, et le gros sacristain se retourna en ricanant, et Thimothina dit à son père:

—Tiens, M. Léonard qui coule par terre!

Son père ricana! Miserere!

Le sacristain me repiqua, rouge de honte et faible d'amour, sur ma chaise rembourrée, et me fit une place. Mais je baissai les yeux, je voulus dormir! Cette société m'était importune, elle ne devinait pas l'amour qui souffrait là dans l'ombre: je voulus dormir! mais j'entendis la conversation se tourner sur moi!...

Je rouvris faiblement les yeux...

Césarin et le sacristain fumaient chacun un cigare maigre, avec toutes les mignardises possibles, ce qui rendait leurs personnes effroyablement ridicules: madame la sacristaine, sur le bord de sa chaise, sa poitrine cave penchée en avant, ayant derrière elle tous les flots de sa robe jaune qui lui bouffaient jusqu'au cou, et épanouissant autour d'elle son unique volant, effeuillait délicieusement une rose: un sourire affreux entr'ouvrait ses lèvres, et montrait à ses gencives maigres deux dents noires, jaunes, comme la faïence d'un vieux poêle.—Toi, Thimothina, tu étais belle, avec ta collerette blanche, tes yeux baissés, et tes bandeaux plats.

—C'est un jeune homme d'avenir; son présent inaugure son futur, disait en laissant aller un flot de fumée grise le sacristain…

—Oh! monsieur Léonard illustrera la robe, nasilla la sacristaine: les deux dents parurent!…

Moi, je rougissais à la façon d'un garçon de bien; je vis que les chaises s'éloignaient de moi, et qu'on chuchotait sur mon compte…

Thimothina regardait toujours mes souliers; les deux sales dents me menaçaient… le sacristain riait ironiquement: j'avais toujours la tête baissée!…

—Lamartine est mort… dit tout à coup Thimothina.

Chère Thimothina! C'était pour ton adorateur, pour ton pauvre poète Léonard, que tu jetais dans la conversation ce nom de Lamartine; alors je relevai le front, je sentis que la pensée seule de la poésie allait refaire une virginité à tous ces profanes, je sentais mes ailes palpiter, et je dis, rayonnant, l'œil sur Thimothina:

—Il avait de beaux fleurons à sa couronne, l'auteur des *Méditations poétiques!*

—Le cygne des vers est défunt! dit la sacristaine.

—Oui, mais il a chanté son chant funèbre, repris-je, enthousiasmé.

—Mais, s'écria la sacristaine, monsieur Léonard est poète aussi! Sa mère m'a montré l'an passé des essais de sa muse…

Je jouai d'audace:

—Oh! Madame je n'ai apporté ni ma lyre ni ma cithare; mais…

—Oh! votre cithare! vous l'apporterez un autre jour…

—Mais, ce néanmoins, si cela ne déplaît pas à l'honorable—et je tirais un morceau de papier de ma poche,—je vais vous lire quelques vers… Je les dédie à mademoiselle Thimothina.

—Oui! oui! jeune homme! très bien! Récitez, récitez, mettez-vous au bout de la salle…

Je me reculai… Thimothina regardait mes souliers… La sacristaine faisait la Madone; les deux messieurs se penchaient l'un vers l'autre… Je rougis, je toussai, et je dis en chantant tendrement:

Dans sa retraite de coton
Dort le zéphyr à douce haleine…
Dans son nid de soie et de laine
Dort le zéphyr au gai menton.

Toute l'assistance pouffa de rire: les messieurs se penchaient l'un vers l'autre en faisant de grossiers calembours; mais ce qui était surtout effroyable, c'était l'air de la sacristaine, qui, l'œil au ciel, faisait la mystique, et souriait avec ses dents affreuses! Thimothina, Thimothina crevait de rire! Cela me perça d'une atteinte mortelle, Thimothina se tenait les côtes!...—Un doux zéphyr dans du coton, c'est suave, c'est suave!...faisait en reniflant le père Césarin...Je crus m'apercevoir de quelque chose...Mais cet éclat de rire ne dura qu'une seconde: tous essayèrent de reprendre leur sérieux, qui pétait encore de temps en temps...

—Continuez, jeune homme, c'est bien, c'est bien!

Quand le zéphyr lève son aile
Dans sa retraite de coton,...
Quand il court où la fleur l'appelle,
Sa douce haleine sent bien bon...

Cette fois, un gros rire secoua mon auditoire; Thimothina regarda mes souliers: j'avais chaud, mes pieds brûlaient sous son regard, et nageaient dans la sueur; car je disais: ces chaussettes que je porte depuis un mois, c'est un don de son amour, ces regards qu'elle jette sur mes pieds, c'est un témoignage de son amour: elle m'adore!

Et voici que je ne sais quel petit goût me parut sortir de mes souliers: oh! je compris les rires horribles de l'assemblée! Je compris qu'égarée dans cette société méchante, Thimothina Labinette, Thimothina ne pourrait jamais donner un libre cours à sa passion! Je compris qu'il me fallait dévorer, à moi aussi, cet amour douloureux éclos dans mon cœur une après-midi de mai, dans une cuisine des Labinette, devant le tortillement postérieur de la Vierge au bol!

Quatre heures, l'heure de la rentrée, sonnaient à la pendule du salon; éperdu, brûlant d'amour et fou de douleur, je saisis mon chapeau, je m'enfuis en renversant une chaise, je traversai le corridor en murmurant: J'adore Thimothina, et je m'enfuis au séminaire sans m'arrêter...

Les basques de mon habit noir volaient derrière moi, dans le vent, comme des oiseaux sinistres!...

. . . .

. . . .

30 juin. Désormais, je laisse à la muse divine le soin de bercer ma douleur; martyr d'amour à dix-huit ans, et, dans mon affliction, pensant à un autre martyr du sexe qui fait nos joies et nos bonheurs, n'ayant plus celle que j'aime, je vais aimer la foi! Que le Christ, que Marie me prennent sur leur sein: je les suis; je ne suis pas digne de dénouer les cordons des souliers de Jésus; mais ma douleur! mais mon supplice! Moi aussi, à dix-huit ans et sept mois, je porte une croix, une couronne d'épines! mais, dans la main, au lieu d'un roseau, j'ai une cithare! Là sera le dictame à ma plaie!

. . . .

—Un an après, 1er août.—Aujourd'hui, on m'a revêtu de la robe sacrée; je vais servir Dieu; j'aurai une cure et une modeste servante dans un riche village. J'ai la foi; je ferai mon salut, et sans être dispendieux, je vivrai comme un bon serviteur de Dieu avec sa servante. Ma Mère la sainte Église me réchauffera dans son sein: qu'elle soit bénie! que Dieu soit béni!

... Quant à cette passion cruellement chérie que je renferme au fond de mon cœur, je saurai la supporter avec constance: sans la raviver précisément, je pourrai m'en rappeler quelquefois le souvenir; ces choses-là sont bien douces!—Moi, du reste, j'étais né pour l'amour et pour la foi!—Peut-être un jour, revenu dans cette ville, aurai-je le bonheur de confesser ma chère Thimothina? Puis, je conserve d'elle un doux souvenir: depuis un an, je n'ai pas défait les chaussettes qu'elle m'a données...

Ces chaussettes-là, mon Dieu! je les garderai à mes pieds jusque dans votre saint Paradis!...

III. 1871
Les Déserts de l'amour

LES DÉSERTS DE L'AMOUR

Avertissement

Ces écritures-ci sont d'un jeune, tout jeune *homme*, dont la vie s'est développée n'importe où; sans mère, sans pays, insoucieux de tout ce qu'on connaît, fuyant toute force morale, comme furent déjà plusieurs pitoyables jeunes hommes. Mais, lui, si ennuyé et si troublé, qu'il ne fit que s'amener à la mort comme à une pudeur terrible et fatale. N'ayant pas aimé de femmes,—quoique plein de sang!—il eut son âme et son cœur, toute sa force, élevés en des erreurs étranges et tristes. Des rêves suivants,—ses amours!—qui lui vinrent dans ses lits ou dans les rues, et de leur suite et de leur fin, de douces considérations religieuses se dégagent—peut-être se rappellera-t-on le sommeil continu des Mahométans légendaires,—braves pourtant et circoncis! Mais, cette bizarre souffrance possédant une autorité inquiétante, il faut sincèrement désirer que cette âme, égarée parmi nous tous, et qui veut la mort, ce semble, rencontre en cet instant-là des consolations sérieuses et soit digne!

I

C'est certes la même campagne. La même maison rustique de mes parents: la salle même où les dessus de porte sont des bergeries roussies, avec des armes et des lions. Au dîner, il y a un salon, avec des bougies et des vins et des boiseries rustiques. La table à manger est très-grande. Les servantes! Elles étaient plusieurs, autant que je m'en suis souvenu.—Il y avait là un de mes jeunes amis anciens, prêtre et vêtu en prêtre, maintenant: c'était pour être plus libre. Je me souviens de sa chambre de pourpre, à vitres de papier jaune: et ses livres, cachés, qui avaient trempé dans l'océan!

Moi j'étais abandonné, dans cette maison de campagne sans fin: lisant dans la cuisine, séchant la boue de mes habits devant les hôtes, aux conversations du salon: ému jusqu'à la mort par le murmure du lait du matin et de la nuit du siècle dernier.

J'étais dans une chambre très sombre: que faisais-je? Une servante vint près de moi:

je puis dire que c'était un petit chien: quoiqu'elle fût belle, et d'une noblesse maternelle inexprimable pour moi: pure, connue, toute charmante! Elle me pinça le bras.

Je ne me rappelle même plus bien sa figure: ce n'est pas pour me rappeler son bras, dont je roulai la peau dans mes deux doigts: ni sa bouche, que la mienne saisit comme une petite vague désespérée, minant sans fin quelque chose. Je la renversai dans une corbeille de coussins et de toiles de navire, en un coin noir. Je ne me rappelle plus que son pantalon à dentelles blanches.—Puis, ô désespoir, la cloison devint vaguement l'ombre des arbres, et je me suis abîmé sous la tristesse amoureuse de la nuit.

II

Cette fois, c'est la Femme que j'ai vue dans la ville, et à qui j'ai parlé et qui me parle.

J'étais dans une chambre sans lumière. On vint me dire qu'elle était chez moi: et je la vis dans mon lit, toute à moi, sans lumière! Je fus très ému, et beaucoup parce que c'était la maison de famille: aussi une détresse me prit! j'étais en haillons, moi, et elle, mondaine, qui se donnait; il lui fallait s'en aller! Une détresse sans nom, je la pris, et la laissai tomber hors du lit, presque nue; et dans ma faiblesse indicible, je tombai sur elle et me traînai avec elle parmi les tapis sans lumière. La lampe de la famille rougissait l'une après l'autre les chambres voisines. Alors la femme disparut. Je versai plus de larmes que Dieu n'en a pu jamais demander.

Je sortis dans la ville sans fin. Ô Fatigue! Noyé dans la nuit sourde et dans la fuite du bonheur. C'était comme une nuit d'hiver, avec une neige pour étouffer le monde décidément. Les amis auxquels je criais: où reste-t-elle, répondaient faussement. Je fus devant les vitrages de là où elle va tous les soirs: je courais dans un jardin enseveli. On m'a repoussé. Je pleurais énormément, à tout cela. Enfin je suis descendu dans un lieu plein de poussière, et assis sur des charpentes, j'ai laissé finir toutes les larmes de mon corps avec cette nuit.—Et mon épuisement me revenait pourtant toujours.

J'ai compris qu'elle était à sa vie de tous les jours; et que le tour de bonté serait plus long à se reproduire qu'une étoile. Elle n'est pas revenue, et ne reviendra jamais, l'Adorable qui s'était rendue chez moi,—ce que je n'aurais jamais présumé.—Vrai, cette fois, j'ai pleuré plus que tous les enfants du monde.

IV. 1872

Proses évangeliques

I

À Samarie, plusieurs ont manifesté leur foi en lui. Il ne les a pas vus. Samarie la parvenue, l'égoïste, plus rigide observatrice de sa loi protestante que Juda des tables antiques. Là la richesse universelle permettait bien peu de discussion éclairée. Le sophisme, esclave et soldat de la routine, y avait déjà, après les avoir flattés, égorgé plusieurs prophètes.

C'était un mot sinistre, celui de la femme à la fontaine: «Vous êtes prophète, vous savez ce que j'ai fait».

Les femmes et les hommes croyaient aux prophètes. Maintenant on croit à l'homme d'état.

À deux pas de la ville étrangère, incapable de la menacer matériellement, s'il était pris comme prophète, puisqu'il s'était montré là si bizarre, qu'aurait-il fait?

Jésus n'a rien pu dire à Samarie.

II

L'air léger et charmant de la Galilée: les habitants le reçurent avec une joie curieuse: ils l'avaient vu, secoué par la sainte colère, fouetter les changeurs et les marchands de gibier du temple. Miracle de la jeunesse pâle et furieuse, croyaient-ils.

Il sentit sa main aux mains chargées de bagues et à la bouche d'un officier. L'officier était à genoux dans la poudre: et sa tête était assez plaisante, quoique à demi chauve.

Les voitures filaient dans les étroites rues; un mouvement, assez fort pour ce bourg; tout semblait devoir être trop content ce soir-là.

Jésus retira sa main: il eut un mouvement d'orgueil enfantin et féminin. «Vous autres, si vous ne voyez des miracles, vous ne croyez point.»

Jésus n'avait point encor fait de miracles. Il avait, dans une noce, dans une salle à manger verte et rose, parlé un peu hautement à la Sainte Vierge. Et personne n'avait parlé du vin de Cana à Capharnaüm, ni sur le marché, ni sur les quais. Les bourgeois peut-être.

Jésus dit: «Allez, votre fils se porte bien». L'officier s'en alla, comme on porte quelque pharmacie légère, et Jésus continua par les rues moins fréquentées. Des liserons, des bourraches montraient leur lueur magique entre les pavés. Enfin il vit au loin la prairie poussiéreuse, et les boutons d'or et les marguerites demandant grâce au jour.

III

Bethsaïda, la piscine des cinq galeries, était un point d'ennui. Il me semblait que ce fût un sinistre lavoir, toujours accablé de la pluie et noir, et les mendiants s'agitant sur les marches intérieures,—blêmies par ces lueurs d'orages précurseurs des éclairs d'enfer, en plaisantant sur leurs yeux bleus aveugles, sur les linges blancs ou bleus dont s'entouraient leurs moignons. Ô buanderie militaire, ô bain populaire. L'eau était toujours noire, et nul infirme n'y tombait même en songe.

C'est là que Jésus fit la première action grave; avec les infâmes infirmes. Il y avait un jour, de février, mars ou avril, où le soleil de 2 h. ap. midi, laissait s'étaler une grande faux de lumière sur l'eau ensevelie; et comme, là-bas, loin derrière les infirmes, j'aurais pu voir tout ce que ce rayon seul éveillait de bourgeons et de cristaux et de vers, dans ce reflet, pareil à un ange blanc couché sur le côté, tous les reflets infiniment pâles remuaient.

Alors tous les péchés, fils légers et tenaces du démon, qui pour les cœurs un peu sensibles, rendaient ces hommes plus effrayants que les monstres, voulaient se jeter à cette eau. Les infirmes descendaient, ne raillant plus; mais avec envie.

Les premiers entrés sortaient guéris, disait-on. Non. Les péchés les rejetaient sur les marches, et les forçaient de chercher d'autres postes: car leur Démon ne peut rester qu'aux lieux où l'aumône est sûre.

Jésus entra aussitôt après l'heure de midi. Personne ne lavait ni ne descendait de bêtes. La lumière dans la piscine était jaune comme les dernières feuilles des vignes. Le divin maître se tenait contre une colonne: il regardait les fils du Péché; le démon tirait sa langue en leur langue; et riait ou niait.

Le Paralytique se leva, qui était resté couché sur le flanc, franchit la galerie, et ce fut d'un pas singulièrement assuré qu'ils le virent franchir la galerie et disparaître dans la ville, les Damnés.

V. 1873

Une saison en enfer

★ ★ ★ ★

Jadis, si je me souviens bien, ma vie était un festin où s' ouvraient tous les cœurs, où tous les vins coulaient.

Un soir, j'ai assis la Beauté sur mes genoux.—Et je l'ai trouvée amère.—Et je l'ai injuriée.

Je me suis armé contre la justice.

Je me suis enfui. Ô sorcières, ô misère, ô haine, c'est à vous que mon trésor a été confié!

Je parvins à faire s'évanouir dans mon esprit toute l'espérance humaine. Sur toute joie pour l'étrangler j'ai fait le bond sourd de la bête féroce.

J'ai appelé les bourreaux pour, en périssant, mordre la crosse de leurs fusils. J'ai appelé les fléaux, pour m'étouffer avec le sable, le sang. Le malheur a été mon dieu. Je me suis allongé dans la boue. Je me suis séché à l'air du crime. Et j'ai joué de bons tours à la folie.

Et le printemps m'a apporté l'affreux rire de l'idiot.

Or, tout dernièrement m'étant trouvé sur le point de faire le dernier *couac!* j'ai songé à rechercher la clef du festin ancien, où je reprendrais peut-être appétit.

La charité est cette clef.—Cette inspiration prouve que j'ai rêvé!

«Tu resteras hyène, etc...», se récrie le démon qui me couronna de si aimables pavots. «Gagne la mort avec tous tes appétits, et ton égoïsme et tous les péchés capitaux.»

Ah! j'en ai trop pris:—Mais, cher Satan, je vous en conjure, une prunelle moins irritée! et en attendant les quelques petites lâchetés en retard, vous qui aimez dans l'écrivain l'absence des facultés descriptives ou instructives, je vous détache ces quelques hideux feuillets de mon carnet de damné.

MAUVAIS SANG

J'ai de mes ancêtres gaulois l'œil bleu blanc, la cervelle étroite, et la maladresse dans la lutte. Je trouve mon habillement aussi barbare que le leur. Mais je ne beurre pas ma chevelure.

Les Gaulois étaient les écorcheurs de bêtes, les brûleurs d'herbes les plus ineptes de leur temps.

D'eux, j'ai: l'idolâtrie et l'amour du sacrilège;—oh! tous les vices, colère, luxure,—magnifique, la luxure;—surtout mensonge et paresse.

J'ai horreur de tous les métiers. Maîtres et ouvriers, tous paysans, ignobles. La main à plume vaut la main à charrue.—Quel siècle à mains!—Je n'aurai jamais ma main. Après, la domesticité mène trop loin. L'honnêteté de la mendicité me navre. Les criminels dégoûtent comme des châtrés: moi, je suis intact, et ça m'est égal.

Mais! qui a fait ma langue perfide tellement, qu'elle ait guidé et sauvegardé jusqu'ici ma paresse? Sans me servir pour vivre même de mon corps, et plus oisif que le crapaud, j'ai vécu partout. Pas une famille d'Europe que je ne connaisse.—J'entends des familles comme la mienne, qui tiennent tout de la déclaration des Droits de l'Homme.—J'ai connu chaque fils de famille!

Si j'avais des antécédents à un point quelconque de l'histoire de France!

Mais non, rien.

Il m'est bien évident que j'ai toujours été race inférieure. Je ne puis comprendre la révolte. Ma race ne se souleva jamais que pour piller: tels les loups à la bête qu'ils n'ont pas tuée.

Je me rappelle l'histoire de la France fille aînée de l'Église. J'aurais fait, manant, le voyage de terre sainte; j'ai dans la tête des routes dans les plaines souabes, des vues de Byzance, des remparts de Solyme; le culte de Marie, l'attendrissement sur le crucifié s'éveillent en moi parmi mille féeries profanes.—Je suis assis, lépreux, sur les pots cassés et les orties, au pied d'un mur rongé par le soleil.—Plus tard, reître, j'aurais bivaqué sous les nuits d'Allemagne.

Ah! encore: je danse le sabbat dans une rouge clairière, avec des vieilles et des enfants.

Je ne me souviens pas plus loin que cette terre-ci et le christianisme. Je n'en finirais pas de me revoir dans ce passé. Mais toujours seul; sans famille; même, quelle langue parlais-je? Je ne me vois jamais dans les conseils du Christ; ni dans les conseils des Seigneurs,—représentants du Christ.

Qu'étais-je au siècle dernier: je ne me retrouve qu'aujourd'hui. Plus de vagabonds, plus de guerres vagues. La race inférieure a tout couvert—le peuple, comme on dit, la raison; la nation et la science.

Oh! la science! On a tout repris. Pour le corps et pour l'âme,—le viatique,—on a la médecine et la philosophie,—les remèdes de bonnes femmes et les chansons populaires arrangées. Et les divertissements des princes et les jeux qu'ils interdisaient! Géographie, cosmographie, mécanique, chimie!...

La science, la nouvelle noblesse! Le progrès. Le monde marche! Pourquoi ne tournerait-il pas?

C'est la vision des nombres. Nous allons à l'*Esprit.* C'est très-certain, c'est oracle, ce que je dis. Je comprends, et ne sachant m'expliquer sans paroles païennes, je voudrais me taire.

Le sang païen revient! L'Esprit est proche, pourquoi Christ ne m'aide-t-il pas, en donnant à mon âme noblesse et liberté. Hélas! l'Évangile a passé! l'Évangile! l'Évangile.

J'attends Dieu avec gourmandise. Je suis de race inférieure de toute éternité.

Me voici sur la plage armoricaine. Que les villes s'allument dans le soir. Ma journée est faite; je quitte l'Europe. L'air marin brûlera mes poumons; les climats perdus me tanneront. Nager, broyer l'herbe, chasser, fumer surtout; boire des liqueurs fortes comme du métal bouillant,—comme faisaient ces chers ancêtres autour des feux.

Je reviendrai, avec des membres de fer, la peau sombre, l'œil furieux: sur mon masque, on me jugera d'une race forte. J'aurai de l'or: je serai oisif et brutal. Les femmes soignent ces féroces infirmes retour des pays chauds. Je serai mêlé aux affaires politiques. Sauvé.

Maintenant je suis maudit, j'ai horreur de la patrie. Le meilleur, c'est un sommeil bien ivre, sur la grève.

On ne part pas.—Reprenons les chemins d'ici, chargé de mon vice, le vice qui a poussé ses racines de souffrance à mon côté, dès l'âge de raison—qui monte au ciel, me bat, me renverse, me traîne.

La dernière innocence et la dernière timidité. C'est dit. Ne pas porter au monde mes dégoûts et mes trahisons.

Allons! La marche, le fardeau, le désert, l'ennui et la colère.

À qui me louer? Quelle bête faut-il adorer? Quelle sainte image attaque-t-on? Quels cœurs briserai-je? Quel mensonge dois-je tenir?—Dans quel sang marcher?

Plutôt, se garder de la justice.—La vie dure, l'abrutissement simple,—soulever, le poing desséché, le couvercle du cercueil, s'asseoir, s'étouffer. Ainsi point de vieillesse, ni de dangers: la terreur n'est pas française.

—Ah! je suis tellement délaissé que j'offre à n'importe quelle divine image des élans vers la perfection.

Ô mon abnégation, ô ma charité merveilleuse! ici-bas, pourtant!

De profundis Domine, suis-je bête!

Encore tout enfant, j'admirais le forçat intraitable sur qui se referme toujours le bagne; je visitais les auberges et les garnis qu'il aurait sacrés par son séjour; je voyais *avec son idée* le ciel bleu et le travail fleuri de la campagne; je flairais sa fatalité dans les villes. Il avait plus de force qu'un saint, plus de bon sens qu'un voyageur—et lui, lui seul! pour témoin de sa gloire et de sa raison.

Sur les routes, par des nuits d'hiver, sans gîte, sans habits, sans pain, une voix étreignait mon cœur gelé: «Faiblesse ou force: te voilà, c'est la force. Tu ne sais ni où tu vas ni pourquoi tu vas, entre partout, réponds à tout. On ne te tuera pas plus que si tu étais cadavre.» Au matin j'avais le regard si perdu et la contenance si morte, que ceux que j'ai rencontrés *ne m'ont peut-être pas vu.*

Dans les villes la boue m'apparaissait soudainement rouge et noire, comme une glace quand la lampe circule dans la chambre voisine, comme un trésor dans la forêt! Bonne chance, criais-je, et je voyais une mer de flammes et de fumée au ciel; et, à gauche, à droite, toutes les richesses flambant comme un milliard de tonnerres.

Mais l'orgie et la camaraderie des femmes m'étaient interdites. Pas même un compagnon. Je me voyais devant une foule exaspérée, en face du peloton d'exécution, pleurant du malheur qu'ils n'aient pu comprendre, et pardonnant!—Comme Jeanne d'Arc!—«Prêtres, professeurs, maîtres, vous vous trompez en me livrant à la justice. Je n'ai jamais été de ce peuple-ci; je n'ai jamais été chrétien; je suis de la race qui chantait dans le supplice; je ne comprends pas les lois; je n'ai pas le sens moral, je suis une brute: vous vous trompez...»

Oui, j'ai les yeux fermés à votre lumière. Je suis une bête, un nègre. Mais je puis être sauvé. Vous êtes de faux nègres, vous maniaques, féroces, avares. Marchand, tu es nègre; magistrat, tu es nègre; général, tu es nègre; empereur, vieille démangeaison, tu es nègre: tu as bu d'une liqueur non taxée, de la fabrique de Satan.—Ce peuple est inspiré par la fièvre et le cancer. Infirmes et vieillards sont tellement respectables qu'ils demandent à être bouillis.—Le plus malin est de quitter ce continent, où la folie rôde pour pourvoir d'otages ces misérables. J'entre au vrai royaume des enfants de Cham.

Connais-je encore la nature? me connais-je?—*Plus de mots.* J'ensevelis les morts dans mon ventre. Cris, tambour, danse, danse, danse, danse! Je ne vois même pas l'heure où, les blancs débarquant, je tomberai au néant.

Faim, soif, cris, danse, danse, danse, danse!

Les blancs débarquent. Le canon! Il faut se soumettre au baptême, s'habiller, travailler.

J'ai reçu au cœur le coup de la grâce. Ah! je ne l'avais pas prévu!

Je n'ai point fait le mal. Les jours vont m'être légers, le repentir me sera épargné. Je n'aurai pas eu les tourments de l'âme presque morte au bien, où remonte la lumière sévère comme les cierges funéraires. Le sort du fils de famille, cercueil prématuré couvert de limpides larmes. Sans doute la débauche est bête, le vice est bête; il faut jeter la pourriture à l'écart. Mais l'horloge ne sera pas arrivée à ne plus sonner que l'heure de la pure douleur! Vais-je être enlevé comme un enfant, pour jouer au paradis dans l'oubli de tout le malheur!

Vite! est-il d'autres vies?—Le sommeil dans la richesse est impossible. La richesse a toujours été bien public. L'amour divin seul octroie les clefs de la science. Je vois que la nature n'est qu'un spectacle de bonté. Adieu chimères, idéals, erreurs.

Le chant raisonnable des anges s'élève du navire sauveur: c'est l'amour divin.—Deux amours! je puis mourir de l'amour terrestre, mourir de dévouement. J'ai laissé des âmes dont la peine s'accroîtra de mon départ! Vous me choisissez parmi les naufragés; ceux qui restent sont-ils pas mes amis?

Sauvez-les!

La raison m'est née. Le monde est bon. Je bénirai la vie. J'aimerai mes frères. Ce ne sont plus des promesses d'enfance. Ni l'espoir d'échapper à la vieillesse et à la mort. Dieu fait ma force, et je loue Dieu.

L'ennui n'est plus mon amour. Les rages, les débauches, la folie, dont je sais tous les élans et les désastres,—tout mon fardeau est déposé. Apprécions sans vertige l'étendue de mon innocence.

Je ne serais plus capable de demander le réconfort d'une bastonnade. Je ne me crois pas embarqué pour une noce avec Jésus-Christ pour beau-père.

Je ne suis pas prisonnier de ma raison. J'ai dit: Dieu. Je veux la liberté dans le salut: comment la poursuivre? Les goûts frivoles m'ont quitté. Plus besoin de dévouement ni d'amour divin. Je ne regrette pas le siècle des cœurs sensibles. Chacun a sa raison, mépris et charité: je retiens ma place au sommet de cette angélique échelle de bon sens.

Quant au bonheur établi, domestique ou non… non, je ne peux pas. Je suis trop dissipé, trop faible. La vie fleurit par le travail, vieille vérité: moi, ma vie n'est pas assez pesante, elle s'envole et flotte loin au-dessus de l'action, ce cher point du monde.

Comme je deviens vieille fille, à manquer du courage d'aimer la mort!

Si Dieu m'accordait le calme céleste, aérien, la prière,—comme les anciens saints.—Les saints! des forts! les anachorètes, des artistes comme il n'en faut plus!

Farce continuelle! Mon innocence me ferait pleurer. La vie est la farce à mener par tous.

Assez! voici la punition.—*En marche!*

Ah! les poumons brûlent, les tempes grondent! la nuit roule dans mes yeux, par ce soleil! le cœur… les membres…

Où va-t-on? au combat? Je suis faible! les autres avancent. Les outils, les armes… le temps!…

Feu! feu sur moi! Là! ou je me rends.—Lâches!—Je me tue! Je me jette aux pieds des chevaux!

Ah!…

—Je m'y habituerai.

Ce serait la vie française, le sentier de l'honneur!

NUIT DE L'ENFER

J'ai avalé une fameuse gorgée de poison.—Trois fois béni soit le conseil qui m'est arrivé!—Les entrailles me brûlent. La violence du venin tord mes membres, me rend difforme, me terrasse. Je meurs de soif, j'étouffe, je ne puis crier. C'est l'enfer, l'éternelle peine! Voyez comme le feu se relève! Je brûle comme il faut. Va, démon!

J'avais entrevu la conversion au bien et au bonheur, le salut. Puis-je décrire la vision, l'air de l'enfer ne souffre pas les hymnes! C'était des millions de créatures charmantes, un suave concert spirituel, la force et la paix, les nobles ambitions, que sais-je?

Les nobles ambitions!

Et c'est encore la vie!—Si la damnation est éternelle! Un homme qui veut se mutiler est bien damné, n'est-ce pas? Je me crois en enfer, donc j'y suis. C'est l'exécution du catéchisme. Je suis esclave de mon baptême. Parents, vous avez fait mon malheur et vous avez fait le vôtre. Pauvre innocent!—L'enfer ne peut attaquer les païens.—C'est la vie encore! Plus tard, les délices de la damnation seront plus profondes. Un crime, vite, que je tombe au néant, de par la loi humaine.

Tais-toi, mais tais-toi!... C'est la honte, le reproche, ici: Satan qui dit que le feu est ignoble, que ma colère est affreusement sotte.—Assez!... Des erreurs qu'on me souffle, magies, parfums faux, musiques puériles.—Et dire que je tiens la vérité, que je vois la justice: j'ai un jugement sain et arrêté, je suis prêt pour la perfection... Orgueil.—La peau de ma tête se dessèche. Pitié! Seigneur, j'ai peur. J'ai soif, si soif! Ah! l'enfance, l'herbe, la pluie, le lac sur les pierres, *le clair de lune quand le clocher sonnait douze*... le diable est au clocher, à cette heure. Marie! Sainte-Vierge!...—Horreur de ma bêtise.

Là-bas, ne sont-ce pas des âmes honnêtes, qui me veulent du bien... Venez... J'ai un oreiller sur la bouche, elles ne m'entendent pas, ce sont des fantômes. Puis, jamais personne ne pense à autrui. Qu'on n'approche pas. Je sens le roussi, c'est certain.

Les hallucinations sont innombrables. C'est bien ce que j'ai toujours eu: plus de foi en l'histoire, l'oubli des principes. Je m'en tairai: poètes et visionnaires seraient jaloux. Je suis mille fois le plus riche, soyons avare comme la mer.

Ah çà! l'horloge de la vie s'est arrêtée tout à l'heure. Je ne suis plus au monde.—La théologic est sérieuse, l'enfer est certainement *en bas*—et le ciel en haut.—Extase, cauchemar, sommeil dans un nid de flammes.

Que de malices dans l'attention dans la campagne... Satan, Ferdinand, court avec les graines sauvages... Jésus marche sur les ronces purpurines, sans les courber... Jésus marchait sur les eaux irritées. La lanterne nous le montra debout, blanc et des tresses brunes, au flanc d'une vague d'émeraude...

Je vais dévoiler tous les mystères: mystères religieux ou naturels, mort, naissance, avenir, passé, cosmogonie, néant. Je suis maître en fantasmagories.

Écoutez!...

J'ai tous les talents!—Il n'y a personne ici et il y a quelqu'un: je ne voudrais pas répandre mon trésor.—Veut-on des chants nègres, des danses de houris? Veut-on que je disparaisse, que je plonge à la recherche de l'*anneau?* Veut-on? Je ferai de l'or, des remèdes.

Fiez-vous donc à moi, la foi soulage, guide, guérit. Tous, venez,—même les petits enfants,—que je vous console, qu'on répande pour vous son cœur,—le cœur merveilleux!—Pauvres hommes, travailleurs! Je ne demande pas de prières; avec votre confiance seulement, je serai heureux.

—Et pensons à moi. Ceci me fait peu regretter le monde. J'ai de la chance de ne pas souffrir plus. Ma vie ne fut que folies douces, c'est regrettable.

Bah! faisons toutes les grimaces imaginables.

Décidément, nous sommes hors du monde. Plus aucun son. Mon tact a disparu. Ah! mon château, ma Saxe, mon bois de saules. Les soirs, les matins, les nuits, les jours... Suis-je las!

Je devrais avoir mon enfer pour la colère, mon enfer pour l'orgueil,—et l'enfer de la caresse; un concert d'enfers.

Je meurs de lassitude. C'est le tombeau, je m'en vais aux vers, horreur de l'horreur! Satan, farceur, tu veux me dissoudre, avec tes charmes. Je réclame. Je réclame! un coup de fourche, une goutte de feu.

Ah! remonter à la vie! Jeter les yeux sur nos difformités. Et ce poison, ce baiser mille fois maudit! Ma faiblesse, la cruauté du monde! Mon Dieu, pitié, cachez-moi, je me tiens trop mal!—Je suis caché et je ne le suis pas.

C'est le feu qui se relève avec son damné.

DÉLIRES

I
Vierge folle

L'ÉPOUX INFERNAL

Écoutons la confession d'un compagnon d'enfer:

«Ô divin Époux, mon Seigneur, ne refusez pas la confession de la plus triste de vos servantes. Je suis perdue. Je suis soûle. Je suis impure. Quelle vie!

«Pardon, divin Seigneur, pardon! Ah! pardon! Que de larmes! Et que de larmes encore plus tard, j'espère!

«Plus tard, je connaîtrai le divin Époux! Je suis née soumise à Lui.—L'autre peut me battre maintenant!

«À présent, je suis au fond du monde! Ô mes amies!... non, pas mes amies... Jamais délires ni tortures semblables... Est-ce bête!

«Ah! je souffre, je crie. Je souffre vraiment. Tout pourtant m'est permis, chargée du mépris des plus méprisables cœurs.

«Enfin, faisons cette confidence, quitte à la répéter vingt autres fois,—aussi morne, aussi insignifiante!

«Je suis esclave de l'Époux infernal, celui qui a perdu les vierges folles. C'est bien ce démon-là. Ce n'est pas un spectre, ce n'est pas un fantôme. Mais moi qui ai perdu la sagesse, qui suis damnée et morte au monde,—on ne me tuera pas!—Comment vous le décrire! Je ne sais même plus parler. Je suis en deuil, je pleure, j'ai peur. Un peu de fraîcheur, Seigneur, si vous voulez, si vous voulez bien!

«Je suis veuve...—J'étais veuve...—mais oui, j'ai été bien sérieuse jadis, et je ne suis pas née pour devenir squelette!...—Lui était presque un enfant... Ses délicatesses mystérieuses m'avaient séduite. J'ai oublié tout mon devoir humain pour le suivre. Quelle vie! La vraie vie est absente. Nous ne sommes pas au monde. Je vais où il va, il le faut. Et souvent il s'emporte contre moi, *moi, la pauvre âme.* Le Démon!—C'est un Démon, vous savez, *ce n'est pas un homme.*

«Il dit: "Je n'aime pas les femmes. L'amour est à réinventer, on le sait. Elles ne peuvent plus que vouloir une position assurée. La position gagnée, cœur et beauté sont mis de côté: il ne reste que froid dédain, l'aliment du mariage, aujourd'hui. Ou bien je vois des femmes, avec les signes du bonheur, dont, moi, j'aurais pu faire de bonnes camarades, dévorées tout d'abord par des brutes sensibles comme des bûchers..."

«Je l'écoute faisant de l'infamie une gloire, de la cruauté un charme. "Je suis de race lointaine: mes pères étaient Scandinaves: ils se perçaient les côtes, buvaient leur sang.—Je me ferai des entailles partout le corps, je me tatouerai, je veux devenir hideux comme un Mongol: tu verras, je hurlerai dans les rues. Je veux devenir bien fou de rage. Ne me montre jamais de bijoux, je ramperais et me tordrais sur le tapis. Ma richesse, je la voudrais tachée de sang partout. Jamais je ne travaillerai..." Plusieurs nuits, son démon me saisissant, nous nous roulions, je luttais avec lui!—Les nuits, souvent, ivre, il se poste dans des rues ou dans des maisons, pour m'épouvanter mortellement.—"On me coupera vraiment le cou; ce sera dégoûtant." Oh! ces jours où il veut marcher avec l'air du crime!

«Parfois il parle, en une façon de patois attendri, de la mort qui fait repentir, des malheureux qui existent certainement, des travaux pénibles, des départs qui déchirent les cœurs. Dans les bouges où nous nous enivrions, il pleurait en considérant ceux qui nous entouraient, bétail de la misère. Il relevait les ivrognes dans les rues noires. Il avait la pitié d'une mère méchante pour les petits enfants.—Il s'en allait avec des gentillesses de petite fille au catéchisme.—Il feignait d'être éclairé sur tout, commerce, art, médecine.—Je le suivais, il le faut!

«Je voyais tout le décor dont, en esprit, il s'entourait; vêtements, draps, meubles: je lui prêtais des armes, une autre figure. Je voyais tout ce qui le touchait, comme il aurait voulu le créer pour lui. Quand il me semblait avoir l'esprit inerte, je le suivais, moi, dans des actions étranges et compliquées, loin, bonnes ou mauvaises: j'étais sûre de ne jamais entrer dans son monde. À côté de son cher corps endormi, que d'heures des nuits j'ai veillé, cherchant pourquoi il voulait tant s'évader de la réalité. Jamais homme n'eut pareil vœu. Je reconnaissais,—sans craindre pour lui,—qu'il pouvait être un sérieux danger dans la société.—Il a peut-être des secrets pour *changer la vie?* Non, il ne fait qu'en chercher, me répliquais-je. Enfin sa charité est ensorcelée, et j'en suis la prisonnière. Aucune autre âme n'aurait assez de force,—force de désespoir!—pour la supporter,—pour être protégée et aimée par lui. D'ailleurs, je ne me le figurais pas avec une autre âme: on voit son Ange, jamais l'Ange d'un autre,—je crois. J'étais dans son âme comme dans un palais qu'on a vidé pour ne pas voir une personne si peu noble que vous: voilà tout. Hélas! je dépendais bien de lui. Mais que voulait-il avec mon existence terne et lâche? Il ne me rendait pas meilleure, s'il ne me faisait pas mourir! Tristement dépitée, je lui dis quelquefois: "Je te comprends." Il haussait les épaules.

«Ainsi, mon chagrin se renouvelant sans cesse, et me trouvant plus égarée à mes yeux,—comme à tous les yeux qui auraient voulu me fixer, si je n'eusse été condamnée pour jamais à l'oubli de tous!—j'avais de plus en plus faim de sa bonté. Avec ses baisers et ses étreintes amies, c'était bien un ciel, un sombre ciel, où j'entrais, et où j'aurais voulu être laissée, pauvre, sourde, muette, aveugle. Déjà j'en prenais l'habitude. Je nous voyais comme deux bons enfants, libres de se promener dans le Paradis de tristesse. Nous nous accordions. Bien émus, nous travaillions ensemble. Mais, après une pénétrante caresse, il disait: "Comme ça te paraîtra drôle, quand je n'y serai plus, ce par quoi tu as passé. Quand tu n'auras plus mes bras sous ton cou, ni mon cœur pour t'y reposer, ni cette bouche sur tes yeux. Parce qu'il faudra que je m'en aille, très loin, un jour. Puis il faut que j'en aide d'autres: c'est mon devoir. Quoique ce ne soit guère ragoûtant…, chère âme…" Tout de suite je me pressentais, lui parti, en proie au vertige, précipitée dans l'ombre la plus affreuse: la mort. Je lui faisais promettre qu'il ne me lâcherait pas. Il l'a faite vingt fois, cette promesse d'amant. C'était aussi frivole que moi lui disant: "Je te comprends."

«Ah! je n'ai jamais été jalouse de lui. Il ne me quittera pas, je crois. Que devenir? Il n'a pas une connaissance, il ne travaillera jamais. Il veut vivre somnambule. Seules, sa bonté et sa charité lui donneraient-elles droit dans le monde réel? Par instants, j'oublie la pitié où je suis tombée: lui me rendra forte, nous voyagerons, nous chasserons dans les déserts, nous dormirons sur les pavés des villes inconnues, sans soins, sans peines. Ou je me réveillerai, et les lois et les mœurs auront changé,—grâce à son pouvoir magique,—le monde, en restant le même, me laissera à mes désirs, joies, nonchalances. Oh! la vie d'aventures qui existe dans les livres des enfants, pour me récompenser, j'ai tant souffert, me la donneras-tu? Il ne peut pas. J'ignore son idéal. Il m'a dit avoir des regrets, des espoirs: cela ne doit pas me regarder. Parle-t-il à Dieu? Peut-être devrais-je m'adresser à Dieu. Je suis au plus profond de l'abîme, et je ne sais plus prier.

«S'il m'expliquait ses tristesses, les comprendrais-je plus que ses railleries? Il m'attaque, il passe des heures à me faire honte de tout ce qui m'a pu toucher au monde, et s'indigne si je pleure.

«"Tu vois cet élégant jeune homme, entrant dans la belle et calme maison: il s'appelle Duval, Dufour, Armand, Maurice, que sais-je? Une femme s'est dévouée à aimer ce méchant idiot: elle est morte, c'est certes une sainte au ciel, à présent. Tu me feras mourir comme il a fait mourir cette femme. C'est notre sort, à nous, cœurs charitables..." Hélas! il avait des jours où tous les hommes agissant lui paraissaient les jouets de délires grotesques: il riait affreusement, longtemps.—Puis, il reprenait ses manières de jeune mère, de sœur aimée. S'il était moins sauvage, nous serions sauvés! Mais sa douceur aussi est mortelle. Je lui suis soumise.—Ah! je suis folle!

«Un jour peut-être il disparaîtra merveilleusement; mais il faut que je sache, s'il doit remonter à un ciel, que je voie un peu l'assomption de mon petit ami!»

Drôle de ménage!

DÉLIRES

II

Alchimie du verbe

À moi. L'histoire d'une de mes folies.

Depuis longtemps je me vantais de posséder tous les paysages possibles, et trouvais dérisoires les célébrités de la peinture et de la poésie moderne.

J'aimais les peintures idiotes, dessus de portes, décors, toiles de saltimbanques, enseignes, enluminures populaires; la littérature démodée, latin d'église, livres érotiques sans orthographe, romans de nos aïeules, contes de fées, petits livres de l'enfance, opéras vieux, refrains niais, rhythmes naïfs.

Je rêvais croisades, voyages de découvertes dont on n'a pas de relations, républiques sans histoires, guerres de religion étouffées, révolutions de mœurs, déplacements de races et de continents: je croyais à tous les enchantements.

J'inventai la couleur des voyelles!—*A* noir, *E* blanc, *I* rouge, *O* bleu, *U* vert.—Je réglai la forme et le mouvement de chaque consonne, et, avec des rhythmes instinctifs, je me flattai d'inventer un verbe poétique accessible, un jour ou l'autre, à tous les sens. Je réservais la traduction.

Ce fut d'abord une étude. J'écrivais des silences, des nuits, je notais l'inexprimable. Je fixais des vertiges.

Loin des oiseaux, des troupeaux, des villageoises,
Que buvais-je, à genoux dans cette bruyère
Entourée de tendres bois de noisetiers,
Dans un brouillard d'après-midi tiède et vert?

Que pouvais-je boire dans cette jeune Oise,
—Ormeaux sans voix, gazon sans fleurs, ciel couvert!—
Boire à ces gourdes jaunes, loin de ma case
Chérie? Quelque liqueur d'or qui fait suer.

Je faisais une louche enseigne d'auberge.
—Un orage vint chasser le ciel. Au soir
L'eau des bois se perdait sur les sables vierges,
Le vent de Dieu jetait des glaçons aux mares;

Pleurant, je voyais de l'or—et ne pus boire.—

À quatre heures du matin, l'été,
Le sommeil d'amour dure encore.
Sous les bocages s'évapore
        L'odeur du soir fêté.

Là-bas, dans leur vaste chantier
Au soleil des Hespérides,
Déjà s'agitent—en bras de chemise—
        Les Charpentiers.

Dans leurs Déserts de mousse, tranquilles,
Ils préparent les lambris précieux
Où la ville
        Peindra de faux cieux.

Ô, pour ces Ouvriers charmants
Sujets d'un roi de Babylone,
Vénus! quitte un instant les Amants
        Dont l'âme est en couronne.

        Ô Reine des Bergers,
Porte aux travailleurs l'eau-de-vie,
Que leurs forces soient en paix
En attendant le bain dans la mer à midi.

La vieillerie poétique avait une bonne part dans mon alchimie du verbe.

Je m'habituai à l'hallucination simple: je voyais très-franchement une mosquée à la place d'une usine, une école de tambours faite par des anges, des calèches sur les routes du ciel, un salon au fond d'un lac; les monstres, les mystères; un titre de vaudeville dressait des épouvantes devant moi.

Puis j'expliquai mes sophismes magiques avec l'hallucination des mots!

Je finis par trouver sacré le désordre de mon esprit. J'étais oisif, en proie à une lourde fièvre: j'enviais la félicité des bêtes,—les chenilles, qui représentent l'innocence des limbes, les taupes, le sommeil de la virginité!

Mon caractère s'aigrissait. Je disais adieu au monde dans d'espèces de romances:

CHANSON DE LA PLUS HAUTE TOUR

Qu'il vienne, qu'il vienne,
Le temps dont on s'éprenne.

J'ai tant fait patience
Qu'à jamais j'oublie.
Craintes et souffrances
Aux cieux sont parties.
Et la soif malsaine
Obscurcit mes veines.

Qu'il vienne, qu'il vienne,
Le temps dont on s'éprenne.

Telle la prairie
À l'oubli livrée,
Grandie, et fleurie
D'encens et d'ivraies,
Au bourdon farouche
Des sales mouches.

Qu'il vienne, qu'il vienne,
Le temps dont on s'éprenne.

J'aimai le désert, les vergers brûlés, les boutiques fanées, les boissons tiédies. Je me traînais dans les ruelles puantes et, les yeux fermés, je m'offrais au soleil, dieu de feu.

«Général, s'il reste un vieux canon sur tes remparts en ruines, bombarde-nous avec des blocs de terre sèche. Aux glaces des magasins splendides! dans les salons! Fais manger sa poussière à la ville. Oxyde les gargouilles. Emplis les boudoirs de poudre de rubis brûlante . . .»

Oh! le moucheron enivré à la pissotière de l'auberge, amoureux de la bourrache, et que dissout un rayon!

FAIM

Si j'ai du goût, ce n'est guère
Que pour la terre et les pierres.
Je déjeune toujours d'air,
De roc, de charbons, de fer.

Mes faims, tournez. Paissez, faims,
	Le pré des sons.
Attirez le gai venin
	Des liserons.

Mangez les cailloux qu'on brise,
Les vieilles pierres d'églises;
Les galets des vieux déluges,
Pains semés dans les vallées grises.

Le loup criait sous les feuilles
En crachant les belles plumes
De son repas de volailles:
Comme lui je me consume.

Les salades, les fruits
N'attendent que la cueillette;
Mais l'araignée de la haie
Ne mange que des violettes.

Que je dorme! que je bouille
Aux autels de Salomon.
Le bouillon court sur la rouille,
Et se mêle au Cédron.

Enfin, ô bonheur, ô raison, j'écartai du ciel l'azur, qui est du noir, et je vécus, étincelle d'or de la lumière *nature.* De joie, je prenais une expression bouffonne et égarée au possible:

Elle est retrouvée!
Quoi? l'éternité.
C'est la mer mêlée
	Au soleil.

Mon âme éternelle,
Observe ton vœu
Malgré la nuit seule
Et le jour en feu.

Donc tu te dégages
Des humains suffrages,

Des communs élans!
Tu voles selon…

—Jamais l'espérance.
        Pas d'*orietur.*
Science et patience,
Le supplice est sûr.

Plus de lendemain,
Braises de satin,
        Votre ardeur
        Est le devoir.

Elle est retrouvée!
—Quoi?—l'Éternité.
C'est la mer mêlée
        Au soleil.

Je devins un opéra fabuleux: je vis que tous les êtres ont une fatalité de bonheur: l'action n'est pas la vie, mais une façon de gâcher quelque force, un énervement. La morale est la faiblesse de la cervelle.

À chaque être, plusieurs *autres* vies me semblaient dues. Ce monsieur ne sait ce qu'il fait: il est un ange. Cette famille est une nichée de chiens. Devant plusieurs hommes, je causai tout haut avec un moment d'une de leurs autres vies.—Ainsi, j'ai aimé un porc.

Aucun des sophismes de la folie,—la folie qu'on enferme,—n'a été oublié par moi: je pourrais les redire tous, je tiens le système.

Ma santé fut menacée. La terreur venait. Je tombais dans des sommeils de plusieurs jours, et, levé, je continuais les rêves les plus tristes. J'étais mûr pour le trépas, et par une route de dangers ma faiblesse me menait aux confins du monde et de la Cimmérie, patrie de l'ombre et des tourbillons.

Je dus voyager, distraire les enchantements assemblés sur mon cerveau. Sur la mer, que j'aimais comme si elle eût dû me laver d'une souillure, je voyais se lever la croix consolatrice. J'avais été damné par l'arc-en-ciel. Le Bonheur était ma fatalité, mon remords, mon ver: ma vie serait toujours trop immense pour être dévouée à la force et à la beauté.

Le Bonheur! Sa dent, douce à la mort, m'avertissait au chant du coq,—*ad matutinum,* au *Christus venit,*—dans les plus sombres villes:

Ô saisons, ô châteaux!
Quelle âme est sans défauts?

J'ai fait la magique étude
Du bonheur, qu'aucun n'élude.

Salut à lui, chaque fois
Que chante le coq gaulois.

Ah! je n'aurai plus d'envie:
Il s'est chargé de ma vie.

Ce charme a pris âme et corps
Et dispersé les efforts.

Ô saisons, ô châteaux!
L'heure de sa fuite, hélas!
Sera l'heure du trépas.

Ô saisons, ô châteaux!

Cela s'est passé. Je sais aujourd'hui saluer la beauté.

L'IMPOSSIBLE

Ah! cette vie de mon enfance, la grande route par tous les temps, sobre surnaturellement, plus désintéressé que le meilleur des mendiants, fier de n'avoir ni pays, ni amis, quelle sottise c'était.—Et je m'en aperçois seulement!

—J'ai eu raison de mépriser ces bonshommes qui ne perdraient pas l'occasion d'une caresse, parasites de la propreté et de la santé de nos femmes, aujourd'hui qu'elles sont si peu d'accord avec nous.

J'ai eu raison dans tous mes dédains: puisque je m'évade!

Je m'évade!

Je m'explique.

Hier encore, je soupirais: «Ciel! sommes-nous assez de damnés ici-bas! Moi j'ai tant de temps déjà dans leur troupe! Je les connais tous. Nous nous reconnaissons toujours; nous nous dégoûtons. La charité nous est inconnue. Mais nous sommes polis; nos relations avec le monde sont très-convenables.» Est-ce étonnant? Le monde! les marchands, les naïfs!—Nous ne sommes pas déshonorés.—Mais les élus, comment nous recevraient-ils? Or il y a des gens hargneux et joyeux, de faux élus, puisqu'il nous faut de l'audace ou de l'humilité pour les aborder. Ce sont les seuls élus. Ce ne sont pas des bénisseurs!

M'étant retrouvé deux sous de raison—ça passe vite!—je vois que mes malaises viennent de ne m'être pas figuré assez tôt que nous sommes à l'Occident. Les marais occidentaux! Non que je croie la lumière altérée, la forme exténuée, le mouvement égaré... Bon! voici que mon esprit veut absolument se charger de tous les développements cruels qu'a subis l'esprit depuis la fin de l'Orient... Il en veut, mon esprit!

...Mes deux sous de raison sont finis!—L'esprit est autorité, il veut que je sois en Occident Il faudrait le faire taire pour conclure comme je voulais.

J'envoyais au diable les palmes des martyrs, les rayons de l'art, l'orgueil des inventeurs, l'ardeur des pillards; je retournais à l'Orient et à la sagesse première et éternelle.—Il paraît que c'est un rêve de paresse grossière!

Pourtant, je ne songeais guère au plaisir d'échapper aux souffrances modernes. Je n'avais pas en vue la sagesse bâtarde du Coran.—Mais n'y a-t-il pas un supplice réel en ce que, depuis cette déclaration de la science, le christianisme, l'homme *se joue*, se prouve les évidences, se gonfle du plaisir de répéter ces preuves, et ne vit que comme cela! Torture subtile, niaise; source de mes divagations spirituelles. La nature pourrait s'ennuyer, peut-être~! M. Prudhomme est né avec le Christ.

N'est-ce pas parce que nous cultivons la brume! Nous mangeons la fièvre avec nos légumes aqueux. Et l'ivrognerie! et le tabac! et l'ignorance! et les dévouements!—Tout cela est-il assez loin de la pensée de la sagesse de l'Orient, la patrie primitive? Pourquoi un monde moderne, si de pareils poisons s'inventent!

Les gens d'Église diront: C'est compris. Mais vous voulez parler de l'Éden. Rien pour vous dans l'histoire des peuples orientaux.—C'est vrai; c'est à l'Éden que je songeais! Qu'est-ce que c'est pour mon rêve, cette pureté des races antiques!

Les philosophes: Le monde n'a pas d'âge. L'humanité se déplace, simplement. Vous êtes en Occident, mais libre d'habiter dans votre Orient, quelque ancien qu'il vous le faille,—et d'y habiter bien. Ne soyez pas un vaincu. Philosophes, vous êtes de votre Occident.

Mon esprit, prends garde. Pas de partis de salut violents. Exerce-toi!—Ah! la science ne va pas assez vite pour nous!

—Mais je m'aperçois que mon esprit dort.

S'il était bien éveillé toujours à partir de ce moment, nous serions bientôt à la vérité, qui peut-être nous entoure avec ses anges pleurant!...—S'il avait été éveillé jusqu'à ce moment-ci, c'est que je n'aurais pas cédé aux instincts délétères, à une époque immémoriale!...—S'il avait toujours été bien éveillé, je voguerais en pleine sagesse!...

Ô pureté! pureté!

C'est cette minute d'éveil qui m'a donné la vision de la pureté!—Par l'esprit on va à Dieu!

Déchirante infortune!

L'ÉCLAIR

Le travail humain! c'est l'explosion qui éclaire mon abîme de temps en temps.

«Rien n'est vanité; à la science, et en avant!» crie l'Ecclésiaste moderne, c'est-à-dire *Tout le monde.* Et pourtant les cadavres des méchants et des fainéants tombent sur le cœur des autres... Ah! vite, vite un peu; là-bas, par delà la nuit, ces récompenses futures, éternelles... les échappons-nous?...

—Qu'y puis-je? Je connais le travail; et la science est trop lente. Que la prière galope et que la lumière gronde... je le vois bien. C'est trop simple, et il fait trop chaud; on se passera de moi. J'ai mon devoir, j'en serai fier à la façon de plusieurs, en le mettant de côté.

Ma vie est usée. Allons! feignons, fainéantons, ô pitié! Et nous existerons en nous amusant, en rêvant amours monstres et univers fantastiques, en nous plaignant et en querellant les apparences du monde, saltimbanque, mendiant, artiste, bandit,—prêtre! Sur mon lit d'hôpital, l'odeur de l'encens m'est revenue si puissante; gardien des aromates sacrés, confesseur, martyr...

Je reconnais là ma sale éducation d'enfance. Puis quoi!... Aller mes vingt ans, si les autres vont vingt ans...

Non! non! à présent je me révolte contre la mort! Le travail paraît trop léger à mon orgueil: ma trahison au monde serait un supplice trop court. Au dernier moment, j'attaquerais à droite, à gauche...

Alors,—oh!—chère pauvre âme, l'éternité serait-elle pas perdue pour nous!

MATIN

N'eus-je pas *une fois* une jeunesse aimable, héroïque, fabuleuse, à écrire sur des feuilles d'or,—trop de chance! Par quel crime, par quelle erreur, ai-je mérité ma faiblesse actuelle? Vous qui prétendez que des bêtes poussent des sanglots de chagrin, que des malades désespèrent, que des morts rêvent mal, tâchez de raconter ma chute et mon sommeil. Moi, je ne puis pas plus m'expliquer que le mendiant avec ses continuels *Pater* et *Ave Maria. Je ne sais plus parler!*

Pourtant, aujourd'hui, je crois avoir fini la relation de mon enfer. C'était bien l'enfer; l'ancien, celui dont le fils de l'homme ouvrit les portes.

Du même désert, à la même nuit, toujours mes yeux las se réveillent à l'étoile d'argent, toujours, sans que s'émeuvent les Rois de la vie, les trois mages, le cœur, l'âme, l'esprit. Quand irons-nous, par delà les grèves et les monts, saluer la naissance du travail nouveau, la sagesse nouvelle, la fuite des tyrans et des démons, la fin de la superstition, adorer—les premiers!—Noël sur la terre!

Le chant des cieux, la marche des peuples! Esclaves, ne maudissons pas la vie.

ADIEU

L'automne déjà!—Mais pourquoi regretter un éternel soleil, si nous sommes engagés à la découverte de la clarté divine,—loin des gens qui meurent sur les saisons.

L'automne. Notre barque élevée dans les brumes immobiles tourne vers le port de la misère, la cité énorme au ciel taché de feu et de boue. Ah! les haillons pourris, le pain trempé de pluie, l'ivresse, les mille amours qui m'ont crucifié! Elle ne finira donc point cette goule reine de millions d'âmes et de corps morts *et qui seront jugés!* Je me revois la peau rongée par la boue et la peste, des vers plein les cheveux et les aisselles et encore de plus gros vers dans le cœur, étendu parmi les inconnus sans âge, sans sentiment... J'aurais pu y mourir... L'affreuse évocation! J'exècre la misère.

Et je redoute l'hiver parce que c'est la saison du comfort!

—Quelquefois je vois au ciel des plages sans fin couvertes de blanches nations en joie. Un grand vaisseau d'or, au-dessus de moi, agite ses pavillons multicolores sous les brises du matin. J'ai créé toutes les fêtes, tous les triomphes, tous les drames. J'ai essayé d'inventer de nouvelles fleurs, de nouveaux astres, de nouvelles chairs, de nouvelles langues. J'ai cru acquérir des pouvoirs surnaturels. Eh bien! je dois enterrer mon imagination et mes souvenirs! Une belle gloire d'artiste et de conteur emportée!

Moi! moi qui me suis dit mage ou ange, dispensé de toute morale, je suis rendu au sol, avec un devoir à chercher, et la réalité rugueuse à étreindre! Paysan!

Suis-je trompé? la charité serait-elle sœur de la mort, pour moi?

Enfin, je demanderai pardon pour m'être nourri de mensonge. Et allons.

Mais pas une main amie! et où puiser le secours?

Oui, l'heure nouvelle est au moins très sévère.

Car je puis dire que la victoire m'est acquise: les grincements de dents, les sifflements de feu, les soupirs empestés se modèrent. Tous les souvenirs immondes s'effacent. Mes derniers regrets détalent,—des jalousies pour les mendiants, les brigands, les amis de la mort, les arriérés de toutes sortes.—Damnés, si je me vengeais!

Il faut être absolument moderne.

Point de cantiques: tenir le pas gagné. Dure nuit! le sang séché fume sur ma face, et je n'ai rien derrière moi, que cet horrible arbrisseau!... Le combat spirituel est aussi brutal que la bataille d'hommes; mais la vision de la justice est le plaisir de Dieu seul.

Cependant c'est la veille. Recevons tous les influx de vigueur et de tendresse réelle. Et à l'aurore, armés d'une ardente patience, nous entrerons aux splendides villes.

Que parlais-je de main amie! Un bel avantage, c'est que je puis rire des vieilles amours mensongères, et frapper de honte ces couples menteurs,—j'ai vu l'enfer des femmes là-bas;—et il me sera loisible de *posséder la vérité dans une âme et un corps.*

Avril-août, 1873

VI. 1872–1874

Illuminations

APRÈS LE DÉLUGE

Aussitôt que l'idée du Déluge se fut rassise,

Un lièvre s'arrêta dans les sainfoins et les clochettes mouvantes et dit sa prière à l'arc-en-ciel à travers la toile de l'araignée.

Oh les pierres précieuses qui se cachaient,—les fleurs qui regardaient déjà.

Dans la grande rue sale les étals se dressèrent, et l'on tira les barques vers la mer étagée là-haut comme sur les gravures.

Le sang coula, chez Barbe-Bleue,—aux abattoirs,—dans les cirques, où le sceau de Dieu blêmit les fenêtres. Le sang et le lait coulèrent.

Les castors bâtirent. Les «mazagrans» fumèrent dans les estaminets.

Dans la grande maison de vitres encore ruisselante les enfants en deuil regardèrent les merveilleuses images.

Une porte claqua, et sur la place du hameau, l'enfant tourna ses bras compris des girouettes et des coqs des clochers de partout, sous l'éclatante giboulée.

Madame*** établit un piano dans les Alpes. La messe et les premières communions se célébrèrent aux cent mille autels de la cathédrale.

Les caravanes partirent. Et le Splendide Hôtel fut bâti dans le chaos de glaces et de nuit du pôle.

Depuis lors, la Lune entendit les chacals piaulant par les déserts de thym,—et les églogues en sabots grognant dans le verger. Puis, dans la futaie violette, bourgeonnante, Eucharis me dit que c'était le printemps.

Sourds, étang,—Écume, roule sur le pont et par-dessus les bois;—draps noirs et orgues,—éclairs et tonnerres,—montez et roulez;—Eaux et tristesses, montez et relevez les Déluges.

Car depuis qu'ils se sont dissipés,—oh les pierres précieuses s'enfouissant, et les fleurs ouvertes!—c'est un ennui! et la Reine, la Sorcière qui allume sa braise dans le pot de terre, ne voudra jamais nous raconter ce qu'elle sait, et que nous ignorons.

ENFANCE

I

Cette idole, yeux noirs et crin jaune, sans parents ni cour, plus noble que la fable, mexicaine et flamande; son domaine, azur et verdure insolents, court sur des plages nommées, par des vagues sans vaisseaux, de noms férocement grecs, slaves, celtiques.

À la lisière de la forêt—les fleurs de rêve tintent, éclatent, éclairent,—la fille à lèvre d'orange, les genoux croisés dans le clair déluge qui sourd des prés, nudité qu'ombrent, traversent et habillent les arcs-en-ciel, la flore, la mer.

Dames qui tournoient sur les terrasses voisines de la mer; enfantes et géantes, superbes noires dans la mousse vert-de-gris, bijoux debout sur le sol gras des bosquets et des jardinets dégelés—jeunes mères et grandes sœurs aux regards pleins de pèlerinages, sultanes, princesses de démarche et de costume tyranniques[,] petites étrangères et personnes doucement malheureuses.

Quel ennui, l'heure du «cher corps» et «cher cœur».

II

C'est elle, la petite morte, derrière les rosiers.—La jeune maman trépassée descend le perron—La calèche du cousin crie sur le sable—Le petit frère—(il est aux Indes!) là, devant le couchant, sur le pré d'œillets.—Les vieux qu'on a enterrés tout droits dans le rempart aux giroflées.

L'essaim des feuilles d'or entoure la maison du général. Ils sont dans le midi.—On suit la route rouge pour arriver à l'auberge vide. Le château est à vendre; les persiennes sont détachées.—Le curé aura emporté la clef de l'église.—Autour du parc, les loges des gardes sont inhabitées... Les palissades sont si hautes qu'on ne voit que les cimes bruissantes. D'ailleurs il n'y a rien à voir là dedans.

Les prés remontent aux hameaux sans coqs, sans enclumes. L'écluse est levée. Ô les calvaires et les moulins du désert, les îles et les meules.

Des fleurs magiques bourdonnaient. Les talus *le* berçaient. Des bêtes d'une élégance fabuleuse circulaient. Les nuées s'amassaient sur la haute mer faite d'une éternité de chaudes larmes.

III

Au bois il y a un oiseau, son chant vous arrête et vous fait rougir.

Il y a une horloge qui ne sonne pas.

Il y a une fondrière avec un nid de bêtes blanches.

Il y a une cathédrale qui descend et un lac qui monte.

Il y a une petite voiture abandonnée dans le taillis, ou qui descend le sentier en courant, enrubannée.

Il y a une troupe de petits comédiens en costumes, aperçus sur la route à travers la lisière du bois.

Il y a enfin, quand l'on a faim et soif, quelqu'un qui vous chasse.

IV

Je suis le saint, en prière sur la terrasse,—comme les bêtes pacifiques paissent jusqu'à la mer de Palestine.

Je suis le savant au fauteuil sombre. Les branches et la pluie se jettent à la croisée de la bibliothèque.

Je suis le piéton de la grand'route par les bois nains; la rumeur des écluses couvre mes pas. Je vois longtemps la mélancolique lessive d'or du couchant.

Je serais bien l'enfant abandonné sur la jetée partie à la haute mer, le petit valet, suivant l'allée dont le front touche le ciel.

Les sentiers sont âpres. Les monticules se couvrent de genêts. L'air est immobile. Que les oiseaux et les sources sont loin! Ce ne peut être que la fin du monde, en avançant.

V

Qu'on me loue enfin ce tombeau, blanchi à la chaux avec les lignes du ciment en relief—très loin sous terre.

Je m'accoude à la table, la lampe éclaire très vivement ces journaux que je suis idiot de relire, ces livres sans intérêt.—

À une distance énorme au dessus de mon salon souterrain, les maisons s'implantent, les brumes s'assemblent. La boue est rouge ou noire. Ville monstrueuse, nuit sans fin!

Moins haut, sont des égouts. Aux côtés, rien que l'épaisseur du globe. Peut-être les gouffres d'azur, des puits de feu. C'est peut-être sur ces plans que se rencontrent lunes et comètes, mers et fables.

Aux heures d'amertume je m'imagine des boules de saphir, de métal. Je suis maître du silence. Pourquoi une apparence de soupirail blêmirait-elle au coin de la voûte?

CONTE

Un Prince était vexé de ne s'être employé jamais qu'à la perfection des générosités vulgaires. Il prévoyait d'étonnantes révolutions de l'amour, et soupçonnait ses femmes de pouvoir mieux que cette complaisance agrémentée de ciel et de luxe. Il voulait voir la vérité, l'heure du désir et de la satisfaction essentiels. Que ce fût ou non une aberration de piété, il voulut. Il possédait au moins un assez large pouvoir humain.

—Toutes les femmes qui l'avaient connu furent assassinées. Quel saccage du jardin de la beauté! Sous le sabre, elles le bénirent. Il n'en commanda point de nouvelles.—Les femmes réapparurent.

Il tua tous ceux qui le suivaient, après la chasse ou les libations.—Tous le suivaient.

Il s'amusa à égorger les bêtes de luxe. Il fit flamber les palais. Il se ruait sur les gens et les taillait en pièces.—La foule, les toits d'or, les belles bêtes existaient encore.

Peut-on s'extasier dans la destruction, se rajeunir par la cruauté! Le peuple ne murmura pas. Personne n'offrit le concours de ses vues.

Un soir il galopait fièrement. Un Génie apparut, d'une beauté ineffable, inavouable même. De sa physionomie et de son maintien ressortait la promesse d'un amour multiple et complexe! d'un bonheur indicible, insupportable même! Le Prince et le Génie s'anéantirent probablement dans la santé essentielle. Comment n'auraient-ils pas pu en mourir? Ensemble donc ils moururent.

Mais ce Prince décéda, dans son palais, à un âge ordinaire. Le prince était le Génie. Le Génie était le Prince.

La musique savante manque à notre désir.

PARADE

Des drôles très solides. Plusieurs ont exploité vos mondes. Sans besoins, et peu pressés de mettre en œuvre leurs brillantes facultés et leur expérience de vos consciences. Quels hommes mûrs! Des yeux hébétés à la façon de la nuit d'été, rouges et noirs, tricolores, d'acier piqué d'étoiles d'or; des faciès déformés, plombés, blêmis[,] incendiés; des enrouements folâtres! La démarche cruelle des oripeaux!—Il y a quelques jeunes,—comment regarderaient-ils Chérubin?—pourvus de voix effrayantes et de quelques ressources dangereuses. On les envoie prendre du dos en ville, affublés d'un *luxe* dégoûtant.

Ô le plus violent Paradis de la grimace enragée! Pas de comparaison avec vos Fakirs et les autres bouffonneries scéniques. Dans des costumes improvisés avec le goût du mauvais rêve ils jouent des complaintes, des tragédies de malandrins et de demi-dieux spirituels comme l'histoire ou les religions ne l'ont jamais été, Chinois, Hottentots, bohémiens, niais, hyènes, Molochs, vieilles démences, démons sinistres, ils mêlent les tours populaires, maternels, avec les poses et les tendresses bestiales. Ils interpréteraient des pièces nouvelles et des chansons «bonnes filles». Maîtres jongleurs, ils transforment le lieu et les personnes et usent de la comédie magnétique. Les yeux flambent, le sang chante, les os s'élargissent, les larmes et des filets rouges ruissellent. Leur raillerie ou leur terreur dure une minute, ou des mois entiers.

J'ai seul la clef de cette parade sauvage.

ANTIQUE

Gracieux fils de Pan! Autour de ton front couronné de fleurettes et de baies tes yeux, des boules précieuses, remuent. Tachées de lies brunes, tes joues se creusent. Tes crocs luisent. Ta poitrine ressemble à une cithare, des tintements circulent dans tes bras blonds. Ton cœur bat dans ce ventre où dort le double sexe. Promène-toi, la nuit, en mouvant doucement cette cuisse, cette seconde cuisse et cette jambe de gauche.

BEING BEAUTEOUS

Devant une neige un Être de Beauté de haute taille. Des sifflements de mort et des cercles de musique sourde font monter, s'élargir et trembler comme un spectre ce corps adoré; des blessures écarlates et noires éclatent dans les chairs superbes. Les couleurs propres de la vie se foncent, dansent, et se dégagent autour de la Vision, sur le chantier. Et les frissons s'élèvent et grondent et la saveur forcenée de ces effets se chargeant avec les sifflements mortels et les rauques musiques que le monde, loin derrière nous, lance sur notre mère de beauté,—elle recule, elle se dresse. Oh! nos os sont revêtus d'un nouveau corps amoureux.

* * * *

Ô la face cendrée, l'écusson de crin, les bras de cristal! le canon sur lequel je dois m'abattre à travers la mêlée des arbres et de l'air léger!

VIES

I

Ô les énormes avenues du pays saint, les terrasses du temple! Qu'a-t-on fait du brahmane qui m'expliqua les Proverbes? D'alors, de là-bas, je vois encore même les vieilles! Je me souviens des heures d'argent et de soleil vers les fleuves, la main de la campagne sur mon épaule, et de nos caresses debout dans les plaines poivrées.—Un envol de pigeons écarlates tonne autour de ma pensée.—Exilé ici j'ai eu une scène où jouer les chefs-d'œuvre dramatiques de toutes les littératures. Je vous indiquerais les richesses inouïes. J'observe l'histoire des trésors que vous trouvâtes. Je vois la suite! Ma sagesse est aussi dédaignée que le chaos. Qu'est mon néant, auprès de la stupeur qui vous attend?

II

Je suis un inventeur bien autrement méritant que tous ceux qui m'ont précédé; un musicien même, qui ai trouvé quelque chose comme la clef de l'amour. À présent, gentilhomme d'une campagne aigre au ciel sobre j'essaie de m'émouvoir au souvenir de l'enfance mendiante, de l'apprentissage ou de l'arrivée en sabots, des polémiques, des cinq ou six veuvages, et quelques noces où ma forte tête m'empêcha de monter au diapason des camarades. Je ne regrette pas ma vieille part de gaîté divine: l'air sobre de cette aigre campagne alimente fort activement mon atroce scepticisme. Mais comme ce scepticisme ne peut désormais être mis en œuvre, et que d'ailleurs je suis dévoué à un trouble nouveau,—j'attends de devenir un très méchant fou.

III

Dans un grenier où je fus enfermé à douze ans j'ai connu le monde, j'ai illustré la comédie humaine. Dans un cellier j'ai appris l'histoire. À quelque fête de nuit dans une cité du Nord j'ai rencontré toutes les femmes des anciens peintres. Dans un vieux passage à Paris on m'a enseigné les sciences classiques. Dans une magnifique demeure cernée par l'Orient entier j'ai accompli mon immense œuvre et passé mon illustre retraite. J'ai brassé mon sang. Mon devoir m'est remis. Il ne faut même plus songer à cela. Je suis réellement d'outre-tombe, et pas de commissions.

DÉPART

Assez vu. La vision s'est rencontrée à tous les airs.
Assez eu. Rumeurs des villes, le soir, et au soleil, et toujours.
Assez connu. Les arrêts de la vie.—Ô Rumeurs et Visions!
Départ dans l'affection et le bruit neufs!

ROYAUTÉ

Un beau matin, chez un peuple fort doux, un homme et une femme superbes criaient sur la place publique. «Mes amis, je veux qu'elle soit reine!» «Je veux être reine!» Elle riait et tremblait. Il parlait aux amis de révélation, d'épreuve terminée. Ils se pâmaient l'un contre l'autre.

En effet ils furent rois toute une matinée où les tentures carminées se relevèrent sur les maisons, et toute l'après-midi, où ils s'avancèrent du côté des jardins de palmes.

À UNE RAISON

Un coup de ton doigt sur le tambour décharge tous les sons et commence la nouvelle harmonie.

Un pas de toi, c'est la levée des nouveaux hommes et leur en-marche.

Ta tête se détourne: le nouvel amour! Ta tête se retourne,—le nouvel amour!

«Change nos lots, crible les fléaux, à commencer par le temps», te chantent ces enfants. «Élève n'importe où la substance de nos fortunes et de nos vœux» on t'en prie,

Arrivée de toujours, qui t'en iras partout.

MATINÉE D'IVRESSE

Ô *mon* Bien! Ô *mon* Beau! Fanfare atroce où je ne trébuche point! Chevalet féerique! Hourra pour l'œuvre inouïe et pour le corps merveilleux, pour la première fois! Cela commença sous les rires des enfants, cela finira par eux. Ce poison va rester dans toutes nos veines même quand, la fanfare tournant, nous serons rendu à l'ancienne inharmonie. Ô maintenant nous si digne de ces tortures! rassemblons fervemment cette promesse surhumaine faite à notre corps et à notre âme créés: cette promesse, cette démence! L'élégance, la science, la violence! On nous a promis d'enterrer dans l'ombre l'arbre du bien et du mal, de déporter les honnêtetés tyranniques, afin que nous amenions notre très pur amour. Cela commença par quelques dégoûts et cela finit,—ne pouvant nous saisir sur[-]le[-]champ de cette éternité,—cela finit par une débandade de parfums.

Rire des enfants, discrétion des esclaves, austérité des vierges, horreur des figures et des objets d'ici, sacrés soyez-vous par le souvenir de cette veille. Cela commençait par toute la rustrerie, voici que cela finit par des anges de flamme et de glace.

Petite veille d'ivresse, sainte! quand ce ne serait que pour le masque dont tu nous a[s] gratifié. Nous t'affirmons, méthode! Nous n'oublions pas que tu as glorifié hier chacun de nos âges. Nous avons foi au poison. Nous savons donner notre vie tout entière tous les jours.

Voici le temps des *Assassins.*

PHRASES

Quand le monde sera réduit en un seul bois noir pour nos quatre yeux étonnés,—en une plage pour deux enfants fidèles—en une maison musicale pour notre claire sympathie,—je vous trouverai.

Qu'il n'y ait ici[-]bas qu'un vieillard seul, calme et beau, entouré d'un «luxe inouï»,—et je suis à vos genoux.

Que j'aie réalisé tous vos souvenirs,—que je sois celle qui sait vous garrotter,—je vous étoufferai.

Quand nous sommes très forts,—qui recule? très gais, qui tombe de ridicule? Quand nous sommes très méchants, que ferait-on de nous.

Parez-vous, dansez, riez.—Je ne pourrai jamais envoyer l'Amour par la fenêtre.

—Ma camarade, mendiante, enfant monstre! comme ça t'est égal, ces malheureuses et ces manœuvres, et mes embarras. Attache-toi à nous avec ta voix impossible, ta voix! unique flatteur de ce vil désespoir.

FRAGMENTS SANS TITRE

Une matinée couverte, en Juillet. Un goût de cendres vole dans l'air;—une odeur de bois suant dans l'âtre,—les fleurs rouies—le saccage des promenades—la bruine des canaux par les champs,—pourquoi pas déjà les joujoux et l'encens?

J'ai tendu des cordes de clocher à clocher; des guirlandes de fenêtre à fenêtre; des chaînes d'or d'étoile à étoile, et je danse.

Le haut étang fume continuellement. Quelle sorcière va se dresser sur le couchant blanc? Quelles violettes frondaisons vont descendre?

Pendant que les fonds publics s'écoulent en fêtes de fraternité, il sonne une cloche de feu rose dans les nuages.

Avivant un agréable goût d'encre de Chine une poudre noire pleut doucement sur ma veillée.—Je baisse les feux du lustre, je me jette sur le lit, et tourné du côté de l'ombre je vous vois, mes filles! mes reines!

OUVRIERS

Ô cette chaude matinée de février. Le Sud inopportun vint relever nos souvenirs d'indigents absurdes, notre jeune misère.

Henrika avait une jupe de coton à carreau blanc et brun, qui a dû être portée au siècle dernier, un bonnet à rubans et un foulard de soie. C'était bien plus triste qu'un deuil. Nous faisions un tour dans la banlieue. Le temps était couvert et ce vent du Sud excitait toutes les vilaines odeurs des jardins ravagés et des prés desséchés.

Cela ne devait pas fatiguer ma femme au même point que moi. Dans une flache laissée par l'inondation du mois précédent à un sentier assez haut elle me fit remarquer de très petits poissons.

La ville, avec sa fumée et ses bruits de métiers, nous suivait très loin dans les chemins. Ô l'autre monde, l'habitation bénie par le ciel et les ombrages! Le sud me rappelait les misérables incidents de mon enfance, mes désespoirs d'été, l'horrible quantité de force et de science que le sort a toujours éloignée de moi. Non! Nous ne passerons pas l'été dans cet avare pays où nous ne serons jamais que des orphelins fiancés. Je veux que ce bras durci ne traîne plus *une chère image.*

LES PONTS

Des ciels gris de cristal. Un bizarre dessin de ponts, ceux-ci droits, ceux-là bombés, d'autres descendant ou obliquant en angles sur les premiers, et ces figures se renouvelant dans les autres circuits éclairés du canal, mais tous tellement longs et légers que les rives, chargées de dômes[,] s'abaissent et s'amoindrissent. Quelques-uns de ces ponts sont encore chargés de masures. D'autres soutiennent des mâts, des signaux, de frêles parapets. Des accords mineurs se croisent, et filent, des cordes montent des berges. On distingue une veste rouge, peut-être d'autres costumes et des instruments de musique. Sont-ce des airs populaires, des bouts de concerts seigneuriaux, des restants d'hymnes publics? L'eau est grise et bleue, large comme un bras de mer.—Un rayon blanc, tombant du haut du ciel, anéantit cette comédie.

VILLE

Je suis un éphémère et point trop mécontent citoyen d'une métropole crue moderne parce que tout goût connu a été éludé dans les ameublements et l'extérieur des maisons aussi bien que dans le plan de la ville. Ici vous ne signaleriez les traces d'aucun monument de superstition. La morale et la langue sont réduites à leur plus simple expression, enfin! Ces millions de gens qui n'ont pas besoin de se connaître amènent si pareillement l'éducation, le métier et la vieillesse, que ce cours de vie doit être plusieurs fois moins long que ce qu'une statistique folle trouve pour les peuples du continent. Aussi comme, de ma fenêtre, je vois des spectres nouveaux roulant à travers l'épaisse et éternelle fumée de charbon,—notre ombre des bois, notre nuit d'été!—des Érynnies nouvelles, devant mon cottage qui est ma patrie et tout mon cœur puisque tout ici ressemble à ceci,—la Mort sans pleurs, notre active fille et servante, et un Amour désespéré, et un joli Crime piaulant dans la boue de la rue.

ORNIÈRES

À droite l'aube d'été éveille les feuilles et les vapeurs et les bruits de ce coin du parc, et les talus de gauche tiennent dans leur ombre violette les mille rapides ornières de la route humide. Défilé de féeries. En effet: des chars chargés d'animaux de bois doré, de mâts et de toiles bariolées, au grand galop de vingt chevaux de cirque tachetés, et les enfants et les hommes sur leurs bêtes les plus étonnantes;—vingt véhicules, bossés, pavoisés et fleuris comme des carrosses anciens ou de contes, pleins d'enfants attifés pour une pastorale suburbaine;—Même des cercueils sous leur dais de nuit dressant les panaches d'ébène, filant au trot des grandes juments bleues et noirs.

VILLES [I]

Ce sont des villes! C'est un peuple pour qui se sont montés ces Alleghanys et ces Libans de rêve! Des chalets de cristal et de bois qui se meuvent sur des rails et des poulies invisibles. Les vieux cratères ceints de colosses et de palmiers de cuivre rugissent mélodieusement dans les feux. Des fêtes amoureuses sonnent sur les canaux pendus derrière les chalets. La chasse des carillons crie dans les gorges. Des corporations de chanteurs géants accourent dans des vêtements et des oriflammes éclatants comme la lumière des cimes. Sur les plate[s-]formes au milieu des gouffres les Rolands sonnent leur bravoure. Sur les passerelles de l'abîme et les toits des auberges l'ardeur du ciel pavoise les mâts. L'écroulement des apothéoses rejoint les champs des hauteurs où les centauresses séraphiques évoluent parmi les avalanches. Au[-]dessus du niveau des plus hautes crêtes une mer troublée par la naissance éternelle de Vénus, chargée de flottes orphéoniques et de la rumeur des perles et des conques précieuses,—la mer s'assombrit parfois avec des éclats mortels. Sur les versants des moissons de fleurs grandes comme nos armes et nos coupes, mugissent. Des cortèges de Mabs en robes rousses, opalines, montent des ravines. Là[-]haut, les pieds dans la cascade et les ronces, les cerfs tettent Diane. Les Bacchantes des banlieues sanglotent et la lune brûle et hurle. Vénus entre dans les cavernes des forgerons et des ermites. Des groupes de beffrois chantent les idées des peuples. Des châteaux bâtis en os sort la musique inconnue. Toutes les légendes évoluent et les élans se ruent dans les bourgs. Le paradis des orages s'effondre. Les sauvages dansent sans cesse la fête de la nuit. Et une heure je suis descendu dans le mouvement d'un boulevard de Bagdad où des compagnies ont chanté la joie du travail nouveau, sous une brise épaisse, circulant sans pouvoir éluder les fabuleux fantômes des monts où l'on a dû se retrouver.

Quels bons bras, quelle belle heure me rendront cette région d'où viennent mes sommeils et mes moindres mouvements?

VAGABONDS

Pitoyable frère! Que d'atroces veillées je lui dus! «Je ne me saisissais pas fervemment de cette entreprise. Je m'étais joué de son infirmité. Par ma faute nous retournerions en exil, en esclavage.» Il me supposait un guignon et une innocence très-bizarres, et il ajoutait des raisons inquiétantes.

Je répondais en ricanant à ce satanique docteur, et finissais par gagner la fenêtre. Je créais, par delà la campagne traversée par des bandes de musique rare, les fantômes du futur luxe nocturne.

Après cette distraction vaguement hygiénique, je m'étendais sur une paillasse. Et, presque chaque nuit, aussitôt endormi, le pauvre frère se levait, la bouche pourrie, les yeux arrachés,—tel qu'il se rêvait!—et me tirait dans la salle en hurlant son songe de chagrin idiot.

J'avais en effet, en toute sincérité d'esprit, pris l'engagement de le rendre à son état primitif de fils du soleil,—et nous errions, nourris du vin des cavernes et du biscuit de la route, moi pressé de trouver le lieu et la formule.

VILLES[II]

L'acropole officielle outre les conceptions de la barbarie moderne les plus colossales. Impossible d'exprimer le jour mat produit par ce ciel immuablement gris, l'éclat impérial des bâtisses, et la neige éternelle du sol. On a reproduit dans un goût d'énormité singulier toutes les merveilles classiques de l'architecture. J'assiste à des expositions de peinture dans des locaux vingt fois plus vastes qu'Hampton-Court. Quelle peinture! Un Nabuchodonosor norwégien a fait construire les escaliers des ministères; les subalternes que j'ai pu voir sont déjà plus fiers que des Brahmas et j'ai tremblé à l'aspect des gardiens de colosses et officiers de constructions. Par le groupement des bâtiments en squares, cours et terrasses fermées, on [a] évincé les cochers. Les parcs représentent la nature primitive travaillée par un art superbe. Le haut quartier a des parties inexplicables: un bras de mer, sans bateaux, roule sa nappe de grésil bleu entre des quais chargés de candélabres géants. Un pont court conduit à une poterne immédiatement sous le dôme de la Sainte-Chapelle. Ce dôme est une armature d'acier artistique de quinze mille pieds de diamètre environ.

Sur quelques points des passerelles de cuivre, des plates-formes, des escaliers qui contournent les halles et les piliers, j'ai cru pouvoir juger la profondeur de la ville. C'est le prodige dont je n'ai pu me rendre compte: quels sont les niveaux des autres quartiers sur ou sous l'acropole? Pour l'étranger de notre temps la reconnaissance est impossible. Le quartier commerçant est un circus d'un seul style, avec galeries à arcades. On ne voit pas de boutiques. Mais la neige de la chaussée est écrasée; quelques nababs aussi rares que les promeneurs d'un matin de dimanche à Londres, se dirigent vers une diligence de diamants. Quelques divans de velours rouge: on sert des boissons polaires dont le prix varie de huit cent[s] à huit mille roupies. À l'idée de chercher des théâtres sur ce circus, je me réponds que les boutiques doivent contenir des drames assez-sombres. Je pense qu'il y a une police; mais la loi doit être tellement étrange, que je renonce à me faire une idée des aventuriers d'ici.

Le faubourg aussi élégant qu'une belle rue de Paris est favorisé d'un air de lumière. L'élément démocratique compte quelques cents âmes. Là encore les maisons ne se suivent pas; le faubourg se perd bizarrement dans la campagne, le «Comté» qui remplit l'occident éternel des forêts et des plantations prodigieuses où les gentilshommes sauvages chassent leurs chroniques sous la lumière qu'on a créée.

VEILLÉES

I

C'est le repos éclairé, ni fièvre ni langueur, sur le lit ou sur le pré.
C'est l'ami ni ardent ni faible. L'ami.
C'est l'aimée ni tourmentante ni tourmentée. L'aimée.
L'air et le monde point cherchés. La vie.
—Était-ce donc ceci?
—Et le rêve fraîchit.

II

L'éclairage revient à l'arbre de bâtisse. Des deux extrémités de la salle, décors quelconques, des élévations harmoniques se joignent. La muraille en face du veilleur est une succession psychologique de coupes de frises, de bandes atmosphériques et d'accidences géologiques.—Rêve intense et rapide de groupes sentimentaux avec des êtres de tous les caractères parmi toutes les apparences.

———

III

Les lampes et les tapis de la veillée font le bruit des vagues, la nuit, le long de la coque et autour du steerage.

La mer de la veillée, telle que les seins d'Amélie.

Les tapisseries, jusqu'à mi-hauteur, des taillis de dentelle, teinte d'émeraude, où se jettent les tourterelles de la veillée.

. . . .

La plaque du foyer noir, de réels soleils des grèves: ah! puits des magies; seule vue d'aurore, cette fois.

MYSTIQUE

Sur la pente du talus les anges tournent leurs robes de laine dans les herbages d'acier et d'émeraude.

Des prés de flammes bondissent jusqu'au sommet du mamelon. À gauche le terreau de l'arête est piétiné par tous les homicides et toutes les batailles, et tous les bruits désastreux filent leur courbe. Derrière l'arête de droite la ligne des orients, des progrès.

Et tandis que la bande en haut du tableau est formée de la rumeur tournante et bondissante des conques des mers et des nuits humaines,

La douceur fleurie des étoiles et du ciel et du reste descend en face du talus, comme un panier,—contre notre face, et fait l'abîme fleurant et bleu là-dessous.

AUBE

J'ai embrassé l'aube d'été.

Rien ne bougeait encore au front des palais. L'eau était morte. Les camps d'ombres ne quittaient pas la route du bois. J'ai marché, réveillant les haleines vives et tièdes, et les pierreries regardèrent, et les ailes se levèrent sans bruit.

La première entreprise fut, dans le sentier déjà empli de frais et blêmes éclats, une fleur qui me dit son nom.

Je ris au wasserfall blond qui s'échevela à travers les sapins: à la cime argentée je reconnus la déesse.

Alors je levai un à un les voiles. Dans l'allée, en agitant les bras. Par la plaine, où je l'ai dénoncée au coq. À la grand'ville elle fuyait parmi les clochers et les dômes, et courant comme un mendiant sur les quais de marbre, je la chassais.

En haut de la route, près d'un bois de lauriers, je l'ai entourée avec ses voiles amassés, et j'ai senti un peu son immense corps. L'aube et l'enfant tombèrent au bas du bois.

Au réveil il était midi.

FLEURS

D'un gradin d'or,—parmi les cordons de soie, les gazes grises, les velours verts et les disques de cristal qui noircissent comme du bronze au soleil,—je vois la digitale s'ouvrir sur un tapis de filigranes d'argent, d'yeux et de chevelures.

Des pièces d'or jaune semées sur l'agate, des piliers d'acajou supportant un dôme d'émeraudes, des bouquets de satin blanc et de fines verges de rubis entourent la rose d'eau.

Tels qu'un dieu aux énormes yeux bleus et aux formes de neige, la mer et le ciel attirent aux terrasses de marbre la foule des jeunes et fortes roses.

NOCTURNE VULGAIRE

Un souffle ouvre des brèches opéradiques dans les cloisons,—brouille le pivotement des toits rongés,—disperse les limites de foyers,—éclipse les croisées.—Le long de la vigne, m'étant appuyé du pied à une gargouille,—je suis descendu dans ce carrosse dont l'époque est assez indiquée par les glaces convexes, les panneaux bombés et les sophas contournés—Corbillard de mon sommeil, isolé, maison de berger de ma niaiserie, le véhicule vire sur le gazon de la grande route effacée: et dans un défaut en haut de la glace de droite tournoient les blêmes figures lunaires, feuilles, seins;—Un vert et un bleu très foncés envahissent l'image. Dételage aux environs d'une tache de gravier.

—Ici va-t-on siffler pour l'orage, et les Sodomes,—et les Solymes,—et les bêtes féroces et les armées,

(—Postillon et bêtes de Songe reprendront-ils sous les plus suffocantes futaies, pour m'enfoncer jusqu'aux yeux dans la source de soie.)

—Et nous envoyer, fouettés à travers les eaux clapotantes et les boissons répandues, rouler sur l'aboi des dogues...

—Un souffle disperse les limites du foyer.

MARINE

Les chars d'argent et de cuivre—
Les proues d'acier et d'argent—
Battent l'écume,—
Soulèvent les souches des ronces—
        Les courants de la lande,
Et les ornières immenses du reflux
Filent circulairement vers l'est,
Vers les piliers de la forêt,—
Vers les fûts de la jetée,
Dont l'angle est heurté par des tourbillons de lumière

FÊTE D'HIVER

La cascade sonne derrière les huttes d'opéra-comique. Des girandoles prolongent, dans les vergers et les allées voisins du Méandre,—les verts et les rouges du couchant. Nymphes d'Horace coiffées au Premier Empire,—Rondes Sibériennes, Chinoises de Boucher.

ANGOISSE

Se peut-il qu'Elle me fasse pardonner les ambitions continuellement écrasées,—qu'une fin aisée répare les âges d'indigence,—qu'un jour de succès nous endorme sur la honte de notre inhabileté fatale,

(Ô palmes! diamant!—Amour, force!—plus haut que toutes joies et gloires!—de toutes façons, partout,—démon, dieu,—Jeunesse de cet être-ci; moi!)

Que des accidents de féerie scientifique et des mouvements de fraternité sociale soient chéris comme restitution progressive de la franchise première? . . .

Mais la Vampire qui nous rend gentils commande que nous nous amusions avec ce qu'elle nous laisse, ou qu'autrement nous soyons plus drôles.

Rouler aux blessures, par l'air lassant et la mer; aux supplices, par le silence des eaux et de l'air meurtriers; aux tortures qui rient, dans leur silence atrocement houleux.

MÉTROPOLITAIN

Du détroit d'indigo aux mers d'Ossian, sur le sable rose et orange qu'a lavé le ciel vineux viennent de monter et de se croiser des boulevards de cristal habités incontinent par des jeunes familles pauvres qui s'alimentent chez les fruitiers. Rien de riche.—La ville!

Du désert de bitume fuient droit en déroute avec les nappes de brumes échelonnées en bandes affreuses au ciel qui se recourbe, se recule et descend, formé de la plus sinistre fumée noire que puisse faire l'Océan en deuil, les casques, les roues, les barques, les croupes.—La bataille!

Lève la tête: ce pont de bois, arqué; les derniers potagers de Samarie; ces masques enluminés sous la lanterne fouettée par la nuit froide; l'ondine niaise à la robe bruyante, au bas de la rivière; les crânes lumineux dans les plan[t]s de pois,—et les autres fantasmagories—la campagne.

Des routes bordées de grilles et de murs, contenant à peine leurs bosquets, et les atroces fleurs qu'on appellerait cœurs et sœurs, Damas damnant de long[u]eur,—possessions de féeriques aristocraties ultra-Rhénanes, Japonaises, Guaranies, propres encore à recevoir la musique des anciens—et il y a des auberges qui pour toujours n'ouvrent déjà plus—il y a des princesses, et si tu n'es pas trop accablé, l'étude des astres—le ciel.

Le matin où avec Elle vous vous débattîtes parmi les éclats de neige, les lèvres vertes, les glaces[,] les drapeaux noirs et les rayons bleus, et les parfums pourpres du soleil des pôles,—ta force.

BARBARE

Bien après les jours et les saisons, et les êtres et les pays,

Le pavillon en viande saignante sur la soie des mers et des fleurs arctiques; (elles n'existent pas.)

Remis des vieilles fanfares d'héroïsme—qui nous attaquent encore le cœur et la tête—loin des anciens assassins—

Oh! le pavillon en viande saignante sur la soie des mers et des fleurs arctiques; (elles n'existent pas)

Douceurs!

Les brasiers, pleuvant aux rafales de givre,—Douceurs!—les feux à la pluie du vent de diamants—jetée par le cœur terrestre éternellement carbonisé pour nous.—Ô monde!—

(Loin des vieilles retraites et des vieilles flammes, qu'on entend, qu'on sent,)

Les brasiers et les écumes. La musique, virement des gouffres et choc des glaçons aux astres.

Ô Douceurs, ô monde, ô musique! Et là, les formes, les sueurs, les chevelures et les yeux, flottant. Et les larmes blanches, bouillantes,—ô douceurs!—et la voix féminine arrivée au fond des volcans et des grottes arctiques.

Le pavillon…

FAIRY

Pour Hélène se conjurèrent les sèves ornamentales dans les ombres vierges et les clartés impassibles dans le silence astral. L'ardeur de l'été fut confiée à des oiseaux muets et l'indolence requise à une barque de deuils sans prix par des anses d'amours morts et de parfums affaissés.

—Après le moment de l'air des bûcheronnes à la rumeur du torrent sous la ruine des bois, de la sonnerie des bestiaux à l'écho des vals, et des cris des steppes.—

Pour l'enfance d'Hélène frissonnèrent les fourrures et les ombres,—et le sein des pauvres, et les légendes du ciel.

Et ses yeux et sa danse supérieurs encore aux éclats précieux, aux influences froides, au plaisir du décor et de l'heure uniques.

GUERRE

Enfant, certains ciels ont affiné mon optique: tous les caractères nuancèrent ma physionomie. Les Phénomènes s'émurent.—À présent, l'inflexion éternelle des moments et l'infini des mathématiques me chassent par ce monde où je subis tous les succès civils, respecté de l'enfance étrange et des affections énormes.—Je songe à une Guerre, de droit ou de force, de logique bien imprévue.

C'est aussi simple qu'une phrase musicale.

SOLDE

À vendre ce que les Juifs n'ont pas vendu, ce que noblesse ni crime n'ont goûté, ce qu'ignore l'amour maudit et la probité infernale des masses: ce que le temps ni la science n'ont pas à reconnaître;

Les Voix reconstituées; l'éveil fraternel de toutes les énergies chorales et orchestrales et leurs applications instantanées; l'occasion, unique, de dégager nos sens!

À vendre les Corps sans prix, hors de toute race, de tout monde, de tout sexe, de toute descendance! Les richesses jaillissant à chaque démarche! Solde de diamants sans contrôle!

À vendre l'anarchie pour les masses; la satisfaction irrépressible pour les amateurs supérieurs; la mort atroce pour les fidèles et les amants!

À vendre les habitations et les migrations, sports, féeries et comforts parfaits, et le bruit, le mouvement et l'avenir qu'ils font!

À vendre les applications de calcul et les sauts d'harmonie inouïs. Les trouvailles et les termes non soupçonnés, possession immédiate.

Élan insensé et infini aux splendeurs invisibles, aux délices insensibles,—et ses secrets affolants pour chaque vice—et sa gaîté effrayante pour la foule—

À vendre les Corps, les voix, l'immense opulence inquestionable, ce qu'on ne vendra jamais. Les vendeurs ne sont pas à bout de solde! Les voyageurs n'ont pas à rendre leur commission de si tôt!

JEUNESSE

I

Dimanche

Les calculs de côté, l'inévitable descente du ciel, et la visite des souvenirs et la séance des rhythmes occupent la demeure, la tête et le monde de l'esprit.

—Un cheval détale sur le turf suburbain et le long des cultures et des boisements percé par la peste carbonique. Une misérable femme de drame, quelque part dans le monde, soupire après des abandons improbables. Les desperadoes languissent après l'orage, l'ivresse et les blessures. De petits enfants étouffent des malédictions le long des rivières.—

Reprenons l'étude au bruit de l'œuvre dévorante qui se rassemble et remonte dans les masses.

II

Sonnet

Homme de constitution ordinaire, la chair
n'était-elle pas un fruit pendu dans le verger,—ô
journées enfantes! le corps un trésor à prodiguer;—ô
aimer, le péril ou la force de Psyché? La terre
avait des versants fertiles en princes et en artistes,

et la descendance et la race vous poussaient aux
crimes et aux deuils: le monde votre fortune et votre
péril. Mais à présent, ce labeur comblé, toi, tes calculs,
—toi, tes impatiences—ne sont plus que votre danse et
votre voix, non fixées et point forcées, quoique d'un double
événement d'invention et de succès une saison,
—en l'humanité fraternelle et discrète par l'univers
sans images;—la force et le droit réfléchissent la danse
et la voix à présent seulement appréciées.

III

Vingt ans

Les voix instructives exilées... L'ingénuité physique amèrement rassise...—Adagio—Ah! l'égoïsme infini de l'adolescence, l'optimisme studieux: que le monde était plein de fleurs cet été! Les airs et les formes mourant... Un chœur, pour calmer l'impuissance et l'absence! Un chœur de verres de mélodies nocturnes... En effet les nerfs vont vite chasser.

IV

Tu en es encore à la tentation d'Antoine. L'ébat du zèle écourté, les tics d'orgueil puéril, l'affaissement et l'effroi.

Mais tu te mettras à ce travail: toutes les possibilités harmoniques et architecturales s'émouvront autour de ton siège. Des êtres parfaits, imprévus, s'offriront à tes expériences. Dans tes environs affluera rêveusement la curiosité d'anciennes foules et de luxes oisifs. Ta mémoire et tes sens ne seront que la nourriture de ton impulsion créatrice. Quant au monde, quand tu sortiras, que sera-t-il devenu? En tout cas, rien des apparences actuelles.

PROMONTOIRE

L'aube d'or et la soirée frissonnante trouvent notre brick en large en face de cette Villa et de ses dépendances, qui forment un promontoire aussi étendu que l'Épire et le Péloponnèse, ou que la grande île du Japon, ou que l'Arabie! Des fanums qu'éclaire la rentrée des théories, d'immenses vues de la défense des côtes modernes; des dunes illustrées de chaudes fleurs et de bacchanales; de grands canaux de Carthage et des Embankments d'une Venise louche, de molles éruptions d'Etnas et des crevasses de fleurs et d'eaux des glaciers, des lavoirs entourés de peupliers d'Allemagne; des talus de parcs singuliers penchant des têtes d'Arbre du Japon, et les façades circulaires des «Royal» ou des «Grand» de Scarbro' ou de Brooklyn; et leurs railways flanquent, creusent, surplombent les dispositions dans cet Hôtel, choisies dans l'histoire des plus élégantes et des plus colossales constructions de l'Italie, de l'Amérique et de l'Asie, dont les fenêtres et les terrasses à présent pleines d'éclairages, de boissons et de brises riches, sont ouvertes à l'esprit des voyageurs et des nobles—qui permettent, aux heures du jour, à toutes les tarentelles des côtes,—et même aux ritournelles des vallées illustres de l'art, de décorer merveilleusement les façades du Palais-Promontoire.

DÉVOTION

À ma sœur Louise Vanaen de Voringhem:—Sa cornette bleue tournée à la mer du Nord.—Pour les naufragés.

À ma sœur Léonie Aubois d'Ashby. Baou—l'herbe d'été bourdonnante et puante.—Pour la fièvre des mères et des enfants.

À Lulu,—démon—qui a conservé un goût pour les oratoires du temps des Amies et de son éducation incomplète. Pour les hommes! À madame***.

À l'adolescent que je fus. À ce saint vieillard, ermitage ou mission.

À l'esprit des pauvres. Et à un très haut clergé.

Aussi bien à tout culte en telle place de culte mémoriale et parmi tels événements qu'il faille se rendre, suivant les aspirations du moment ou bien notre propre vice sérieux.

Ce soir, à Circeto des hautes glaces, grasse comme le poisson, et enluminée comme les dix mois de la nuit rouge—(son cœur ambre et spunk),—pour ma seule prière muette comme ces régions de nuit et précédant des bravoures plus violentes que ce chaos polaire.

À tout prix et avec tous les airs, même dans des voyages métaphysiques.—Mais plus *alors.*

DÉMOCRATIE

«Le drapeau va au paysage immonde, et notre patois étouffe le tambour.

«Aux centres nous alimenterons la plus cynique prostitution. Nous massacrerons les révoltes logiques.

«Aux pays poivrés et détrempés!—au service des plus monstrueuses exploitations industrielles ou militaires.

«Au revoir ici, n'importe où, Conscrits du bon vouloir, nous aurons la philosophie féroce; ignorants pour la science, roués pour le confort; la crevaison pour le monde qui va. C'est la vraie marche. En avant, route!»

SCÈNES

L'ancienne Comédie poursuit ses accords et divise ses Idylles:

Des boulevards de tréteaux.

Un long pier en bois d'un bout à l'autre d'un champ rocailleux où la foule barbare évolue sous les arbres dépouillés.

Dans des corridors de gaze noire suivant le pas des promeneurs aux lanternes et aux feuilles.

Des oiseaux des mystères s'abattent sur un ponton de maçonnerie mû par l'archipel couvert des embarcations des spectateurs.

Des scènes lyriques accompagnées de flûte et de tambour s'inclinent dans des réduits ménagés sous les plafonds, autour des salons de clubs modernes ou des salles de l'Orient ancien.

La féerie manœuvre au sommet d'un amphithéâtre couronné par les taillis—Ou s'agite et module pour les Béotiens, dans l'ombre des futaies mouvantes sur l'arête des cultures.

L'opéra-comique se divise sur une scène à l'arête d'intersection de dix cloisons dressées de la galerie aux feux.

SOIR HISTORIQUE

En quelque soir, par exemple, que se trouve le touriste naïf, retiré de nos horreurs économiques, la main d'un maître anime le clavecin des prés; on joue aux cartes au fond de l'étang, miroir évocateur des reines et des mignonnes; on a les saintes, les voiles, et les fils d'harmonie, et les chromatismes légendaires, sur le couchant.

Il frissonne au passage des chasses et des hordes. La comédie goutte sur les tréteaux de gazon. Et l'embarras des pauvres et des faibles sur ces plans stupides!

À sa vision esclave, l'Allemagne s'échafaude vers des lunes; les déserts tartares s'éclairent; les révoltes anciennes grouillent dans le centre du Céleste Empire; par les escaliers et les fauteuils de rois—un petit monde blême et plat, Afrique et Occidents, va s'édifier. Puis un ballet de mers et de nuits connues, une chimie sans valeur, et des mélodies impossibles.

La même magie bourgeoise à tous les points où la malle nous déposera! Le plus élémentaire physicien sent qu'il n'est plus possible de se soumettre à cette atmosphère personnelle, brume de remords physiques, dont la constatation est déjà une affliction.

Non! Le moment de l'étuve, des mers enlevées, des embrasements souterrains, de la planète emportée, et des exterminations conséquentes, certitudes si peu malignement indiquées dans la Bible et par les Nornes et qu'il sera donné à l'être sérieux de surveiller.—Cependant ce ne sera point un effet de légende!

BOTTOM

La réalité étant trop épineuse pour mon grand caractère,—je me trouvai néanmoins chez Madame, en gros oiseau gris bleu s'essorant vers les moulures du plafond et traînant l'aile dans les ombres de la soirée.

Je fus, au pied du baldaquin supportant ses bijoux adorés et ses chefs-d'œuvre physiques, un gros ours aux gencives violettes et au poil chenu de chagrin, les yeux aux cristaux et aux argents des consoles.

Tout se fit ombre et aquarium ardent. Au matin,—aube de juin batailleuse,—je courus aux champs, âne, claironnant et brandissant mon grief, jusqu'à ce que les Sabines de la banlieue vinrent se jeter à mon poitrail.

H

Toutes les monstruosités violent les gestes atroces d'Hortense. Sa solitude est la mécanique érotique, sa lassitude, la dynamique amoureuse. Sous la surveillance d'une enfance, elle a été, à des époques nombreuses, l'ardente hygiène des races. Sa porte est ouverte à la misère. Là, la moralité des êtres actuels se décorpore en sa passion, ou en son action.—Ô terrible frisson des amours novice[s] sur le sol sanglant et par l'hydrogène clarteux! trouvez Hortense.

MOUVEMENT

Le mouvement de lacet sur la berge des chutes du fleuve,
Le gouffre à l'étambot,
La célérité de la rampe,
L'énorme passade du courant
Mènent par les lumières inouïes

Et la nouveauté chimique
Les voyageurs entourés des trombes du val
Et du strom.

Ce sont les conquérants du monde
Cherchant la fortune chimique personnelle;
Le sport et le comfort voyagent avec eux;
Ils emmènent l'éducation
Des races, des classes et des bêtes, sur ce Vaisseau.
Repos et vertige
À la lumière diluvienne,
Aux terribles soirs d'étude.

Car de la causerie parmi les appareils,—le sang, les fleurs, le feu, les bijoux,—
Des comptes agités à ce bord fuyard,
On voit, roulant comme une digue au delà de la route hydraulique motrice:
Monstrueux, s'éclairant sans fin,—leur stock d'études;
Eux chassés dans l'extase harmonique,
Et l'héroïsme de la découverte.
Aux accidents atmosphériques les plus surprenants
Un couple de jeunesse s'isole sur l'arche,
—Est-ce ancienne sauvagerie qu'on pardonne?
Et chante et se poste.

GÉNIE

Il est l'affection et le présent puisqu'il a fait la maison ouverte à l'hiver écumeux et à la rumeur de l'été, lui qui a purifié les boissons et les aliments, lui qui est le charme des lieux fuyants et le délice surhumain des stations. Il est l'affection et l'avenir, la force et l'amour que nous, debout dans les rages et les ennuis, nous voyons passer dans le ciel de tempête et les drapeaux d'extase.

Il est l'amour, mesure parfaite et réinventée, raison merveilleuse et imprévue, et l'éternité: machine aimée des qualités fatales. Nous avons tous eu l'épouvante de sa concession et de la nôtre: ô jouissance de notre santé, élan de nos facultés, affection égoïste et passion pour lui, lui qui nous aime pour sa vie infinie...

Et nous nous le rappelons et il voyage... Et si l'Adoration s'en va, sonne, sa promesse sonne: «Arrière ces superstitions, ces anciens corps, ces ménages et ces âges. C'est cette époque-ci qui a sombré!»

Il ne s'en ira pas, il ne redescendra pas d'un ciel, il n'accomplira pas la rédemption des colères de femmes et des gaîtés des hommes et de tout ce péché: car c'est fait, lui étant, et étant aimé.

Ô ses souffles, ses têtes, ses courses; la terrible célérité de la perfection des formes et de l'action.

Ô fécondité de l'esprit et immensité de l'univers!

Son corps! le dégagement rêvé, le brisement de la grâce croisée de violence nouvelle!

Sa vue, sa vue! tous les agenouillages anciens et les peines *relevés* à sa suite.

Son jour! l'abolition de toutes souffrances sonores et mouvantes dans la musique plus intense.

Son pas! les migrations plus énormes que les anciennes invasions.

Ô Lui et nous! l'orgueil plus bienveillant que les charités perdues.

Ô monde! et le chant clair des malheurs nouveaux!

Il nous a connus tous et nous a tous aimés. Sachons, cette nuit d'hiver, de cap en cap, du pôle tumultueux au château, de la foule à la plage, de regards en regards, forces et sentiments las, le héler et le voir, et le renvoyer, et, sous les marées et au haut des déserts de neige, suivre ses vues, ses souffles, son corps, son jour.

ŒUVRES DIVERSES

I. COMPOSITIONS D'ÉCOLE

"VER ERAT . . ."

Ver erat, et morbo Romae languebat inerti
Orbilius: diri tacuerunt tela magistri
Plagarumque sonus non jam veniebat ad aures,
Nec ferula assiduo cruciabat membra dolore.
Arripui tempus: ridentia rura petivi
Immemor; a studio moti curisque soluti
Blanda fatigatam recrearunt gaudia mentem.
Nescio qua laeta captum dulcedine pectus
Taedia jam ludi, jam tristia verba magistri
Oblitum, campos late spectare juvabat
Lætaque vernantis miracula cernere terræ.
Nec ruris tantum puer otia vana petebam:
Majores parvo capiebam pectore sensus:
Nescio lymphatis quæ mens divinior alas
Sensibus addebat: tacito spectacula visu
Attonitus contemplabar: pectusque calentis
Insinuabat amor ruris: ceu ferreus olim
Annulus, arcana quem vi Magnesia cautes
Attrahit, et cæcis tacitum sibi colligat hamis.

Interea longis fessos erroribus artus
Deponens, jacui viridanti in fluminis orâ
Murmure languidulo sopitus, et otia duxi,
Permulsus volucrum concentu aurâque Favoni.
Ecce per ætheream vallem incessere columbæ,
Alba manus, rostro florentia serta gerentes
Quæ Venus in Cypriis redolentia carpserat hortis.
Gramen, ubi fusus recreabar turba petivit
Molli remigio: circum plaudentibus alis
Inde meum cinxere caput, vincloque virenti
Devinxere manus, et olenti tempora myrto

Nostra coronantes, pondus per inane tenellum
Erexere ... Cohors per nubila celsa vehebat
Languidulum roseâ sub fronde: cubilia ventus
Ore remulcebat molli nutantia motu.
Ut patrias tetigere domos, rapidoque volatu
Monte sub ærio pendentia tecta columbæ
Intravere, breve positum vigilemque relinquunt.
Ô dulcem volucrum nidum! ... Lux candida puris
Circumfusa humeros radiis mea corpora vestit:
Nec vero obscuræ lux illa simillima luci,
Quæ nostros hebetat mixta caligine visus:
Terrenæ nil lucis habet cælestis origo!
Nescio quid cæleste mihi per pectora semper
Insinuat, pleno currens ceu flumine, numen.

Interea redeunt volucres, rostroque coronam
Laurea serta gerunt, quali redimitus Apollo
Argutas gaudet compellere pollice chordas.
Ast ubi lauriferâ frontem cinxere coronâ,
Ecce mihi patuit cælum, visuque repente
Attonito, volitans super aurea nubila, Phæbus
Divina vocale manu prætendere plectrum.
Tum capiti inscripsit cælesti hæc nomina flammâ:
TU VATES ERIS ... In nostros se subjicit artus
Tum calor insolitus, ceu, puro splendida vitro,
Solis inardescit radiis vis limpida fontis.
Tunc etiam priscam speciem liquere columbæ:
Musarum chorus apparet, modulamina dulci
Ore sonans, blandisque exceptum sustulit ulnis,
Omina ter fundens ter lauro tempora cingens.

Rimbaud Arthur.
Externe libre du collège de Charleville.
Né à Charleville, le 20 octobre 1854.

"JAMQUE NOVUS ..."

Jamque novus primam lucem consumpserat annus,
Jucundam pueris lucem, longumque petitam,
Oblitamque brevi: risu somnoque sepultus,

Languidulus tacuit puer; illum lectulus ambit
Plumeus, et circa crepitacula garrula terrâ,
Illorumque memor, felicia somnia carpit,
Donaque cælicolum, matris post dona, receptat.
Os hiat arridens, et semadaperta videntur
Labra vocare Deum: juxta caput angelus adstat
Pronus, et innocui languentia murmura cordis
Captat, et ipse suâ pendens ab imagine, vultus
Aethereos contemplatur; frontisque serenæ
Gaudia miratus, miratus gaudia mentis,
Intactumque Notis florem:
«Puer æmule nobis,
I, mecum conscende polos, cælestia regna
Ingredere; in somnis conspecta palatia dignus
Incole; cælestem tellus ne claudat alumnum!
Nulli tuta fides: numquam sincera remulcent
Gaudia mortales; ex ipso floris odore
Surgit amari aliquid, commotaque corda juvantur
Tristi lætitia; numquam sine nube voluptas
Gaudet et in dubio sublucet lacryma risu.
Quid? Frons pura tibi vitâ marceret amarâ,
Curaque cæruleos lacrymis turbaret ocellos,
Atque rosas vultus depelleret umbra cupressi?
Non ita: Divinas mecum penetrabis in oras,
Cælicolumque tuam vocem concentibus addes,
Subjectosque homines, hominumque tuebere fluctus.
I: tibi perrumpit vitalia vincula Numen.
At non lugubri veletur tegmine mater:
Haud alio visu feretrum ac cunabula cernat;
Triste supercilium pellat, nec funera vultum
Constristent: manibus potius det lilia plenis:
Ultima namque dies puro pulcherrima mansit.»
Vix ea: purpureo pennam levis admovet ori,
Demetit ignarum, demessique excipit alis
Cæruleis animam, superis et sedibus infert
Molli remigio: nunc tantum lectulus artus
Servat pallidulos, quibus haud sua gratia cessit,
Sed non almus alit flatus, vitamque ministrat;
Interiit... Sed adhuc redolentibus oscula labris
Exspirant risus, et matris nomen oberrat,
Donaque nascentis moriens reminiscitur anni.
Clausa putes placido languentia lumina somno;

Sed sopor ille, novo plus quam mortalis honore,
Nescio quo cingit cælesti lumine frontem,
Nec terræ sobolem at cæli testatur alumnum.

Oh! quanto genitrix luctu deplanxit ademptum,
Et carum inspersit, fletu manante, sepulcrum!
At quoties dulci declinat lumina somno,
Parvulus affulget, roseo de limine cæli,
Angelus, et dulcem gaudet vocitare parentem.
Subridet subridenti: mox, aere lapsus,
Attonitam niveis matrem circumvolat alis,
Illaque divinis connectit labra labellis.

Rimbaud Arthur.
Né le 20 octobre 1854 à Charleville.

"NASCITUR ARABIIS . . ."

La Providence fait quelquefois reparaître le même homme à travers plusieurs siècles.
BALZAC, *Lettres.*

I
Nascitur Arabiis ingens in collibus infans
Et dixit levis aura: «Nepos est ille Jugurthae . . .»

Fugit pauca dies ex quo surrexit in auras
Qui mox Arabiæ genti patriæque Jugurtha
Ipse futurus erat, quum visa parentibus umbra
Attonitis, puerum super, ipsius umbra Jugurthæ,
Et vitam narrare suam, fatumque referre:
«Ô patria! ô nostro tellus defensa labore!»
Et paulum zephyro vox interrupta silebat.
«Roma, prius multi sedes impura latronis,
Ruperat angustos muros, effusaque circum
Vicinas scelerata sibi constrinxerat oras:
Fortibus hinc orbem fuerat complexa lacertis

Reddideratque suum! Multæ depellere gentes
Nolebant fatale jugum: quæque arma parassent
Nequidquam patriâ pro libertate cruorem
Fundere certabant; ingentior objice Roma
Frangebat populos, quum non acceperat urbes!...»

Nascitur Arabiis ingens in collibus infans
Et dixit levis aura: «Nepos est ille Jugurthæ...»

«Ipse diu hanc plebem generosas volvere mentes
Credideram; sed quum propius discernere gentem
Jam juveni licuit, magnum sub pectore vulnus
Ingenti patuit!...—Dirum per membra venenum,
Auri sacra fames, influxerat... omnis in armis
Visa erat...—Urbs meretrix toto regnabat in orbe!
Ille ego reginæ statui contendere Romæ;
Despexi populum, totus cui paruit orbis!...»

Nascitur Arabiis ingens in collibus infans
Et dixit levis aura: «Nepos est ille Jugurthæ...»

«Nam quum consiliis sese immiscere Jugurthæ
Roma aggressa fuit, sensim sensimque latente
Captatura dolo patriam, impendentia vincla
Conscius adspexi, statuique resistere Romæ,
Ima laborantis cognoscens vulnera cordis!
Ô vulgus sublime! viri! plebecula sancta!
Illa, ferox mundi late regina decusque,
Illa meis jacuit, jacuit terra ebria donis!
Ô quantum Numidæ Romanam risimus urbem!
—Ille ferus cuncto volitabat in ore Jugurtha:
Nullus erat Numidas qui contra surgere posset!»

Nascitur Arabiis ingens in collibus infans
Et dixit levis aura: «Nepos est ille Jugurthæ...»

«Ille ego Romanos aditus Urbemque vocatus
Sustinui penetrare, Nomas!—frontique superbæ
Injeci colaphum, venaliaque agmina tempsi!...
—Oblita hic tandem populus surrexit ad arma:
Hand ego projeci gladios: mihi nulla triumphi
Spes erat: At saltem potui contendere Romæ!
Objeci fluvios, objeci saxa catervis

Romulidum; Lybicis nunc colluctantur arenis,
Nunc posita expugnant sublimi in culmine castra:
Sæpe meos fuso tinxerunt sanguine campos...
—Atque hostem insueti tandem stupuere tenacem!»

Nascitur Arabiis ingens in collibus infans
Et dixit levis aura: «Nepos est ille Jugurthæ...»

«Forsan et hostiles vicissem denique turmas...
Perfidia at Bocchi...—Quid vero plura revolvam?
Contentus patriam et regni fastigia liqui,
Contentus colapho Romam signasse rebelli!
—At novus Arabii victor nunc imperatoris,
Gallia!.. Tu, fili, si quâ fata aspera rumpas,
Ultor eris patriæ... Gentes, capite arma, subactæ!...
Prisca reviviscat domito sub pectore virtus!...
Ô gladios torquete iterum, memoresque Jugurthæ
Pellite victores, patria libate cruorem!...
Ô utinam Arabii surgant in bella leones,
Hostiles lacerent ultrici dente catervas!
—Et tu! cresce, puer! faveat fortuna labori.
Nec dein Arabiis insultet Gallicus oris!...»

—Atque puer ridens gladio ludebat adunco!...

II

Napoleo! proh Napoleo! novus ille Jugurtha
Vincitur: indigno devinctus carcere languet...
Ecce Jugurtha viro rursus consurgit in umbris
Et tales placido demurmurat ore loquelas:
«Cede novo, tu, nate, Deo! Jam linque querelas.
Nunc ætas melior surgit!...—Tua vincula solvet
Gallia, et Arabiam, Gallo dominante, videbis
Lætitiam: accipies generosæ fædera gentis...
—Ilicet immensa magnus tellure, sacerdos
Justitiæ fideique!...—Patrem tu corde Jugurtham
Dilige, et illius semper reminiscere sortem!

III

Ille tibi Arabii genius nam littoris extat!...

Rimbaud Jean-Nicolas-Arthur.
Externe au collège de Charleville.

"OLIM INFLATUS . . ."

Olim inflatus aquis, ingenti Acheloüs ab alveo
Turbidus in pronas valles erupit, et undis
Involvit pecudes et flavæ messis honorem.
Humanæ periere domus, desertaque late
Arva extenduntur: vallem sua nympha reliquit,
Faunorumque cessere chori, cunctique furentem
Amnem adspectabant; miseratâ mente querelas
Audiit Alcides: fluvii frenare furores
Tentat et in tumidos immania corpora fluctus
Projicit, et validis spumantes dejicit ulnis,
Et debellatos proprium deflectit in alveum.
Indignata fremit devicti fluminis unda:
Protinus anguinos fluvii deus induit artus,
Sibilat et stridens liventia terga retorquet
Et tremebunda quatit turgenti littora candâ.
Irruit Alcides, robustaque bracchia collo
Circumdat stringens, obluctantemque lacertis
Frangit, et enecto torquentem tergore truncum
Projicit, et nigrâ moribundum extendit arenâ,
Erigiturque ferox: «Audes tentare lacertos
Herculeos, fremit, imprudens? Hos dextera ludos
(Tunc ego parvus adhuc cunabula prima tenebam)
Extulit: hanc geminos nescis vicisse dracones?»

At pudor instimulat numen fluviale, decusque
Nominis eversi, presso sub corde dolore,
Restitit: ardenti fulgent fera lumina luce:
Frons exsurgit atrox ventosque armata lacessit;
Mugit, et horrendis mugitibus adfremit æther.
At satus Alcmena furialia prælia ridet,
Advolat, arreptumque quatit, tremebundaque membra
Sternit humi, pressatque genu crepitantia colla
Atque lacertoso complexus guttura nexu
Frangit anhelantis, singultantemque premit vi.
Tum monstro expirante ferox insigne tropæi
Sanguinea Alcides cornu de fronte revellit.
Tum Fauni, Dryadumque chori, Nymphæque sorores
Quorum divitias victor patriosque recessus
Ultus erat, molles recubantem ad roboris umbras,
Et priscos lætâ revocantem mente triumphos

Agmine circumeunt alacri, frontemque coronâ
Florigerâ variant, sertisque virentibus ornant.
Tum cornu, quod forte solo propiore jacebat
Communi cepere manu, spoliumque cruentum
Uberibus pomis et odoris floribus implent.

Rimbaud.
Externe au collège de Charleville.

"TEMPUS ERAT . . ."

Tempus erat quo Nazareth habitabat Iesus:
Crescebat virtute puer, crescebat et annis.
Mane novo quondam, vici quum tecta ruberent
Exiit a lecto per cuncta oppressa sopore,
Munus ut exactum surgens reperieret Ioseph.
In cæptum jam pronus opus, vultuque sereno
Ingentem impellens serram, serramque retractans,
Plurima cædebat puerili ligna lacerto.
Late apparebat nitidus sol montibus altis,
Intrabatque humiles argentea flamma fenestras.
Jam vero ad pastum cogunt armenta bubulci,
Et tenerum artificem matutinique laboris
Murmura certanti studio mirantur euntes.
«Quis puer ille?» ferunt; olli nempe eminet ore
Mixta venustate gravitas; vigor emicat armis.
Parvulus ille opifex cedrum, ut vetus, arte laborat
Nec magis Hirami fuerit labor improbus olim,
Quum validis prudens, Salomone adstante, lacertis
Ingentes cedros et templi ligna secaret.
Attamen hinc gracili curvatur arundine corpus
Lentius, æquaretque humeros arrecta securis.

At genitrix, serræ stridentia lamina captans,
Exierat lecto, sensimque ingressa silensque,
Multa laborantem et versantem ingentia ligna
Conspexit puerum pendens . . . ; pressisque labellis
Spectabat, natumque suum complexa sereno
Intuitu, tremulis errabant murmura labris;
Lucebant risus lacrymis . . . At serra repente

Frangitur, et digitos incauti vulnere fædat:
Candida purpureo maculatum sanguine vestis...
Exsilit ore levis gemitus; matremque repente
Respiciens, digitos condit sub veste rubentes
Atque arridenti similis, matrem ore salutat.
. . . .

At genibus nati Genitrix allapsa fovebat
Heu! digitos digitis, teneris dabat oscula palmis,
Multa gemens, guttisque humectans grandibus ora.
At puer immotus: «Quid ploras, nescia mater?
Quod tetigit digitos acies extrema securis?...
Non jam tempus adest quo te plorare decebit!»
Tum cæptum repetivit opus, materque silescens
Candentes ad humum demisit pallida vultus,
Multa putans, rursusque in natum tristia tollens
Lumina: «Summe Deus, fiat tua sancta voluntas!»

A. Rimbaud.

VERBA APOLLONII DE MARCO CICERONE

Audistis hanc, discipuli, Ciceronis orationem, in qua fecit, ut omnino græcus in graeca oratione, ut in vana re verus, ut in schola minime scholasticus videretur: Quanta jam in argumento prudentia, quantum in narratione acumen et judicium, quam vivida, quam paqhtic˜h peroratio! At quanta praesertim in dicendo concinnitas et abundantia; quantus verborum numerus! Quanta magnificentia sententiae devolvuntur! non Ciceronem omnibus suis natura donis nequidquam ornatum voluit: poscit illum Roma, qui Gracchorum, qui Bruti eloquentiam revocet: poscunt veræ ad tribunal causae, quibus nunc praedatores arguat, nunc innocentiae, forsan et litterarum causam resuscitet. Macte igitur, adolescens: qui nunc vocem intra scholam hanc emittis, modo in foro concionari poteris, et persuasum habeo, te non majores a plebe, quam nunc a me, plausus percepturum. Me nempe gloriari licet, quod talis orator e schola mea evadat; hoc maximum mihi decus erit, te optimarum artium disciplina et studio formavisse, vel ipsius ingenii adolescentiam observavisse: quod majus dulcius ve mihi pretium esse potest, quam quod Ciceronis magister fuisse dicar? haec forsan mihi et apud posteros laus supererit. Vos autem, discipuli, satis justos esse reor, qui Ciceronis praestantiam egregiasque virtutes agnoscatis. Illum igitur eisdem, quibus ego, laudibus ornate, praesertimque imitemini: nempe vobis olim cum Cicerone studuisse gloriosum erit.

Sed in tanta lætitia nescio quis maeror subit et desiderium; nec, etsi ingenium eloquentiamque maximis laudibus ea tollere non dubito, Marcum Tullium Romanum esse possum oblivisci. Romanus es, qui ceteris istis praestat discipulis! Romanum ego informavi et exercui! Graecia Romanorum armis jam tota victa est; quæ libertatis jacturam studio solari poterat, et se terrarum orbi si non armis, ingenio saltem dominari rebatur; ultimo illi solatio, illi dominationi, Romani, invidetis; et nos a litterarum fastigio deturbare, et quod unum vobis hactenus alienum erat, vestrum facere vultis! Romani quondam opes, Corintho ceterisque Graeciae urbibus expugnatis, eripuere, tabulas, aurum atque argentum Romae transtulere, quibus nunc templa nunc publicae aedes exornantur: mox et gloriam eripient, quae urbium expugnationi supererat, inter patriae ruinam integra! dum scriptores nostros vel non imitandos remur, dum Periclis aetatem unicam fore persuasum habemus, en altera aetas Romae incipit aemulari, quae vates, quamvis Sophoclem Euripidemque Periclis una aetas tulerit, quae oratores, quamvis illa Lysiam et Isocratem, quae philosophos, quamvis Platonem et Xenophonta, majores pariat et doctrina magis imbutos pariat! Nec dubium est, quin de graecis litteris jam Roma triumphet: jampridem nobis aemulatur, quippe quae Plautium Rudium Aristophani illi nostro, Terentiumque suum Menandro illi composuerit: nempe Terentius ille, quem apud nos jam celeberrimum video, quum dimidiatus Menander vocetur, in summis poneretur, Graecisque forsan non impar esset, si tam concinni quam puro sermoni vim comicam adjecisset: Quin etiam nova genera instituunt; satyram totam suam esse contendunt: primus nempe Lucilius mores hoc modo castigare docuit, nec dubium est, quin alii vates illud genus mox retractent illustrentque. Quod vero de oratoribus loquar? Nonne jam Gracchorum ingenium et eloquentiam, nonne Bruti illius oratoris facundiam audivistis? nonne tu quoque, Marce Tulli, orato-ribus nostris aemularis? Hoc est igitur, quod nos quidem Romanos adolescentes e Roma in nostram hanc Graeciam transmigrantes intra scholas gymnasiaque accipimus, et optimarum artium studiis ac disciplina formamus, et praeclarorum oratorum exemplo erudimus? Nempe, si dii ita jusserunt, ut nobis ipsi victores instituamus, jam de Graecis litteris actum erit: Romanis enim ad pugnam nova omnia; nos autem degeneres ac scholastici sumus; quid aliud quam veteres laudamus miramurque? Nulli jam in Graecia futuri sunt oratores, nulli vates futuri sunt; Roma autem novis nunc et egregiis scriptoribus gravis: ita ut omnino jam extinctum Graecum ingenium esse videatur. Quomodo enim aliter accedere potuisset? Quid ego nunc queror, quod vos victores fore praevideo, ac non eloquentiam cum libertate nostra simul amissam potius fateor: floruit vere eloquentia, quum liberi rem nostram gerebamus; nune, contrita et pedibus calcata libertate, impositi proconsulis vectigales sumus: Scilicet Pericles ille noster cæsos pro patria cives laudabat: nos pro Romano imperio abductos et caesos in extremis terrarum orbis partibus cives laudaremus? Scilicet Demosthenes Philippum vehementissimis impugnabat sermonibus, urbisque proditores infames faciebat; nos hostem nunc impugnaremus, qui patriam hosti tradidimus? Floruit eloquentia, quum leges in foro promulgarentur quum singuli oratores concionabundi, Deos patrios, plebem virorum simulacra alloquerentur: nunc leges nobis a Romano proconsule imponuntur, nec est, quod obsistamus! perit inter lictorum virgas, ut libertas, eloquentia: nîl jam nisi veterum scripta versare, et quæ in foro declamabantur, legere possumus: non jam de rebus nostris disserimus; at nescio quæ vana et arcessita tractamus, quae victoribus nostris haud nefas videantur! Olim Romae quoque Tullii desideriumerit, quum, a tyrannis e foro in scholam expelletur eloquentia: libertatis enim eloquentia vox est; quomodo igitur eloquentia tyrannorum jugum importunum pati posset?

Hoc ne vos tamen a studiis deterreat, discipuli, et quos semper studiosos compertus sum, eosdem semper comperiar; nobis quidem nullum amissae gloriae solatium est, quippe qui virorum nostrorum simulacra etiam amiserimus; nonne, si memoriam revocaremus illorum temporum, quibus omni rerum copia florebamus, quam velut ex uberrimis fontibus in universum etiam orbem profundebant tot illæ civitates et coloniae nostrae; quibus totam Asiam, imo fere totam Italiam subegimus, quid aliud quam desiderium subiret, quum gloriae et prosperitatis memores essemus, quam ira et dolor, quum præsentem servitutem res quam luctus maerorque, quum quae fata Galliam nostram maneant, conspiceremus. Gloriam itaque, quando ab ineluctabili superorum lege ita decretum est, ut Graecia illa virorum parens et nutrix, nunc domita et despecta jaceat, gloriam a memoria omnino abjiciamus! Supererit litterarum nobis solatium doctrinaeque studium, quod vel in dolore laetitia, vel in servitute nescio quæ libertatis umbra redditur; oculos ab hac nostra humilitate in illam veterum scriptorum dignitatem deferemus: et inter illorum libros semoti, nunc Homeri, nunc Platonis, non jam de rebus publicis, quod ad alios nunc pertinet, at de carmine, de diis immortalibus, de omnibus scilicet, quibus illi mire disseruere, dulci colloquio fruemur! Tu quoque, Tulli, quem tam egregio ingenio praeditum compertus sum, meam hanc tui exspectationem, si diis libet, quum in patriam redux forum experiere, non falles; at inter populares plausus, noli hujus Apollonii Graeci, qui te optimarum artium studio disciplinaque formavit, memoriam abjicere, et hoc semper persuasum habeto, nanquam te majorem quam ego, ex illis plausibus latitiam superbiamque percepturum!

Rimbaud.

INVOCATION À VÉNUS

Mère des fils d'Énée, ô délices des Dieux,
Délices des mortels, sous les astres des cieux,
Vénus, tu peuples tout: l'onde où court le navire,
Le sol fécond: par toi tout être qui respire
Germe, se dresse, et voit le soleil lumineux!
Tu parais... À l'aspect de ton front radieux
Disparaissent les vents et les sombres nuages:
L'Océan te sourit; fertile en beaux ouvrages,
La Terre étend les fleurs suaves sous tes pieds;

Le jour brille plus pur sous les cieux azurés!
Dès qu'Avril reparaît, et, qu'enflé de jeunesse,
Prêt à porter à tous une douce tendresse,
Le souffle du zéphir a forcé sa prison,
Le peuple aérien annonce ta saison:
L'oiseau charmé subit ton pouvoir, ô Déesse;
Le sauvage troupeau bondit dans l'herbe épaisse,
Et fend l'onde à la nage, et tout être vivant,
À ta grâce enchaîné, brûle en te poursuivant!
C'est toi qui, par les mers, les torrents, les montagnes,
Les bois peuplés de nids et les vertes campagnes,
Versant au cœur de tous l'amour cher et puissant,
Les portes d'âge en âge à propager leur sang!
Le monde ne connaît, Vénus, que ton empire!
Rien ne pourrait sans toi se lever vers le jour:
Nul n'inspire sans toi, ni ne ressent d'amour!
À ton divin concours dans mon œuvre j'aspire!...

A. Rimbaud.
Externe au collège de Charleville.

"SIRE, LE TEMPS A LAISSÉ..."

Sire, le temps a laissé son manteau de pluie; les fouriers d'été sont venus: donnons l'huys au visage à Mérencolie! Vivent les lays et ballades! moralités et joyeulsetés! Que les clercs de la basoche nous montent les folles soties: allons ouyr la moralité du Bien-Advisé et Mal-Advisé, et la conversion du clerc Théophilus, et come alèrent à Rome Saint Père et Saint Pol, et comment furent martirez! Vivent les dames à rebrassés collets, portant atours et broderyes! N'est-ce pas, Sire, qu'il fait bon dire sous les arbres, quand les cieux sont vêtus de bleu, quand le soleil cler luit, les doux rondeaux, les ballades haut et cler chantées? *J'ai une arbre de la plante d'amours,* ou *Une fois me dites ouy, ma dame,* ou *Riche amoureux a toujours l'advantage*... Mais me voilà bien esbaudi, Sire, et vous allez l'être comme moi: Maistre François Villon, le bon folastre, le gentil raillart qui rima tout cela, engrillonné, nourri d'une miche et d'eau, pleure et se lamente maintenant au fond du Châtelet! Pendu serez! lui a-t-on dit devant notaire: et le pauvre folet tout transi a fait son épitaphe pour lui et ses compagnons: et les gratieux gallans dont vous aimez tant les rimes, s'attendent danser à Montfaulcon, plus becquetés d'oiseaux que dés à coudre, dans la bruine et le soleil!

Oh! Sire, ce n'est pas pour folle plaisance qu'est là Villon! Pauvres housseurs ont assez de peine! Clergeons attendant leur nomination de l'Université, musards, montreurs de synges, joueurs de rebec qui payent leur escot en chansons, chevaucheurs d'escuryes, sires de deux écus, reîtres cachant leur nez en pots d'étain mieux qu'en casques de guerre*; tous ces pauvres enfants secs et noirs comme escouvillons, qui ne voient de pain qu'aux fenêtres, que l'hiver emmitoufle d'onglée, ont choisi maistre François pour mère nourricière! Or nécessité fait gens méprendre, et faim saillir le loup du bois: peut-être l'Escollier, ung jour de famine, a-t-il pris des tripes au baquet des bouchers, pour les fricasser à l'Abreuvoir Popin ou à la taverne du Pestel? Peut-être a-t-il pipé une douzaine de pains au boulanger, ou changé à la Pomme du Pin un broc d'eau claire pour un broc de vin de Baigneux? Peut-être, un soir de grande galle au Plat-d'Étain, a-t-il rossé le guet à son arrivée; ou les a-t-on surpris, autour de Montfaulcon, dans un souper conquis par noise, avec une dixaine de ribaudes? Ce sont les méfaits de maistre François! Parce qu'il nous montre ung gras chanoine mignonnant avec sa dame en chambre bien nattée, parce qu'il dit que le chappelain n'a cure de confesser, sinon chambrières et dames, et qu'il conseille aux dévotes, par bonne mocque, parler contemplation sous les courtines, l'escollier fol, si bien riant, si bien chantant, gent comme esmerillon, tremble sous les griffes des grands juges, ces terribles oiseaux noirs que suivent corbeaux et pies! Lui et ses compagnons, pauvres piteux! accrocheront un nouveau chapelet de pendus aux bras de la forêt: le vent leur fera chandeaux dans le doux feuillage sonore: et vous, Sire, et tous ceux qui aiment le poète, ne pourront rire qu'en pleurs en lisant ses joyeuses ballades: ils songeront qu'ils ont laissé mourir le gentil clerc qui chantait si follement, et ne pourront chasser Mérencolie!

Pipeur, larron, maistre François est pourtant le meilleur fils du monde: il rit des grasses souppes jacobines: mais il honore ce qu'a honoré l'église de Dieu, et madame la vierge, et la très sainte trinité! Il honore la Cour de Parlement, mère des bons, et sœur des benoitz anges; aux médisants du royaume de France, il veut presque autant de mal qu'aux taverniers qui brouillent le vin. Et dea! Il sait bien qu'il a trop gallé au temps de sa jeunesse folle! L'hiver, les soirs de famine, auprès de la fontaine Maubuay ou dans quelque piscine ruinée, assis à croppetons devant petit feu de chenevottes, qui flambe par instants pour rougir sa face maigre, il songe qu'il aurait maison et couche molle, s'il eût estudié!... Souvent, noir et flou comme chevaucheur d'escovettes, il regarde dans les logis par des mortaises: «—Ô, ces morceaulx savoureux et frians! ces tartes, ces flans, ces grasses gelines dorées!—Je suis plus affamé que Tantalus!—Du rost! du rost!—Oh! cela sent plus doux qu'ambre et civettes!—Du vin de Beaulne dans de grandes aiguières d'argent!—Haro, la gorge m'ard!... Ô, si j'eusse estudié!...—Et mes chausses qui tirent la langue, et ma hucque qui ouvre toutes ses fenêtres, et mon feautre en dents de scie~!—Si je rencontrais un piteux Alexander, pour que je puisse, bien recueilli, bien débouté, chanter à mon aise comme Orpheus le doux ménétrier! Si je pouvais vivre en honneur une fois avant que de mourir!...» Mais, voilà: souper de

*Olivier Basselin, *Vaux-de-Vire.*

rondeaux, d'effets de lune sur les vieux toits, d'effets de lanternes sur le sol, c'est très maigre, très maigre; puis passent, en justes cottes, les mignottes villotières qui font chosettes mignardes pour attirer les passants; puis le regret des tavernes flamboyantes, pleines du cri des buveurs heurtant les pots d'étain et souvent les flamberges, du ricanement des ribaudes, et du chant aspre des rebecs mendiants; le regret des vieilles ruelles noires où saillent follement, pour s'embrasser, des étages de maisons et des poutres énormes; où, dans la nuit épaisse, passent, avec des sons de rapières traînées, des rires et des braieries abominables... Et l'oiseau rentre au vieux nid: Tout aux tavernes et aux filles!...

Oh! Sire, ne pouvoir mettre plumail au vent par ce temps de joie! La corde est bien triste en mai, quand tout chante, quand tout rit, quand le soleil rayonne sur les murs les plus lépreux! Pendus seront, pour une franche repeue! Villon est aux mains de la Cour de Parlement: le corbel n'écoutera pas le petit oiseau! Sire, ce serait vraiment méfait de pendre ces gentils clercs: ces poètes-là, voyez-vous, ne sont pas d'ici-bas: laissez-les vivre leur vie étrange; laissez-les avoir froid et faim, laissez-les courir, aimer et chanter: ils sont aussi riches que Jacques Cœur, tous ces fols enfants, car ils ont des rimes plein l'âme, des rimes qui rient et qui pleurent, qui nous font rire ou pleurer: Laissez-les vivre: Dieu bénit tous les miséricords, et le monde bénit les poètes.

A. Rimbaud.
(Printemps de 1870.)

II. D'UN CAHIER D'ÉCOLIER

[1, 1re]

conspecto, Tunc legatus sic
allocatus est vela corpus imquit, ut
proferam tibi mandate senatus
populique romani,
Aristomene se souleve, etend
sa main et rencontre la peau
velue d'unanimal de grande
taille. c'était un renard que l'odeur
des cadavres attirait et qui faisait
sa pature habituelle des malheureux
précipités dans le gouffre. alors une
lieur d'espoir, quelque legere que'lle
fut, brilla pour aristome il jugea
que cet animal devait connaitre
une issue et qu'il pourrait se tirer
ainsi de ce lieu d'horreur. il saisit aussitot
la queue du renard qui se retoura pour
le mordre mais aristomene lui presenta
la partie anterieure de son bras gauche
recouverte d'un lambeau d'etoffe qu'il
avait ● ramassé pour se couvrir la
nuit. le renard, desesperant de
vaincre son ennemi, que ne pouvai.... ●
arrenter ni les contusions camsées
par les anfractuosités des rochers, ni
les affreuses dechirures que lui faisai......
les ronces et les epines, il finit par apercevoir
un orifice aveuglé par ou passait la
lumiere et par où penetra... sans doute
le renards: alors aristomene le lâcha et

cherchait a fuir mais en meme temps
il entraînait presque alors aisto

pavenu a cette ouverture, il l'agrandit avec toute la fougue possible. Pour l'espoir de la vie et l'amour de la liberté, il alla aussitôt rejoindre (les) Lacedonom, se mit de nouvea.....

[1, 2e]

a leur tête, et apparut aux Lacédémoniens comme une vision vengeresse, sortie pour les punir de leur odieuse lacheté

Creseus

Creseus va n'oser se conformer aux recommandations de l'oracle, quoiqu'il eut pleine confiance qu'avec ses seules forces il serait en etat de vaincre Cyrus, eut soin d'envoyer des ambassadeurs a Sparte, pour engager les lacedemoniens a faire alliance avec eux ils parlerent aimsi: «Creseus, roi des lydiens, vous dit par notre bouche: ô Lacedemoniens, Le dieu de Delphes m'a ordonné de contracter amitié avec les Grecs, et je m'adresse a vous parce que j'apprends que vous êtes le 1∞ peuple de la Grece. je desire que nous fassions alliance sans fraude ni tromperie: rien ne s'opposera a ce que les lacedemoniens, avides de gloire acceptassent les proposition du roi des lydiens; d'ailleus ils avaient entendu la reponse de l'oracle, et ils furent bien flattés de ce que les lydiens étaient venu chez eux aussi ne fait-il pas difficile de les persuader d'entrer dans l'amitié de Creseus, et ils promiren.....de lui envoyer d'abord des deputés, et bientôt après un corps d'arme.....

Creseus

de revenir a sardes de venir en

toure . . . . . . Laceda . . . . . . pendant que
roi de Babiylone, n'ouv.....
Mais Cyrus n'attendit pas quils eussent
recu tous ces renforts,

[2, 1re]

de petites mouches si Jolies que l'envie
me prit de les decrire. le lendemain
j'en vis d'une autre sorte que je decriv
j'en observai ainsi pendant trois sema
trente sept espèces toutes extrême
ment différente mais il en
vint a la fin un si grand
nombre et d'aussi grande variété,
que je laissai là cette études
quoique très amusante, parceque
je manquais de loisir, ou, pour
dire la verité, d'expressions. les
mouches que j'avais obsevees
etaient toutes distingues l'une
de l'autre par leur couleurs,
leurs formes et leurs allur . . . . . .
il y en avait de dorees,
dargentées, ou bronzées,
de tigrées, de rayées
de bleu, de verte de
rembrunies de chatoyantes
les unes avaient le tete
arrondie comme un turban
les autres alongées en pointes
chez quelques unes elles parais
saient obscures comme
un coin de velour noir
et elle étincelait ●
d'autres comme ●
rubis il n'y avait pas moi . . . . . .
de variétes dans leur aile';
Quelques unes en avaient
de longues et de brillantes
comme des lames de nacre
d'autre, de courtes et de larges

qui ressemblaient a des
réseaux de la plus
fine gaze celles ci

[2, 2e]

planaient tourbillonnant
celles là s'élevaient en
se dirigent contre le vent,
par un mecanisme a peu
près semblable a celui des
cerfs volants de papier
qui s'elevent, en faisant
avec l'axe du vent
un angle, je crois, de
degrés et demi

[4, 1re]

nullius il n'est aucun animal excepté l'hom● qui ait quelque est notion de dieu mais parmi les homm il n'est aucune nation si sauvage que celle qui ne sent que il existe un Dieu mais parceque dans toutes chose ●e consentement des nations on doit avouer que quelque puissance divine existe L'habitude de disputer contre les dieux est mauvaise et inique soit que cela soit fait sérieusement soit en plaisantan c'est pourquoi protagoras le plus grand sophiste de son temps nia au commencement q d'un livre que les dieux existaient, et fut chassé de la ville sur l'ordre des Atheniens et ses livres furent brules sur les places publiques. On raconte meme qu'on avait promis un talent d'argent a celui qui le tuerait ainsi nenne le doute de l'existence des dieux ne put eviter son chatiment qui est si intense que celui qui, lorsqu'il ara vu le ciel ne sente pas que il est un dieu. la beauté du monde l'ordre des choses et les revolutions du soleil de la lune et de tous les astres indiqu...... assez par leur aspect q. ne sont pas l'effet du hasard et nous prouve avec quel que quelque nature superieure et eternelle existe qui doit étre ●admirer par le genre humain
rimbaud arthur *deinde pendata gens indica nonne petebent* A
rimbaud arthur *deinde pendata gens indica nonne petebent* A
deinde
deinde Secur quod est preciperam
Secur quod est preciperam
Secur quod est preciperam
Secur quod est preciperam
Secur quod est preciperam
Secur quod est preciperam
Secur quod est preciperam

Secur quod est preciperam
Secur quod est preciperam
Secur quod est preciperam

[5, 1re]

Lousque la replubblique romaine fut administrée par ceux auxquels elle s'était confiée, Ciceron lui portait toute ses pensées et ses soins et il mettait plus de soin a agir qu'a ecrire Lorsque le pouvoir tomba aux mains de Jules Cesars il ne s'abandonna pas aux chagrins par lesquels il était accablé, ni auxplaisirs d'un homme indigne

Arthur
Les infiniments petis

Quelques petits que fussent ces insectes, ils etaient dignes de mon attention, puisque ils avaient herité celle du createur. je continuai donc mes observations, toutes inexactes qu'elles devaient ètre; car je devais toujours ignorer quels etaient les insectes qui frequentaient mon fraisier pendant la nuit, attirés peut-etre par des lumieres phosphoriques qui nous echappent. en examinant de plus pres les feuilles de ● on vegetal au moyen d'un micros copie, je les trouvai divisées en compartiments herissés de poil et separés par des canaux...... ces compartiments m'ont paru semblables a de grands tapis de verdure et leurs poiles a des végétaux, parmi lesquels il y en avait de droits d'enfilés de fourchus Or, la nature n'a rien fait en vain. quand elle dispose des lieux propres a ètre habités, elle y met des animaux. ce n'est jamais elle qu'on verra borner par un espace resserré; on peut donc croire, sans f● d'hypothèse que il y a des animaux

[5, 2e]

qui pessent sur les feuilles de Art
plantes comme les bestiaux

dans nos prairies; qui se
couchent à l'ombre de leurs
arbr. inperceptibles et qui
trouvent dans des plaines
de quelques millimètres
des spectacles dont nous n'avo……
pas l'idée les antères jaunes
des fleurs, suspendue.....sur
des filets blancs, leur présentent
des doubles solives d'or en
equilibre sur des colonnes
plus belles que l'ivoire poli;
les corolles des voutes de rubis et
de topazie d'une grandeur
incommensurable; les nectars
des fleuves de sucre; les autres parties
de la floraison des coupes, des
urnes, des pavillons, des domes
que l'architecture ni l'orfevreri……
des hommes n'ont point encore
imités.
on trouve dans les discours
invenitur in virtutes
de Caton toutes les qualités
Catoni omes qualitates
de l'orateur. on dit que les abeilles
auctoris
ont un roi. Quand on sert les lois
on sert Dieu, on rapporte
que le lion s'epouvante
au chant du coq. quand
on aime les autes on a suf
fisamant de vertus.
Quand on donne au pauvre,
on donne a Dieu de meme

[6, 1re]

On vend sa liberté quand on
accepte un bienfait. quand
on interroge avec fourberie,
on ne merite pas d'entendre

la vérité. on peut à peine
changer l'opinion du vul
gaire quand on desire la paix,
on prepare la guerre on ne s'est
jamais repenti d'avoir gardé
le silence. dans les choses grandes
et dignes de memoire, on exami
ne d'abord les projets, ensuite les
succès

Arthur

[7, 1re]

Quand Esope etait l'esclave d'un tiran,
il lui fut ordonné de preparer le diner.
Cherchant donc du feu, il alla de maison......
en maisons. enfin il trouva où
poser sa lanterne
●
peut tu te croire egale a moi toi et moi
● n'avons certes pas obtenu la meme
Destinée, moi je passe ma
vie dans les temples dans les palais
des rois, où il me plait. je me fais 14
rien, et je jouis des meilleures choses 13
toi aucontraire tu travailles sans 2
relache et tu mene une existence 2
fort dure». La fourmi repondit: «tu 3
ne fais rien, il est vrai et tu jouis mainte —
nant de beaucoup d'avantages; mais 34
quand la saison rigoureuse sera venue,
ton sort sera bien changé alors le froid
et la faim t'auront bientôt emporté
moi, aucontraire, je trouverai une maison
bien pourvue et je passerai l'hiver
en securité. il est glorieux, dis tu, de
vivre parmi les rois et les dieux; il est plus
utile et plus sur de travailler.»

[7, 2e]

quelle est la contenance d'une piece de terre de la longueur
de 252 m 80 et de la largeur de 78 m 600 au bout et 84 m 20 à l'ai

si on a payé 20 litres 3250 dites quel est le prix de 7 deci

Si on a payé 2 steres de bois

Esope (suiite
alors, parce qu'il avait été tres longtemps
a continuer son chemin, il se hata
de revenir par la place alors un bavard

de la foule lui dit: Esope, que fais tu en plein midi avec une lanterne je cherche un homme, dit il et il se hata de s'en aller a la maison

[8, 1re]

Si on a payé deux steres de bois 32 f
combien couteront 7 decisteres

32	2		1 f 60
12	16	10	7
00	60	1 f 60	11,30
		000	

àmesure que l'homme approche
des elements de la matiere, les principes
de sa science s'evanouissent et
quand il cherche a avancer dans
l'espace de l'infini, son intelli
gence confondue se perd a la vue
de tant de merveilles d'un ordre
different. en effet, prenez une loupe,
et voyez la matiere redoubler, pour
ainsidire, de soins a mesure que
ses œuvres diminuent de volume
voyez l'or, la pourpre, l'azur, la nacre
et tous les emaux, dont elle embellit
quelquefois la cuirasse du plus vil
insecte. voyez le reseau chatoyant
dont elle tapisse l'aile du Ciron
voyez cette multitude d'yeux, ces
diademes clairvoyants dont elle
s'est plu a ceindre la tete de la

mouche il semble a qui......
contemple la creation, qui avec
delicatesse essaye partout de
l'emporter sur la magnifi
cence. l'œil de la baleine ou
de l'elephant presente a l'exam

[8, 2e]

des details que leur petitesse
derobent a nos regards; et ces
details ne sont pas, a beaucoup près,
les derniers où le travail sarrete
art
Dans la genese, les commence
ments du monde ont été ainsi
racontés par moise. la lumiere,
dit-il virgule, le firmament
la terre les plantes, le soleil,
les poissons, les oiseaux et
tous les animaux furent suc
cessivement crées par Dieu
puis l'homme fut fait.
Adam, ce premier homme,
et eve, la premiere fenne,
furent placées dans un jardin
délicieux, là ils étaient libre......
et heureux. mais ce bonheur
ne fut pas de longue durée.
Eve fut séduite par le serpent,
adam fut entrainé par Eve dans
le mal; l'epoux et l'epouse
coupables furent chassés
du paradis par le seigneur......
irrité et dès lors le travail......
la douleur, les maladies, les mau......
et toutes les miseres furent
attachés a eux.
Le prejugé
les athemiens etaient reunis dans
un theatre, appelés a juger un
celebre histrion qui s'etait

dejà fait une grande reno……
mée dans les differentes villes
de la grèce, par l'adresse qu'il
deployait a imiter le cri

[9, 1re]

des animaux, j'essayerais en vain de vous
depeindre l'enthousiasme avec lequel
on accueillait on accueillait sa présence
c'etait des applaudissements, des arth
trepignemants des rires entrainants
auxquels tout le monde aurait cédé:
l'homme morose que rien ne recreerait
aurait été forcé de rire et d'applaudir
comme les autres. cependant, au milieu
de la satisfaction et de la joie gene
rale, un paysan trouva a redire, et se
plaignit d'une admiration qu'il re
gardait comme peu méritée je projette,
dit-il, de vous prouver que cet homme
ne merite pas que vous le louiez, ni
que vous le choyiez tant.

Les maximes
fili mi ne judicas homines
quun vides illorum conspectun
nam saepe, si divites sunt, mali
sunt. Rimbaud athur de Charleville
n° loqueris hominis impis nam
mox illi similis eris
volo tibi fabulam narrare
ut conservas prœceptum
discipulus posuerat malum ma
lam in mensà et circum mi
serat aliorum malorum
bonarum mox illœ malœ
fient. est sic hominis
frequentas impias. arthur……

Le cerf et les bœu……
un cerf chassé des forets
qui lui servaient de retraite gagna
avec une crainte aveugle la

ferme voisine afin d'eviter la
mort imminente dont le mena
caient les chasseurs et se cacha
dans un etable a bœufs qui s'offrit
a lui fort a propos. Rimbaud arthur
charleville *illusar ipse ab illud isp*......
iniqui serius aut ocius dant pœmas
malifici

[10, 1re]

I
Prologue

Le soleil était encore chaud;
cependant il n'eclairait pres
queplus la teirre; comme
un flambeau placé devant
les voutes gigantesque ne les
eclaire plus que par une
faible lueur ainsi le so
leil flambeau terrestre
s'eteignait en laissant echap
per de son corps de feu une
dernière et faible lueur
laissant encore cependant
voir les feuilles vertes des ar
bres les petites fleurs qui se
fletrissaient et le somnet
gigantesque des pins, des
peupliers et des chenes séculai
res. le vent rafraichissant, c'est
a dire une brise fraiche agitait
les feuilles des arbres avec un bruis
sement apeuprès semblable
a celui que faisait le bruit des
eaux argentées du ruisseau qui
coulait a mes pieds. les fougeres
courbaient leur front vert devan......
le vent, je m'endormis non
sans métre abreuvé de l'eau
du ruisseau. II

je rêvai que . . . .
. . . .

. . . j'etais né a Reims l'an 1503
Reims etait alors une petite ville
où pour mieux dire un bourg
cependant renommé a cause de
sa belle cathedrale, temoin
du sacre du roi Clovis.

[10, 2e]

Mes parents etaient peu riches
mais très honnetes; il n'avaient
pour tout bien qu'une petite
maison qui leur avait tou
jours appartenu et qui etait
en leur possession vingt
ans avant que je ne fus encore
né en plus quelques mille francs
et il faut encore y ajouter les
petites louis provenant des eco
nomies de ma mere . . . . . .
mon père etait officier dans
les armées du roi, c'était un
homme grand, maigre,
chevelure noire, barbe, yeux, peau
de mem couleur. . . . . .quoi qu'il
n'eût guère quand je suis né
que 48 ou cinquante ans on
lui en aurait certainement . . . . . .
bien donné 60 ou . . . . . . 58 il etait
d'un caractère vif, bouillant,
souvent en colère et ne voulant
rien souffrir qui lui deplut
ma mere etait bien diffe
rente femme douce, calme,
s'effrayant de peu de chose, et
cependant tenant la maison dans
un ordre parfait..elle etait
si calme, que mon père l'a
musait comme une jeune
demoiselle. j'etais le plus

aimé mes frères etaient moins
vaillants que moi et cepen
dant plus grands: j'aimais peu
l'etude c'est a dire d'apprendre
a lire, écrire et compter......

[11, 1re]

mais si c'etait pour arranger une mai
son, cultiver un jardin, faire des
commissions, a la bonne heure, je
me plaisais a cela.
je me rappelle encore qu'un jour
monpère m'avait promis vingt
sous si je lui faisais bien une
division; je commençai; mais je
ne pus finir. ah! combien de fois
ne m'a-t-il pas promis de......sous
des jouets des friandises meme
un fois cinq francs si je pouvais
lui......lire quelque chose......mal
gré cela mon père me nit en
classe des que j'eus 10 ans.
pourquoi, me disais-je, apprendre du
grec du latin? je ne le sais. enfin
on n'a pas besoin de cela que m'in
porte a moi, que je sois reçu......a quoi
cela sert-il d'être recu a rien n'estce
pas? si pourtant on dit qu'on n'a
une place que lorsqu'on est reçu moi
je ne veux pas de place je serai rentier
quand menne on en voudrait une
pourquoi apprendre le latin; person
nene parle cette langue quelquefois
j'en vois sur les journaux mais
Dieu merci je ne serai pas journaliste
pourquoi apprendre et de l'histoire
et de la geographie? on a il est vrai
besoin de savoir que paris est en france
mais on ne demande pas a quel
degré de latitude del'histoire
apprendre la vie de Chinaldon

de nabopolassar de Darius de
Cyrus et d'alexandre

[11, 2e]

et de leurs autres comperes remarquables
par leurs noms diabolique, est un sup
plice?
Que m'inporte moiqu'alexandre
ait été célebre? que m'inporte... 2
que sait-on si les latins ont existé?
c'est peut-etre quel que langue forgée
et quand meme ils auraient existé
qu'ils me laissent rentier et conservent
leur langue pour eux. quel mal leur
—ai-je fait pour qu'ils me flanquent
au supplice. passonsau grec.... cette
sale langue n'est parlée par personne
personne au monde!......
ah saperlipotte de saperlopopette ●
sapristi moi je serai rentier il ne fait
pas si bon de s'user les culottes sur les bancs......
saperlipopettouille!
pour etre decrotteur gagner la place de
decrotteuril faut passer un exanen
car les places qui vous sont accordées sont
d'être ou décrotteur ou porcher ou bouvier
dieu merci je n'en veux pas moi
saperlipouille!
avec ça des soufflets vous sont acco
dés pour recompense on vous appelle
animal ce qui n'est pas vrai
bout d'homme etc
La suite prochainement
ah saperpouillotte!»
Arth......

[12, 2e]

III
post vivenda res, expectas finem.
Le pacte
il me reste encore des choses a

ecrire mais je m'en abstiens
sciemment 1∞ de peur que je ne
te paraisse importun qui' occupe
la grande varieté de tes affair
ensuite, si quelque'un veut essayer
par hasard la meme chose,
il trouve des exemples dans le
teste de l'ouvrage car la natiere
abonde tellement que c'est
plutôt le'artisan qui manque au
travail que le travail à l'artisan [...]

III. FRAGMENTS ET RECONSTITUTIONS

A. FRAGMENTS DE RIMBAUD

CREDO IN UNAM

. . . .

Ô! L'Homme a relevé sa tête libre et fière!
Et le rayon soudain de la beauté première
Fait palpiter le dieu dans l'autel de la chair!
Heureux du bien présent, pâle du mal souffert,
L'Homme veut tout sonder,—et savoir! La Pensée,
La cavale longtemps, si longtemps oppressée
S'élance de son front! Elle saura Pourquoi!...
Qu'elle bondisse libre, et l'Homme aura la Foi!
—Pourquoi l'azur muet et l'espace insondable?
Pourquoi les astres d'or fourmillant comme un sable?
Si l'on montait toujours, que verrait-on là-haut?
Un Pasteur mène-t-il cet immense troupeau
De mondes cheminant dans l'horreur de l'espace?
Et tous ces mondes-là, que l'éther vaste embrasse,
Vibrent-ils aux accents d'une éternelle voix?
—Et l'Homme, peut-il voir? peut-il dire: Je crois?
La voix de la pensée est-elle plus qu'un rêve?
Si l'homme naît si tôt, si la vie est si brève,
D'où vient-il? Sombre-t-il dans l'Océan profond
Des Germes, des Fœtus, des Embryons, au fond
De l'immense Creuset d'où la Mère-Nature
Le ressuscitera, vivante créature,
Pour aimer dans la rose, et croître dans les blés?...

Nous ne pouvons savoir!—Nous sommes accablés
D'un manteau d'ignorance et d'étroites chimères!
Singes d'hommes tombés de la vulve des mères,
Notre pâle raison nous cache l'infini!

Nous voulons regarder:—le Doute nous punit!
Le doute, morne oiseau, nous frappe de son aile . . .
—Et l'horizon s'enfuit d'une fuite éternelle! . . .
. . . .

Le grand ciel est ouvert! les mystères sont morts
Devant l'Homme, debout, qui croise ses bras forts
Dans l'immense splendeur de la riche nature!
Il chante . . . et le bois chante, et le fleuve murmure
Un chant plein de bonheur qui monte vers le jour! . . .
—C'est la Rédemption! c'est l'amour! c'est l'amour! . . .
. . . .

"L'ENFANT QUI RAMASSA LES BALLES . . ."

L'Enfant qui ramassa les balles, le Pubère
Où circule le sang de l'exil et d'un Père
Illustre entend germer sa vie avec l'espoir
De sa figure et de sa stature et veut voir
Des rideaux autres que ceux du Trône et des Crèches.
Aussi son buste exquis n'aspire pas aux brèches
De l'Avenir!—Il a laissé l'ancien jouet.—
O son doux rêve ô son bel Enghien*! Son œil est
Approfondi par quelque immense solitude;
«Pauvre jeune homme, il a sans doute l'Habitude!»

François Coppée
†

"ON A FAIM DANS LA CHAMBRÉE . . ."

On a faim dans la chambrée —
        C'est vrai . . .
    Émanations, explosions. Un génie:
    «Je suis le gruère! —
Lefêbvre: «Keller!»
Le Génie: «Je suis le Brie!»
Les soldats coupent sur leur pain:
        «C'est la vie!

---

*parce que: «Enghien chez soi»!

Le Génie — «Je suis le Roquefort!
　　— «Ça s'ra not' mort! . . .
　　— Je suis le gruère
　　Et la Brie . . . etc.
　　—Valse
On nous a joints, Lefêvbre et moi, etc.

B. RECONSTITUTIONS PAR VERLAINE

VERS POUR LES LIEUX

De ce siège si mal tourné
Qu'il fait s'embrouiller nos entrailles,
Le trou dut être maçonné
Par de véritables canailles.

Albert Mérat
Paris, 1872.

Quand le fameux Tropmann détruisit Henri Kink,
Cet assassin avait dû s'asseoir sur ce siège,
Car le con de Badingue et le con d'Henri V
Sont bien dignes vraiment de cet état de siège.

Paris, 1872

★ ★ ★ ★

"IL PLEUT DOUCEMENT SUR LA VILLE"

Il pleut doucement sur la ville.

★ ★ ★ ★

C. RECONSTITUTIONS PAR ERNEST DELAHAYE

DEUX SONNETS

1.
"LES ANCIENS ANIMAUX SAILLISSAIENT . . ."

Les anciens animaux saillissaient, même en course,
Avec des glands bardés de sang et d'excrément.
Nos pères étalaient leur membre fièrement
Par le pli de la gaine et le grain de la bourse.

Au moyen âge pour la femelle, ange ou pource,
Il fallait un gaillard de solide grément;
Même un Kléber, d'après la culotte qui ment
Peut-être un peu, n'a pas dû manquer de ressource.

D'ailleurs l'homme au plus fier mammifère est égal;
L'énormité de leur membre à tort nous étonne;
Mais une heure stérile a sonné: le cheval

Et le bœuf ont bridé leurs ardeurs, et personne
N'osera plus dresser son orgueil génital
Dans les bosquets où grouille une enfance bouffonne.

2
"NOS FESSES NE SONT PAS LES LEURS . . ."

Nos fesses ne sont pas les leurs. Souvent j'ai vu
Des gens déboutonnés derrière quelque haie,
Et, dans ces bains sans gêne où l'enfance s'égaie,
J'observais le plan et l'effet de notre cul.

Plus ferme, blême en bien des cas, il est pourvu
De méplats évidents que tapisse la claie
Des poils; pour elles, c'est seulement dans la raie
Charmante que fleurit le long satin touffu.

Une ingéniosité touchante et merveilleuse
Comme l'on ne voit qu'aux anges des saints tableaux
Imite la joue où le sourire se creuse.

Oh! de même être nus, chercher joie et repos,
Le front tourné vers sa portion glorieuse,
Et libres tous les deux murmurer des sanglots?

"OH! SI LES CLOCHES SONT DE BRONZE..."

Oh! si les cloches sont de bronze,
Nos cœurs sont pleins de désespoir!
En juin mil huit cent soixante-onze,
Trucidés par un être noir,
Nous Jean Baudry, nous Jean Balouche,
Ayant accompli nos souhaits,
Mourûmes en ce clocher louche
En abominant Desdouets!...

"AU PIED DES SOMBRES MURS..."

Au pied des sombres murs, battant les maigres chiens...

"DERRIÈRE TRESSAUTAIT EN DES HOQUETS GROTESQUES..."

Derrière tressautait en des hoquets grotesques,
Une rose avalée au ventre du portier...

"BRUNE, ELLE AVAIT SEIZE ANS..."

Brune, elle avait seize ans quand on la maria
. . . .

. . . .

Car elle aime d'amour son fils de dix-sept ans.

"VOUS AVEZ MENTI..."

.... Vous avez
Menti, sur mon fémur, vous avez menti, fauve
Apôtre! Vous voulez faire des décavés
De nous? Vous voudriez peler notre front chauve?
Mais moi, j'ai deux fémurs bistournés et gravés!
. . . .

Parce que vous suintez tous les jours au collège
Sur vos collets d'habit de quoi faire un beignet,
Que vous êtes un masque à dentiste, au manège

Un cheval épilé qui bave en un cornet,
Vous croyez effacer mes quarante ans de siège!
. . . .

J'ai mon fémur! J'ai mon fémur! J'ai mon fémur!
C'est cela que depuis quarante ans je bistourne
Sur le bord de ma chaise aimée en noyer dur;
L'impression du bois pour toujours y séjourne;
Et quand j'apercevrai, moi, ton organe impur,
A tous tes abonnés, pitre, à tes abonnées,
Pertractant cet organe avachi de leurs mains, [...]
Je ferai retoucher, pour tous les lendemains,
Ce fémur travaillé depuis quarante années!

LA PLAINTE DES ÉPICIERS

Qu'il entre au magasin, quand la lune miroite
    A ses vitrages bleus,
Qu'il empoigne à nos yeux la chicorée en boîte.
. . . .

D. RECONSTITUTIONS PAR LABARRIÈRE

.................................Sont-ce
........(des tonneaux?).... qu'on défonce?
.... Non!
C'est un chef cuisinier ronflant comme un basson.

★ ★ ★ ★

    Oh! les vignettes pérennelles!

★ ★ ★ ★

.......Parmi les ors, les quartz, les porcelaines,
.......................un pot de nuit banal,
Reliquaire indécent des vieilles châtelaines,
Courbe ses flancs honteux sur l'acajou royal.

★ ★ ★ ★

Et le poète soûl engueulait l'Univers!

E. RECONSTITUTIONS PAR P. ARNOULT ET JEAN RICHEPIN

"QUAND S'ARRÊTA LA CARAVANE..."

[...] Quand s'arrêta la caravane d'Iran à la fontaine de Ctésiphon, elle fut au désespoir de la trouver tarie. Les uns en accusèrent les mages, les autres les imans. Les chameliers s'unirent en imprécations[...] Ils s'étaient mis en route depuis plusieurs lunes avec[...] charge-ment d'encens, de myrrhe et d'or. Leur chef s'écria[...] décida de supprimer[...] Certains acceptèrent.

F. PHRASE

Prends-y garde, Ô ma vie absente!

G. FRAGMENTS DE L'*ALBUM ZUTIQUE*

BOUTS-RIMÉS

lévitiques,
ur fauve *fessier,*
matiques,
enou *grossier,*

apoplectiques,
nassier,
mnastiques,
ux membre d'*acier.*

et peinte en *bile,*
a *sébile*
in,

n fruit d'*Asie,*
saisie,
ve d'*airain.*

A.R.

"MAIS ENFIN…"

Mais enfin, c'
Qu'ayant p
Je puisse,
Et du mon
Rêver le sé
Le tableau
Des animau
Et, loin du
L'élaborat
D'un *Choler*

IV. BROUILLON D'*UNE SAISON EN ENFER*

MAUVAIS SANG

Oui c'est un vice que j'ai, qui s'arrête et qui ~~reprend~~ avec moi, et, ma poitrine ouverte, je verrais un horrible cœur infirme. Dans mon enfance, j'entends ses racines de souffrance jetée à mon flanc: aujourd'hui elle a ~~poussé~~ au ciel, elle bien plus forte que moi, elle me bat, me traîne, me jette à terre.

Donc c'est dit, renier la joie, éviter le devoir, ne pas porter au monde mon dégoût et mes trahisons supérieures la dernière innocence, la dernière timidité.

Allons, la marche! le désert, le fardeau, les coups, le malheur, l'ennui, la colère.—L'enfer, là sûrement les délires de mes peurs et se disperse.

À quel démon ~~je suis à~~ me louer? Quelle bête faut-il adorer? dans quel sang faut-il marcher? Quels cris faut-il pousser? Quel mensonge faut-il soutenir? ~~A~~ Quelle Sainte image faut-il attaquer? Quels cœurs faut-il briser?

Plutôt ~~éviter d'offrir la main br~~ stupide justice, de la mort. J'entendrai ~~les la~~ complainte chantée ~~aujourd'hui~~ jadis ~~dans~~ sur les marchés. Point de popularité.

La dure vie, l'abrutissement pur,—et puis soulever d'un poing séché le couvercle du cercueil, s'asseoir et s'étouffer. ~~Je ne vieillirai~~ pas de vieillesse. Point de dangers la terreur n'est pas française.

Ah! je suis tellement délaissé, que j'offre à n'importe quelle divine image des élans vers la perfection. Autre marché grotesque.

~~À quoi servent~~ Ô mon abnégation Ô ma charité inouïes De profundis Domine! je suis bête?

Assez. Voici la punition! Plus à parler d'innocence. En marche. Oh! les reins se déplantent, le cœur gronde, la poitrine brûle, la tête est battue, la nuit roule dans les yeux, au Soleil.

~~Sais je où je vais~~ Où va-t-on, à la bataille?

Ah! mon âme ma sale jeunesse. Va!... va, les autres avancent ~~remuent~~ les outils, les armes.

Oh! oh. C'est la faiblesse, c'est la bêtise, moi!

Allons, feu sur moi. Ou je me rends! ~~qu'on laisse~~ blessé, je me jette à plat ventre, foulé aux pieds des chevaux.

Ah!

Je m'y habituerai.

Ah çà, je mènerais la vie française, et je tiendrais le Sentier de l'honneur.

FAUSSE CONVERSION

Jour de malheur! J'ai avalé un fameux ~~verre~~ gorgée de poison. La rage du désespoir m'emporte contre tout la nature les objets, moi, que je veux déchirer. Trois fois béni soit le conseil qui m'est arrivé. ~~M~~ Les entrailles me brûlent, la violence du venin tord mes membres, me rend difforme. Je meurs de soif. J'étouffe. Je ne puis crier. C'est l'enfer l'éternité de la peine. Voilà comme le feu se relève. Va, démon, va, diable, va Satan attise-le. Je brûle ~~bien~~ comme il faut, c'est un bon (bel et bon) enfer.

J'avais entrevu ~~le salut~~ la conversion, le bien, le bonheur, le salut. Puis-je décrire la vision, on n'est pas poète ~~dans~~ en enfer.

~~Dès que~~ C'était ~~l'apparition~~ des milliers de ~~'Apsaras?~~ charmantes, un admirable concert spirituel, la force et la paix, les nobles ambitions, que sais-je!

Ah: les nobles ambitions! ma haine. ~~R~~ Je recommence l'existence enragée la colère dans le sang, la vie bestiale, l'abêtissement, le ~~malheur . . . mon malh et les malheurs des autres~~ qui m'importe peu et c'est encore la vie! Si la damnation est éternelle. C'est ~~encore~~ ~~la vie encore~~. C'est l'exécution des lois religieuses pourquoi a-t-on semé une foi pareille dans mon esprit? ~~On a~~ ~~Les~~ Mes parents ont fait mon malheur, et le leur, ce qui m'importe peu. On a abusé de mon innocence. Oh! l'idée du baptême. Il y en a qui ont vécu mal, qui vivent mal, et qui ne sentent rien! C'est ~~le~~ mon baptême et ma faiblesse dont je suis esclave. C'est la vie encore!

Plus tard, les délices de la damnation seront plus profondes. Je reconnais bien la damnation. ~~Quand~~ Un homme qui veut se mutiler est bien damné, n'est-ce pas? Je me crois en enfer, donc j'y suis.—Un crime, vite, que je tombe au néant, par la loi des hommes.

Tais-toi. Mais tais-toi! C'est la honte et le reproche, ~~qui~~ à côté de moi; c'est Satan qui me dit que son feu est ignoble, idiot; et que ma colère est affreusement laide. Assez. Tais-toi! ce sont des erreurs qu'on me souffle à l'oreille, ~~la~~ les magies, ~~l'~~ les alchimies, les mysticismes, les parfums ~~fleuris?~~ faux, les musiques naïves, ~~les~~. C'est Satan qui se charge de cela. Alors les poètes sont damnés. Non ce n'est pas cela.

Et dire que je tiens la vérité. Que j'ai un jugement sain et arrêté sur toute chose, que je suis tout prêt pour la perfection. ~~Tais-toi, c'est~~ l'orgueil! à présent. Je ne suis qu'un bonhomme en bois, la peau de ma tête se dessèche. Ô Dieu! mon Dieu! mon Dieu! J'ai peur, pitié. Ah! j'ai soif. Ô mon enfance, mon village, les prés, le lac sur la grève le clair de lune quand le clocher sonnait douze. ~~Satan a ri~~. Et c'est au clocher.—Que je deviens bête! Ô Marie, Sainte-Vierge, faux sentiment, fausse prière.

DÉLIRES II: ALCHIMIE DU VERBE

Enfin mon esprit devin[t]. . . . . . .
de Londres ou de Pékin, ou Ber. . . . . . .

qui ~~disparaissent je plaisante sur~~........
de réjouissance populaire. ~~Voilà~~........
les ~~petits~~ fournaises........
J'aurais voulu le désert crayeux de....

J'adorai les boissons tiédies, les boutiques fanées, les vergers brûlés. Je restais de longues heures la langue pendante, comme les bêtes harassées: je me traînais dans les ruelles puantes, et, les yeux fermés, je ~~priais le~~ m'offrais au soleil, Dieu de feu, qu'il me renversât ~~et~~, Général, roi, disais-je, si tu as encore un vieux canons sur tes remparts qui dégringolent, bombarde les hommes avec des ~~monceau~~ mottes de terre sèche Aux glaces des magasins splendides! Dans les salons frais! Que les ~~araignées À la~~ manger sa poussière à la ville! Oxyde des gargouilles. À l'heure exacte après boudoirs ~~du~~ brules sable de rubis les

~~Je portais des vêtements de toile.~~ Je me ~~mot illisible~~ j'allais cassais ~~sie~~ des pierres sur des routes balayées toujours. Le soleil souverain ~~descendait~~ donnait vers ~~la~~ une merde, dans la vallée de la ~~illisible~~, son moucheron enivré au centre
à la pissotière de l'auberge isolée, amoureux de la bourrache,
et dissous au soleil
et
qui va se fondre en un rayon

FAIM

J'ai réfléchis aux bonheur des bêtes; les chenilles étaient les foule ~~petits corps blancs~~ innocen des limbes: romantique envahie par l'aube opale; la punaise, brune personne, attendait ~~mots illisibles~~ passionné. Heureuse ~~le somm~~ la taupe, sommeil de toute la Virginité!

Je m'éloignais ~~du contact~~ Étonnante virginité d'essay l'écrire, avec une espèce de romance. Chanson de la plus haute tour.

Je crus avoir trouvé raison et bonheur. J'écartais le ciel, l'azur, qui est du noir, et je vivais, étincelle d'or de la lumière *nature*. C'était très sérieux. J'exprimai, ~~le plus~~ bêtement.

ÉTERNITÉ

~~Et pour comble~~ De joie, je devins un opéra fabuleux.

ÂGE D'OR

À cette ~~période, c'était~~ c'était ma vie éternelle, non écrite, non chantée,—quelque chose comme la Providence ~~les lois du monde un~~ à laquelle on croit et qui ne chante pas.

Après ces nobles minutes, ~~vint~~ stupidité complète. Je ~~n~~ vis une fatalité de bonheur dans tous les êtres: l'action n'était ~~pas la vie mauvaise~~ qu'une façon ~~de~~ instinctive de gâcher une insatiété de vie: ~~seulement moi, je laissai la sachant~~, au hasard sinistre et doux, ~~un~~ énervement, ~~déviation~~ errement. Le savoir était la faiblesse et la cervelle. . . . . . .

. . . . êtres et toutes choses m'apparaissaient
. . . . d'autres vies autour d'elles. Ce monsieur
. . . . un ange. Cette famille n'est pas
. . . . Avec plusieurs hommes
. . . . .moment d'une de leurs autres vies.
. . . .~~histoire~~ plus de principes. Pas un des sophismes qui. . . . . . .la folie enfermée.

Je pourrais les redire tous ~~et d'autres~~ et bien d'autres ~~et d'autres~~, je sais le système. Je n'éprouvais plus rien. Les ~~hallucinations étaient tourbillonnaient trop~~. Mais maintenant je ~~ne voudrais~~ n'essaierais pas de me faire écouter.

Un mois de cet exercice, ~~je crus~~ Ma santé ~~s'ébranla~~ fut menacée.

J'avais bien autre chose à faire que de vivre. Les hallucinations étaient plus vives ~~plus épouvantes~~ la terreur ~~plus~~ venait! Je faisais des sommeils de plusieurs jours, et, levé, continuais les rêves les plus tristes (les égarés) partout.

MÉMOIRE

Je me trouvais mûr pour ~~la mort~~ le trépas et ma faiblesse me tirait jusqu'aux confins du monde et de la vie, ~~où le tourbillon~~ dans la Cimmérie noire, patrie des morts, où un grand... a pris une route de dangers laissé presque toute chez une sur emb... tion épouvantes.

CONFINS DU MONDE

Je voyageai un peu. J'allai au nord: je ~~rappelai au~~ (fermai mon cerveau) Je voulus reconnaître là toutes mes odeurs féodales, bergères, sources sauvages. J'aimais la mer ~~bonhomme le sol et les principes~~ l'anneau magique dans l'eau lumineuse ~~éclairée~~ comme si elle dût me laver d'un ~~me laver de ces aberrations~~ souillures. Je voyais la croix consolante. J'avais été damné par l'arc-en-ciel et les ~~bes~~ magies religieuses; et par le Bonheur, ~~mon remor~~ ma fatalité, mon ver, et qui ~~je~~ quoique ~~le monde me parut très nouveau, à moi qui avais~~ levé toutes les impressions possibles: faisant ma vie trop immense énervait même après que ma ~~illisible~~ pour armer (sincer) (seulement) bien réellement la force et la beauté.

Dans les plus grandes villes, à l'aube, ad ~~diluculum~~ matutinum, au Christus venit, ~~quand pour les hommes forts le Christ vient~~ sa dent, douce à ~~la~~ mort, m'avertissait avec le chant du coq.

BONR

Si faible, je ne me crus plus supportable dans la société, qu'à force de ~~pitié~~ Quel malheur Quel cloître possible pour ce beau dégoût?

Cela s'est passé peu à peu.

Je hais maintenant les élans mystiques et les bizarreries de style.

Maintenant je puis dire que l'art est une sottise.

Nos grands poètes aussi facile: l'art est une sottise.

Salut à la bont.

V. LETTRES CHOISIES

À THÉODORE DE BANVILLE

Charleville (Ardennes), le 24 mai 1870.

À Monsieur Théodore de Banville.

Cher Maître,

Nous sommes aux mois d'amour; j'ai dix-sept ans. L'âge des espérances et des chimères, comme on dit,—et voici que je me suis mis, enfant touché par le doigt de la Muse,—pardon si c'est banal,—à dire mes bonnes croyances, mes espérances, mes sensations, toutes ces choses des poètes—moi j'appelle cela du printemps.

Que si je vous envoie quelques-uns de ces vers,—et cela en passant par Alph. Lemerre, le bon éditeur,—c'est que j'aime tous les poètes, tous les bons Parnassiens,—puisque le poète est un Parnassien,—épris de la beauté idéale; c'est que j'aime en vous, bien naïvement, un descendant de Ronsard, un frère de nos maîtres de 1830, un vrai romantique, un vrai poète. Voilà pourquoi.—C'est bête, n'est-ce pas, mais enfin? . . .

Dans deux ans, dans un an peut-être, je serai à Paris.

—Anch'io, messieurs du journal, je serai Parnassien!—Je ne sais ce que j'ai là . . . qui veut monter . . . —Je jure, cher maître, d'adorer toujours les deux déesses, Muse et Liberté.

Ne faites pas trop la moue en lisant ces vers: . . . Vous me rendriez fou de joie et d'espérance, si vous vouliez, cher Maître, *faire faire* à la pièce *Credo in unam* une petite place entre les Parnassiens . . . Je viendrais à la dernière série du *Parnasse:* cela ferait le Credo des poètes! . . . —Ambition! ô Folle!

Arthur Rimbaud.

Si ces vers trouvaient place au *Parnasse contemporain?*
—Ne sont-ils pas la foi des poètes?
—Je ne suis pas connu; qu'importe? les poètes sont frères. Ces vers croient; ils aiment; ils espèrent: c'est tout.

—Cher maître, à moi: Levez-moi un peu: je suis jeune: tendez-moi la main . . .

À GEORGES IZAMBARD

Charleville, [13] mai 1871.

Cher Monsieur!

Vous revoilà professeur. On se doit à la Société, m'avez-vous dit; vous faites partie des corps enseignants: vous roulez dans la bonne ornière.—Moi aussi, je suis le principe: je me fais cyniquement *entretenir*; je déterre d'anciens imbéciles de collège: tout ce que je puis inventer de bête, de sale, de mauvais, en action et en paroles, je le leur livre: on me paie en bocks et en filles. *Stat mater dolorosa, dum pendet filius,*—Je me dois à la Société, c'est juste;—et j'ai raison.—Vous aussi, vous avez raison, pour aujourd'hui. Au fond, vous ne voyez en votre principe que poésie subjective: votre obstination à regagner le râtelier universitaire—pardon!—le prouve. Mais vous finirez toujours comme un satisfait qui n'a rien fait, n'ayant rien voulu faire. Sans compter que votre poésie subjective sera toujours horriblement fadasse. Un jour, j'espère,—bien d'autres espèrent la même chose,—je verrai dans votre principe la poésie objective, je la verrai plus sincèrement que vous ne le feriez!—Je serai un travailleur: c'est l'idée qui me retient, quand les colères folles me poussent vers la bataille de Paris,—où tant de travailleurs meurent pourtant encore tandis que je vous écris! Travailler maintenant, jamais, jamais; je suis en grève.

Maintenant, je m'encrapule le plus possible. Pourquoi? Je veux être poète, et je travaille à me rendre *Voyant:* vous ne comprendrez pas du tout, et je ne saurais presque vous expliquer. Il s'agit d'arriver à l'inconnu par le dérèglement de *tous les sens.* Les souffrances sont énormes, mais il faut être fort, être né poète, et je me suis reconnu poète. Ce n'est pas du tout ma faute. C'est faux de dire: Je pense: on devrait dire on me pense.—Pardon du jeu de mots.

JE est un autre. Tant pis pour le bois qui se trouve violon, et Nargue aux inconscients, qui ergotent sur ce qu'ils ignorent tout à fait!

Vous n'êtes pas *Enseignant* pour moi. Je vous donne ceci: est-ce de la satire, comme vous diriez? Est-ce de la poésie? C'est de la fantaisie, toujours.—Mais, je vous en supplie, ne soulignez ni du crayon, ni trop de la pensée:

LE CŒUR SUPPLICIÉ [p. 406]

Ça ne veut pas rien dire.—RÉPONDEZ-MOI
Bonjour de cœur,

Ar. Rimbaud.

À PAUL DEMENY

Charleville, 15 mai 1871.

J'ai résolu de vous donner une heure de littérature nouvelle; je commence de suite par un psaume d'actualité:

—Voici de la prose sur l'avenir de la poésie—

Toute poésie antique aboutit à la poésie grecque, Vie harmonieuse.—De la Grèce au mouvement romantique,—moyen âge,—il y a des lettrés, des versificateurs. D'Ennius à Theroldus, de Theroldus à Casimir Delavigne, tout est prose rimée, un jeu, avachissement et gloire d'innombrables générations idiotes: Racine est le pur, le fort, le grand.—On eût soufflé sur ses rimes, brouillé ses hémistiches, que le Divin Sot serait aujourd'hui aussi ignoré que le premier venu auteur d'*Origines*.—Après Racine, le jeu moisit. Il a duré deux mille ans.

Ni plaisanterie, ni paradoxe. La raison m'inspire plus de certitudes sur le sujet que n'aurait jamais eu de colères un Jeune-France. Du reste, libre aux *nouveaux!* d'exécrer les ancêtres: on est chez soi et l'on a le temps.

On n'a jamais bien jugé le romantisme. Qui l'aurait jugé? Les critiques!! Les romantiques, qui prouvent si bien que la chanson est si peu souvent l'œuvre, c'est-à-dire la pensée chantée *et comprise* du chanteur?

Car Je est un autre. Si le cuivre s'éveille clairon, il n'y a rien de sa faute. Cela m'est évident: j'assiste à l'éclosion de ma pensée: je la regarde, je l'écoute: je lance un coup d'archet: la symphonie fait son remuement dans les profondeurs, ou vient d'un bond sur la scène.

Si les vieux imbéciles n'avaient pas trouvé du moi que la signification fausse, nous n'aurions pas à balayer ces millions de squelettes qui, depuis un temps infini, ont accumulé les produits de leur intelligence borgnesse, en s'en clamant les auteurs!

En Grèce, ai-je dit, vers et lyres *rythment l'Action*. Après, musique et rimes sont jeux, délassements. L'étude de ce passé charme les curieux: plusieurs s'éjouissent à renouveler ces antiquités:—c'est pour eux. L'intelligence universelle a toujours jeté ses idées, naturellement; les hommes ramassaient une partie de ces fruits du cerveau: on agissait par, on en écrivait des livres: telle allait la marche, l'homme ne se travaillant pas, n'étant pas encore éveillé, ou pas encore dans la plénitude du grand songe. Des fonctionnaires, des écrivains: auteur, créateur, poète, cet homme n'a jamais existé!

La première étude de l'homme qui veut être poète est sa propre connaissance, entière; il cherche son âme, il l'inspecte, il la tente, l'apprend. Dès qu'il la sait, il doit la cultiver; cela semble simple: en tout cerveau s'accomplit un développement naturel; tant d'*égoïstes* se proclament auteurs; il en est bien d'autres qui *s*'attribuent leur progrès intellectuel!—Mais il s'agit de faire l'âme monstrueuse: à l'instar des comprachicos, quoi~! Imaginez un homme s'implantant et se cultivant des verrues sur le visage.

Je dis qu'il faut être *voyant*, se faire *voyant*.

Le Poète se fait *voyant* par un long, immense et raisonné *dérèglement* de *tous les sens*. Toutes les formes d'amour, de souffrance, de folie; il cherche lui-même, il épuise en lui tous les poisons, pour n'en garder que les quintessences. Ineffable torture où il a besoin de toute la foi, de toute la force surhumaine, où il devient entre tous le grand malade, le grand criminel, le grand maudit,—et le suprême Savant!—Car il arrive à l'*inconnu!* Puisqu'il a cultivé son âme, déjà riche, plus qu'aucun! Il arrive à l'inconnu, et quand, affolé, il finirait par perdre l'intelligence de ses visions, il les a vues! Qu'il crève dans son bondissement par les choses inouïes et innommables: viendront d'autres horribles travailleurs; ils commenceront par les horizons où l'autre s'est affaissé!

—La suite à six minutes—

Ici j'intercale un second psaume *hors du texte:* veuillez tendre une oreille complaisante,—et tout le monde sera charmé.—J'ai l'archet en main, je commence:

Voilà. Et remarquez bien que, si je ne craignais de vous faire débourser plus de 60 c. de port,—moi pauvre effaré qui, depuis sept mois, n'ai pas tenu un seul rond de bronze!—je vous livrerais encore mes *Amants de Paris,* cent hexamètres, Monsieur, et ma *Mort de Paris,* deux cents hexamètres!—

Je reprends:

Donc le poète est vraiment voleur de feu.

Il est chargé de l'humanité, des *animaux* même; il devra faire sentir, palper, écouter ses inventions; si ce qu'il rapporte de *là-bas* a forme, il donne forme; si c'est informe, il donne de l'informe. Trouver une langue;

—Du reste, toute parole étant idée, le temps d'un langage universel viendra! Il faut être académicien,—plus mort qu'un fossile,—pour parfaire un dictionnaire, de quelque langue que ce soit. Des faibles se mettraient *à penser* sur la première lettre de l'alphabet, qui pourraient vite ruer dans la folie!—

Cette langue sera de l'âme pour l'âme, résumant tout, parfums, sons, couleurs, de la pensée accrochant la pensée et tirant. Le poète définirait la quantité d'inconnu s'éveillant en son temps dans l'âme universelle: il donnerait plus—que la formule de sa pensée, que la notation *de sa marche au Progrès!* Énormité devenant norme, absorbée par tous, il serait vraiment *un multiplicateur de progrès!*

Cet avenir sera matérialiste, vous le voyez;—Toujours pleins du *Nombre* et de l'*Harmonie,* ces poèmes seront faits pour rester.—Au fond, ce serait encore un peu la Poésie grecque.

L'art éternel aurait ses fonctions, comme les poètes sont citoyens. La Poésie ne rythmera plus l'action; elle *sera en avant.*

Ces poètes seront! Quand sera brisé l'infini servage de la femme, quand elle vivra pour elle et par elle, l'homme,—jusqu'ici abominable,—lui ayant donné son renvoi, elle sera poète, elle aussi! La femme trouvera de l'inconnu! Ses mondes d'idées différeront-ils des nôtres?—Elle trouvera des choses étranges, insondables, repoussantes, délicieuses; nous les prendrons, nous les comprendrons.

En attendant, demandons aux *poètes* du *nouveau,*—idées et formes. Tous les habiles croiraient bientôt avoir satisfait à cette demande.—Ce n'est pas cela!

Les premiers romantiques ont été *voyants* sans trop bien s'en rendre compte: la culture de leurs âmes s'est commencée aux accidents: locomotives abandonnées, mais brûlantes, que prennent quelque temps les rails.—Lamartine est quelquefois voyant, mais étranglé par la forme vieille.—Hugo, *trop cabochard,* a bien du VU dans les derniers volumes: *Les Misérables* sont un vrai *poème.* J'ai *Les Châtiments* sous main; *Stella* donne à peu près la mesure de la *vue* de Hugo. Trop de Belmontet et de Lamennais, de Jehovahs et de colonnes, vieilles énormités crevées.

Musset est quatorze fois exécrable pour nous, générations douloureuses et prises de visions,—que sa paresse d'ange a insultées! Ô! les contes et les proverbes fadasses! ô les nuits! ô Rolla, ô Namouna, ô la Coupe! tout est français, c'est-à-dire haïssable au suprême degré; français, pas parisien! Encore une œuvre de cet odieux génie qui a inspiré Rabelais, Voltaire, Jean La Fontaine, commenté par M. Taine! Printanier, l'esprit de Musset! Charmant, son amour! En voilà, de la peinture à l'émail, de la poésie solide! On savourera longtemps la poésie *française,* mais en France. Tout garçon épicier est en mesure de débobiner une apostrophe Rollaque; tout séminariste en porte les cinq cents rimes dans le secret d'un carnet. À quinze ans, ces élans de passion mettent les jeunes en rut; à seize ans, ils se contentent déjà de les réciter avec *cœur;* à dix-huit ans, à dix-sept même, tout collégien qui a le moyen fait le Rolla, écrit un Rolla! Quelques-uns en meurent peut-être encore. Musset n'a rien su faire: il y avait des visions derrière la gaze des rideaux: il a fermé les yeux. Français, panadif, traîné de l'estaminet au pupitre de collège, le beau mort est mort, et, désormais, ne nous donnons même plus la peine de le réveiller par nos abominations!

Les seconds romantiques sont très *voyants:* Th. Gautier, Lec[onte] de Lisle, Th. de Banville. Mais inspecter l'invisible et entendre l'inouï étant autre chose que reprendre l'esprit des choses mortes, Baudelaire est le premier voyant, roi des poètes, *un vrai Dieu.* Encore a-t-il vécu dans un milieu trop artiste; et la forme si vantée en lui est mesquine: les inventions d'inconnu réclament des formes nouvelles.

Rompue aux formes vieilles, parmi les innocents, A. Renaud,—a fait son Rolla;—L. Grandet,—a fait son Rolla;—Les gaulois et les Musset, G. Lafenestre, Coran, Cl. Popelin, Soulary, L. Salles; Les écoliers, Marc, Aicard, Theuriet; les morts et les imbéciles, Autran, Barbier, L. Pichat, Lemoyne, les Deschamps, les Desessarts; Les journalistes, L. Cladel, Robert Luzarches, X. de Ricard; les fantaisistes, C. Mendès; les bohèmes; les femmes; les talents, Léon Dierx et Sully-Prudhomme, Coppée,—la nouvelle école, dite parnassienne, a deux voyants, Albert Mérat et Paul Verlaine, un vrai poète.—Voilà. Ainsi je travaille à me rendre *voyant.*—Et finissons par un chant pieux.

ACCROUPISSEMENTS [p. 409]

. . . .

Vous seriez exécrable de ne pas répondre: vite, car dans huit jours, je serai à Paris, peut-être.

Au revoir,

A. Rimbaud.

Monsieur Paul Demeny,
À Douai.

À PAUL DEMENY

Charleville, 10 juin 1871.

À M. P. DEMENY

LES POÈTES DE SEPT ANS [p. 413]

LES PAUVRES À L'ÉGLISE [p. 416]

Voici,—ne vous fâchez pas,—un motif à dessins drôles: c'est une antithèse aux douces vignettes pérennelles où batifolent les cupidons, où s'essorent les cœurs panachés de flammes, fleurs vertes, oiseaux mouillés, promontoires de Leucade, etc . . . —Ces triolets, eux aussi, au reste, iront

Où les vignettes pérennelles,
Où les doux vers.

Voici:—ne vous fâchez pas—

LE CŒUR DU PITRE [p. 406]

Voilà ce que je fais.

J'ai trois prières à vous adresser

Brûlez, *je le veux,* et je crois que vous respecterez ma volonté comme celle d'un mort, brûlez *tous les vers que je fus assez sot* pour vous donner lors de mon séjour à Douai: ayez la bonté de m'envoyer, s'il vous est possible et s'il vous plaît, un exemplaire de vos *Glaneuses,* que je voudrais relire et qu'il m'est impossible d'acheter, ma mère ne m'ayant gratifié d'aucun rond de bronze depuis six mois,—pitié! enfin, veuillez bien me répondre, quoi que ce soit, pour cet envoi et pour le précédent.

Je vous souhaite un bon jour, ce qui est bien bon.

Écrivez à: M. Deverrière, 95, sous les Allées, pour

A. Rimbaud.

Monsieur Paul Demeny,
À Paris.

À THÉODORE DE BANVILLE

Charleville, Ardennes, 15 août 1871.

À Monsieur Théodore de Banville.

CE QU'ON DIT AU POÈTE À PROPOS DE FLEURS [p. 421]

. . . .

Monsieur et cher Maître,

Vous rappelez-vous avoir reçu de province, en juin 1870, cent ou cent cinquante hexamètres mythologiques intitulés *Credo in unam?* Vous fûtes assez bon pour répondre!

C'est le même imbécile qui vous envoie les vers ci-dessus, signés Alcide Bava.—Pardon.

J'ai dix-huit ans.—J'aimerai toujours les vers de Banville.

L'an passé je n'avais que dix-sept ans!

Ai-je progressé?

Alcide Bava.
A. R.

ACKNOWLEDGMENTS

Translation is a fundamentally solitary pursuit, yet I wouldn't be able to manage it without the frequent good company of the generous colleagues and friends who make my working life a joy. I have little doubt that what is best in my efforts is attributable in some real way to everyone mentioned below.

Several individuals and institutions previously known to me only through their work graciously responded to my requests for assistance during the course of this project. Michel Tourneux, curator of the Rimbaud Museum in Charleville, provided the images in the book from the collection of his excellent museum. Robert Greer Cohn answered a query regarding "L'Homme juste," resolving an old confusion. Paul Auster answered an inquiry with very helpful, timely advice. Michael Attias furnished useful information about contemporary French editions of Rimbaud's work, as well as an insightful reading of "Les Corbeaux." John Sullivan kindly volunteered his considerable editorial gifts in the service of my lesser, writerly ones. Lydia Davis generously examined a few clumsy drafts of early versions of my translations: her suggestions were invaluable, as anyone familiar with her work could only expect. And the wonderful UCROSS Foundation provided a perfectly timed, altogether opulent, residency.

Many people who I have depended on in the past once again gave freely of their time and expertise. French author Pierre Michon, whose books I have been lucky to translate, answered many questions about Rimbaud's schoolwork: he was instrumental in helping me decode Rimbaud's pastiche of Villon's French. Critic Jean-Yves Pouilloux, who long ago introduced me to the fun of translation, was yet again indispensable on a range of issues, particularly on the matter of Rimbaud's register in the *Illuminations*. Lee Fahnestock—a patron saint of starving translators—continues to heap encouragements upon me greater than I warrant, and to read more of my bad early drafts than she should have to. Kirsten Janene-Nelson has time and again proved willing to lend a hand as both reader and friend, two roles at which she excels equally. My agent, Elizabeth Sheinkman, has shown an interest in my work and commitment to its success that seem greatly out of proportion with what I can provide her. Leonard Michaels's scrupulousness as a reader and writer has lately been an example to me, and the generosity of his suggestions a reward. Roger Shattuck's interest in my earliest translations was as reassuring as it was unexpected; his continued attention is a great encouragement. And Guy Davenport's unstinting enthusiasm for my grapplings remains bread in the wilderness.

At the Modern Library, everyone involved has gone to unusual lengths to ensure the book's best form. My thanks to designers Gabrielle Bordwin (cover) and Gabriel Levine (guts), who turned my plain manuscript into something this reader finds very beautiful. Publicist Ericka Muncy has overflowed with kind words about, and excellent ideas for, the project. Production editor Vincent La Scala labored tirelessly to ensure that my many waves of revision made their way into type. And both my editor, Will Murphy, and Modern Library's publishing director, David Ebershoff, have repeatedly shown me personal kindness and professional enthusiasm well beyond any of my expectations.

Some people in my life have been spared any direct involvement in the making of this book. I can assure them, though, that this endeavor would have been without much pleasure for me absent the thought of them eventually reading it. Thanks then to Mark Barry, Roger Berkowitz, David Bezmozgis, Ilan Bohm, Diana Colbert, Thea DeSando, Greg Djanikian, Chris Elam, the Gavrils, Mia Hatgis, Annie Hermann, Barbara Kastakova, Jon Mandel, the Panitches, Jon Stein, Rondell Sarrett, and Susanne Ziegler, all of whom have offered every kindness during a difficult season.

Four friends—Patricia Ackerman, Charles Bock, David Koff, and Thomas Maffeo—have been generous to me in so many outsized ways that to attempt to enumerate any of them is to clarify none. What I provide them with in return for their interest and affection is unknown to me, beyond the joy I take in sharing their successes, and the delight I find in their company.

Thanks above all thanking go to my folks, to whom this work is lovingly dedicated. Most parents would rightly see their son's impractical enthusiasms as a source of real concern. Instead, they have responded with tireless encouragement, and unending generosity. I am—and in every sense will be—forever in their debt.

—Wyatt Mason
December 2001

SELECTED BIBLIOGRAPHY

By no means exhaustive, this gathering mentions those volumes that have been of particular use, and which therefore may prove interesting to readers.

I. FRENCH EDITIONS OF RIMBAUD'S WORKS

Œuvres complètes, ed. Rolland de Renéville and Jules Mouquet, Gallimard, Pléiade, 1954.

Œuvres complètes, ed. Antoine Adam, Gallimard, Pléiade, 1972.

Œuvres complètes, ed. Pierre Brunel, Livre de Poche, 1999.

Œuvres complètes, I: Poésies, ed. Steve Murphy. Honoré Champion, 1999.

The editions above offer an evolutionary view of Rimbaud scholarship of the last half century, each arriving at different strategies for making order out of the chaos in which Rimbaud left his posterity. While the first Pléiade listed is incomplete, it is important for Mouquet's translations of Rimbaud's Latin poems and because all previous English translations of the works depend upon the volume. The second Pléiade, and the remaining *OC*s, all vary in numerous ways that delight scholars, each of whom may be seen battling it out in the footnotes. Steve Murphy's editorial approach, a chronological presentation of all existing manuscript versions of the poems, has been immensely useful in the preparation of this volume.

II. COMPLETE ENGLISH TRANSLATIONS OF RIMBAUD'S WORKS

Collected Poems. Tr. Oliver Bernard. Penguin, 1962.

Complete Works, Selected Letters. Tr. Wallace Fowlie, University of Chicago, 1966.

Complete Works. Tr. Paul Schmidt. Harper & Row, 1976.

While dozens of different translators have taken aim at the biggest targets in Rimbaud's output (*Illuminations* and *Season in Hell*), only the translators of the three editions above (all still in print) have attempted to offer complete views of

Rimbaud's works, though each omits, both by design and taste, items of potential interest to readers. Bernard offers plain prose translations that strive for literalness. Fowlie offers literal, line-for-line versions. Schmidt's edition is a freer approach, containing many beautiful readings.

III. PARTIAL ENGLISH TRANSLATIONS OF RIMBAUD'S WORKS

Samuel Beckett, tr. *A Translation of Arthur Rimbaud's Poem* Le Bateau ivre. James Knowlson and Felix Leakey, eds. Whiteknights Press, 1976.

Davenport, Guy. *A Table of Green Fields.* New Directions, 1993.

———. *The Cardiff Team.* New Directions, 1995.

Angel Flores, ed. *The Anchor Anthology of French Poetry.* Anchor, 1958.

Bertrand Matthieu, tr. *A Season in Hell & Illuminations.* BOA, 1991.

Nabokov, Vladimir. *Ada.* McGraw Hill, 1969.

Pound, Ezra. *Translations.* New Directions, 1963.

Louise Varese, tr. *Illuminations.* New Directions, 1941.

IV. WORKS ON RIMBAUD'S LIFE AND POETRY

Alain Borer, ed. *Œuvre/vie.* Arléa, 1991.

Briet, Suzanne. *Rimbaud notre prochain.* Nouvelles Éditions latines, 1956.

William Carter and Robert Vines, eds. *A Concordance to the* Œuvres complètes *of Arthur Rimbaud.* Ohio University Press, 1978

Cohn, Robert Greer. *The Poetry of Rimbaud.* University of South Carolina Press, 1999.

Delahaye, Ernest. *Souvenirs familiers.* Messein, 1925.

Robb, Graham. *Rimbaud.* Norton, 2000.

Starkie, Enid. *Rimbaud.* Norton, 1947.

Lefrère, Jean Jacques. *Arthur Rimbaud.* Fayard, 2001.

V. ON SUBJECTS RELATING TO THE TRANSLATION

William Arrowsmith and Roger Shattuck, eds. *Craft and Context of Translation.* University of Texas, 1961.

Auden, W. H. *Collected Shorter Poems, 1927–1957.* Faber, 1966.

Paul Auster, ed. *The Random House Book of 20th Century Poetry.* Random House, 1981.

Baudelaire, Charles. *Les Fleurs du Mal.* Richard Howard, tr. Godine, 1980.

Borges, Jorge Luis. *This Craft of Verse.* Harvard, 2000.

Davenport, Guy. *The Geography of the Imagination.* North Point, 1981.

———. *Seven Greeks.* New Directions, 1995.

Davenport, Guy and Benjamin Urrutia. *The Logia of Yeshua.* Counterpoint, 1996.

Eliot, T. S. *Four Quartets.* Harcourt Brace, 1943.

Gass, William. *Reading Rilke.* Ecco, 2000.

Michon, Pierre. *Rimbaud le fils.* Gallimard, 1990.

Nabokov, Vladimir. *Lectures on Russian Literature.* Harcourt Brace, 1981.

Rilke, Rainer Maria. *Selected Poetry.* Stephen Mitchell, tr. Vintage, 1983.

INDEX OF TITLES AND FIRST LINES (ENGLISH)

All page numbers in Roman refer to the translations; all page numbers in italic refer to the originals.

A breath of air opens operatic breaches in walls, 251, *516*
A broad carved sideboard, 33, *393*
A brunette, just sixteen when she was married, 334, *561*
Adv't., 259, *519*
After the Flood, 223, *503*
After the idea of the Flood had receded, 223, *503*
A green hole where a river sings, 37, *395*
A humble scrub brush, too coarse, 145, *461*
Album Zutique, 133, 339, *457*, *563*
Alchemy of the Word, 208, 347, *494*, *566*
Ancient animals sullied themselves, even on the run, 331, *559*
And so off I went, fists thrust in the torn pockets, 49, *403*
And the mother, closing the workbook, 65, *413*
And the new year had already begun, 280, *529*
Anguish, 254, *517*
Antique, 229, *507*
A pale man in black, cigar in moue, 51, *404*
Apollonius the Greek Speaks of Marcus Cicero, 291, *536*
A Prince was troubled by his habit, 227, *505*
Aristomanes lifted himself up, 303, *542*
As a child, certain skies sharpened my sight, 258, *519*
As if from a green tin coffin, 19, *384*
A teary tincture slops, 58, *408*
At four in the morning, in summer, 110, *441*
At the Cabaret-Vert, Five P.M., 36, *394*
At the feet of dark walls, beating skinny dogs, 333, *561*
At Twenty, 261, *521*
Autumn already!, 219, *502*
A very big baby was born in the mountains of Arabia, 283, *531*

Bad Blood, 196, 343, *485*, *565*
Barbarian, 256, *518*
Barracks at Night, The, 328, *558*
Because he has opened the house to foaming winter, 270, *525*

Be honest, these village churches are a joke, 72, *417*
Being Beauteous, 230, *507*
Beneath the sky's unalterable collapse, 260, *520*
Black A, White E, Red I, Green U, Blue O: vowels, 104, *438*
Blacksmith, The, 43, *399*
Black wens, pockmarks, green bags, 97, *434*
Blankets of blood, coalfires, a thousand murders, 123, *450*
Bl[is]s, 353, *569*
Bluish roofs and white doors, 147, *462*
Bottom, 267, *524*
Bridges, 240, *511*
Brush, The, 145, *461*
But…, 340, *564*

Caesar's Rage, 51, *404*
Chariots of silver and copper, 252, *517*
Cheerful, one-armed, and black, 40, *397*
Childhood, 224, *504*
Cities [I], 243, *512*
Cities [II], 245, *513*
City, 241, *511*
Clear water, like salt from childhood's tears, 130, *454*
Clever Girl, 35, *394*
Come: wines beat the beaches, 108, *440*
Comedy of Thirst, 107, *439*
Common Nocturne, 251, *516*
Cowards, behold! Spill from the stations!, 62, *410*
Credo in Unam, 325, *557*
Crows, 122, *450*
Crystal gray skies. A strange pattern of bridges, 240, *511*
Customs Men, 100, *436*

Dark and wrinkled like a violet carnation, 135, *457*
Dawn, 249, *515*
Dead of ninety-two and ninety-three, 27, *389*
Deliria I: Foolish Virgin, 204, *491*
Deliria II: Alchemy of the Word, 208, 347, *494*, *566*
Democracy, 264, *522*
Departure, 233, *508*
Deserts of Love, 183, *481*
Devotion, 263, *522*
Doubtless I prefer outdoor cafés in spring, 140, *459*

Drunk Driver, 142, *460*
Drunken Boat, The, 85, *426*
Drunken Morning, 236, *509*

Eight days of shredding my boots, 36, *394*
Ends of the Earth, 352, *568*
Enlightened leisure, neither fever nor languor, in a meadow or a bed, 247, *514*
Eternal water-nymphs, 108, *440*
Eternity, 115, 349, *445*, *567*
Evening Prayer, 102, *437*
Evil, 50, *404*
Exile, 146, *461*

Fairy, 257, *519*
Fallen Cherub, 147, *462*
False Conversion, 345, *566*
Farewell, 219, *502*
Far from birds, herds, and village girls, 112, *443*
Faun's Head, 103, *437*
Feast of Love, 138, *458*
First Communion, 72, *417*
First Night, 20, *384*
Flowerbeds of amaranths stretching, 124, *451*
Flowers, 250, *516*
Foolish Virgin, 204, *491*
For a Reason, 235, *509*
Forebears, 107, *439*
For example, an evening when a humble traveler withdraws, 266, *523*
Forgive me, father!, 151, *463*
For sale: what the Jews haven't sold, 259, *519*
Free and proud, Man raised his head!, 325, *557*
Friends, 108, *440*
From a golden slope, 250, *516*
From indigo straights to Ossian seas, 255, *518*
Frozen in Fear, 28, *390*

Genius, 270, *525*
Golden Age, 116, 350, *446*, *568*
Golden dawn and shivering night, 262, *521*
Good Morning Thoughts, 110, *441*
Goodness and Beauty, and they're *mine*, 236, *509*
Gospels, 189, *483*

Graceful son of Pan!, 229, *507*
[Grocers' Gripes], 335, *562*

H, 268, *524*
Hanged Men Dancing, 40, *397*
Hear a hellmate's confession, 204, *491*
Heart Under a Cassock, A, 165, *470*
Hellish Husband, 204, *491*
Historic Evening, 266, *523*
Hortense's every gesture is violated by every atrocity, 268, *524*
Humanity tied the shoes of Progress, that enormous child, 141, *459*
Hunger, 348, *567*
Hunger Celebrated, 121, *449*

I am a transient, and not altogether unhappy, 241, *511*
Idle youth, 114, *444*
If the knife has yet, 129, *454*
I held the summer dawn in my arms, 249, *515*
I live my life sitting like an angel in a barber's chair, 102, *437*
Illuminations, 221, *503*
Impossible, The, 215, *499*
In April, listen, 126, *452*
In back, the porter leapt in grotesque hiccups, 333, *561*
In Dreams, Babbit, 138, *458*
In Rome, in the Sistine, 137, *458*
In Samaria, many had shown their faith in him, 189, *483*
In snow and fog, 28, *390*
In starry silence, virgin shadow, and impassive light, 257, *519*
Instructive voices exiled, 261, *521*
In the brown dining room, brimming, 35, *394*
In the middle, the Emperor, in an apotheosis, 34, *393*
In those days, Jesus lived in Nazareth, 289, *535*
Invocation to Venus, 295, *538*
Is she a dancer?, 120, *448*
I swallowed a gollup of poison, 202, *490*
It rained softly on the city, 330, *559*
It was spring; illness kept Orbilius immobilized in Rome, 277, *528*
It would stink if the sun left our shores!, 127, *453*
I was in a third-class compartment, 139, *459*

Jeanne-Marie has strong hands, 92, *431*
Jeanne-Marie's Hands, 92, *431*

Later, when he feels his stomach grumble, 60, *409*
Let him enter the store, 335, *562*
Lice Hunters, 99, *435*
Lightning, 217, *501*
Lily, 136, *457*
Lines, 237, *509*
Lives, 231, *507*
Long after the seasons and days, 256, *518*
Long ago, Achelous' swollen waters rose from his broad bed, 287, *534*
Long ago, if my memory serves, life was a feast, 195, *485*

Man of ordinary make, 260, *520*
Man's labors! Explosions that, from time to time, illuminate my abyss, 217, *501*
May Banners, 113, *444*
Memory, 130, 351, *454*, *568*
Metropolitan, 255, *518*
Michel and Christine, 127, *453*
Might it be She could forgive my eternally dashed ambitions, 254, *517*
Morning, 218, *501*
Movement, 269, *524*
Muscle-bound goons. The kind that rape the world, 228, *506*
My Bohemia, 49, *403*
My dear Conneau—, 146, *461*
My Gallic forebears gave me pale blue eyes, 196, *485*
My high youth!, 215, *499*
My hunger, Anne, Anne, 121, *449*
My Little Loves, 58, *408*
My sad heart drools on deck, 55, *406*
Mystic, 248, *515*
My turn. A tale of one of my follies, 208, *494*

Night in Hell, 202, *490*
Nina Replies, 22, *385*
Nonsense, 142, *460*
No one's serious at seventeen, 30, *391*
Novel, 30, *391*

O Godly delights, mortal delights, 295, *538*
Oh if the bells are bronze!, 333, *560*
Old Woman's Old Man, The, 143, *460*
On calm black waters filled with sleeping stars, 17, *383*
Once upon a time wasn't my childhood pleasant, 218, *501*

One arm wields a giant hammer, enormous, 43, *399*
One day as he walked happily along, 42, *398*
One fine morning, in a land of very decent people, 234, *508*
One of these voices, 116, *446*
One winter, we'll take a train, a little rose-colored car, 32, *392*
On summer nights, beneath shop windows' ardent eyes, 148, *462*
On the hillside, angels twirl their wool dresses, 248, *515*
On the right, the summer dawn stirs the leaves and mists, 242, *512*
On the Subject of Flowers: Remarks, Addressed to the Poet, 78, *421*
Ophelia, 17, *383*
Orphans' New Year's Gifts, The, 5, *376*
O seasons, o châteaux, 132, 355, *456*
O swaying lilies! O silver enemas!, 136, *457*
O the vast avenues of the holy land, 231, *507*
O the warm February morning, 239, *511*
O Thimothina Labinette!, 165, *470*
Our asses aren't like theirs, 332, *560*
Out of the snow rises a Beautiful Being, 230, *507*

Paris, 142, *460*
Parisian Battle Song, 56, *407*
Parisian Orgy or The Repopulation of Paris, 62, *410*
Parked on oak benches in church corners, 68, *414*
Pathetic brother! What wretched sleepless nights he caused!, 244, *513*
Patience Celebrated, 113, *443*
Pauper Dreams, A, 109, *441*
Perhaps a Night awaits me, 109, *441*
Pidgeons tremble in the prairie, 109, *441*
Piglet, 142, *460*
Poem in Set Rhymes, 339, *563*
Poets, Age Seven, 65, *413*
Poor at Church, The, 68, *414*
Promontory, 262, *521*
Pruned into stingy plots of grass, the public square, 38, *396*

Reality always too troublesome for my exalted character, 267, *524*
Recollection, 153, *465*
Rediscovered, 115, *445*
Remembrances of an Old Idiot, 151, *463*
River Cassis, 111, *442*
Royalty, 234, *508*
Ruts, 242, *512*

Saturnine Hypotyposes, Via Belmontet, 150, *463*
Seascape, 252, *517*
Season in Hell, A, 193, 341, *485*, *565*
Seen enough. Visions confronted in every weather, 233, *508*
Seen in Rome, 137, *458*
Sensation, 11, *379*
Shame, 129, *454*
She was almost undressed, 20, *384*
Sideboard, The, 33, *393*
Sideshow, 228, *506*
Sire, time has abandoned his raincoat, 297, *539*
Sisters of Charity, 70, *416*
Sitting Men, 97, *434*
Sleeper in the Valley, A, 37, *395*
Soldiers, sailors, imperial rabble, even pensioners, 100, *436*
Song from the Tallest Tower, 114, *444*
Sonnet, 260, *520*
Sonnet to an Asshole, 135, *457*
Soul, 108, *440*
So what is this dark and impenetrable mystery?, 150, *463*
Spring is here, plain as day, 56, *407*
Squatting, 60, *409*
Stages, 265, *523*
Stolen Heart, 55, *406*
Striking your finger on a drum discharges all sound, 235, *509*
Stunning Victory at Saarbrücken, The, 34, *393*
Such cities! Alleghenies and Lebanons out of a dream, 243, *512*
Sun and Flesh, 12, *379*
Sunday, 260, *520*

Take heed, o absent life of mine!, 338, *563*
Tale, 227, *505*
Tartufe Undone, 42, *398*
Tear, 112, *443*
The bedroom stands open to the turquoise sky, 119, *448*
The call of the kill dies feebly, 113, *444*
The child who gathered bullets, the Pubescent Boy, 327, *558*
The comedy of old perpetuates itself, 265, *523*
The flag fits the filthy land, 264, *522*
The hole of this seat is poorly made, 329, *559*
The official acropolis surpasses our most colossal conceptions, 245, *513*
The poor driver, beneath the tin canopy, 144, *460*

The Righteous Man sat up on his heavy hips, 89, *429*
The room is full of shadow, 5, *376*
The star wept rose into the heart of your ears, 101, *436*
The sun, hearth of tenderness and life, 12, *379*
The sun was still hot, 159, *468*
The wagging movement along the banks of the river's falls, 269, *524*
The waterfall sings behind opera-buffa shacks, 253, *517*
The year the imperial Prince was born, 153, *465*
The young man with shining eyes and brown skin, 70, *416*
There, bordering blue black skies, 78, *421*
This idol, black-eyed and blond-topped, 224, *504*
Through blue summer nights I will pass along paths, 11, *379*
To bedside books, placidly artful books, 149, *463*
To Music, 38, *396*
To my Sister Louise Vanaen de Voringhem, 263, *522*
To the peasants of the emperor!, 143, *460*
Two Sonnets, 331, *559*

Under Siege?, 144, *460*
Unnoticed, the River Cassis streams, 111, *442*

Vagabonds, 244, *513*
Venus Anadyomene, 19, *384*
Verses for Bathroom Walls, 329, *559*
Vigils, 247, *514*
Vowels, 104, *438*

War, 258, *519*
We are your Grandparents, 107, *439*
What follows is the work of a young—very young—*man*, 183, *481*
When the cannon's red spittle, 50, *404*
When the child's forehead full of red torments, 99, *435*
When the famous Tropmann destroyed Henri Kink, 330, *559*
When the Iranian caravan stopped, 337, *563*
When the world is no more than a lone dark wood, 237, *509*
When your meadows lie cold, O Lord, 122, *450*
While swept downstream on indifferent Rivers, 85, *426*
Winter Celebrated, 253, *517*
Winter Dream, 32, *392*
Within the leaves, this gilded bower, 103, *437*
Workers, 239, *511*

You get hungry in the barracks, 328, *558*
You have heard, my disciples, Cicero's speech, 291, *536*
You lied, on my femur, you lied, 334, *561*
Young Coupledom, 119, *448*
Your breast on my breast, 22, *385*
Youth, 260, *520*

INDEX OF TITLES AND FIRST LINES (FRENCH)

All page numbers in Roman refer to the translations; all page numbers in italic refer to the originals.

À droite l'aube d'été éveille les feuilles et les vapeurs, 242, *512*
À la Musique, 38, *396*
À ma sœur Louise Vanaen de Voringhem, 263, *522*
À moi. L'histoire d'une de mes folies, 208, *494*
A noir, E blanc, I rouge, U vert, O bleu, voyelles, 104, *438*
À quatre heures du matin, l'été, 110, *441*
À Samarie, 189, *483*
À une Raison, 235, *509*
À vendre ce que les Juifs n'ont pas vendu, 259, *519*
Accroupissements, 60, *409*
Adieu, 219, *502*
Âge d'or, 116, 350, *446*, *568*
Ah! cette vie de mon enfance, la grande route par tous les temps, 215, *499*
Ainsi, toujours, vers l'azur noir, 78, *421*
Album Zutique, L', 133, 339, *457*, *563*
Alchimie du verbe (Délires II), 208, 347, *494*, *566*
Amis, Les, 108, *440*
Angelot maudit, L', 147, *462*
Angoisse, 254, *517*
Antique, 229, *507*
Après le Déluge, 223, *503*
Aristomene se souleve, 303, *542*
Assez vu. La vision s'est rencontrée à tous les airs, 233, *508*
Assis, Les, 97, *434*
Au Cabaret-Vert, cinq heures du soir, 36, *394*
Au gibet noir, manchot aimable, 40, *397*
Au milieu, l'Empereur, dans une apothéose, 34, *393*
Au pied des sombres murs, battant les maigres chiens, 333, *561*
Aube, 249, *515*
Audistis hanc, discipuli, Ciceronis orationem, 291, *536*
Aussitôt que l'idée du Deluge se fut rassise, 223, *503*
Aux branches claires des tilleuls, 113, *444*
Aux livres de chevet, livres de l'art serein, 149, *463*
Aux paysans de l'empereur!, 143, *460*

Bal des pendus, 40, *397*
Balai, Le, 145, *461*
Bannières de mai, 113, *444*
Barbare, 256, *518*
Bateau ivre, Le, 85, *426*
Being Beauteous, 230, *507*
Bethsaïda, la piscine des cinq galeries, 190, *484*
Bien après les jours et les saisons, 256, *518*
Bien tard, quand il se sent l'estomac écœuré, 60, *409*
Bonne pensée du matin, 110, *441*
Bonr, 353, *569*
Bottom, 267, *524*
Bouts-rimés, 339, *563*
Brune, elle avait seize ans quand on la maria, 334, *561*
Buffet, Le, 33, *393*

Ce qu'on dit au poète à propos de fleurs, 78, *421*
Ce sont des villes!, 243, *512*
Ces écritures-ci sont d'un jeune, tout jeune *homme,* 183, *481*
C'est le repos éclairé, ni fièvre ni langueur, 247, *514*
C'est un humble balai de chiendent, trop dur, 145, *461*
C'est un large buffet sculpté, 33, *393*
C'est un trou de verdure où chante une rivière, 37, *395*
Cette année où naquit le Prince impérial, 153, *465*
Cette idole, yeux noirs et crin jaune, sans parents ni cour, 224, *504*
Ceux qui disent Cré Nom, ceux qui disent macache, 100, *436*
Chanson de la plus haute tour, 114, *444*
Chant de guerre parisien, 56, *407*
Châtiment de Tartufe, Le, 42, *398*
Chercheuses de poux, Les, 99, *435*
Cocher ivre, 142, *460*
Cœur sous une Soutane, Un, 163, *470*
Cœur volé, Le, 55, *406*
Comédie de la Soif, 107, *439*
Comme d'un cercueil vert en fer blanc, une tête, 19, *384*
Comme je descendais des Fleuves impassibles, 85, *426*
Confins du monde, 352, *568*
Conneries, 142, *460*
Conte, 227, *505*
Corbeaux, Les, 122, *450*

Dans la feuillée, écrin vert taché d'or, 103, *437*
Dans la salle à manger brune, 35, *394*

De ce siège si mal tourné, 329, *559*
Délires I: Vierge folle. L'Époux infernal, 204, *491*
Délires II: Alchimie du verbe, 208, 347, *494, 566*
Démocratie, 264, *522*
Départ, 233, *508*
Depuis huit jours, j'avais déchiré mes bottines, 36, *394*
Derrière tressautiat en des hoquets grotesques, 333, *561*
Des ciels gris de cristal, 240, *511*
Des drôles très solides, 228, *506*
Déserts de l'amour, Les, 181, *481*
Deux Sonnets, 331, *560*
Devant une neige un Être de Beauté de haute taille, 230, *507*
Dévotion, 263, *522*
Dimanche, 260, *520*
Dormeur du Val, Le, 37, *395*
Douaniers, Les, 100, *436*
Du détroit d'indigo aux mers d'Ossian, 255, *518*
D'un gradin d'or, —parmi les cordons de soie, 250, *516*

Éclair, L', 217, *501*
Éclatante victoire de Saarebrück, L', 34, *393*
Écoutons la confessions d'un compagnon d'enfer, 204, *491*
Effarés, Les, 28, *390*
Elle est retrouvée, 115, *445*
Elle était fort déshabillée, 20, *384*
En quelque soit, par exemple, que se trouve, 266, *523*
Enfance, 224, *504*
Enfant, certains ciels ont affiné mon optique, 258, *519*
Enfant qui ramassa les balles, 329, *558*
Entends comme brame, 126, *452*
Époux Infernal, L', 204, *491*
Esprit, L', 108, *440*
Est-elle almée?, 120, *448*
Et la Mère, fermant le livre du devoir, 65, *413*
Etat de siége?, 144, *460*
Éternelles Ondines, 108, *440*
Éternité, L', 115, 349, *445, 567*
Étrennes des orphelins, Les, 5, *376*
Exil, 146, *461*

Faim, 348, *567*
Fairy, 257, *519*
Fausse Conversion, 345, *566*

Fête d'hiver, 253, *517*
Fête Galante, 138, *458*
Fêtes de la faim, 121, *449*
Fêtes de la patience, 113, *443*
Fleurs, 250, *516*
Forgeron, Le, 43, *399*

Génie, 270, *525*
Gracieux fils de Pan!, 229, *507*
Guerre, 258, *519*

H, 268, *524*
Homme de constitution ordinaire, 260, *520*
Homme juste, L', 89, *429*
Honte, 129, *454*
Hypotyposes saturniennes, ex Belmontet, 150, *463*

Idole, L'. Sonnet du Trou du Cul, 135, *457*
Il est, à Rome, à la Sixtine, 137, *458*
Il est l'affection et le présent, 270, *525*
Il pleut doucement sur la ville, 330, *559*
Illuminations, 221, *503*
Impossible, L', 215, *499*
Invocation à Vénus, 295, *538*

Jadis, si je me souviens bien, ma vie était un festin, 195, *485*
J'ai avalé une fameuse gorgée de poison, 202, *490*
J'ai de mes ancêtres gaulois l'œil bleu blanc, 196, *485*
J'ai embrassé l'aube d'été, 249, *515*
Jamque novus primam lucem consumpsetat annus, 280, *529*
Je m'en allais, les poings dan mes poches crevées, 49, *403*
Je préfère sans doute, 140, *459*
Je suis un éphémère et point trop mécontent citoyen, 241, *511*
Je vis assis, tel qu'un ange aux mains d'un barbier, 102, *437*
Jeanne-Marie a des mains fortes, 92, *431*
Jeune goinfre, 142, *460*
Jeune ménage, 119, *448*
Jeunesse, 260, *520*
J'occupais un wagon de troisième un vieux prêtre, 139, *459*

La cascade sonne derrière les huttes d'opéra-comique, 253, *517*
La chambre est ouverte au ciel bleu-turquin, 119, *448*

La chambre est pleine d'ombre, 5, 376
La réalité étant trop épineuse pour mon grand caractère, 267, *524*
La Rivière de Cassis roule ignorée, 111, *442*
L'acropole officielle outre les conceptions, 245, *513*
L'air léger et charmant de la Galilée, 189, *483*
L'ancienne Comédie poursuit ses accords, 265, *523*
Larme, 112, *443*
L'aube d'or et la soirée frissonnante, 262, *521*
L'automne déjà!, 219, *502*
Le bras sur un marteau gigantesque effrayant, 43, *399*
Le drapeau va au paysage immonde, 264, *522*
Le jeune homme dont l'œil est brillant, la peau brune, 70, *416*
Le Juste restait droit sur ses hanches solides, 89, *429*
Le mouvement de lacet sur la barge des chutes du fleuve, 269, *524*
Le pauvre postillon, sous le dais de ferblanc, 144, *460*
Le Printemps est évident, car, 56, *407*
Le Soleil, le foyer de tendresse et de vie, 12, *379*
Le soleil était encore chaud, 157, *468*
Le travail humain! c'est l'explosion qui éclaire mon abîme, 217, *501*
L'eau claire, comme le sel des larmes d'enfance, 130, *454*
Les anciens animaux saillissaient, même en course, 331, *560*
Les calculs de côté, 260, *520*
Les chars d'argent et de cuivre, 252, *517*
Les pigeons qui tremblent dans la prairie, 109, *441*
Les soirs d'été, sous l'œil ardent des devantures, 148, *462*
Les voix instructives exilées, 261, *521*
L'étoile a pleuré rose au cœur de tes oreilles, 101, *436*
L'hiver, nous irons dans un petit wagon rose, 32, *392*
L'homme pâle, le long des pelouses fleuries, 51, *404*
L'Humanité chaussait le vaste enfant Progrès, 141, *459*
Loin des oiseaux, des troupeaux, des villageoises, 112, *443*
Lys, 136, *457*

Ma Bohême (Fantaisie), 49, *403*
Ma faim, Anne, Anne, 121, *449*
Mains de Jeanne-Marie, Les, 92, *431*
Mais enfin, 340, *564*
Mal, Le, 50, *404*
Maline, La, 35, *394*
Marine, 252, *517*
Matin, 218, *501*
Matinée d'ivresse, 236, *509*

Mauvais sang, 196, 343, *485*, *565*
Mémoire, 130, 351, *454*, *568*
Mère des fils d'Ènée, ô delices des Dieux, 295, *538*
Mes Petites amoureuses, 58, *408*
Métropolitain, 255, *518*
Michel et Christine, 127, *453*
Mon triste cœur bave à la poupe, 55, *406*
Morts de Quatre-vingt-douze, 27, *389*
Mouvement, 269, *524*
Mystique, 248, *515*

Nascitur Arabiis ingens in collibus infans, 283, *531*
N'eus-je pas *une fois* une jeunesse aimable, héroïque, fabuleuse, 218, *501*
Nocturne vulgaire, 251, *516*
Noirs dans la neige en dans la brume, 28, *390*
Noirs de loupes, grêlés, les yeux cerclés de bagues, 97, *434*
Nos fesses ne sont pas le leurs, 332, *560*
Nous sommes tes Grandes-Parents, 107, *439*
Nuit de l'enfer, 202, *490*

O balançoirs! o lys! clysopompes d'argent!, 136, *457*
Ô cette chaude matinée de février, 239, *511*
Ô lâches, la voilà! Dégorgez dans les gares!, 62, *410*
Ô les énormes avenues du pays saint, 231, *507*
Ô! L'Homme a relevé sa tête libre et fière!, 325, *557*
Ô *mon* Bien! Ô *mon* Beau!, 236, *509*
O saisons, ô châteaux, 132, 355, *456*
Ô Thimothina Labinette!, 163, *470*
Obscur et froncé comme un œillet violet, 135, *457*
Oh! si les cloches sont de bronze, 333, *561*
Oisive jeunesse, 114, *444*
Olim inflatus aquis, ingenti Acheloüs ab alveo, 287, *534*
On a faim dans la chambrée, 328, *558*
On n'est pas sérieux, quand on a dix-sept ans, 30, *391*
Ophélie, 17, *383*
Oraison du soir, 102, *437*
Orgie parisienne, L', 62, *410*
Ornières, 242, *512*
Ouvriers, 239, *511*

Par les soirs bleus d'été, j'irai dans les sentiers, 11, *379*
Parade, 228, *506*

Pardon mon père, 151, *463*
Parents, Les, 107, *439*
Paris, 142, *460*
Parqués entre des bancs de chêne, aux coins d'église, 68, *414*
Pauvre songe, Le, 109, *441*
Pauvres à L'église, les, 68, *414*
Peut-être un Soir m'attend, 109, *441*
Phrases, 237, *509*
Pitoyable frère! Que d'atroces veillées, 244, *513*
Plainte des épiciers, La, 335, *562*
Plates-bandes d'amarantes jusqu'a, 124, *451*
Poètes de sept ans, Les, 65, *413*
Ponts, Les, 240, *511*
Pour Hélène se conjurèrent les sèves ornamentales, 257, *519*
Première soirée, 20, *384*
Premières Communions, Les, 72, *417*
Prends-y garde, Ô ma vie absente!, 338, *563*
Promontoire, 262, *521*
Proses évangeliques, 187, *483*

Quand le fameux Tropmann détruisit Henri Kink, 330, *559*
Quand le front de l'enfant, plein de rouges tourmentes, 99, *435*
Quand le monde sera réduit en un seul bois noir, 237, *509*
Quand s'arrêta la caravane, 337, *563*
Que l'on s'intéressa souvent, mon cher Conneau!, 146, *461*
Quel est donc ce mystère impénétrable et sombre?, 150, *463*
Quelqu'une des voix, 116, *446*
Qu'est-ce pour nous, non cœur, que les nappes de sang, 123, *450*
Qu'il entre au magasin, quand la lune miroite, 335, *562*

Rages de Césars, 51, *404*
Remembrances du vieillard idiot, Les, 151, *463*
Reparties de Nina, Les, 22, *385*
Ressouvenir, 153, *465*
Rêvé pour l'hiver, 32, *392*
Rêveur, Scapin, 138, *458*
Rivière de Cassis, La, 111, *442*
Roman, 30, *391*
Royauté, 234, *508*

Saison en enfer, Une, 193, 341, *485*, *565*
Scènes, 265, *523*

Se peut-il qu'Elle me fasse pardonner les ambitions, 254, *517*
Seigneur, quand froide est la prairie, 122, *450*
Sensation, 11, *379*
Sire, le temps a laissé son manteau de pluie, 297, *539*
Sœurs de charité, Les, 70, *416*
Soir historique, 266, *523*
Solde, 259, *519*
Soleil et Chair, 12, *379*
Sonnet du Trou du Cul (L'Idole), 260, *520*
Sur la pente du talus les anges tournent leurs robes, 248, *515*
Sur la place taillée en mesquines pelouses, 38, *396*
Sur l'onde calme et noire où dorment les étoiles, 17, *383*

Ta poitrine sur ma poitrine, 22, *385*
Tandis que les crachats rouges de la mitraille, 50, *404*
Tant que la lame n'aura, 129, *454*
Tempus erat quo Nazareth habitabat Iesus, 289, *535*
Tête de faune, 103, *437*
Tisonnant, tisonnant son cœur amoureux sous, 42, *398*
Toits bleuâtres et portes blanches, 147, *462*
Toutes les monstruositées violent les gestes atroces d'Hortense, 268, *524*

Un beau matin, chez un people fort doux, 234, *508*
Un coup de ton doigt sur le tambour, 235, *509*
Un hydrolat lacrymal lave, 58, *408*
Un Prince était vexé de n s'être employé, 227, *505*
Un souffle ouvre des brèches opéradiques, 251, *516*

Vagabonds, 244, *513*
Veillées, 247, *514*
Vénus Anadyomène, 19, *384*
Ver erat, et morbo Romae languibat inerti, 277, *528*
Verba Apollonii de Marco Cicerone, 291, *536*
Vers pour les lieux, 329, *559*
Viens, les vins vont aux plages, 108, *440*
Vierge folle (Délires I), 204, *491*
Vies, 231, *507*
Vieux de la Vieille!, 143, *460*
Ville, 241, *511*
Villes I, 243, *512*
Villes II, 245, *513*
Vingt Ans, 261, *521*

Vous aves menti, sur mon fémut, vous aves menti, 334, *561*
Voyelles, 104, *438*
Vraiment, c'est bête, ces églises des villages, 72, *417*
Vu à Rome, 137, *458*

Zut alors si le soleil quitte ces bords!, 127, *453*

ABOUT THE TRANSLATOR

WYATT MASON studied literature at the University of Pennsylvania, Columbia University, and the University of Paris. His first translation, Pierre Michon's *Masters and Servants*, was a finalist for the French-American Foundation Translation Prize. He has translated five books by Michon, including *The Origin of the World.* His current projects include a translation of Arthur Rimbaud's complete correspondence, and a new edition of Dante's *La Vita Nuova*, also for the Modern Library.